LONG
AWAITED
WEST

Tina S. Kracke
333 W Hubbard St Apt 313
Chicago, IL 60654-4977

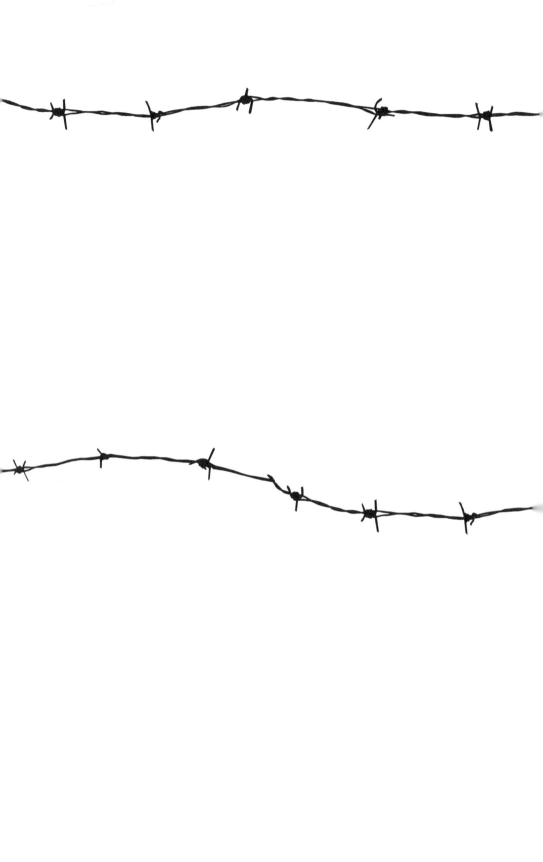

LONG AWAITED WEST

Eastern Europe since 1944

STEFANO BOTTONI

Translated by SEAN LAMBERT

INDIANA UNIVERSITY PRESS

This book is a publication of

Indiana University Press
Office of Scholarly Publishing
Herman B Wells Library 350
1320 East 10th Street
Bloomington, Indiana 47405 USA

iupress.indiana.edu

This book was produced under the auspices of the Research Centre for the Humanities of the Hungarian Academy of Sciences and with the support of the National Bank of Hungary.

Names: Bottoni, Stefano, author.
Title: Long awaited West : Eastern Europe since 1944 / Stefano
    Bottoni ; translated by Sean Lambert.
Other titles: Várva várt Nyugat. English
Description: Bloomington : Indiana University Press, 2017. |
    Includes bibliographical references and index.
Identifiers: LCCN 2017001600 (print) | LCCN 2017031128 (ebook) |
    ISBN 9780253030207 (eb) | ISBN 9780253026958 (cloth : alkaline
    paper) | ISBN 9780253030016 (paperback : alkaline paper)
Subjects: LCSH: Europe, Eastern—History—1945– | Europe,
    Eastern—Economic policy. | Europe, Eastern—Social policy. |
    Europe, Eastern—Relations—Europe, Western. | Europe,
    Western—Relations—Europe, Eastern.
Classification: LCC DJK50 (ebook) | LCC DJK50 .B68813 2017 (print) |
    DDC 947.0009/045—dc23
LC record available at https://lccn.loc.gov/2017001600

1 2 3 4 5   22 21 20 19 18 17

To my family, with love

CONTENTS

ACKNOWLEDGMENTS

HABENT FATA SUA LIBELLI. The seminal idea of this book originates from the bold proposal an Italian editor made to me, a fresh PhD with a limited conceptual horizon, around ten years ago. Although I was relieved after declining this offer to write nothing less than a general history of contemporary Eastern Europe, I had to admit to myself that it would be wonderful if a celebrated scholar were to produce such a work. To my greatest surprise, in 2009 another editor made me a tempting offer on a similar issue. I accepted it with a pinch of rational skepticism and spent the following year reflecting on how to narrate the recent past of this region to an academic and nonacademic audience. The result of that effort was a book published in 2011 by Carocci Editore in Rome (*Un altro Novecento: L'Europa orientale dal 1919 ad oggi*), which soon became a popular college textbook in my home country. A deeply revised, chronologically more concentrated version of that book came out three years later under the auspices of my new academic base, the Hungarian Academy of Sciences in Budapest. Shortly after, I was offered the privilege to make it accessible to the international public by a leading scholarly publisher, Indiana University Press. As a result of a hard year of work that included not only the translation but also the narrative and conceptual reframing of the previous manuscripts, the reader finds here a new self-standing book, and not a mere revision of the previous editions. I have adapted the narrative style and reduced the amount of details and background information to the needs of an international public of area scholars and students interested in getting sense of the somber, often controversial, and indeed very fascinating history of the people of Eastern Europe since the end of the Second World War.

Because of the unconventionally complex genesis of this book, the list of persons and institutions to whom and which I owe my deepest expressions of gratitude is unbearably long. Thus, I will mention only those who contributed to the making of this most recent manuscript, while I also extend my gratitude to the multitude of scholars, colleagues, and students with whom I have discussed the topics covered in this book over the past decade. My first thanks are addressed to the general director of my workplace, the Research Center for the Humanities: Pál Fodor has placed great belief in this project, providing me with the financial resources needed for translating the Hungarian edition. My colleague László Borhi has played an invaluable role in making possible the advancement of the process. A special thanks to Sean Lambert, my translator, who has also been a valuable intellectual partner and a patient critic during the laborious stages of developing a new manuscript. I am deeply indebted to the colleagues with whom I had the privilege to spend an unforgettable period of research at the Imre Kertész Kolleg of the University of Jena in 2015. Among the many people whose enthusiasm and competence made my stay in Jena so productive and pleasant, I would like to address my sincere thanks to professors Joachim von Puttkamer and Włodzimierz Borodziej and to the colleagues who participated in this intellectual journey with me. Although this book project was not originally linked to my stay in Jena, I am certain that they will find some of the seminars we attended and the lengthy conversations we carried out on world affairs reflected in the pages to follow. I also wish to express my gratitude to those who have read and made insightful comments on the manuscript or parts of it: Ferenc Laczó, Tom Junes, Valentina Fava, Guido Franzinetti, and Zoltán Pogátsa. Last but not least, I would like to thank the editorial staff of Indiana University Press for handling the publication process with professionalism and the optimal amount of flexibility. I take full responsibility for any errors or omissions that may have remained in the book, notwithstanding the contribution of so many benevolent colleagues to improve the final version of the manuscript.

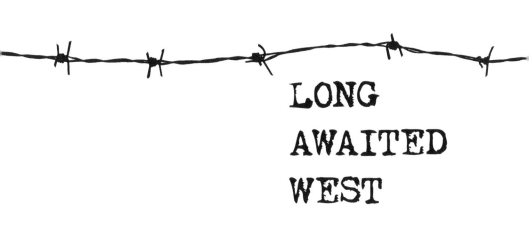

LONG
AWAITED
WEST

Introduction

Reframing the Debated Concept of Eastern Europe

WHEN WAS THE CONCEPT of Eastern Europe born, which territories of Europe were meant to be included in it, and what has remained of it after the end of the Cold War? The meaning of *Eastern Europe* has been changing continuously. Each scholarly community and political group interprets this expression differently. This might not be surprising, since the term is related to questions of (self-)legitimization and emotions more than to scholarly considerations. As any non–Eastern European historian who deals with Eastern Europe may have already experienced, the difficulty regarding this term tends to arise when "Eastern European" colleagues reject the notion on the ground that it is unsuitable to describe their homeland (though are willing to admit that it might perhaps be meaningfully applied to neighboring countries). While the concept of Eastern Europe is viewed in the West as corresponding to a self-evident reality, many "Eastern Europeans" consider it little more than a historical and moral stigma. This serves to explain the paradox that whereas in the West many distinguished universities offer an area studies program focused on Eastern Europe, thereby recognizing the legitimacy of regional approaches, in the states of the former Soviet Bloc, consciousness of the shared trajectory of Eastern Europe from 1944 to 1989 is gradually fading.

Debates surrounding the geographical, political, and cultural borders of Eastern Europe have produced a large amount of literature in the fields of history, political science, cultural anthropology, and literary studies.[1] The author of the present volume would like to highlight as an introduction to this synthesis three of the previously mentioned issues: the historical and political borders of the region; the original causes of the historical, economic, and social underdevelopment of Eastern Europe; and the complex relationship between the logic of the nation-state and the traditionally multinational character of the region.

Even the most authoritative international organizations appear to disagree over the definition of Eastern Europe, and in the early 1990s this conceptual vagueness produced some bewildering subregional designations: the European Union introduced the category of "Western Balkans" to refer to Albania and the states of the former Yugoslavia with the exception of Slovenia, which as a result of its higher level of development was implicitly regarded as more European.

It should be clear that *Eastern Europe* is far from a consensual geographical or geopolitical term. Recently, the end of the Cold War and rapprochement with the West deprived the region of its ideological distinctiveness and internal legitimacy. The entire region of what used to be called Eastern Europe has for decades engaged itself primarily with issues surrounding its relationship with Western civilization, and its borders have been adapted to changes in the political environment. Despite its large geographical size, Eastern Europe does not constitute an independent pole under any terms, whether political, economic, or cultural. The region measures itself against the West and awaits the decisive impulses from this direction as a result of pattern-following behavior inherited from the nineteenth century.

The conceptual confusion regarding Eastern Europe manifests itself in terminological debates as well. The German expression *Zwischeneuropa* qualifies the region as the intermediate part of Europe. This does not refer to the same geographical area as the term *Mitteleuropa*, which composed part of the theoretical horizon of such pre–First World War thinkers as Friedrich List, Walter Rathenau, and Friedrich Neumann, all of whom regarded Middle Europe as an independent region extending from the Baltic Sea through the Black Sea and all the way to the Mediterranean. In its original usage, the designation *Mitteleuropa* implied the possibility of political and economic alliance among the German, Hungarian, and Slavic peoples under the leadership of Germany. Far from the territory of the former Austria-Hungary, National Socialism used the political concept of *Mitteleuropa* as the foundation for its policy of territorial expansion. The collapse of the Nazi system therefore brought an end to both German plans to gain hegemony over large parts of the continent as well as a series of geopolitical conceptions—many of which had previously enjoyed much legitimacy.[2] Many historians nevertheless agree that the eastern half of Europe displays many divergent developmental patterns as compared to the western half.

An important though often overlooked fact must be borne in mind: before the Second World War, Eastern Europe simply did not exist as a political region. According to Larry Wolff, Enlightenment thought was the first to depict the "Eastern" mentality in contrast to the achievements of "Western" civilization.[3] The increasingly fashionable narratives of "Easternness" in travel diaries of the nineteenth century primarily reflected the intellectual perceptions and preconceptions of their authors rather than the political or social realities of the described territories. More recently, a scholar of Slavic literature made the same point speaking about how Eastern Europe came into being in the Western discourse:

> "Eastern Europe" was always simultaneously both the other Europe and Europe's "Other," and in this sense dependent on images produced in the West. Even the new entrants to the EU struggled to shed the tag of "poor relation." That being the case, there can be no Eastern Europe in an objective sense. The term makes sense only if we use it neutrally, recognizing the diversity that it subsumes.[4]

As late as the interwar period there were no perceptible common political and economic characteristics of Eastern Europe. Not even the still-confident political officials could define the region's internal and external borders. For example, the founder of the Czechoslovak state, Tomáš Garrigue Masaryk, regarded *Střední Evropa*—the Czech-language equivalent of *Zwischeneuropa*—as a "special zone of dispersed small peoples from the North Cape to Cape Matapan" that included Greece and Turkey, although for obvious political reasons excluded Austria and Germany—countries with which Czechoslovakia maintained poor relations.[5] The successor states that emerged from the three expansive multinational monarchies that had existed in the region until the end of the First World War—Austria-Hungary, the Russian Empire, and the Ottoman Empire—differed to a greater degree from one another in terms of economic development than did Eastern Europe from Western Europe. Bohemia, Moravia, and Silesia possessed strong urban middle-class populations and were counted among the industrial centers of Europe, whereas the level of development in Yugoslavia, southeastern Romania, Bulgaria, and Albania resembled that of Mediterranean Europe—Portugal, Spain, and many party of Italy—and impoverished Ireland much more closely than it did that of the peripheral states of Central Europe that played a defining role for the German, Polish, Hungarian, and Italian *Bürgertümer.*[6]

The term *Eastern Europe* can thus be regarded as a by-product of the "short" twentieth century, when the West-East conceptual relation reach the point to transform unclear geographic boundaries into cognitive antipodes and the East came to play an exclusively negative role in the Western discursive field.

With regard to research on Eastern Europe, the maxim that emerged to describe impressionist painting seems to be valid: the picture becomes clear only from a distance. One of the most penetrating comprehensive analyses of the nature and social dysfunctions of Eastern Europe came from Sir Lewis Namier. Although Namier never engaged in academic research in his homeland and did not regard himself as a specialist on Eastern Europe, fundamentally examining the entire region through the prism of Irish nation-building efforts, his socialization on one of the front lines of the nationality struggle, Eastern Galicia, made him sensitive to problems related to the formation of modern nations. During the Second World War, Namier wrote an important essay examining nationality issues.[7] In this work, Namier asserted that discord was an inevitable product of the irreconcilable conflicts of interest that existed among the various Eastern European national movements to which Namier referred as the "European Middle East."[8]

Some years later, Hungarian sociologist and political scientist István Bibó examined the formation of the small nations of Eastern Europe. Bibó considered the national principle—the building and operation of the nation-based state— to be one of the main motors of European social development.[9] Whereas Bibó classified himself among the "populist" thinkers who stood in contrast to the "urban" intellectual orientation in Hungary, he sharply opposed the national-characterological approach to national, minority, and ethnic issues related to Hungarian development. Shortly after the Second World War, Bibó became acquainted with Hugh Seton-Watson, whom he regarded as a personal friend and source of inspiration. Bibó was also presumably familiar with the work of Ernest Gellner, who researched the role that the intellectual élite played in the emergence of post-imperial nationalisms in Eastern Europe.

In their appraisals of nationalism, Bibó, Seton-Watson, and Gellner all expressed the view that there existed no nationalist ideology that could be considered an intellectual achievement. All three thinkers believed that nationalism must be regarded as a political movement largely responsible for the important bond between national consciousness and the quest for modernity in Eastern Europe in the nineteenth century.[10] In his seminal book that appeared in 1944, Hans Kohn had already established a contrast between the "civic" nationalism of the West and the "ethnic" nationalism of the East.[11]

Practically every significant researcher of nationalism expanded on this disparity over the following decades: at the beginning of the 1970s, John Plamenatz discerned the difference between the West and the East in the solidity of differing cultural identities; in the 1980s, A. D. Smith defined a similar boundary, asserting that the civic-territorial principle predominated in the West, while the genealogical-ethnic principle predominated in the East. Bibó, however, identified further demarcation lines within Eastern Europe itself, noting that the nobility had nourished the development of Polish and Hungarian nationalism beginning in the Middle Ages, whereas the bourgeoisie and the industrial proletariat had impelled the building of Czech nationalism and the masses had been the subject of strengthening nationalism in the Balkan nations at the end of the nineteenth century. Peter Sugar's comparative analysis of Eastern European nationalisms published in the late 1960s arrived at a similar conclusion.[12]

The eradication of Eastern European Jewry and the subsequent disappearance of wealthy, self-aware minority communities that possessed strong middle classes, such as the Germans, Poles, and Italians, also played a key role in preparing the ground for the introduction of communist rule in the region. One may surmise that the antipathy that many democratic intellectuals of the Central and Eastern European region felt toward the previous political systems and their appalling experiences during the Second World War prevented them from noticing that the forcible establishment of homogeneous states improved the chances of the Bolshevik alternative at the expense of the democratic one.

It was the Soviet political-military bloc, which emerged in the late 1940s, that created Eastern Europe. The members of this bloc then promoted a historiographical system that validated the differences between Western and Eastern Europe on an ideological plane through a new interpretation of the history of Europe presupposing the existence of irreconcilable conflicts between the two halves of the continent. In the early 1950s, Polish historian Oskar Halecki rejected the a priori classification of his country as part of Eastern Europe primarily on moral grounds, claiming that it created an artificial distance between Poland and the West while intimating the existence of a fraternal spirit between Poland and the Soviet Union. In the 1960s, much of what was original in Hungarian historiography suggested a positive reevaluation of the Austro-Hungarian monarchy from an intellectual standpoint in contrast to its previous vulgar-Marxist interpretation. This reexamination of the Dual Monarchy also generated a new image of Central Europe based on rational arguments.[13] An attempt to break free of the "West-East" dichotomy colored this rediscovery of the imperial order. Scholars began researching the previous millennium of European history and the fault lines that emerged as a result of the nation-building process in Eastern Europe in terms of Fernand Braudel's *longue durée*.[14] Zsigmond Pál Pach identified already in the early 1960s the phenomenon of "cyclical deviation" that Immanuel Wallerstein used in his famous 1979 book *The Capitalist World-Economy* to describe the formation of the partially or wholly peripheral territories connected to the historical centers of capitalism. According to Pach, Hungary would have belonged to one of these historical centers had the codification of serfdom in the sixteenth century not disrupted the country's development.[15] Iván T. Berend and György Ránki utilized Pach's theses in their collaboratively written comparative works regarding the economic history of modern Europe, which projected a positive social-economic image of the Habsburg Empire until the beginning of the First World War.[16] The theses and conclusions of these books held obvious implications regarding both the Austro-Hungarian monarchy's successor states as well as the controversial integration efforts of the Soviet Union in the Eastern Bloc. Another Hungarian historian, Péter Hanák, examined the Dual Monarchy from a cultural perspective, emphasizing the viability of this multinational laboratory.[17]

The contention that Central Europe belonged to the Western sphere of civilization returned to the center of attention with the growing crisis that surrounded the Soviet-type systems in the first half of the 1980s. In 1984, exiled Czech writer Milan Kundera published an essay in which he asserted that Czechoslovakia and the entire region had been betrayed.[18] Public intellectuals such as Václav Havel, Czesław Miłosz, and György Konrád achieved significant success in the West in a much more direct manner through their propagation of the "captive Europe" paradigm in the middle of the 1980s, a paradigm Western scholars helped popularize in the glorious days of the 1989 regime change.[19] As György Schöpflin and Nancy Wood noted, however, the *Mitteleuropa* of which those authors dreamed had nothing to do with interwar German geopolitics. Todorova identified a further weakness of this concept: the "central European" Eastern Europe that was reclaiming its dignity included neither Germany nor Russia and ignored the Balkan region.[20] The exclusive, somewhat elitist particularity of Central Europe that opposition intellectuals proclaimed during the 1980s contributed to the rapid degeneration of discourse regarding the region following the collapse of communism in the Soviet Bloc in 1989. Neither Habsburg nostalgia nor the claim to affiliation with the "civilized" part of Europe managed to produce a conceptual apparatus capable of addressing the challenges of the postcommunist period. The attempt of the more developed and democratically supposedly more mature Visegrád Group countries—Poland, Czechoslovakia, and Hungary—to secede from postcommunist Eastern Europe proved rather short lived and generally unsuccessful. According to Attila Melegh, with the failure of communist systems in Europe, the previous East-West cognitive structure of the imperial-colonial hierarchy supplanted the Cold War interaction between competing modernities. Central and Eastern European semiperipheral strategies can be placed on the incline of civilization sloping toward the East to the extent that their application of the East-West contrast serves to portray themselves as "more Western" and the scorned other as "more Eastern."[21]

As the final chapter of this book shows, the histories of the postcommunist European states contain more common attributes than disparities, although it is exceptionally difficult to describe the forces that continue to bind these countries together in a postideological and increasingly interdependent world. The present volume is based on a pragmatic definition of Eastern Europe as those territories that were exposed to the historical experiences of Soviet communism starting with the Molotov-Ribbentrop Pact and the subsequent outbreak of the Second World War. Following the collapse of the three multinational states (the Soviet Union, Yugoslavia, and Czechoslovakia), the region currently encompasses twenty countries with a total area of nearly 2 million square kilometers and a population of around 180 million people.

This volume represents a comparative, problem-centered overview of the modern history of Eastern Europe. The political, social, and cultural diversity of

Eastern Europe has for decades presented authors of comprehensive works with a profound methodological challenge.[22]

Following the First World War, the majority of the successor states that emerged following the collapse of the multinational empires (see the cases of Poland, Czechoslovakia, and Romania) slowly reproduced the fragmentation of the bygone state entities. They did so, however, within a completely transformed environment and under the pressure of mass nationalism and acting in the name of the principle of self-determination.

Meanwhile, minority groups and their hinterlands, such as Germany, Hungary, and Bulgaria—to borrow Rogers Brubaker's triadic relational interplay between national minorities, the newly nationalizing states, and the "external homelands" to which they still felt themselves to belong—engaged in a counterproductive use of the League of Nations minority-protection system.[23] The lack of loyalty among minorities during the interwar period was, indeed, among the factors that contributed to the outbreak of the Second World War. Similarly, the dissolution of the federal states of Eastern Europe—Czechoslovakia and Yugoslavia—between 1991 and 1993 generated serious debates among scholars. The previously mentioned dilemma addressed the heart of the matter: were multinational state formations viable in a region where the political elite of every state had for 150 years aspired to acquire and preserve its own (exclusive) territory? Some regarded the disintegration of multinational states as a foreordained failure, while others believed that their breakup would serve to promote the spread of nationality conflict, thereby impeding the process of European integration. In fact, neither Czechoslovakia nor Yugoslavia was destined to fail—both states had come into existence, after an extended period of intellectual preparation, as an act of political will during times of crisis. The dissolution of Czechoslovakia and Yugoslavia was primarily the result of the inability of communist systems to adequately address issues related to national differences.

Despite the official ideological premise of internationalism, the Eastern Europe that existed within the Soviet zone of influence never was an authentic, supranational community. The national antagonism and conflicting economic interests that emerged in Eastern Europe after the Second World War were manifest in the policies and discourse of the communist parties that came to power in the region, thus undermining bilateral relations among Eastern European countries and inciting ever-greater tension between those states and the Soviet Union. As this book examines throughout, Eastern Europe depended to a significant degree on the Soviet Union, although the region's position of total subservience to the Soviets in the 1940s and 1950s later transformed into a relationship of conditional loyalty. Events of national reach and local historical paths continued to exercise a significant influence over the course of history in Eastern Europe even under Soviet domination. After 1989, many people maintained the illusion that communism represented a mere historical interlude that could be easily left behind through political democratization and economic privatization. This book presents the author's argument that the communist "deviation" in Eastern Europe can be best understood as the intertwined product of external (Soviet) aggression and unsolved internal contradictions (economic underperformance, social inequality, and nationality conflicts) that had become since the interwar period ingrained in the collective thought of Eastern European people and the social systems of their states. The common legacy of their uncomfortable past likely constitutes the only truly profound connection that the Soviet Union managed to create among its reluctant allies.

This book attempts to combine chronological narration of main historical turning points with a thematic examination of various topics of importance to an understanding of the region, notably the economic and social development of the various Eastern European states. The author believes that analysis of the statistically measurable economic and social underdevelopment of Eastern Europe is essential to understand the unique complexity of the regional mosaic. Only through this comprehensive approach can one find an answer to the most important question that has emerged with regard to Eastern Europe in recent decades: why has the distance that separates this region from Western Europe decreased only so slightly despite strenuous efforts to reduce it? This book argues that the unintended preservation of this distance results from two inseparable factors. The first is linked to the socioeconomic development of the central-eastern European and post-Soviet region, whose integration in the European Union has been a surface success. But even more important, the everyday use of the obsolete term *Eastern Europe* also reflects the fact that the deep mental and psychological gap that divides it from the core countries of Europe has not narrowed significantly over the past decades, and seems to have widened again after the global economic crisis of 2008–2009. As a consequence, the growing influence of anti-Western feelings among the Eastern European elites should sound an alarm on the risk that the region turn from a gloomy but comfortable buffer zone into an openly disputed area between a distracted West and an increasingly assertive Russia. In his study regarding the disappearance of traditional political borders within the expanding European Union, Karl Schlögel maintained that Mikhail Bakhtin's concept of the *chronotope*—the manner in which configurations of time and space are represented in language and discourse—revealed a significant phase delay when applied to East-West relations.[24] The critical impetus behind this book seeks to acquaint the reader with those apparently residual memory strata that to the present day hold Eastern Europe together and hinder the region's long-desired convergence with the West.

Notes

1. See the following fundamental works: Halecki, *Borderlands of Western Civilization*. See also Szűcs, *Vázlat Európa három történeti régiójáról*; Schöpflin and Wood, *In Search of Central Europe*; Wolff, *Inventing Eastern Europe*. For the image of the Balkans in European culture, see Maria Todorova, *Immaginando i Balcani*, particularly 232–265 on the Balkans and the myth of Central Europe. On the scholarly debate, see Franzinetti, "Mitteleuropa in East-Central Europe," 219–235; Janowski, Iordachi, and Trencsényi, "Why Bother about Historical Regions?," 5–58.
2. Bugge, "Use of the Middle," 15–35.
3. Wolff, *Inventing Eastern Europe*, 12.
4. Grob, "Concept of Eastern Europe in Past and Present," 17.
5. Masaryk quote from Todorova, *Immaginando i Balcani*, 249.
6. Graziosi, "Il mondo in Europa," 193–228.
7. Namier, *Conflicts*.
8. Franzinetti, "Irish and East European Questions," 67–96.
9. Bibó, *Válogatott Tanulmányok IV, 1935–1979*, 344.
10. Kovács, *Az európai egyensúlytól a kölcsönös szolgáltatások társadalmáig*, 364–371.
11. Kohn, *Idea of Nationalism*.
12. Sugar and Lederer, *Nationalism in Eastern Europe*.
13. For the Hungarian debate, see Pók, *Politics of Hatred*, 103–117.
14. See Niederhauser, *History of Eastern Europe since the Middle Ages*, as well as important comparative works that this author wrote regarding the national awakening during the romantic era, notably *Nemzetek születése Kelet-Európában*, and *A nemzeti megújulási mozgalmak Kelet-Európában*.
15. Pach, *Nyugat-európai és magyarországi agrárfejlődés a XV–XVII században*. See also Wallerstein's argument in *The Capitalist World-Economy*.
16. Berend and Ránki, *Economic Development in East-Central Europe in the 19th and 20th Centuries*.
17. Hanák, *Garden and the Workshop*.
18. Szűcs, *Vázlat*; Kundera, "Tragedy of Central Europe," 33–38.
19. Ash, *Uses of Adversity*.
20. Todorova, *Immaginando i Balcani*, 248–254.
21. Melegh, *On the East-West Slope*.
22. The works of Joseph Rothschild regarding the interwar and communist periods rank among the most significant internationally used handbooks on Eastern Europe: *East Central Europe Between the Two World* Wars and *Return to Diversity*. See also Crampton, *Eastern Europe in the Twentieth Century*. The following book abandons the chronological approach to focus greater attention on cultural and economic history: Bideleux and Jeffries, *A History of Eastern Europe*. For detail on economic issues, see Berend, *Central and Eastern Europe, 1944–1993*. The following book concentrates on social transformation: Pittaway, *Eastern Europe 1939–2000*. See also Magocsi's monumental historical atlas, *Historical Atlas of Central Europe*. For a useful historical database (terminological introduction, statistics and chronology), see Webb, *Routledge Companion to Central and Eastern Europe since 1919*.
23. Brubaker, *Nationalism Reframed*.
24. Schlögel, *Leggere il tempo nello spazio*.

Chapter 1

On Soviet Turf (1944–1948)

Eastern Europe in the Shadow of Genocidal War

> The maid came in and began clearing the table, wearing white gloves, as she did when serving, because this was also one of the rules of the house. I went to my room and sat down at the old desk. Before the windows, the city was silent in the spring night. Only occasionally did a tank rumble on its way to Castle Hill, carrying members of the Gestapo to occupy the offices. I listened to the clattering tanks and smoked cigarettes. The room was pleasantly lukewarm. I looked absent-mindedly at the books lining the walls, the six thousand volumes I had gathered together in various places in the world. Here was that Marcus Aurelius I bought from a second-hand dealer on the banks of the Seine, Eckermann's *Conversations*, and an old Hungarian edition of the Bible. And six thousand more books. From a wall my father, grandfather, and deceased relatives looked down at me.
>
> —Sándor Márai, *Memoir of Hungary, 1944–1948*

The recent history of Eastern Europe is inseparable from the human, material, and moral devastation of the Second World War. The offensive launched by Nazi Germany and its allies against the Soviet Union in the summer of 1941 transformed the military conflict that began in 1939 into a total, genocidal war. The opening of the Eastern Front provided the idea of "New Europe," which had long played a role in National Socialist public discourse, with a decisive push toward practical application. Over the following three and a half years, the effort to implement this concept led to the methodical genocide of Jews and Roma, as well as serial crimes committed against Poles, Ukrainians, and Russians.[1] Ghettos were established in Germany in 1940 following the implementation of anti-Semitic policies throughout Eastern Europe that had been codified in the 1935 Nuremberg Laws; the establishment of mobile "deployment groups" (*Einsatzgruppen*) in 1941 represented the beginning of the next phase. These units followed Axis troops advancing along the Soviet front in order to carry out their nominal duty of cleansing occupied territory of presumed communist elements, which in practice turned out to be primarily Jews. These *Einsatzgruppen*, which included local auxiliary units, committed acts of genocide that in fewer than three years resulted in the deaths of 2 million people, primarily Jews in the Ukraine and the Baltic, who had inhabited the shtetl located in the former Pale of Settlement established in czarist Russia.[2]

Among the German allies, the Romanian occupational forces also cooperated in the massacres that occurred in Bessarabia, Bukovina, and the city of Odessa during the invasion of the Soviet Union. Romania contributed to the atrocities committed on the Eastern Front with death brigades of its own. The government of Romania, led by Marshal Ion Antonescu, independently planned and carried out the deportation and execution of 280,000 Jews from occupied territories beyond the Dniester River, as well as 10,000 Roma from Bessarabia and northern Bukovina.[3] The diplomatic and armed struggle between Hungary and Romania for control of Transylvania provides a clear illustration of the ground that the concept of national exclusivity had gained in Europe at this time. Holly Case demonstrates that the collapse of the Versailles system and the outbreak of the Second World War placed Romania, the previous defender of the territorial status quo, and Hungary, one of the primary losers in the post–First World War peace agreements, in a new situation. Before the Second Vienna Award both countries endeavored to win the favor of the expanding Germany that had proclaimed the "new European order"; then after the pact they fought alongside the Germans on the Soviet front while making continual preparations to attack each other. The two allied countries joined the war not primarily to fight against the Soviet Union or Bolshevism but as a means of acquiring territory, above all Transylvania.[4]

The attempt to establish the New Europe assumed an extremely brutal character in large areas of the Soviet Union. The genocidal nature of the German invasion was reflected in the treatment of Soviet prisoners of war, above all in Ukraine, Belarus, and the Volga region. The mortality rate among prisoners held in concentration and internment camps was very high in the winter of 1942, and only 1.1 million of the nearly 4 million soldiers held captive in these camps survived. Famine and the brutality of the invading forces decimated the civilian population of major occupied cities.

Several authors have emphasized that by 1944 the cruelty of the Axis occupation of the Soviet Union had generated nearly universal hostility toward the local German administration, even among those such as the supporters of the Stepan Bandera–led militant wing of the Organization of Ukrainian Nationalists, which in 1941 had greeted Wehrmacht forces as liberators and launched the recruitment of an anti-Bolshevik national army that failed precisely because of initial opposition from the German military leadership. The Germans subsequently approved the Ukrainian request to form armed military units, though only in 1943. The resulting Kraków-based Ukrainian National Committee fought under German command as part of the 14th Galician SS-Volunteer Division in Ukraine, in anti-partisan operations in the Balkan Peninsula as well as in Slovakia at the time of the August 1944 Slovak National Uprising. Before the collapse of the Third Reich, this force grew to include more than 70,000 active personnel and was trans-formed into the First Division of the Ukrainian National Army.[5]

In the Baltics, the local civilian population largely supported collabora-tion with German authorities. This was not only because of the historically significant German presence in the region, but also due to the anti-Soviet at-titudes that had permeated throughout nearly the entire population of Estonia, Latvia, and Lithuania following the Soviet occupation of 1940. The Germans incorporated these countries and part of Poland and Belarus into the Riga-based Reichskommissariat Ostland in 1941. The German occupation therefore provided the Baltic states with some degree, albeit largely formal, of autonomy. Moreover, the Germans partially reprivatized the economies of the Baltic re-gion, but subordinated them to the war effort and permitted local farmers only to rent land that had been expropriated at the time of the Soviet occupation. Around 250,000 Jews were murdered in the Baltic states during the Second World War. Estonian and Latvian SS regiments committed the majority of these killings. The population of Lithuania, which also possessed a large Jewish community, regarded the occupational forces with a hostility that frequently evolved into active resistance.

German oppression appeared in its most violent form in Poland. In addition to the fact that the extermination of Jews assumed its most horrifying forms and dimensions in the annexed territories of Poland, the war that the Third Reich launched against the country's entire population made no distinctions with re-gard to nationality or political affiliation. Hitler did not merely want to defeat Poland—he wanted to obliterate it. Because Poland was the home of the larg-est Jewish community in Europe, the German-occupied country was doomed to serve as the final destination of deportations and the primary site of the physical destruction of European Jewry. The residents of Jewish ghettos in major cities in Poland were deported to the country's largest camp, Auschwitz-Birkenau (those from the Lwów/Lemberg Ghetto in March 1942, those from Warsaw Ghetto be-tween July and September 1943, and those from Łódź Ghetto in the summer of 1944). Jews from the Netherlands, the Protectorate of Bohemia and Moravia, Slo-vakia, Austria, Hungary, and Greece were also deported to Auschwitz-Birkenau. Nearly 450,000 Hungarian Jews were the final significant transport to the exter-mination camp in the spring and early summer of 1944. Several hundred thou-sand Poles, Russians, and other Slavs, as well as Roma, homosexuals, and political prisoners, died at Nazi death camps as well.

In the Baltic states, Poland, Belarus, Ukraine, and western Russia, the "blood-lands" that suffered appalling devastation at the hands of both Hitler and Stalin from 1933 to 1945, around 14 million noncombatants were killed over this twelve-year period. In his recent and much-discussed books on the German and Soviet rule over that region, Timothy Snyder seeks to explain the extraordinary amount of physical violence perpetrated against ordinary people.[6] Snyder challenges the "Auschwitz paradox" and claims that the mass killing camps of Eastern Europe should be regarded as the epistemological center of the tragedy; instead, it was not the lethality of modern bureaucracy—as previously claimed by standard his-toriography of the Holocaust, but rather the removal of bureaucracy or deporta-tion of Jews to "bureaucracy-free zones in the East" that was fatal to the East European Jewry.[7] According to Snyder, many Jews avoided deportation because dependent satellites of Nazi Germany (Slovakia and Croatia), conquered states (France, Netherlands, Belgium, Denmark, Norway, Yugoslavia, and Greece), and allied states (Italy, Hungary, Bulgaria, and Romania) all retained varying degrees of sovereignty that protected Jews to some extent from unrestrained German will. However, the domestically arranged mass killings carried out in 1941–42 by the Romanian state administration in occupied Transnistria and Bessarabia, the Roma and Serb Holocaust perpetrated by Croatian authorities during the war, or the involvement at all levels of the Hungarian bureaucracy in the mass deporta-tions of 1944 demonstrate that local agency—that is to say, the role of national or regional bureaucracies—cannot be left out from the set of explanations for the genocidal war.

As mentioned, Nazi-occupied Poland suffered the highest number of casu-alties compared to its overall population. Tadeusz Piotrowski estimates that 5.6 million citizens of Poland—21 percent of the country's total population—fell vic-tim to the cruelties and depravations of war between 1939 and 1945. Three million of those who died as a result of war and genocide during this period were Jews (just 10 percent of Poland's Jewish community survived the war), and 2.5 mil-lion were non-Jews—2 million Poles and around 500,000 Ukrainians and Be-larusians.[8] One-third of the population of Poland was either killed or wounded as the front rolled over the country. The Warsaw Ghetto and its inhabitants were liquidated following the 1943 ghetto uprising, and the Germans and allied Ukrai-nian volunteers completely destroyed the western half of Poland's capital city after suppressing the Polish Home Army–led Warsaw Uprising in October 1944.

The Italian historian Antonio Ferrara believes that with the eradication of Jewish communities throughout Europe, the Nazis had delivered a definitive blow to the continent's old bourgeois world and transnational network. Accord-ing to Ferrara, the obliteration of European Jewry can be defined as "one of Nazi Germany's most revolutionary acts" for its long-standing social and cultural con-sequences.[9]

Liberation or Occupation?

The political and social organization of Europe following the Second World War depended primarily on the balance of power that emerged on the battlefield. The two-pronged Soviet offensive launched in the late summer of 1944—into Poland from the north and into the Balkans and up toward Hungary from the south—ended with the Red Army's occupation of Prague on May 9, 1945, following the Wehrmacht's surrender the previous day. At the end of the war in Europe, Soviet troops occupied half of the continent, including Vienna and Trieste. Yugoslav forces had captured Trieste on May 1, 1945, with the approval of Soviet and Italian communist leaders and maintained control over the city for an entire month.[10]

Norman Davies contends that the Soviet advance through Central Europe represented one of the "largest and most terrible military operations in modern history," which succeeded in ending the cataclysmic war despite almost immediately subjecting Eastern Europe to Stalinist political practices and Soviet geopolitical interests.[11] The end of armed conflict and the beginning of the postwar period entailed a completely different set of circumstances in Red Army–controlled Eastern Europe than in Western Europe. To understand the conditions under which a given city, region, nationality, religious community, or social group reacted to the Soviet presence, one must examine the micro-level effects of the grand narrative of 1944–45 (see map 1.1).

The arrival of the Red Army delivered millions of people from the Nazi genocide, military occupation, and radical right-wing political systems. For the Jews who survived the deportations and camps, for the Slavic nations that Hitler had forced into a state of servitude, for the armed partisans and members of political resistance organizations, and, finally, for a significant portion of the exhausted civilian populations, the appearance of the Soviet army represented true liberation, and often the sole chance for survival. After six years of war, most people simply wanted peace regardless of the political system under which it emerged.

Thus, the paradox of hundreds of thousands of people expressing enthusiasm for the Soviet Union and communist ideology in countries where the end of the Second World War did not by any means signify the end of mass violence was not the sole result of fear and opportunism. The citizens of Czechoslovakia and Bulgaria regarded the Red Army as a liberation force, especially since it quickly withdrew from those countries. For the Germans and their allies, particularly the Hungarians, the arrival of the Soviet army represented not only military defeat and the collapse of a Weltanschauung, but the beginning phase of a more or less spontaneous terror that millions of physically and psychologically devastated soldiers inflicted upon the vanquished. The number of people who suffered injury and abuse with the arrival of Soviet troops, primarily in Germany, Poland, and Hungary, is inestimable. For the several million prisoners of war

Map 1.1. Eastern Europe, 1944. Courtesy Béla Nagy, Hungarian Academy of Sciences.

and defenseless civilians—above all women who for months lived in continual fear of violation and indignity—the year 1945 brought not liberation, but tragedy.[12] According to Andrea Pető, the rapes committed by the soldiers of the Red Army in several Central and Eastern European countries represent a special case of social memory. On the one hand, everybody privately knew that the Soviet soldiers were committing rapes, but this fact became part of the canonized historical knowledge very late, in most cases only after the demise of socialism. Pető maintains that the silence around the Soviet soldiers' mass rapes was not a case of amnesia, but rather a "conspiracy of silence" obtained though the formation of a psychological pattern: keeping silent helped people believe that the events had not even happened, and that silence had a major impact on the formation of new national identity.[13]

These circumstances produced the incongruity between the official qualification in postwar Eastern Europe of the arrival of Soviet troops as liberators and the actual lived experiences of many Eastern Europeans. Not surprisingly, these experiences produced a much more critical appraisal of the Soviet military presence in Eastern Europe, one that has been passed down through the generations and survives in the region's collective memory to this day.

Ethnically Cleansed Europe and the Fate of the Collaborators

The end of the Second World War entailed the aggressive homogenization of both territorial and social space in the eastern half of Europe. During the Second World War, both the Western powers and the Soviet Union arrived at the same conclusion, though based on different considerations, regarding the ethnic tensions that existed in Eastern Europe: beginning in the 1930s, Germany and its allies abused minority rights in both theory and practice. They deemed the guarantees of the Paris peace system to be dangerous and advocated their annulment. The United Nations Universal Declaration of Human Rights, adopted in December 1948, protected only the individual rights of national, linguistic, and religious minorities and made no provision for their collective rights.[14]

According to Mark Mazower, the Allies agreed beginning in 1943 that the political and ethnic borders of postwar Eastern Europe be harmonized to facilitate the formation of nation-states in the region.[15] At the same time, one must recognize the validity of Tony Judt's assertion: "At the conclusion of the First World War it was borders that were invented and adjusted, while people were on the whole left in place (with the significant exception of Greeks and Turks, following the Lausanne Treaty of 1923). After 1945 what happened was rather the opposite: with one major exception boundaries stayed broadly intact and people were moved instead."[16]

The most enduring legacy of the Second World War, the German genocide and Stalinist nationality policy—the categorical and preemptive terror of "guilty peoples"—in Eastern Europe was not the introduction of the Soviet system, but the brutal nationalization of the physical and social spheres.[17] Between 1939 and 1950, nearly 30 million Eastern Europeans fell victim to ethnic cleansing of various forms—from population exchanges and forced expulsion to internment in work camps and mass murder—on the basis of the principle of collective guilt. Around 12 million civilians of German ethnicity were removed from Eastern Europe after the Second World War, including 7 million from Poland, 3 million from Czechoslovakia, and several hundred thousand from Hungary, Yugoslavia, and Romania. According to conservative estimates, more than 1 million of them died during the process of expulsion and resettlement. Stalin, Churchill, and Roosevelt on many occasions referred to this practice during their meetings regarding the future political and territorial organization of Europe.[18] Pro-Soviet authorities in Poland and Czechoslovakia did not wait for permission from the Allied powers attending the Potsdam Conference in the summer of 1945 to unilaterally expel the German inhabitants of these states, who had been declared collectively responsible for the catastrophe of the Second World War. The merciless ethnic cleansing and the mass flight of Germans that had been taking place since early 1945 radically transformed the ethnic composition of East Prussia, Pomerania, the Sudetenland, and Silesia in the period of just a few months. Only a small number of Germans known to be "actively anti-fascist" were permitted to remain in these regions.[19]

In 1946 and 1947 nearly 200,000 Germans were expelled from Hungary—roughly half of the country's German minority population—after being accused of collaborating with fascist authorities during the Second World War.[20] Hungary's communist-controlled Interior Ministry played a central role in the preparation and implementation of the expulsions. With the execution of the expulsion decree, the communists acquired yet another means of exercising power. However, the expulsion of Germans from Hungary according to the principle of collective guilt did not prove to be the foreign and domestic political panacea that Hungarian governments had hoped it would be. In fact, the expulsion of Germans weakened the position of these governments vis-à-vis those of victorious neighboring states, particularly Czechoslovakia. The fact that Prague regarded the expulsion of Germans from Hungary as a precedent exercised a decisive influence on the subsequent fate of their Hungarian minority populations. Moreover, many of the expelled Germans refused to accept the verdict that had been brought against them and later returned to Hungary, which they regarded as their only home.

Although no systematic expulsions took place in Romania, around 200,000 Germans—one-third of the country's German minority population—fled to the Allied occupation zones of former Nazi Germany in 1944 and 1945. In January of the latter year, the Allied Control Commission ordered that the 80,000 Germans living in the Banat and the Partium regions of Romania be transported to the Soviet Union to perform forced labor on the grounds that they had collaborated with the Nazis during the war. As the result of various rescue actions, "only" 69,000 Germans were eventually sent to the Soviet Union in cattle wagons in accordance with this order.[21]

In Yugoslavia particularly brutal forms of ethnic cleansing attended the postwar expulsions. The act of calling to account those accused of collaboration in this country provided the new Yugoslav leadership strata with the means to implement their desired elimination of the established urban middle classes. The Italian-speaking population of Istria and Dalmatia suffered the same fate as the German-language minority in Vojvodina and the Banat, even though the Allied powers had not endorsed the enactment of any measures against them in the name of collective guilt. The severe political, economic, and nationalist retribution to which Yugoslav authorities subjected Italian-speaking inhabitants of Istria and Dalmatia prompted almost all 250,000 of them to flee abroad.[22] Reprisals against the Hungarian minority in Vojvodina claimed around 15,000 lives in the autumn of 1944 and compelled tens of thousands more Hungarians to leave the region permanently.[23]

However, neither the nearly half million Hungarians of Yugoslavia nor the million and a half Hungarians of Romania were subjected to mass expulsion after the Second World War, and they quickly integrated into the new Yugoslav and Romanian political systems, which initially honored their linguistic and cultural rights. Conversely, the 600,000 Hungarians of Czechoslovakia endured the same type of discrimination as the Sudeten Germans. The presidential edicts proclaimed in Czechoslovakia in 1945 known as the Beneš decrees deprived the country's German and Hungarian minorities of their citizenship rights on the basis of the premise that they had collaborated with the Axis powers during the war. The common objective of the Czechoslovak political leadership in Prague and Bratislava shifted from the prosecution of the guilty toward collective punishment of so-called undesirable people. President Beneš had begun taking diplomatic steps already during the Second World War to expedite the unilateral expulsion of undesirable Germans and Hungarians from the reconstituted postwar Czechoslovakia. However, whereas all of the Allied powers endorsed the expulsion of Germans, only the Soviet Union supported the total expulsion of Hungarians. On February 27, 1946, Czechoslovakia and Hungary finally reached an agreement regarding a mutual—though asymmetrical—population exchange. According to this pact, Czechoslovakia would have the right to expel up to the same number of Hungarians as the number of Slovaks who voluntarily moved from Hungary to Czechoslovakia. However, in the end, the population-exchange agreement affected around 110,000 Hungarians compared to only 73,000 Slovaks.[24] Not all ruling parties and governments in Eastern Europe subjected national minorities to such severe measures in the postwar period. The Bulgarian Communist Party, for example, renounced the state nationalism of the interwar period and in the 1950s exercised positive discrimination toward the country's 800,000-strong Turkish minority.[25]

The treatment of minorities in Eastern Europe following the Second World War depended primarily on two factors: the Soviet appraisal of the given minority's past activity and the wartime geopolitical status of the state in which the minority was located. In the case of Hungary, for example, the facts that the country would have been incapable of receiving 2 million refugees and that the fate of Hungarian minorities in neighboring countries could have exercised a negative impact on the Hungarian Communist Party's room for maneuver and degree of social acceptance had to be taken into consideration.

With regard to Poland, where the issue of tense Ukrainian-Polish relations was due to be permanently resolved, Stalin acted exclusively according to Soviet national security interests. In September 1944, the pro-Soviet Polish government concluded an agreement with Soviet authorities that sanctioned the exchange of Poles and Ukrainians living in the territory of eastern Poland that was transferred to the Soviet Union after the war. Nearly 2 million Poles were exchanged for a half million Ukrainians under conditions of severe material deprivation and explosive ethnic antagonism.[26] The undeclared war in eastern Poland between two nations speaking similar languages was the result of complex political disagreements. The strong, illegal Ukrainian nationalist movement was based on territory that had formerly belonged to Poland. Whereas in 1939 most Ukrainians regarded Soviet military forces as liberators from Polish domination, by 1943 many of them elected to cooperate with the Germans to halt the advance of the Red Army. As the author of an important study on Lemberg has stressed, although the Nazis brought unprecedented forms and extremes of violence to that borderland microcosm, with regard to the perceptions and reactions of the local population, Soviet and Nazi policies nonetheless influenced each other and brought about a mounting radicalization against an ethnic and social group, former ruling Poles, who had come under attack from the 1930s onwards.[27]

Tensions surrounding this issue lasted until April 1947, when the Polish government decided to expel the 200,000 Ukrainian-nationality Lemkos from Poland on the grounds that they had collaborated with the anti-communist and anti-Polish Ukrainian resistance. The Czechoslovak- and Soviet-supported Operation Vistula resulted in the forced expulsion of 140,000 people in May and June 1947. According to Orest Subtelny, the Poles and the Soviets were pursuing divergent objectives in the resolution of the Polish-Ukrainian conflict: whereas the Poles, like the Czechoslovaks, wanted to establish a nation-state, the Soviets did not intend to create homogeneous Ukrainian territories, instead replacing the Polish-speaking inhabitants removed from these regions with people imported from European Russia.[28]

Various political forces acting in accordance with similar political motives worked toward the ethnic homogenization of Eastern Europe. In Czechoslovakia, both the large majority of people and all mainstream political parties, from the Beneš-represented civic-nationalist party to the communists, sought retribution against the Germans and the Hungarians living in the country. In Poland, communist leader Władysław Gomułka administered the territory in the western part of the country that had been reacquired from Germany. In Hungary, not all political forces supported the collective punishment of the country's German minority: while the communists and the National Peasant Party—representing the left-wing populist intelligentsia that had been active since the 1930s—advocated the expulsion of the "Swabians" (ethnic Germans in Hungary) and the redistribution of their vacated land, political moderates, some socialist democrats, and the Roman Catholic Church (the head of which, Cardinal József Mindszenty, was of German origin) opposed such action. In both Romania and Bulgaria, left-wing political parties supported the integration of national minorities, while right-wing parties endorsed the "Czechoslovak" solution to the national-minority issue.[29]

The vibrant Jewish communities that had previously existed throughout Eastern Europe were almost totally destroyed in most countries of the region during the Second World War. Of the 5 million Jews who lived in Eastern Europe before the war, only 1 million remained alive in 1945. Jews essentially disappeared from the Baltic states, Czechoslovakia, Ukraine, the Balkan Peninsula, and the Mediterranean region. A significant number of Jews survived the war in only three Eastern European countries: Romania (nearly 400,000), Poland (around 300,000), and Hungary (nearly 200,000). The only large urban Jewish community in Eastern Europe that remained largely intact after the Second World War and has survived until today is that of Budapest.[30]

The defeat of fascism did not bring an end to manifestations of anti-Semitism in Eastern Europe.[31] In 1946, deadly pogroms occurred in places where relatively large Jewish communities continued to exist even after the war, such as Kielce, Poland, and Kunmadaras, Hungary. The Hungarian political theorist István Bibó, who attempted in the immediate postwar period to analyze the trauma of the genocide and provide a rational explanation for the persistence of anti-Semitism, concluded in his seminal 1948 study that the latter phenomenon was the result of two conditions: prejudice based on medieval anti-Judaism, though detached from its religious roots in its modern form, and dissatisfaction arising from an accumulation of unresolved social crises and obstacles to social development as well as the desire to find scapegoats to blame for those adversities.[32] The "new anti-Semitism" was a fusion of traditional political and cultural motives and widespread antipathy toward upwardly mobile communist cadres.

As had occurred so many times in the course of European history, Jews were portrayed as scapegoats, and as a result of rising anti-Semitism, they were forced to
seek refuge, this time in Israel, which had been founded in 1948 with the support
of the Soviet Union. The mass emigration of Jews from Eastern Europe following the Second World War represented the loss of a highly skilled and educated,
economically dynamic social group that was receptive to Western influences and
prepared to meet the challenges of modernity.[33] According to Mark Kramer, the
ethnic cleansing and further erosion of Jewish communities that occurred in
Eastern Europe after the war produced an ethnic stability that helped communist
parties loyal to the Soviet Union take power in the region.[34]

The fate of those who had collaborated with foreign occupiers and fascist
dictatorships was an important issue throughout Europe following the Second
World War. Political purges and legal proceedings were initiated against collaborators across the continent. Extrajudicial killings were also widespread. Armed
civilians and (frequently communist) partisans executed tens of thousands of
people in France in 1944 and northern Italy in 1945. Moreover, the newly installed
authorities in these countries declined to launch investigations of the killings
until only years later, to avoid disturbing the fragile postwar peace; therefore,
most of these unlawful acts remained unpunished. The prosecution of wartime
collaborators in Eastern Europe nevertheless differed in two respects from that
in Western Europe: first, it occurred over a longer period of time—from the fall
of 1944 until 1948; and second, it entailed a significantly greater number of trials
(hundreds of thousands) and executions (thousands) in the region. The communist-led governments that came to power in Eastern Europe following the war
exploited the prosecution of collaborators to eliminate rival groups of political
elites—religious leaders, bourgeois party officials, and even those who had supported the illegal communist movements.

The calling to account of collaborators took place under extralegal conditions
in the months immediately following the collapse of Axis power in Yugoslavia,
Bulgaria, and Albania. The number of people killed and executed on charges of
collaboration in these countries was extremely high, although the precise figure
remains unknown. The war of national liberation in Yugoslavia brought long-
standing ethnic conflict to the surface in various regions of the country, such as
between Serbs and Albanians in Kosovo and between Serbs and Croats in Bosnia
and Herzegovina. Fighting in the territory of Yugoslavia between 1941 and 1945
claimed some 1 million lives. The motives of the warring sides were rooted in
an ever-changing combination of ideological, ethnic, and religious factors that
resulted in a protracted spiral of violence that claimed some 250,000 victims in
Bosnia and Herzegovina alone in 1945 and 1946.[35] The restoration of Yugoslav
administration generated hostility and fear among Kosovo Albanians, many of
whom had supported the German occupation and some of whom even joined

the Waffen-SS Skanderbeg Division to fight against the mostly Serbian Yugoslav partisans. Kosovo Albanians launched a rebellion in the fall of 1944 to unify the region with Albania, then led by Enver Hoxha. This uprising was "pacified" only one year later after Albania's communist leadership accepted Kosovo's reincorporation into Yugoslavia under strong Soviet pressure.[36]

In Yugoslavia, in the autumn of 1944 anti-fascist forces expelled 300,000 Germans accused of collaboration with the Nazis from Vojvodina and the Banat and drove them toward the western border of the country. An estimated 50,000 to 70,000 of these Germans were killed during these death marches.[37] Not only ethnic minorities were subjected to punishment for cooperation with the occupying powers; several tens of thousands of people, primarily Serbian military officers and civilians affiliated with the Chetnik movement, were killed with the arrival of the Yugoslav army and the rise to power of new communist authorities in the newly liberated city of Belgrade during the second half of October 1944. One of the most merciless instances of retaliation against suspected collaborators, one that continues to generate public debate, took place in the village of Bleiburg, located in modern-day southern Austria, near the border of Slovenia, during the second week of May 1945. After Ante Pavelić, the leader of the interwar *Ustaše* movement and the wartime German-sponsored Independent State of Croatia, fled from Zagreb, around 70,000 of his Croatian military and civilian supporters attempted to take refuge in the British zone of occupation in Austria. However, British authorities turned the Croatian refugees, by then numbering near 100,000, away from the border back into Yugoslavia. Local partisan leaders, ignoring Marshal Tito's orders, exceeded general expectations regarding the magnitude of reprisals, executing 10,000 Croatian soldiers and driving the rest of the refugees back through Slovenia in forced marches that claimed 26,500 military victims and 7,000 civilian victims.[38] The partisans thereby administered retribution against fascist collaborators and at the same time eliminated many members of the noncommunist resistance. Chetnik leader Draža Mihailović was executed on July 1946, and the archbishop of Zagreb Aloysius Stepinac was sentenced to sixteen years of hard labor a few months later.

The pro-Soviet government of Poland prosecuted not only those who had collaborated with the German occupying forces but also members of the Home Army who had fought against the Germans since 1939. The Soviet-guided political purges that took place in Poland between 1945 and 1947 resulted in 3,000 death sentences and the temporary imprisonment or deportation to the Soviet Union of around 150,000 Polish citizens.[39]

The new coalition governments in Hungary established people's tribunals in the spring of 1945 to try those accused of collaboration. These courts pronounced around 27,000 convictions and 477 death sentences, of which 189 were carried

out. Four heads of government from the period between 1939 and 1945—Béla Im-
rédy, László Bárdossy, Döme Sztójay, and Ferenc Szálasi—and several dozens of
ministers who had served in their cabinets were executed in 1946, and 62,000
government officials and civil servants were dismissed and placed under judicial investigation as a result of their actions during the deportation of Jews from
Hungary in 1944. According to László Karsai, the trials of suspected collaborators in Hungary manifested a unique duality: while prosecuting authorities,
including many Jewish judicial and police officials, used these cases to portray
wartime collaboration as the most recent episode in a long series of crimes committed against minorities in the country, the tribunals and other bureaucratic
organs simultaneously impeded the progress of legal proceedings.[40]

In Czechoslovakia, political purges before the communist rise to power
resulted in nearly 30,000 legal actions and 713 executions between 1945 and
1948. The focus and outcome of this retribution varied significantly between the
western and eastern halves of the country: in Bohemia and Moravia, 132,000 investigations were launched primarily against Sudeten Germans—while largely
sparing Czechs—on suspicion of "crimes against the nation," resulting in 21,000
convictions; in Slovakia, 100,000 investigations were initiated mainly against
Slovaks accused of cooperation with the pro-German administration of Slovak
Republic president Jozef Tiso, resulting in 8,058 convictions. Tiso himself was
sentenced to death for triple treason (collaboration with the Germans as well as
betrayal of Czechoslovakia and the Slovak National Uprising of 1944) and executed on April 18, 1947.[41] However, the judicial campaign against the Roman
Catholic priest and Slovak national leader Tiso generated long-term conflict
between the government in Prague and the noncommunist political parties in
Slovakia.[42]

Romania was the only state in Eastern Europe to initiate only a small number of people's tribunal proceedings against accused collaborators and war criminals following the Second World War. Courts operating in Bucharest and Iași
sentenced only 668 to prison in 1945 and 1946, and the court in Cluj responsible
for prosecuting Hungarian war criminals condemned many people to death in
absentia. In Romania only four wartime officials were convicted of war crimes,
including genocide committed against Jews in the country: former head of state
and government Marshal Ion Antonescu, former deputy prime minister and foreign minister Mihai Antonescu, and two associates, all of whom were executed
on June 1, 1946.[43] This declaration of essentially singular culpability made it possible for many of those guilty of collaboration and war crimes to evade justice in
Romania following the Second World War. Ironically, the death sentences that
the "revolutionary tribunal" later imposed on Nicolae and Elena Ceaușescu in
1989 produced similar results.

Eastern Europe in the Soviet Zone of Influence

Soviet and Western Peace Plans

Eastern Europe played a secondary role in the strategic plans that the United States and the United Kingdom began preparing with regard to the postwar peace settlement in 1942. The Politburo of the Communist Party of the Soviet Union (CPSU) decided only later, in the fall of 1943, to establish ad hoc committees to formulate future peace plans.

Specialists working for the Allied powers concluded that the nation-states and closed economic structures that had been established in Eastern Europe during the interwar period should be transformed into confederative systems.[44] Prime Minister Władysław Sikorski, of the Polish government-in-exile, and President Edvard Beneš, of the Czechoslovak government-in-exile, presented the Churchill government with a plan to establish two confederative states in Eastern Europe—a Balkan state centered on Yugoslavia and Greece and a Central European state centered on Poland and Czechoslovakia. In June 1942, the Advisory Committee on Post-War Foreign Policy, led by US secretary of state Cordell Hull, introduced a proposal to establish the "Union of East European States" in the territory located between Germany and the Soviet Union that would have included both Austria and Greece. The proposed union was divided into a northern section including the Baltics, Poland, and Czechoslovakia and a southern section centered on Austria and Hungary. According to the US plan, this two-part confederation would have had a common president and joint political and economic decision-making bodies. During the war, the London-based Royal Institute of International Affairs initiated the foundation of the Foreign Research and Press Service at Balliol College in Oxford. The specialists working under the auspices of this organization, who until 1944 did not regard the Soviet occupation of Eastern Europe to be inevitable, determined that the establishment of confederations could serve to curtail the ambitions of the continental powers in the region. Soviet officials not unexpectedly regarded English confederative plans to signify the revival of the notion of an anti-communist cordon sanitaire that emerged at the time of the post–First World War peace talks in Paris.

The counterattack of the Red Army following its pivotal victory at the Battle of Stalingrad in 1943 placed Soviet foreign policy on the offensive as well, thus further encouraging the process of carving out zones of influence. In May 1943, Stalin made the conciliatory gesture toward the West of dissolving the Comintern, which had maintained only a nominal existence since the purges of the late 1930s. Meanwhile, a division was established within the Central Committee of the CPSU to supervise relations among various communist parties. Alexei Filitov contends that the Soviet Union was considering long-term cooperation with the West, notably the United Kingdom. Existing documents from the period 1942–43 do not refer to revolution or democracy, although they frequently employ the term "zone of influence." According to a November 1943 memorandum, the Soviet zone of influence would include Sweden, Finland, Poland, Czechoslovakia, Hungary, Yugoslavia, Romania, Bulgaria, Albania, and Turkey. A January 1944 position paper defined the Soviet Union's primary postwar strategic objective: to lay the foundations for a long-lasting period of peace that would make it possible for the Soviet Union to grow stronger. According to this document, the socialist transformation of Eastern Europe could be achieved within thirty to fifty years, excluding all risk of war. The document furthermore emphasized the importance of establishing militarily defendable borders in Poland and Czechoslovakia.[45] Vojtech Mastny points out that Stalin's strategy was composed of a synthesis of insecurity, which sometimes approached paranoia, and traditional greater Russian aspirations and were therefore much closer to the geopolitical concepts of the czarist period than they were to those of Lenin. Paradoxically, in 1944 the peace committees led by Ivan Maisky and Maxim Litvinov reached even more radical conclusions than Stalin, proposing the creation of a Soviet zone of influence extending all the way to the borders of Western Europe, the dismemberment and economic subordination of Germany, and the immediate communist takeover of Poland.[46] The 1943 treaty of friendship between the Soviet Union and the Czechoslovak government-in-exile stipulated the restoration of Czechoslovakia's pre–Munich Agreement borders and the collective expulsion of Sudeten Germans, thereby allocating to Czechoslovakia a cardinal role in Soviet postwar security arrangements. With regard to the Hungarian-Romanian dispute over Transylvania, the Soviet Union's previously vacillating strategic goals vis-à-vis this region solidified to the benefit of Romania late in the war: in recognition of the military support that the new government of Romania provided the Soviet Union following its overthrow of the Marshal Antonescu–led military dictatorship in August 1944, Soviet officials decided to return northern Transylvania to Romania.[47]

From the "Percentages Agreement" to the 1947 Paris Peace Treaties

The Soviet Union began resolving the contradictions in its European policy with the meeting of Stalin, Churchill, and Roosevelt at the Tehran Conference from November 28 to December 1, 1943. Soviet diplomacy emerged from the conference in a fortified state: the United Kingdom's proposal regarding zones of influence had been rejected, and the United States accepted the Soviet Union's recommended modifications to the borders of Poland. The three great powers agreed, moreover, to establish a new international organization in place of the discredited League of Nations and to divide Germany into occupation zones. Stalin also convinced Churchill to recognize Tito as the military and political leader of the Yugoslav resistance movement. The United Kingdom therefore withdrew its previous support for Chetnik leader Mihailović in 1944, a turning point in the course of Yugoslavia's foreign and domestic politics.[48] The short-term objectives of the main Allied powers remained compatible as long as the United States was interested in maintaining political and economic cooperation with the Soviet Union.

The subsequent bilateral meeting between Stalin and Churchill took place in Moscow on October 9–10, 1944, as the Red Army was fighting its way through Hungary and Slovakia toward Vienna and Prague in its effort to bring Central Europe under Soviet control. The primary outcome of this meeting was the so-called percentages agreement. According to this deal, which Churchill proposed to Stalin at the end of their meeting, the United Kingdom and the Soviet Union would establish spheres of influence in the Balkans. Some observers considered the percentages agreement to be the product of pure realpolitik, founded on the notion of an undivided Europe and was compatible with traditional European balance of power policy. Fraser Harbutt reached a very different and provocative conclusion, arguing that Stalin might have been partly responsible for the forceful division of Europe after 1945, but the main burden of culpability would rest with Britain's wartime prime minister Winston Churchill, who purposely attempted to keep Stalin on his own side, as he was trying to maintain the British Empire through control of the Mediterranean and the Middle East.[49] It is important to note that numerous local military agreements had already been concluded in the summer of 1944; thus, the spheres of influence that Churchill and Stalin defined several months later in many instances, such as that of Romania, served merely to confirm the existing status quo.[50]

László Borhi has argued that already in 1944 the United States considered the Soviet occupation of most of Eastern Europe and its consequences to be unavoidable. The State Department regarded Czechoslovakia and Hungary as the only two countries in the region in which it might manage to retain US influence and thereby prevent their total separation from the Western world. This did not, however, indicate that the United States had accorded these countries—particularly Axis-affiliated Hungary—prominent roles in US foreign policy. Whereas Hungary participated only peripherally in the process of formulating postwar peace treaties, Austria gained much more influence over its own destiny given that the United States had defined the border between the two states as the limit of Soviet expansion and the demarcation line between West and East.[51]

The balance of power in the Balkans was thus clear from the beginning: Western influence in Greece and Soviet predominance in Yugoslavia, Romania, and Bulgaria. The communist rise to power in both Yugoslavia and Bulgaria in October 1944 seemed to create the conditions necessary to establish a confederation between them as Marshal Tito so strongly advocated. Tito furthermore maintained openly hegemonic plans regarding the entire region encompassing the Danube, the Adriatic, and the Balkans: the leader of newly liberated Yugo-slavia wanted to bring Carinthia, the Istrian Peninsula, and the city of Trieste in Austria, the Mecsek coal basin around the city of Pécs in Hungary, Greek Macedonia all the way to the city of Thessaloniki, as well the entire country of Albania under direct Yugoslav influence. After some hesitation, Stalin withdrew his support for Tito's territorial designs, which would have elicited strong an-tipathy from the Western powers and aroused strong doubts among the Georgi Dimitrov–led Bulgarian communists as well.[52]

The situation with regard to Poland was more complicated. Stalin somewhat reluctantly accepted the notion of cooperating with the anti-communist centrist Stanisław Mikołajczyk, to whom the Soviet leader had personally offered the post of prime minister in the new Polish government as well as one-quarter of its cabinet members in 1944. Soviet officials considered the Polish Workers' Party founded in 1942 to be unpopular, sectarian, and too radical in terms of its agri-cultural policy. Mikołajczyk, who served as the head of the Polish government-in-exile during wartime, himself resisted previous Soviet efforts to conclude an alliance, thus convincing Stalin to turn toward the Lublin Committee in the in-terest of forming a future Polish government.

Soviet attempts to establish a new, loyal Eastern Europe encountered in-creasing difficulty during the period between the Yalta Conference in February 1945 and the signing of peace treaties with Nazi Germany's five wartime allies—Finland, Italy, Hungary, Romania, and Bulgaria—on February 10, 1947. At Yalta, the Soviet Union, the United Kingdom, and the United States all supported the proposed division, disarmament, and demilitarization of Germany as a means of ensuring future peace in Europe. The main Allied powers furthermore came to the following agreements with regard to states in Eastern Europe: in Poland to establish a provisional democratic government in Poland, though delay elec-tions until after the war; in Yugoslavia to sanction the June 16, 1944, settlement between Tito and the head of the Yugoslav government-in-exile, Ivan Šubašić, stipulating that the two Yugoslav governmental powers be united under commu-nist leadership and that the Partisans be recognized as the sole Yugoslav national army; and in Romania and Bulgaria to institute Allied Control Commissions to oversee the process of political and economic reconstruction in those countries.

The Yalta Conference did not produce the division of the world into spheres of influence, nor did it ensure the Western loss of Eastern Europe; rather, it re-flected the desire of the Soviet Union, the United Kingdom, and the United States to cooperate despite their increasingly conspicuous ideological and strategic conflicts regarding the future of Europe. In 1945, following two years of work, the Council of Foreign Ministers managed to formulate a peace treaty that, par-tially in accordance with Soviet plans, essentially reestablished the prewar ter-ritorial arrangements. The conference failed to resolve two issues: the zones of

Allied occupation remained in both Germany and the German capital of Berlin, and the city of Trieste and its environs—over which both Italy and Yugoslavia claimed the right of sovereign authority—was divided into two zones of administrative control within an independent territory known as the Free Territory of Trieste, Zone A, under the military administration of the United Kingdom and the United States, and Zone B under the administration of Yugoslavia, which gained de facto sovereignty over this zone.

The German question emerged as the central problem affecting the course of international relations following the Second World War. In February 1945, the major Allied powers agreed to divide Germany as well as its capital city of Berlin into four occupation zones. The main objectives of the Potsdam Agreement concluded between the United States, the United Kingdom, and the Soviet Union in August 1945 were the denazification and democratization of Germany. This agreement also obliged Germany to pay enormous war reparations to several countries. However, there was significant disagreement between the Western powers and the Soviet Union regarding the implementation of the Potsdam Agreement. Over the long term, Stalin sought to establish unified administration over the four zones of occupation in Germany. The Western powers, however, were more interested in rebuilding the economies in their zones of occupation than they were in receiving war reparations; they quickly initiated efforts to realize their long-range objective of establishing economic and administrative unity in western Germany. Before 1948 the Soviet Union did not intend to establish a formally independent satellite state in its German zone of occupation. According to Norman Naimark, the leaders of the Soviet occupation zone in Germany were unfamiliar with institutional structures that diverged from those in the Soviet Union; therefore, their activity inevitably served to promote the Sovietization of this zone.[53] Even after the unification of the Western zones of occupation in Germany, Stalin continued to advocate the preservation of a unified Germany that would play the role of neutral political and economic intermediary between Western Europe and the Eastern Bloc. The Soviet leader attempted to force the Western powers to abandon the notion of dividing Germany by placing Berlin under military blockade and threatening to starve the city's civilian population. The Western powers responded decisively, launching an airlift that both ensured the provision of Berliners for nearly one year and showed the global public that Stalin could be defied with sufficient will.

Following France's declaration of support for the planned western German state, the foundation of the German Federal Republic was proclaimed on May 23, 1949, with its capital in Bonn. The German Democratic Republic was then established in the Soviet zone of occupation on October 7, 1949, thus substantiating the division of Germany that would last for approximately four decades (see map 1.2).

Map 1.2. Germany and Austria, 1945. Courtesy Béla Nagy, Hungarian Academy of Sciences.

Multi-Stage Revolution? People's Democracy and Sovietization

Stalin made the following well-known statement during a meeting in Moscow with a Yugoslav party delegation in April 1945: "This war is not as in the past; whoever occupies a territory also imposes on it his own social system. Everyone imposes his own system as far as his army can reach. It cannot be otherwise."[54] The logic that Stalin expressed raises a question: was the establishment of Soviet-type political systems throughout Eastern Europe unavoidable? The two preeminent early Sovietologists, Hugh Seton-Watson and Zbigniew Brzezinski, concluded that Stalin attempted during the final stages of the Second World War to generate a revolutionary situation that would make it possible for the Soviet Union to bring a large part of Europe under its military and political oversight. Soviet officials implemented carefully prepared plans designed to eliminate all internal opposition in the course of expanding the Soviet zone of influence.[55] Soviet military forces and political advisors were immediately able to eradicate almost all resistance in the states of Eastern Europe. In Czechoslovakia, Hungary, and Romania, Soviet specialists prudently placed local communist parties in control of the given country's interior ministry, police, state-security organs, propaganda mechanisms, and education system. The Soviets made a special effort to quickly bring local youth organizations under their oversight.[56]

According to Brzezinski, Soviet leaders and party ideologists used the expression "people's democracy" to differentiate the system they wanted to introduce in Eastern Europe from both the bourgeois and the socialist political and economic structures it was intended to gradually bridge. However, the Russian historian Leonid Gibiansky maintains that Stalin used the phrase "people's democracy" purely as a means of deceiving the West and noncommunist parties in Eastern Europe.[57] The expression "Sovietization," which is still frequently used to describe the political and social changes that took place in Eastern Europe after the Second World War, misleadingly encompasses several distinct events and periods, notably the Red Army's advance through the region in the years 1944–1945 and the subsequent political, economic, social, and cultural integration of Eastern European states into the Soviet empire. The word *Sovietization* pertains, in fact, to those territories that the Soviet Union conquered between 1939 and 1945—Finnish Karelia, Estonia, Latvia, Lithuania, East Prussia, the western regions of Belarus that were previously part of Poland, Subcarpathia in modern-day Ukraine, Bukovina, and Bessarabia. The Soviet Union employed various methods, ranging from looting and expulsion to agricultural collectivization, to rapidly bring these territories under its control during the Second World War and the immediate postwar period.

State violence and popular resistance continued in these territories for a long period of time following the end of the Second World War. Soviet authorities encountered strong armed resistance, which they attempted to suppress through the deportation of the "bandits" and their family members. Stalin resorted to the same means of eliminating this armed resistance with which he had quelled opposition in these territories between 1939 and 1941, offering concessions to certain strata of society while ruthlessly punishing others. In Lithuania, the Soviets returned land to the peasantry that the Germans had seized following their invasion of the country in 1941 and given to the Roman Catholic Church and the primarily German-nationality major landowners. Lithuania's capital of Vilnius, which had been part of Poland during the interwar period and the population of which was only 2 percent Lithuanian in 1939, became a Lithuanian-Soviet city in which the large majority of the population was Lithuanian within just a few years after the war.[58] Antanas Sniečkus, first secretary of the Lithuanian Communist Party, served as highest-ranking party official in Lithuania until 1974 and nevertheless supported the "Lithuanianization" of the postwar republic. Strengthening the native population was a much lower priority for the Soviets in Estonia and Latvia. Moscow encouraged the immigration of the Russian-speaking population into those republics. During the late Soviet period, Russian speakers came to constitute almost half the residents living in the capital cities of Tallinn (Estonia) and Riga (Latvia).

There was prolonged opposition to Sovietization in the Baltic states that did not end until 1953. Anti-Soviet guerilla groups that had been formed under German direction during the war counted nearly 50,000 members in the Baltics. The Soviets were forced to deploy both the army and security forces to defeat guerillas in Estonia. Armed resistance to Sovietization is a controversial subject in the postwar history of the region. The collective memories of Eastern Europeans living from the Baltic states to Romania have repudiated the communist-era charge that anti-Soviet partisans were guilty of cooperation with the Germans during the Second World War and continue to regard these armed resistance fighters as heroes.[59] The Organization of Ukrainian Nationalists and the Ukrainian Insurgent Army have emerged as an instrument of reinvigorating Ukrainian national identity since the 2014 political change and anti-Russian war. The nationalist resistance has been used more as the metaphor of the anti-Soviet and anti-communist struggle for independence than as historical entity.[60]

The Sovietization of western Ukraine represented one of the most drastic measures of mass oppression that began in the region with the Stalinist purges of the late 1930s. As a result of the Soviet Union's aggressive modification of the Soviet-Polish border and annexation of Subcarpathia from Hungary and northern Bukovina from Romania, the area of the Ukrainian Soviet Socialist Republic grew from 171,800 square miles to 222,400 square miles. According to Roman Szporluk, Stalin transformed Ukraine into a simulacrum of a state via the CPSU Central Committee's mandated establishment of Ukrainian and Belarusian foreign ministries and diplomatic delegations.[61] Szporluk maintains that Stalin took action to increase the political influence of the Soviet Union in the course of peace negotiations. Beginning in 1943, Stalin actively supported the aspiration of Eastern European Ukrainians to unite with a new Soviet republic. It is therefore understandable that the number of Ukrainians living in the already-mentioned traditionally Polish and Jewish city of Lemberg rose from 30 percent of the municipality's population in 1943 to 74 percent in 1946 as the result of the flight of Poles, the deportation and murder of Jews, and the settlement of Ukrainians. In view of the Soviet logic of state building, the fact that Ukrainian CPSU organization leader Nikita Khrushchev asked for the return of the Crimean Peninsula to Ukraine in 1944 and simultaneously directed the brutal persecution of pro-independence Ukrainian nationalists did not represent a political contradiction.

Beginning in 1943, the biggest problem that Ukrainian Bolshevik ideologues faced was the formulation of political doctrines that were national and "Slav" in outlook, though nevertheless differed from those of Ukrainian nationalists. Following the Second World War, the Ukrainian Greek Catholic Church was the most significant victim of Bolshevik ideological syncretism—the combination of internationalism and socialist patriotism. Stalin regarded the Ukrainian Greek Catholic Church, led by metropolitan of Lviv Josyf Slipyj, and its 4 million adherents as one of the greatest impediments to the Soviet integration of Ukraine. The Soviet leader launched a defamation campaign against the Ukrainian Greek Catholic Church clerics through local officials, who accused them of collaboration with the German occupiers during the war. In March 1946, the Soviet government convened a pseudo-synod that sanctified the return of the Ukrainian Greek Catholic Church to the patriarchate of Moscow. Romanian authorities announced the dissolution of the Greek Catholic Church of Transylvania in 1948, and Czechoslovakia banned the Greek Catholic Church of Subcarpathia the following year.[62]

The armed resistance that surfaced in the territories of Galicia and Volhynia following their Soviet occupation turned into a brutal civil war. A 1946 communiqué from the Soviet Interior Ministry regarding the struggle to regain control over Galicia and Volhynia reported the liquidation of 110,000 "bandits" and the arrest of 250,000 more bandits. During the civil war waged between 1944 and 1947, the Ukrainian Insurgent Army (Ukrayins'ka Povstans'ka Armiya) killed 30,000 Soviet soldiers and state functionaries, targeting those civilians suspected of collaboration with the occupying forces as well.[63] In 1953, Soviet minister of internal affairs Lavrenti Beria estimated that a half million people had been killed or arrested in western Ukraine during the postwar period. People living in territories annexed from Hungary and Romania suffered to an even greater degree. The non-Slavic inhabitants of these territories were subjected to systematic oppression, particularly in the previously Romanian-controlled region of Bessarabia. Nearly 500,000 citizens of Romanian nationality were deported from the

Moldavian Soviet Socialist Republic to the interior of the Soviet Union between 1944 and 1960.[64] Moreover, 200,000 inhabitants of the western parts of the Ukrainian Soviet Socialist Republic and the Moldavian Soviet Socialist Republic died of starvation in the great famine of 1946–1947. A Ukrainian committee examining Soviet-era oppression determined that the famine had not been the result of deliberate state policy, but that the indifference of Soviet officials had contributed greatly to the magnitude of the catastrophe.[65]

Deportations took place from the region of Subcarpathia as well in the years 1944–1945. Around 10 percent of the Hungarian population of the region—which had undergone five changes in national sovereignty over the previous century—was deported to labor camps in the Soviet Union in the autumn of 1944, along with 300,000 inhabitants of eastern Hungary.[66] During the late Stalinist period, people living in the regions incorporated directly into the Soviet Union suffered much more as a result of Sovietization than did those living in the nominally independent states of Eastern Europe.

The communist takeover of the states that came under Soviet military control was not implemented uniformly, but it did possess three common attributes: the predominant influence of the Soviet Union and local communist parties on domestic political events; the gradual elimination of noncommunist forces, which the West supported only half-heartedly; and discord between rival military and ideological blocs that emerged in large measure as the result of the deterioration of relations between the main Allied powers. Stalin's principle short-term objective was not to carry out political and social revolution, but "to gain control over weak East-Central European governments that had been purged of their pro-West and anti-Soviet political officials."[67] In the candid words of the future East German communist leader Walter Ulbricht: "It's quite clear—it's got to look democratic, but we must have everything in our control."[68]

Soviet military security played a key role in preparations for political expansion. Stalin's decision in the autumn of 1947 to establish Eastern European governments operating Soviet-type systems was based on tactical factors rather than ideological considerations. Soviet leaders regarded Eastern Europe primarily as a vast security zone. The priority of the Soviet Union was to stabilize the borders and the new state and social structures of countries in Eastern Europe as quickly as possible; thus, its presence served to suppress territorial disputes in the region. From a political perspective, the Soviet Union occupied the power vacuum created in Eastern Europe with the defeat of Nazi Germany, though beginning in 1944—contrary to the interwar period—it was able to bring the region under genuine long-term control. East European communist parties generally emerged fortified from the Second World War, and most of their leaders were loyal to the Soviet Union after having spent many years living there in exile. The Western powers did not hurry to support the Warsaw Uprising in September 1944 and abandoned the notion of liberating Prague ahead of the Soviets in May 1945.[69] In his analysis of Hungary's attempt to conclude a separate peace in March 1944, László Borhi argues that to facilitate the landing in Normandy the United States and United Kingdom put pressure on Budapest and Bucharest to break with Hitler even at the price of a German invasion of Hungary and Romania. Thus, the decision of Hungarian prime minister Miklós Kállay to attempt to withdraw from the Axis alliance took place under pressure from the Allied powers and served the strategic interests of the latter more than it did those of Hungary. From the years 1947–1948 until the mid-1960s, the United States believed that the independence of the small states of Eastern Europe would increase the overall stability and security of Europe. The Eastern European policy of the United States can thus be interpreted within the framework of the paradigm of continental stability versus national self-determination.[70]

Until 1947, Soviet authorities pursued subtle policies in Eastern Europe that to a certain degree recognized local political traditions and existing interests in the region. The Yugoslav and Albanian communist parties were able to monopolize power as early as 1945 because of the roles they had played in the anti-German armed resistance during the war, using their position of dominance to unabashedly liquidate their political opponents and initiate the Stalinist transformation of the economy and society.[71] The realignment of the two Balkan monarchies—Romania and Bulgaria—took place with relative speed as well: although the communist parties in these two countries faced fairly strong peasant parties after Kimon Georgiev became prime minister of Bulgaria on September 9, 1944, and Petru Groza became prime minister of Romania on March 6, 1945, from the very beginning the Soviets ensured that communists would fill every important governmental position in these countries.

The West tried unsuccessfully to influence the course of local politics in Eastern Europe through the Allied Control Commissions. Eduard Mark asserts in his comparative analysis that in many respects the status of Poland resembled that of Romania and Bulgaria, although Stalin focused greater attention on Poland because he considered it the most strategically important country in Eastern Europe. Soviet intervention in Poland therefore assumed a very direct and aggressive form: this country had to become socialist, primarily to satisfy the Soviet Union's strategic interests.[72] In Czechoslovakia and, to a lesser degree, Hungary, the Soviet Union participated with strong support from the Czechoslovak and Hungarian communist parties in the establishment of genuine anti-fascist coalitions and, subsequently, the staging of free elections. To accurately appraise the process of Sovietization in Eastern Europe, one must not fail to consider the internal changes that were taking place in the Soviet Union following the Second World War. The Soviet leadership regarded the subjugation of Eastern Europe to be necessary because it feared that a possible postwar political thaw could trigger a dangerous ideological counterreaction, thus threatening the stability of the Soviet Union.[73]

Politics and Economy in the Years of Transition

Eastern European countries did not constitute a homogeneous territory in either political or economic terms during the prolonged period of postwar transition. One can, however, discern common elements in all the "people's democracies" of Eastern Europe. Extreme right-wing nationalist parties were dissolved and their supporters persecuted. The political spectrum shifted to the left even in countries such as Czechoslovakia and Hungary in which genuine political pluralism existed until 1948. Communist parties strengthened considerably: the Romanian Communist Party (RCP), for example, grew from a marginal political movement into a hegemonic mass party in a period of just a few years. Power struggles that began within communist parties in 1948 introduced an element of grassroots anti-Semitism to the struggle between "Muscovite" and "national" communists, resulting in the gradual expulsion of undesirable minorities from the most sensitive realms of the mechanisms of power. Another common attribute of postwar politics in the states of Eastern Europe was serial land reform in which new governments redistributed the enormous estates of the Church and aristocracy. These land reforms entailed particularly strong political repercussions in Poland and Hungary, countries in which radical land distribution had not taken place after the First World War. In Czechoslovakia, Yugoslavia, and Romania, the process of land redistribution assumed an overtly ethnic quality, focusing predominantly on the ruling classes of German and Hungarian nationality to the benefit of the majority population. The production mechanisms in the various countries of Eastern Europe showed vast disparities until the 1950s, partially the result of previous levels of development (e.g., the economic structures of Bohemia and Moravia were similar to those of Germany and Belgium, whereas hardly any modern industry existed in the Balkan region) and partially the result of the speed with which they adapted their economies to Soviet expectations.

The Vanguard: Yugoslavia and Albania

Yugoslavia pursued model policies during the period 1945–1948 from the perspective of the pace at which it implemented economic and social transformation. The country's new coalition government was formed on March 5, 1945, with Tito as prime minister and monarchist Ivan Šubašić as foreign minister. Aleksandar Ranković, the close Serbian ally of the half-Croatian, half-Slovene Tito, became the interior minister of the government in 1946, holding that key position for twenty years. In October 1945, Šubašić and some of his associates resigned from their posts in this government to protest the dominant role that communists had taken in the administration of all aspects of the economy. The People's Front of Yugoslavia presented a common list of candidates in parliamentary elections held on November 11, 1945: voters participating in the elections could choose between the alternatives of either supporting this list or rejecting it. As John R. Lampe emphasizes, the absence of an organized opposition made it possible for the communists to win these elections: in Slovenia just more than 15 percent of voters cast ballots for non-listed candidates, whereas in Serbia and Vojvodina only 10 percent of voters backed such candidates. The fact that one-quarter of all the electorate boycotted the elections also deprived the opposition of potential support, thus propelling the People's Front to a landslide victory, with 68 percent of the votes.[74]

Introduction of the one-party system in Yugoslavia accelerated following the 1945 elections, bringing the period of political transition to a close in just a few months. The Federal People's Republic of Yugoslavia (FPRY) was proclaimed on November 29, 1945, and the Communist Party of Yugoslavia and its fellow travelers occupied all the seats in the parliament, which adopted the country's new constitution on January 31, 1946. The newly founded FPRY was composed of six federal republics—Slovenia, Croatia, Montenegro, Serbia, Bosnia and Herzegovina, and Macedonia—based on the system of republics in the Soviet Union enshrined in the 1936 Soviet Constitution. The regions of Vojvodina—the population of which was one-quarter Hungarian—and predominantly Albanian Kosovo were incorporated into the Socialist Republic of Serbia as autonomous provinces. However, administrative and fiscal federalism within the FPRY remained purely nominal until the 1960s, thus causing numerous conflicts between the republics and the central government in Belgrade. Although the 1946 constitution made no explicit reference to socialism, Tito initiated the mass nationalization of the means of production, a process that culminated in the First Five-Year Plan launched in April 1947. The estimated US$400 million in funding that the Western powers, primarily Yugoslavia's main ideological enemy, the United States, provided to the FPRY through the United Nations Relief and Rehabilitation Administration (UNRRA) contributed significantly to the short-term successes of the First Five-Year Plan.[75]

The swiftness of Yugoslavia's socialist transformation contributed to the rise in Tito's prestige, particularly in neighboring Albania. From the beginning of the Second World War, Tito regarded Albania and its small communist movement as a mere appendix of Yugoslavia and its communist party. Yugoslav authorities kept the Albanian state under close supervision until 1948. The previous year, Yugoslavia provided Albania with credit amounting to one-half of the country's gross domestic product, and the Communist Party of Yugoslavia represented its Albanian counterpart in the foundation of the Information Bureau of the Communist and Workers' Parties (Cominform). The Albanian communists learned much from Tito, adopting his early radicalism. In 1945, the prime minister of the provisional government and officials operating under the authority of communist party leader Enver Hoxha used Yugoslav methods to eliminate their political rivals. Albania's interior minister Koçi Xoxe initiated merciless reprisals that nominally targeted war criminals and those who had collaborated with the Italian and German occupiers, although they were in fact aimed primarily at the leaders of the northern Gheg clan and prosperous peasants. Most of the new communist leaders not incidentally were southern Albanians of urban *moyenne bourgeoisie* origin. In elections held in Albania on December 2, 1945, the Democratic Forum won 93 percent of the votes with a unified list of candidates. Albania became a people's republic even before Yugoslavia with the adoption of a new constitution that signified an end to the previous kingdom in early January 1946.

"Revolution from Abroad": Poland, Romania, Bulgaria

Whereas internal forces dominated the process of building socialism in Yugoslavia and Albania, Soviet leaders played a decisive role in the establishment of political and economic systems that they deemed suitable in other countries of Eastern Europe. The strategic interests of the Soviet Union predominated especially with regard to the new borders of Poland. Stalin insisted on maintaining control over the territories in eastern Poland that the Soviet Union had acquired in 1939. Even during the war, the Soviet leader actively sought to have these territories cleansed of unreliable elements, notably the Polish middle class and intelligentsia. Stalin compensated Poland for the Soviet Union's retention of these territories with a large section of land that had encompassed the eastern part of Germany. During the final months of the war, the Soviet Union regarded the Polish Committee of National Liberation that had been formed in Lublin under Soviet direction in July 1944 as the sole legitimate government in Poland. The influence of communists within Poland increased enormously after the elimination of noncommunist resistance in the country with the suppression of the Warsaw Uprising in October 1944. The 600,000-member Polish People's Party (Polskie Stronnictwo Ludowe, or PSL), led by Stanisław Mikołajczyk, became the most powerful political force in Poland following the secession of its pro-communist agricultural wing in September 1945. The stipulation of the Yalta agreement prescribing the incorporation of representatives from the people's party, the socialist party, and the democratic party into the government coalition came into effect in June 1945. Nevertheless, armed detachments of the communist party, with the cooperation of the police and secret services, fought fierce battles against the PSL activists in rural areas of Poland.

Polish national resistance stood in a state of dramatic confrontation with Soviet ambitions to exercise total control over political life in Poland during the early postwar years. The so-called Three Times Yes referendum held in Poland on June 30, 1946, was intended to sanction the objectives of the communist-controlled Democratic Bloc: dissolution of the Senate, partial nationalization of the economy, and designation of the new Polish-German border along the Oder-Neisse line. Although the official results of the referendum showed 70 percent approval for the first two propositions and 90 percent approval for the third, archival data reveals that without fraud and manipulation, only the latter proposal regarding the location of the Polish-German border would have received the majority of votes needed for confirmation. The communist Polish Workers' Party–dominated Democratic Bloc that contested Poland's intimidation- and violence-marred parliamentary elections on January 19, 1947, comprised parties that resembled their historical predecessors in name only. According to estimates at the time, the Democratic Bloc would not have obtained the majority of votes in this election had the Soviet occupational forces and the Polish police not conducted a large-scale campaign of fraud and intimidation that served to reduce support for the opposition Polish People's Party (PSL). With the support of tactics such as the exclusion of PSL candidates from several voting districts on spurious grounds, the disqualification of numerous "reactionary elements" from electoral lists, and the arrest of hundreds of opposition candidates, the Democratic Bloc won 80.1 percent of the votes, thus acquiring 394 of 444 seats in parliament, while the PSL received just 28 parliamentary seats.[76] On February 19, 1947, the Polish parliament adopted a new constitution that contained both communist and noncommunist constitutional elements; it would remain in effect until 1952. Following the removal of Stanisław Mikołajczyk from the government, the Edward Osóbka-Morawski–led Polish Socialist Party—which, contrary to the government-allied socialists, had maintained its political independence—represented the only genuine opposition to communist power. However, the socialists were compelled to revoke the membership of one-quarter of its members on charges of reactionary sympathies, and the party was forced to merge with the Polish Workers' Party in December 1948 just as left-wing parties were pressured to unite with communist parties throughout Europe during this year.

Poland's transitional period was complex from an economic standpoint as well. On September 6, 1944, the National Unity Front government enacted land reform that embodied national aspirations, notably the strengthening of the middle peasantry through the redistribution of German-owned land to Polish homesteaders. Banks and large factories were subsequently nationalized as part of the three-year reconstruction plan launched in 1947. This plan was designed to reach the ambitious objective of elevating the Polish standard of living back to its prewar level by the end of 1949. As Joseph Rothschild emphasizes, the three-year reconstruction plan did not implicitly represent the introduction of the socialist system: Poland's economic system was based on the precepts of state capitalism already in the 1930s; therefore, there was significant popular support for the nationalization of banks and factories stipulated in the plan.[77] The collapse of foreign trade networks with the advance of the Cold War caused a greater degree of economic upheaval in Poland than did the reconstruction plan. Moreover, in the summer of 1947 the Soviet Union forced Poland to withdraw from participation in the US Marshall Plan, which provided massive reconstruction aid to countries throughout Western Europe, including former Axis powers Germany, Austria, and Italy. However, the end of the Second World War signified the rebirth of the Polish population despite the political and economic upheaval of the postwar period. There were 3.5 million births in Poland between 1946 and 1950, and the number of marriages recorded in the country rose to a hundred-year high in the two years following the end of the war.

Two related factors served to undermine support among the citizens of Poland for the socialist system being built in the country: first, Stalin's previous anti-Polish policies (e.g., the 1939 Molotov-Ribbentrop Pact, the mass execution of army officers and other Polish nationals in Katyń in 1940, the failure of Soviet troops to help the Polish Home Army during the Warsaw Uprising in 1944), and second, the frustration of Polish independence ambitions as a result of the country's incorporation into the Soviet-Russian external empire via implementation of the Soviet leader's "revolutionarily imperialist" strategy.[78]

The communist takeover proceeded with much less difficulty in Hitler's reluctant Balkan ally of Romania. King Michael I utilized every constitutional means at his disposal to prevent the takeover of Romania, although contrary to the situation in Poland, the main opposition parties—the National Liberal Party and National Peasant Party—were unable to generate a mass base of support. The Soviet Union exploited the issue of dominion over Transylvania to the greatest possible degree as a means of increasing its influence over politics in Romania, and Romanian left-wing forces used the defense of national interests as one of their main sources of legitimacy. The sovereignty of Transylvania continued to provide the Soviet Union with considerable leverage over the course of Romanian domestic politics despite the fact that the September 1944 armistice stipulated that the disputed region—or at least the greater part thereof—be "returned to Romania, subject to confirmation at the peace settlement." The Soviet Union's candidate for prime minister of Romania—Petru Groza—had spent his entire career promoting the processes of Romanian-Hungarian rapprochement, although as a young man he had been involved in the Transylvanian Romanian national movement. In 1933, Groza founded the left-wing agrarian Ploughmen's Front organization, which did not possess a broad social base of support until 1944 but managed to become the most significant political ally of the small Romanian Communist Party after the war and functioned as one of the main advocates of the new government's policies, particularly land reform, in rural Romania.[79]

In February 1945, the Soviet deputy minister of foreign affairs Andrei Vyshin-sky traveled as Stalin's special envoy to Romania, where he issued an open ulti-matum to King Michael I: appoint a "democratic" government or lose the Soviet Union's guarantee of Romania's national sovereignty. Although King Michael was highly reluctant to surrender Northern Bukovina, Bessarabia, and Southern Dobruja (the so-called Cadrilater) and knew that the communists would exercise a significant degree of power in the new cabinet through their control of the Min-istries of the Interior, Justice, and Finance, he decided to approve the Groza gov-ernment on the grounds that the minimal stability of Romania could be ensured in no other way. The young monarch nevertheless continued to passively resist the communist takeover. Confident that the Western powers would support him, King Michael urged that the composition of the Groza government be broadened to include members of opposition "historical parties." Over a period of several months from the summer of 1945 until January 1946, Michael engaged in a royal strike, refusing to sign the Groza government's decrees until Soviet officials ap-proved the primarily formal changes that he demanded.

The citizens of Romania lived under the illusion of political pluralism until the country's first postwar parliamentary election on November 19, 1946. Con-trary to the case in other Eastern European states, the political transformation that took place in Romania shortly after the Second World War did not entail the overhaul of the state administration: during this period, the bureaucracy contin-ued to operate as it had before 1944 with only minor personnel changes.[80]

Apparently irreconcilable demands and expectations managed to coexist in Romania between 1944 and 1947. The Groza government achieved its great-est success with its policy of equilibrium vis-à-vis the Romanian Orthodox Church clergy and the complex nationality issue. The large Hungarian minor-ity, which from the beginning resisted integration into the Romanian state, was the beneficiary of broad cultural and linguistic rights. The Hungarian-language Bolyai University in Cluj was at the time the only university in Europe at which all courses were taught in the language of a national minority. The Hungarian People's Union established in the autumn of 1944 managed to unite the politi-cally diverse representatives of the Hungarian nationality, thus facilitating the integration of the Transylvanian Hungarians into the new state.[81] Romanian Jews recovered the civil rights that they had lost in 1938 and mostly supported the new system despite the fact that many advocates of the Zionist movement planned to immigrate to Palestine.[82] The Germans of Transylvania and the Banat were, however, subjected to political and economic persecution—many of them were expelled from their homes and deprived of their lands as a result of the 1945 land reform, temporarily divested of their right to vote, and prohibited from joining party and mass organizations. At the same time, the Germans of Romania were not exposed to widespread physical violence following the Second World War, as were the Germans of Czechoslovakia and Yugoslavia.

Although modern Romanian historiography often portrays early communism as an anti-national ideology guided from abroad that served foreign interests, deeper investigation of the activities of the postwar Romanian Communist Party reveals that it adeptly managed to build political consensus among a broad range of social strata. The relatively smooth incorporation of Romania into the Soviet empire was partially the result of the subordination of the Romanian economy to the Soviet economy via the establishment of Soviet-Romanian joint enterprises called SovRoms.[83] The Soviet-dominated Allied Control Commission gained immense influence over the postwar transition process in Romania through the exercise of political and economic pressure, while the opposition, led by Iuliu Maniu and Dinu Brătianu, could do no more than issue loud protests intended to draw the attention of the Western powers to the communist takeover that was occurring in the country. Leadership changes within these historical opposition parties and their failure to gain support among young people and the urban working classes contributed to their inability to compete with the increasingly popular Romanian Communist Party. The dominant figures within the RCP following the Second World War were former railway worker and communist home resistance member Gheorghe Gheorghiu-Dej and the Moscow-trained Ana Pauker—who in November 1947 became the first woman in the world to serve as foreign minister—became foreign minister of Romania.[84]

Elections held on November 19, 1946, marked a decisive step toward the communist seizure of power in Romania. According to official results, the Democratic People's Front won more than two-thirds of the vote. As in Poland, the elections took place amid widespread violence and heavy electoral fraud. Although there is no precise data available regarding the genuine results of Romania's November 1946 elections, a confidential report prepared for the Romanian Communist Party estimated that the Democratic People's Front and the Hungarian People's Union together won between 43 percent and 45 percent of the vote; the opposition peasant and liberal parties would have received half of the vote in a fair election.[85] The prevalent opinion that the opposition would have won a large majority of the votes cast in a fair election therefore appears to be inaccurate. In fact, the actual results of the election may well have reflected a deeply divided country.

The formation of a new parliament following the November 1946 elections and the signing of the Paris Peace Treaties in February 1947 enabled the Groza government to abandon its previous tactical concessions and cautious economic policies—notably, respect for individual private property. Several hundred opposition officials were interned by decree in the spring of 1947. National Peasant Party leaders Iuliu Maniu and Ion Mihalache were arrested at a military airport in June 1947 as they prepared to leave Romania and establish a government-in-exile.[86]

The deterioration of the international political situation in the autumn of 1947 provided the communist effort to build a party-state dictatorship in Romania with a further boost. The communist Ana Pauker was appointed to replace liberal foreign minister Gheorghe Tătărescu, who had become a loyal supporter of the Groza government despite his right-wing political past, and the third most powerful official within the RCP, the head of the party's Transylvanian organization, Vasile Luca, became finance minister. On December 30, 1947, King Michael I abdicated and went into exile, and the Romanian People's Republic was declared. In February 1948 the Romanian-Soviet treaty of "friendship and mutual assistance" was signed and the million-member Romanian Workers' Party (Partidul Muncitoresc Român) was formed via the merger of the Romanian Communist Party and the Romanian Social Democratic Party. The People's Democratic Front easily won the single-list legislative elections held on March 28, 1948. Two weeks later, the Great National Assembly adopted Romania's new, Soviet-style constitution.

Whereas Romania moved rapidly in the direction of a one-party political system, no radical reform to the country's economic structure took place until the summer of 1948. Although Romania was compelled to send raw materials as well as industrial and agricultural products to the Soviet Union for years as payment of war reparations, the Romanian Communist Party declined to expose itself to the sharp opposition that nationalization and appropriation of private property would have entailed. The drought and subsequent famine that caused hundreds of thousands of deaths in northeastern Romania during the years 1946–1947 heightened the reluctance of the RCP to undertake open confrontation with a large segment of the population. Even the Soviets encouraged Romanian communists to leave the economy in private hands and to guarantee the country's capitalists minimally reasonable profit.

In Bulgaria, the communist party had retained the international prestige that it had acquired between 1919 and 1923 largely as a result of the activity of Georgi Dimitrov and that provided it with much more domestic popularity than its counterparts in Romania or Hungary. Moreover, Bulgaria, along with Czechoslovakia, was one of the few countries in Eastern Europe in which only a small number of people harbored anti-Russian sentiments. The initial phase of the transitional period in Bulgaria following the Soviet occupation of the country in 1944 was, nevertheless, very violent. Bulgaria's new, communist-led coalition government, which included all domestic anti-Nazi political forces, agreed in the October 28, 1944, armistice with the Soviet Union to provide military support to the Red Army and to establish internal order. At the same time, the coalition government used the people's tribunals established to prosecute war crimes as a political weapon: the investigation of the entire military and state apparatus resulted in 11,000 death sentences, although R. J. Crampton estimates that political reprisals could have claimed between 50,000 and 100,000 victims in Bulgaria during the immediate postwar period. In 1946 alone, people's tribunals convicted two regents, two former prime ministers, twenty-six former government ministers, several dozen former parliamentary representatives, and 2,000 other people. The political and legal assault of the Bulgarian right eliminated the elite that had survived the war and placed the reorganizing communist party in a position of great advantage vis-à-vis its subordinate allies—the Bulgarian Agrarian People's Union, the social democrats, and the Zveno movement, a patriotic military and political organization that had joined the anti-Axis resistance.[87]

The most important opposition leader during this time was Bulgarian Agrarian People's Union official Nikola Petkov, who refused to play the proffered role of communist fellow traveler and called for a boycott of the November 18, 1945, parliamentary elections. The Patriotic Front was the only political force in Bulgaria to participate in the elections, which it won with 86 percent of the vote.

The ratification in July 1947 of the peace treaty with the victorious parties the previous February represented the turning point in the communist political takeover of Bulgaria. The first victim of the subsequent rise in communist power was Nikola Petkov, whose parliamentary immunity was revoked before a people's tribunal found him guilty of espionage and sentenced him to death. The other party opposing the Patriotic Front and the Bulgarian Agrarian People's Union—the Kosta Lulchev–led social democratic party—was allowed to participate in October 27, 1946, elections and the referendum regarding the form of state only as a result of pressure from the West. The opposition parties won nearly 30 percent of the vote in the elections despite pressure that had been placed on eligible participants, although this result did not provide them with enough power to oppose Dimitrov's government. The new constitution, based on the Soviet and Yugoslav model, which went into effect in Bulgaria on December 4, 1947, abolished the monarchy and transformed the country into a people's republic.

Smothered Democracies: Czechoslovakia and Hungary

Czechoslovakia was in a relatively advantageous position compared with the rest of the states of Eastern Europe at the end of the Second World War. In December 1943, Stalin and Beneš signed a Soviet-Czechoslovak treaty of friendship and cooperation that included the following stipulations: restoration of Czechoslovakia's territorial integrity, expulsion of enemy minorities, recognition of Gottwald's communists, free and fair elections, and the formulation of a government of national unity under the leadership of the party that received the greatest number of votes in these elections. At the same time, the Czechoslovak government-in-exile in London enjoyed the support of the Western powers. After 1945, public opinion in the free world looked upon Czechoslovakia with sympathy, primarily as a result of the guilt it felt regarding the 1938 Munich Agreement and the subsequent dismantling of Czechoslovakia. Prague thus found itself on the side of the victors following the war, despite the absence in the country of self-criticism toward the mass collaboration that had taken place in the Protectorate of Bohemia and Moravia and the anti-Jewish actions of the Tiso government in the Slovak Republic from 1939 to 1945.[88] The resolute, sometimes even ruthless, measures against minorities designed to create a Czech and Slovak "Slavic" nation-state obscured all internal debate in Czechoslovakia during the immediate postwar period. Soviet military forces withdrew from the territory of Czechoslovakia in December 1945; thus, the independence of the country seemed to be genuine until the summer of 1947.

After returning to Czechoslovakia from London on April 3, 1945, Beneš established his new headquarters in the city of Košice in Slovakia. There the National Front coalition formed a provisional government under the leadership of the social democrat Zdeněk Fierlinger. The Fierlinger cabinet's Košice Government Program, published on April 5, 1945, called for punitive measures ranging from expulsion to abrogation of civil, cultural, and linguistic rights to be enacted against Czechoslovakia's German and Hungarian minorities. This program reflected the values and convictions of nearly the entire Czechoslovak political establishment and thus elicited broad support. Klement Gottwald, leader of the Communist Party of Czechoslovakia (Komunistická Strana Československa, or CPC), personally drafted some of the questionable stipulations of the Košice Government Program, such as those prescribing the punishment of collaborators and minorities, while Communist Party of Slovakia leader Gustáv Husák extended the scope of such retribution to include Slovak war criminals as well—a measure that the Slovak National Council, which served as the de facto regional government of Slovakia until 1948, subsequently reconfirmed.[89] Following the Second World War, resolution of the national question represented the most important political issue in Czechoslovakia.

The so-called re-Slovakization program intended to promote the assimilation of Hungarians in Slovakia, which was launched in April 1946, constituted the final step in Czechoslovakia's expedited effort to establish a nation-state. Slovak communists participated in the implementation of this program of "Leninist nation-building," which served to imbue Slovak national identity with deeply anti-Hungarian and anti-bourgeois features.[90] An Interior Ministry directive issued in 1946 stipulated that those who declared themselves in the 1930 census to be of Slovak nationality were to be regarded as Slovak nationals and thus Czechoslovak citizens, along with Czechs and members of any other Slavic nationality.[91] Czechoslovak authorities expected around 150,000 requests for citizenship based on these conditions; they had received 410,800 such petitions by the year 1948. However, the re-Slovakization program was a long-term failure because those who had elected to submit statements regarding their nationality did not deny their self-identity. Through the postwar statement of loyalty, members of the Hungarian minority managed to avoid mass expulsion and abrogation of their civil rights while subsequently being able to again identify themselves as Hungarians without risking harm to their citizenship status in the following censuses.

In the years 1946–1947, Czechoslovakia's political system contained both liberal democratic elements, such as multiple parties and an extensive private sector open to Western contacts, and "people's democratic" elements, such as the exclusion of the right-wing parties, a broad nationalization campaign, Soviet friendship, and the steady flow of fellow travelers into coalition parties. With the exception of their exclusion of the non-Slav minorities, the May 20, 1946, parliamentary elections, were held in a free and fair manner and showed that the advocates of Western-type parliamentary democracy still composed the majority of the population. The Communist Party of Czechoslovakia, the membership of which had grown from around 80,000 to 500,000 over the previous year, won only 38 percent of the votes in the elections—40 percent in Bohemia and Moravia and 30 percent in Slovakia, where the conservative, Jozef Lettrich–led Democratic Party received almost twice as many votes as the CPC. In accordance with the 1943 Soviet-Czechoslovak treaty of friendship and cooperation, CPC's leader Klement Gottwald was appointed prime minister, while fellow CPC members received nine ministerial posts in the twenty-two-member government, including those of interior minister, justice minister, and information minister. Through its control of the Justice Ministry, the CPC was able to exert significant influence over the outcome of the enormous number of cases being tried at people's tribunals in Czechoslovakia during the period.

This situation changed in the summer of 1947. Soviet leaders forced the communist-led coalition government of Czechoslovakia to abandon its plan to obtain US reconstruction aid through the Marshall Plan. Referring to his talks with Soviet officials regarding participation in the Marshall Plan, Czechoslovak foreign minister Jan Masaryk—the son of Czechoslovakia's founder, Tomáš Garrigue Masaryk—was claimed to have said, "I went to Moscow as the foreign minister of a sovereign state. I returned as a lackey of the Soviet government." The intervention of Soviet leaders to prevent Czechoslovakia from acquiring Marshall Plan aid signified the end of the country's relatively large degree of sovereignty compared to that of its Eastern European neighbors. Tony Judt argues that his decision to stand aside from the European Recovery Program was "one of Stalin's greatest strategic mistakes," as the Americans "would have had no choice but to include Eastern Europe in the aid program, having made the offer available to all, and the consequences for the future would have been immeasurable."[92]

Thus, rejection of Marshall Plan aid not only served to distance the highly industrialized Czechoslovak economy from those of Western Europe but prepared the ground for impending political changes as well. The Communist Party of Czechoslovakia's loss of popularity as a result of the Soviet intervention did not significantly alter the situation. The seizure of power unavoidably entailed violence and oppression under the circumstances that had prevailed in Czechoslovakia since the CPC's proclamation of a general strike in 1947 against the anti-communist Democratic Party, which continued to hold significant power within the Slovak National Council. Beginning in early 1948, the communists, worried that they might be removed from the government as had occurred in Italy and France, mobilized organized labor and the people's militias. The Czech National Social Party then withdrew from the government, prompting all other parties except the CPC and the Czech Social Democratic Party to do the same. However, the popular mobilization and Soviet political blackmail culminated in a general strike that forced reluctant president Beneš to appoint on February 23 a new government based on a Gottwald-prepared list of appointees. The communist seizure of power in Prague had proceeded successfully in spite of the heavy moral message that the suspicious death of Masaryk on March 10, 1948, carried with regard to the coming period in Czechoslovak political history. The communist-dominated government passed the new "people's" constitution of Czechoslovakia through parliament and on May 30 ended the country's second experiment with democracy via single-list elections. The subsequent death of President Edvard Beneš represented the removal of the final, largely symbolic obstacle to the introduction of the Soviet-style communist system in Czechoslovakia.[93]

Conditions in Hungary were catastrophic in both political and psychological terms at the end of the Second World War. The German occupation had paralyzed Hungary's democratic political forces, which began to increase their activity only after the takeover of the Arrow Cross on October 15, 1944, and the advance of the Red Army toward Budapest later that autumn. A provisional coalition government was formed in the liberated city of Debrecen under the leadership of General Béla Dálnoki Miklós on December 22, 1944, then moved its headquarters to Budapest in April 1945. This government undertook the radical transformation of Hungary within a hostile international environment. The Soviet Allied Control Commission, led by Marshal Kliment Voroshilov, exercised nearly unlimited power in Hungary from 1945 to 1947, essentially operating as a shadow government during this period.[94] Hungary was in a disadvantageous position as compared to all its Soviet-supported neighbors in terms of postwar territorial issues. The provisional coalition government concluded an armistice with the Soviet Union on January 20, 1945, as fighting raged in Budapest and the Arrow Cross retained control of western Hungary. In this armistice the provisional government recognized Hungary's war guilt; agreed to pay immense war reparations to the Soviet Union, Czechoslovakia, and Yugoslavia; and renounced control over territories that had been reincorporated into the Hungarian state beginning in 1938. Hungarian political authorities and public opinion nevertheless maintained naive expectations regarding territorial and minority issues until the Council of Foreign Ministers formally decided in Paris on May 1946 to restore Hungary's interwar borders.[95] Among the members of Hungary's coalition government, the British and US-supported Independent Smallholders Party advocated the redrawing of postwar frontiers based on the ethnic principle, the Hungarian Social Democratic Party vacillated between border correction and territorial-cultural autonomy, and the Hungarian Communist Party attempted to simultaneously satisfy Soviet noninterference dictates and strengthen its weak national legitimacy through expression of support for the Transylvanian Hungarian minority and criticism of the discriminatory policies of the Czechoslovak government toward the Hungarians of Slovakia.[96]

The authority of Hungary's provisional government nominally emanated from the parliament formed in December 1944. However, this assembly—of which 133 members were either communists or social democrats—never convened, thus permitting the provisional government to rule by decree until elections held on November 4, 1945. The two most important measures that Hungary's provisional government enacted during its eleven and a half months in office were to dissolve extreme right-wing organizations and to adopt the land-reform program of communist minister of agriculture Imre Nagy. This land reform served to partially correct the social imbalance that had existed in Hungary since the end of the First World War, redistributing 35 percent of the arable land in Hungary to 642,000 families—most of which derived their subsistence from small-scale farming and agricultural day labor—and reducing the maximum size of private land holdings to slightly more than 50 hectares.[97]

The highly favored Hungarian Communist Party suffered a severe defeat in Hungary's November 1945 parliamentary elections. The Independent Smallholders Party, the most right-wing of the parties in the ruling coalition, won 57 percent of the votes cast in the election; the Hungarian Social Democratic Party, 17.4 percent; the Hungarian Communist Party, just under 16.9 percent; the National Peasant Party, 6.9 percent; and the liberal Civic Democratic Party, 1.6 percent. The poor performance of the communists in this election caused disappointment among Soviet leaders, prompting Stalin to approach impending elections in Yugoslavia and Bulgaria with much greater vigilance. The Soviet-dominated Allied Control Commission and the Hungarian Communist Party devised a plan to establish a government in which it would be possible to eliminate the Independent Smallholders Party majority in parliament through the formation of a government in which all coalition parties would receive equal representation. In

1951, the communist leader Mátyás Rákosi amused himself by using a culinary metaphor to label the gradual elimination of the opposition as "salami tactics."

The law declaring Hungary a republic came into effect on February 1, 1946. Although the modifier *people's* had not yet been appended to the official form of state, authorities in Hungary began to crack down on potential enemies of the new system. The first potential sources of opposition to be dissolved were youth organizations, among them the National Body of Catholic Agrarian Youth Young Men's Associations—the final Roman Catholic political organization operating in Hungary—and the Scout Movement. The purging of the state apparatus and exclusion of "reactionary" Independent Smallholders Party (Független Kisgazdapárt, or FKgP) representatives from the FKgP parliamentary caucus proceeded in a nearly continuous wave. By the autumn of 1946, more than 60,000 so-called B-list government employees had been dismissed and politically reliable people appointed in their place.

In February 1947, just a few days after the conclusion of the Paris Peace Treaties, the press in Hungary announced the exposure of the Hungarian Fraternal Community (Magyar Testvéri Közösség). Béla Kovács, the combative secretary-general of the Independent Smallholders Party, was arrested and deported to the Soviet Union, from where he returned to Hungary only in 1955. A further fifty Independent Smallholders Party parliamentary representatives withdrew from the FKgP to protest Kovács's arrest, thus reducing the party's National Assembly caucus to one-third of its initial size following November 1945 elections. Meanwhile, it became clear that other FKgP representatives were communist fellow travelers. On May 30, 1947, Prime Minister Ferenc Nagy resigned while on a visit to Switzerland after communists had threatened to place his family members in Hungary under arrest.

Multiple parties contested Hungary's subsequent parliamentary elections on August 31, 1947, and confidential party reports acknowledged that communist brigades operating primarily in villages cast 63,000 ballots more than once. In spite of the fraud that had occurred in these so-called blue-ballot elections, the Left Bloc of the Hungarian Communist Party, the Hungarian Social Democratic Party, and the National Peasant Party failed to achieve the anticipated majority. Thus, even with the help of the fraudulent "blue ballots," the three parties of the Left-Wing Bloc received only a slightly higher combined percentage of votes cast in the 1947 elections than they had in the elections held in 1945. However, the more moderate political forces in the coalition had splintered into six parties and were thus unable to profit from the Left-Wing Bloc's failure to win an absolute majority of votes in 1947 elections.[98]

Many Hungarians had interpreted the results of the 1945 elections to indicate that Hungary would become a democratic state rather than a Soviet satellite and were thus unprepared for the conversion to a single-party system. However, economic changes preceded this political transition. The Soviet Union placed Hungary in a state of economic dependence through the required payment of millions of US dollars in war reparations, the conclusion of unfavorable economic treaties, and the dismantling of entire industrial facilities. Moreover, the most intense hyperinflation ever recorded anywhere in the world rattled Hungary's economy. Hungary introduced a new currency, the forint, on August 1, 1946, to reestablish financial stability in the country. At the time of its introduction, the value of the forint to the former currency, the pengő, was fixed at one to 400 quadrillion.[99] Particularly in eastern Hungary, communists and their local allies brazenly exploited the political and economic uncertainty stemming from the hyperinflation and the black market to incite anti-Semitism, which resulted in pogroms that claimed several lives.[100]

Following the August 1947 elections, the government of pro-communist FKgP prime minister Lajos Dinnyés prepared the ground for the dissolution of the multiparty system. The Hungarian Social Democratic Party was forced to merge with the Hungarian Communist Party, thus producing the united Hungarian Workers' Party. The first exclusively communist government in Hungary was formed on December 10, 1948, under the leadership of Mátyás Rákosi. According to László Borhi, the Sovietization of Hungary, by which anti-communist political traditions were infused with anti-Russian independence sentiment, was the unavoidable product of Soviet political will and the hegemony that the Soviet Union had gained over the small country that after the Second World War had been left without allies.[101]

Formation of the Soviet Bloc

From the Fulton Speech to the Establishment of Cominform

The increasingly conspicuous conflicts of interest that emerged in the summer of 1947 between the Western powers and the Soviet Union signified an end to the great alliance against fascism. Differences of opinion regarding the status of Germany and the national affiliation of the city of Trieste essentially paralyzed the peace process, thus providing an indication of the infeasibility of common administration of European affairs. Amid the tense atmosphere of the immediate postwar period, the question of the future of Central Europe contributed to the outbreak of international disputes. Speaking at Westminster College in Fulton, Missouri, on March 5, 1946, Winston Churchill asserted that an Iron Curtain had descended "from Stettin in the Baltic to Trieste in the Adriatic" as a result of increasing Soviet political influence in Eastern Europe.[102] The Soviets resentfully repudiated this claim, though continued to believe until early 1947 that the wartime Allied alliance could endure on the basis of the conditions Stalin had posited: common resolution of the German and Austrian questions, international economic cooperation in exchange for the moderate influence of communist parties over Western governments, and the Soviet Union's total political and economic control over the occupied states of Eastern Europe.

On March 12, 1947, US President Harry S. Truman delivered a speech in which he urged Western governments to take measures to oppose the threat of communism regardless of where it emerged, specifically at this time in Greece and Turkey. The uncertain balance among the allies ended in the spring of 1947. As well-organized communist parties were being expelled from governing coalitions in Italy and France, US Secretary of State George C. Marshall announced a comprehensive plan to provide economic and financial assistance to the countries of Europe. This so-called European Recovery Program, which immediately became known as the Marshall Plan, provided a total of $17 billion in aid to seventeen countries in Western Europe through the year 1951. The ambitious objective of the Marshall Plan—to promote the economic integration of Europe— represented an open challenge to Soviet geopolitical interests. Moreover, in addition to Germany, the Soviet Union and its Eastern European satellite states were also eligible to receive Marshall Plan aid, which would have served to reduce the degree of Soviet influence in Europe.[103] Scholars unanimously agree that the rejection of Marshall Plan aid throughout the countries of Eastern Europe represented a clear indication of the impending establishment of the Soviet Bloc.

The founding of the Communist Information Bureau, or Cominform, in September 1947 to coordinate the activities of the various communist parties of Europe represented the next indication of the emergence of the Soviet Bloc. The primary objective of Cominform was to provide the satellite states of the Soviet empire with a vehicle to strengthen organizational coordination and ideological compatibility. However, Cominform included among its members both communist parties from the "people's democracies" of Eastern Europe as well as those from France and Italy—although it did not invite communists from western Germany and Albania to the organization's founding session in Szklarska Poręba, Poland. Andrei Zhdanov presented the opening address at this event, articulating for the first time during his speech the Stalinist ideological vision of a world divided into two camps. According to this concept, these camps included the "democratic anti-imperialist" powers, or the Soviet-led people's democracies, and the "anti-democratic imperialist" powers, or the US-led capitalist states.

The aggressive anti-West rhetoric of Soviet and Yugoslav representatives at the meeting served to reconfirm the collapse of the former Allied alliance and established the ideological foundation for the introduction of Soviet-type systems in Eastern Europe.[104]

The activity of the Cominform was apparently focused on the international dissemination of Soviet propaganda. However, few of Cominform's operations

On Soviet Turf | 51

were public. Control over the organization's apparatus—secretariat, political lecturers, and specialists—was a Soviet prerogative. Prior to 1950, Cominform held secret consultations in Poland, Romania, and Hungary, and the organization's secretariat held four secret meetings. However, the most important decision Cominform made during these secret deliberations was to expel the Communist Party of Yugoslavia from the international communist movement at its meeting in Bucharest from June 19 to June 23, 1948. This measure signaled the beginning of a previously inconceivable conflict between the Soviet Union and its former star pupil.

The Yugoslav Schism

The extension of Soviet control over Eastern Europe presented Stalin with a new dilemma: should the Soviet Union tolerate states in its new sphere of influence to diverge from the Soviet model and travel their own paths toward establishing the socialist system? This problem emerged for the first time in concrete form with regard to Yugoslavia. Tito occupied a unique position among Stalin's postwar Eastern European allies, having gained independent internal legitimacy and leadership over the region's most powerful communist party as a result of his command of anti-fascist forces in Yugoslavia's four-year partisan war. Until 1947, Yugoslavia benefited from the full diplomatic, military, and economic support of the Soviet Union. The Soviet Union was Yugoslavia's most significant trade partner and helped train the Yugoslav army and secret services. Soviet dissatisfaction with Tito emerged in the autumn of 1947 as a result of Yugoslavia's conclusion of a bilateral treaty of cooperation and mutual assistance with Bulgaria in August of that year. Tito obviously regarded the Yugoslav-Bulgarian treaty, which had been concluded without prior Soviet approval, as the first step toward the creation of a future Balkan bloc. Within the tense international climate, Stalin objected to the treaty, the signing of which was delayed for several months by vehement Soviet protests. In January 1948, the Bulgarian Communist Party's general secretary Georgi Dimitrov raised the possibility of establishing a Balkan confederation and customs union that would have included not only the "people's democracies" of Yugoslavia and Bulgaria but Greece as well. On January 19, Tito prepared to annex Albania without the prior approval of the Soviet Union, prompting the CPSU's daily *Pravda* to publish an article criticizing the Yugoslav leader. Stalin harshly denounced Tito's hegemonic ambitions during a secret meeting with Yugoslav and Bulgarian leaders in Moscow on February 10, 1948.

The growing dispute between the Soviet Union and Yugoslavia led to a political split between the two countries in the spring of 1948.[105] In March, Stalin abruptly recalled Soviet military and political advisers from Yugoslavia amid the

Map 1.3. Eastern Europe, 1949. Courtesy Béla Nagy, Hungarian Academy of Sciences.

intensive exchange of correspondence between the CPSU and the Communist Party of Yugoslavia. The Soviets accused Tito and his followers of opportunism and deviation, and the Yugoslavs argued that they maintained the right to diverge from the Soviet model of socialism.[106] The intensification of the conflict became unavoidable with Cominform's June 22, 1948, condemnation of Yugoslavia for nationalism. Eastern European communist parties and governments launched a sweeping anti-Yugoslav propaganda campaign under the direction of the Soviet Union. In Hungary, where Tito was widely popular among communists, party leader Mátyás Rákosi referred to his Yugoslav counterpart as a "chained dog of the imperialists." Borders with Yugoslavia were sealed and trade relations broken. However, Stalin was unable to realize his objective of quickly replacing Tito and his closest political allies. The Yugoslav Communist Party leadership remained unified behind Tito, initiating a merciless police crackdown on so-called Cominformists, that is, communists who had remained loyal to the Soviet Union. The Stalin-Tito split provided the West with an unexpected opportunity to undermine the internal cohesion of the Soviet Bloc. To achieve that objective, the Western powers provided Yugoslavia with economic support that enabled Tito to proclaim the ideology of the "Yugoslav road to socialism" founded on the principle of economic self-determination. This doctrine served as the basis of Tito's legitimacy for decades following its inception in the 1950s. The conflict between Stalin and Tito ended without a clear winner, although the Yugoslav leader's model did not attract any followers (map 1.3).

Notes

1. Mazower, *Hitler's Empire*, 142–143.
2. Ibid., 173–178.
3. Ioanid, *Holocaust in Romania*; and Solonari, *Purifying the Nation*.
4. Case, *Between States*.
5. Boeckh and Völkl, *Ucraina*, 141.
6. Snyder, *Bloodlands*; and id., *Black Earth*. A critical review of the latter in Browning, "New Vision of the Holocaust," 41–43.
7. Snyder, *Black Earth*, 177–216.
8. Piotrowski, *Poland's Holocaust*, 305.
9. Ferrara, "Esodi, deportazioni e stermini,'" 659.
10. On the Italian-Soviet wartime relations, see Zaslavsky and Aga-Rossi, *Togliatti e Stalin*, 136–156.
11. Davies, *Storia d'Europa*, 1157.
12. For a description of the mass violence in the Soviet occupation zone in Germany, see Naimark, *Russians in Germany*, 69–140. On the same issue in postwar Hungary, see Ungváry, *Battle for Budapest*, 279–295; and Mark, "Remembering Rape," 133–161.
13. Pető, "Memory and the Narrative of Rape in Budapest and Vienna," 129–149.

14. Cassese, *I diritti umani nel mondo contemporaneo*, 26–49.

15. Mazower, *Le ombre dell'Europa*, 219.

16. Judt, *Postwar*. 27.

17. Polian, *Against Their Will*, especially 115–153.

18. Naimark, *La politica dell'odio*, 128–132.

19. Ther and Siljak, *Redrawing Nations*.

20. Tóth, *Telepítések Magyarországon 1945–1948 között*.

21. Tismăneanu, Vasile, and Dobrincu, *Raport Final*, 355–359.

22. Pupo, *Il lungo esodo*. From a comparative perspective, see Pirjevec, *Foibe*.

23. The anti-Hungarian reprisals of 1944 have been the subject of a long historical controversy. A mixed historical commission helped find a scholarly consensus. See Glatz, *Magyarok és szerbek*.

24. Vadkerty, *A kitelepítéstől a reszlovakizációig*, 19–25, 123–130, 145–150, and 303–385.

25. *Human Rights of Muslims in Bulgaria*, 36–48.

26. Naimark, *La politica dell'odio*, 155.

27. Amar, *Paradox of Ukrainian Lviv*.

28. Naimark, *La politica dell'odio*, 157.

29. Bottoni, *Transilvania rossa*, 31–60.

30. Stark, *Hungarian Jews during the Holocaust, 1939–1949*.

31. On the survival of the concept of a Christian Europe in postwar Hungary, see Hanebrink, *In Defense of Christian Hungary*, 222–237.

32. Bibó, *Zsidókerdés Magyarországon 1944 után*, 2–261.

33. Wasserstein, *Vanishing Diaspora*.

34. See Kramer's introductory study in Ther and Siljak, *Redrawing Nations*, 8.

35. Malcom, *Storia della Bosnia*, 259.

36. Malcom, *Storia del Kosovo*, 349–358.

37. Zeljko and Lukic, "Migrations on the Territory of Vojvodina," 69–93.

38. Grahek Ravancic, "Controversies about the Croatian Victims," 27–46.

39. Courtois, *Il libro nero del comunismo*, 352.

40. Karsai, "People's Courts and Revolutionary Justice in Hungary," 233–252.

41. Ward, *Priest, Politician, Collaborator*, pp. 287–288.

42. Adams, "The Politics of Retribution," 252–290.

43. Ioanid, *Lotul Antonescu în ancheta SMERȘ*."

44. Romsics, *Wartime American Plans for a New Hungary*; and Bán, *Pax Britannica*.

45. Filitov, "Problems of Post-War Construction in Soviet Foreign Policy Conceptions," 3–22.

46. Mastny, *Il dittatore insicuro*, 20.

47. M. Fülöp, *La paix inachevée*; and A. Fülöp, *La Transylvanie dans les relations roumano-hongroises*.

48. Bettanin, *Stalin e l'Europa*, 114–116.

49. Harbutt, *Yalta 1945*, especially chapter 3.

50. On the Romanian case, see Percival, "Churchill and Romania," 41–61.

51. Borhi, *Magyar-amerikai kapcsolatok*," 19–20.

52. Bettanin, *Stalin e l'Europa*, 145.

53. Naimark, *Russians in Germany*, 353–364.

54. Djilas, *Conversations with Stalin*, 114.

55. Seton-Watson, *East European Revolution*; and Brzezinski, *Soviet Bloc*.

56. Applebaum, *Iron Curtain*, chapter 7.

57. Naimark and Gibiansky, *Establishment of Communist Regimes in Eastern Europe.*

58. Graziosi, *L'URSS dal trionfo al degrado*, 32.

59. Anušanskas, *Anti-Soviet Resistance in the Baltic States.* On anti-Soviet resistance in Romania, see Dobre, *Bande, bandiți și eroi.* On resistance movements in the western Soviet Union, see Rieber, "Civil War in the Soviet Union," 129–162.

60. Yurchuk, *Reordering of Meaningful Worlds*, 200.

61. Graziosi, *L'URSS dal trionfo al degrado*, 44.

62. Boeckh and Völkl, *Ucraina*, 159–162.

63. Graziosi, *L'URSS dal trionfo al degrado*, 45–46.

64. Cașu, *Dușmanul de clasă.* See also Cașu, "Political Repressions in Moldavian SSR after 1956," 89–127.

65. Tismăneanu, Vasile, and Dobrincu, *Raport Final*, 749–764.

66. Stark, "Deportation of Civilians from Hungary to the Soviet Union," 605–618.

67. Bettanin, *Stalin e l'Europa*, 159.

68. Judt, *Postwar*, 131.

69. Kramer, "Stalin, Soviet Policy, and Consolidation of the Communist Bloc," 59–71.

70. Borhi, *Dealing with Dictators*, chapters 2 and 3.

71. Bettanin, *Stalin e l'Europa*, 125–129.

72. Mark, "Revolution by Degrees."

73. Graziosi, *L'URSS dal trionfo al degrado*, 23–27.

74. Lampe, *Yugoslavia as History*, 231.

75. Ibid., 239–240.

76. Wróbel, *Historical Dictionary of Poland*, 89–90.

77. Rothschild, *Return to Diversity*, 82.

78. Behrends, "Nations and Empire," 443–466.

79. Bîtfoi, *Petru Groza, ultimul burghez.*

80. On administrative practices, see Bottoni, "Reassessing the Communist Takeover in Romania," 59–89.

81. Olti and Nagy, *Érdekképviselet vagy pártpolitika?*

82. Nastasă, *Evreii din România (1945–1965).*

83. Banu, *Asalt asupra economiei României.*

84. Levy, *Ana Pauker*, 84.

85. Bottoni, "Reassessing the Communist Takeover in Romania," 78–79.

86. Deletant, *Communist Terror in Romania*, 80.

87. Crampton, *Eastern Europe in the Twentieth Century*, 225–226.

88. I follow here the revisionist interpretation of Mary Heimann, although a group of Czech scholars criticized her for the biased approach to Czechoslovak history. See Heimann, *Czechoslovakia*, especially chapters 4 and 5.

89. Frommer, *National Cleansing*, 73–76.

90. Cohen, *Politics without a Past*, 93–100.

91. Vadkerty, *A kitelepítéstől a reszlovakizációig*, 346–348.

92. Judt, *Postwar*, 92–93.

93. Abrams, "Hope Died Last," 352–359.

94. Cseh, *Documents of the Meetings of the Allied Control Commission for Hungary.*

95. See Békés, *Európából Európába*, 53–128.

96. For a fine analysis of the dilemma that Hungarian communists faced regarding the minority issues, see Mevius, *Agents of Moscow*, 136–160.

97. Romsics, *Hungary in the Twentieth Century*, 228–229.

98.   Mevius, *Agents of Moscow*, 188–189.

99.   Romsics, *Hungary in the Twentieth Century*, 230.

100.   On anti-Semitism in Hungary during the postwar period, see Kenez, *Hungary from the Nazis to the Soviets*, 157–161.

101.   Borhi, *Hungary in the Cold War*, 53.

102.   Churchill's full speech is available at the website http://www.winstonchurchill.org /resources/speeches/1946-1963-elder-statesman/the-sinews-of-peace.

103.   Bettanin, *Stalin e l'Europa*, 225.

104.   Procacci, *Cominform*.

105.   Gibiansky, "The Soviet-Jugoslav Conflict and the Soviet Bloc," 224–225.

106.   Rothschild, *Return to Diversity*, 130–131.

Chapter 2

Terror and Thaw (1949–1955)

Institutional Isomorphism and Cultural Revolution

New Bureaucracy, New Cultural Codes

Radical political, economic, and social transformations aimed at reproducing the system that Stalin had created in the Soviet Union took place in Eastern Europe from the introduction of one-party rule until the Soviet dictator's death in 1953.

According to Arfon E. Rees, the new political system established in Eastern Europe during this period was the product of Soviet self-defense requirements, in preparation for possible military conflict with the West, and the rational utopia of socialist modernization occurring in the economically and culturally diverse states of the region.[1] Although the process of Sovietization did not entail the disappearance of all national characteristics, the new leaders of countries in Eastern Europe attempted to adapt political systems and economic as well as social structures to Soviet norms. Viktor Zaslavasky described such integration as "institutional isomorphism."[2] Constitutions based word for word on the 1936 Soviet constitution were adopted throughout Eastern Europe. Criminal and civil codes were rewritten and amended according to the Soviet model in all states of the region. Although members of the state apparatus in the countries of Eastern Europe were carefully selected after the Second World War, purges of public-sector employees began in the region in 1948.

During this period, entire government ministries and organizations were eliminated in the states of Eastern Europe. Young civil servants of working-class origin, who often lacked experience and training, were chosen to replace those who had lost their jobs as the result of the public-sector purges. The "revolution" that had taken place in Eastern Europe emphasized the priority of productive work over state administration and therefore rapidly transformed the social composition of the leadership in the countries of the region. The importance of political loyalty exceeded and replaced that of technical knowledge and skill, thus temporarily ending the centuries-long process of professionalizing state employees. Eastern European communist parties, which in accordance with the Soviet model gained control over state administration, either substituted for or complemented traditional governing bodies such as ministries and government offices. The commonly used term *nomenklatura* designated party-approved officials who held positions of significant authority.

The organizational pyramid of the party was built on a dual structure of territory and production. Communist Party members were eligible to join the primary organizations in factories, municipalities, or municipal districts. The duality was present at the highest echelons of administration as well. Although a certain internal dialectic prevailed at these levels and the resolutions of the most powerful party organizations assumed statutory force, party decisions were nevertheless substantiated in the form of government decree. The party's central-committee sections—propaganda, organization, cadre, heavy industry, light industry, agriculture, external affairs, culture, and education—were given the authority to supervise enactment of approved laws. With the help of external institutions, these central-committee sections essentially performed the duties of government ministries. The immense party apparatus nearly overturned the existing official pyramid, causing frequent conflicts of authority among the various bureaucracies. Official organs that were supposed to cooperate often competed to gain jurisdiction over important administrative measures and duties. In the countries of Eastern Europe, the administrative chaos that emerged following the communist takeover typically displayed all the dysfunctions of the later Stalinist period, from Bolshevik "legal nihilism"—that is, negative attitudes toward the rule of law—to the intimidation of society. Over the long run, the introduction of this immoderate and inefficient state mechanism produced structural defects that no subsequent reform efforts were able to remedy.

The Stalinist Ecosystem

The rules, values, and symbols that predominated in Europe at the height of the Cold War in the years before Stalin's death—which David L. Hoffmann depicted as the "Stalinist ecosystem"—persisted long after the Soviet dictator's death.[3] Throughout most of Europe, modes of mass communication such as newspapers, radio programs, and propaganda posters were imbued to an unprecedented degree with ideological expectations and the need to establish uniformity. The same themes and personalities appeared repeatedly in newspaper headlines, humor magazines, movies, and cultural events. Cultural planning was not confined exclusively to the censorship of information disseminated to the general public; it also served to define the style of newspaper journalism, thus providing readers with an all-encompassing interpretation of reality. A new, ideologically charged idiom confronted ordinary citizens in the public sector, at Communist Party assemblies, and during political debates: this language steadfastly portrayed the West as "tainted," "decadent," and "imperialist" while presenting the working class as the "vanguard" of socialism, fighting a continuous battle against both internal and external enemies. The latter category included the remnants of capitalism—the kulaks, the bourgeoisie, and the large landowners who sabotaged economic progress. The new political systems in Eastern Europe even meddled in the designation of geographical locations: in 1950, for example, authorities in Romania rechristened the Transylvanian city of Braşov as Oraşul Stalin (Stalin City), which reverted to its original name only a decade later. Stalin and the communist leaders of Eastern Europe, with the possible exception of Polish United Workers' Party (PUWP) leader Bolesław Bierut, were revered as supernatural beings—Hungarian Workers' Party General Secretary Mátyás Rákosi quickly received the title of "Stalin's best student," and Bulgarian Communist Party General Secretary Vulko Chervenkov was said to have radiated "the light reflected from Stalin's cult of personality."[4] The birthdays of these leaders were celebrated with enormous pomp, and their personalities honored with poetry, novels, paintings, and statues.[5] Vanguard workers and Stakhanovites were celebrated as heroes in the press after setting production records in nationalized factories.

Cities and factories organized labor competitions in recognition of official public holidays—notably the November 7 anniversary of the Great October Socialist Revolution and the various dates on which the Soviet Red Army had liberated the states of Eastern Europe in 1944 and 1945. A grotesque competition emerged among these states in their effort to emulate Soviet social and cultural models. Soviet science was regarded as unquestionably superior to that of the West: Soviet discoveries and technological innovation were hailed as triumphs of socialist progress, and Western scientific achievements were either ridiculed or disregarded. The intelligentsia was forced into highly politicized professional associations, such as the various writers' unions. Artists were compelled to adapt to the single legitimate aesthetic style—Soviet-inspired socialist realism, which, according to Andrei Zhdanov, strove to create a historically accurate and truth-confirming depiction of the "revolutionary development of reality."[6] Modern and abstract painting, symbolist poetry, dodecaphonic music, and, naturally, jazz— the typical capitalist artistic import—were ignored and their most prominent practitioners and proponents persecuted and forced to repudiate their artistic principles. Stalinism totally engulfed education, which, along with research, was subjected to revolutionary transformation throughout Eastern Europe beginning in the 1948–1949 academic year to make it conform more closely to the Soviet model. New scientific academies were founded, and existing ones were brought under strict official supervision and purged of their undesirable members to ensure that the state would exercise an absolute monopoly over the propagation of classical culture and the social sciences. In accordance with the Soviet model, universities were relegated to be institutes of higher learning that did not engage in scientific research. Class-based discrimination was practiced in the selection of new students until the 1960s. However, John Connelly's comparative study of the development of universities in East Germany, Poland, and Czechoslovakia in the 1950s reveals that the academic community engaged in forceful cultural resistance against homogenization and leveling. This intergroup solidarity frequently prevailed over ideological dictates even during the late Stalinist period.[7]

The introduction of the communist state also entailed the reorganization of the administrative sphere as well as the use of revolutionary utopian urban architecture. The area of many major cities in Eastern Europe was enlarged through the incorporation of surrounding communities. The objective was to transform these cities into highly developed metropolises to which suburban municipalities were appended to produce agglomerations that functioned as vectors of modernization to accommodate the quickly growing working classes. Stalinist socialist classicism replaced the strictly rationalist Western architecture of the interwar period and was embodied in buildings such as the Palace of Culture and Science in Warsaw, the Stalinallee boulevard in East Berlin, and the House of Scînteia (the title of the Romanian Workers' Party daily newspaper) central press headquarters in Bucharest. Important cities, university towns, and municipalities serving as religious centers were demoted to rural status on purely political grounds, which resulted in their rapid decline. At the same time, enormous investments were made to build new "socialist cities" such as Nowa Huta (New Steel Mill) on the outskirts of Kraków in southern Poland; Sztálinváros (Stalin City), now called Dunaújváros, in central Hungary; and Stalinstadt, now known as Eisenhüttenstadt, in eastern Germany.[8] These multifunction urban complexes designed according to the concept of communist utopia represented, along with existing industrial plants, the forward outposts of socialism. In his study of the first socialist city in Hungary, Sándor Horváth concluded that Sztálinváros scarcely resembled the revolutionary phalanstery that communist authorities had envisioned. People whom prevailing ideology described as "declassed elements" were overrepresented within the original population of Sztálinváros.[9]

The new system placed great emphasis on political education, which was obligatory for citizens of all ages, to prevent the emergence of popular dissatisfaction resulting from economic hardship. For the majority of Eastern Europeans, particularly those of peasant origin, instruction in the foundations of socialist ideology did not exceed the boundaries of general informative pedagogy. People were taught to wash their hands and brush their teeth in courses on basic hygiene, and working women received instruction in the modes of reconciling their maternal and workplace duties. Party activists held lectures on the origin of humans in which they attempted to convince their audiences of the supremacy of Darwinism over creationism. From the perspective of the communist elite, which League of Communists of Yugoslavia official and theorist Milovan Đilas described as a "new class," the Soviet Union represented both a military and political center and a new social vortex. During the early socialist period, thousands of young Eastern Europeans, primarily those of working-class and peasant origin, studied at Soviet universities and research institutes. These young students regarded themselves as the vanguard of a political and cultural elite imbued with the duty to disseminate the messages of the new era. The new leadership class of Eastern Europe—political officials, party functionaries and intellectuals, university students, economists, and artists—met in the city of Moscow, which had become the diplomatic and cultural crossroads of the Soviet Bloc.   *isolation*

The Cold War separated the Eastern Bloc from Western Europe both physically (the closing of borders, the introduction of visa requirements, and the rejection of passport applications) and culturally. Western embassies operating in Eastern Europe were forced to reduce their diplomatic personnel and activity to the bare minimum. Cultural centers and Western-operated libraries were closed in many Eastern European cities. Written correspondence and telephone communications were placed under strict supervision. Borders, even those lying within the Soviet empire, became nearly impassable, thus dividing family members and friends, who would often be unable to meet for decades. Western radio broadcasts represented the only reliable contact that people from the region maintained with the outside world, although listening to such transmissions entailed both personal risk and significant technical obstacles. Radio Free Europe, which began operations with a broadcast aimed at Czechoslovakia on July 4, 1950, was the most prominent of the Western radio stations targeting Eastern European audiences. Hundreds of editors, reporters, and technicians prepared the programming of Radio Free Europe, which the US Congress funded directly through the Central Intelligence Agency until 1971.[10]

The Nationality Question and Church Policy

The creation of an international proletariat devoid of national constraints represented one of the myths of the communist concept of society. However, the civil war that followed the 1917 Bolshevik Revolution forced the multinational Soviet state to confront the fact that the introduction of communism would not automatically resolve existing ethnic conflict. The foundation of the Soviet Union in 1922 entailed the division of the new federative state into autonomous republics, oblasts, and raions. Terry Martin refers to 1920s Soviet Union as the "affirmative action empire," which actively supported the preservation of the cultural self-identity of the various nationalities and ethnic groups in the country. At its Tenth

Congress, held in March 1921, the Russian Communist Party decided that follow-ing the end of the Russian Civil War, it would be necessary to make changes to both economic policy (NEP) and nationality policy. The Bolsheviks attempted to implement the policy of *korenizatsiya* ("putting down roots"), or education and administration conducted in the language of the predominant local nation-ality and the promotion of non-Russians to positions of political power in the autonomous republics.[11] Although the Bolsheviks continued to reject the Aus-tromarxist notion of cultural autonomy, they did provide the nationalities of the Soviet Union with extensive linguistic rights, contrary to the classic communist-internationalist approach. Majority nationality groups, which were frequently national minorities as well, were regarded as titular nations in each adminis-trative district. Even as these titular nations integrated politically and socially into the Soviet state, they were permitted to develop their national self-identities, freely use their native languages, and nurture their national cultures. Neither Lenin's nor Stalin's regime attempted to forge a supranational Soviet national-ity, or *Homo sovieticus*. The policy of *korenizatsiya* reinforced ethnic identity, as stipulated by the introduction of native local administration and party organiza-tions, engaging members of the titular nation to fill positions within those.[12] In the years following its foundation, the Soviet state pursued an integrative policy that Yuri Slezkine described as the Soviet "communal apartment," providing people belonging to different nationalities with a place to live together.[13] Dur-ing his early years in power, Stalin—who was of mixed Georgian and Ossetian ancestry—utilized the sharp criticism of greater Russian chauvinism, which he had borrowed from Lenin, as the basis for the nationality policy of the Soviet Union.

Beginning in the 1930s, however, political authorities in Moscow came into frequent conflict with the Soviet Union's non-Russian elites, primarily Ukrai-nians, thus prompting Stalin to initiate a drastic change in cultural policy. The rewriting of history books engendered a new national-Bolshevik outlook, the foundation of which Stalin had constructed as early as 1913 with his written defi-nition of the political and cultural nation: "A nation is a historically constituted, stable community of people, formed on the basis of a common language, terri-tory, economic life, and psychological make-up manifested in a common cul-ture."[14] Immediately following the Second World War, the recognized leading position of the Russian people assumed a central role in Soviet nationality policy, which later became supplemented with state-supported anti-Semitism and xe-nophobia.

Eastern European communist parties confronted a similar practical prob-lem, the intractability of the nationality issue, during the post–Second World War period. As was shown in the previous chapter, a broad range of policies— from integration to open discrimination—was applied to the various national minorities in Eastern Europe between 1945 and 1948. The establishment of the Soviet Bloc served merely to temporarily suspend national conflict in the region. A dense network of bilateral friendship treaties and economic-cultural contacts regulated relations between the Soviet Union and the "people's democracies." Czechoslovakia and Hungary became the final two states of the Eastern Bloc to conclude such bilateral treaties of friendship and cooperation in 1949 after Soviet leaders prompted their Czechoslovak counterparts to revise their discriminatory policies vis-à-vis the Hungarian minority in Slovakia. In 1949, the Cultural Association of Czechoslovak Hungarian Workers (Czehszlovákiai Magyar Dolgozók Kultúregyesülete) was founded to enlist Hungarian members in the Communist Party of Czechoslovakia, and Hungarian-language instruction in primary and secondary schools was resumed.[15]

Contrary to what had occurred Czechoslovakia, Romania adopted an integrative minority policy immediately after the Second World War. The pro-communist government that operated in the country under the leadership of Prime Minister Petru Groza had invested the 1.5 million Hungarians living in Transylvania with full civil rights already in 1945. Hungarians in Romania achieved significant success in their effort to gain linguistic rights, although those living in the northern part of Transylvania attempted chiefly to preserve the conditions that had existed during the period from 1940 to 1944, when the region had again been part of Hungary. Moreover, several tens of thousands of Hungarians joined the Romanian Communist Party—the membership of which was 12 percent Hungarian in 1947—and assumed positions within the state administration.[16] Beginning in 1948, the Romanian state nationalized schools and other institutions and took total control over denominational education. The state dissolved prominent social organizations and gained the exclusive right to publish periodicals and operate theaters, museums, and publishing houses, thus placing Romania's Hungarian minority in a vulnerable position over the long term. Minority institutions, formerly dependent on private charity, came to be totally dependent on the benevolence of the communist authorities.[17]

The communist takeovers that took place in the states of Eastern Europe brought significant changes to minority policy in the region. Ethnic issues became strictly internal affairs: with the end of the League of Nations right to petition and the acceptance of the principle of collective guilt, states lost their means of influencing the nationality policies of neighboring countries that possessed conational minority populations. At the same time, the Soviet Union expected Eastern European states to abandon openly discriminatory policies toward national minorities. The political and cultural integration of minorities superseded the sharp ethnic conflict that had taken place in Eastern Europe over the previous decades, notably with regard to the Turks of Bulgaria and the Hungarians of Romania. In 1952, Stalin encouraged the Romanian Workers' Party leadership to introduce territorial autonomy based on the Soviet model for the Hungarians living in the Székely Land of southeastern Transylvania. The resulting Hungarian Autonomous Region (HAR) functioned as a "greenhouse" for the Hungarian minority living in the region. The educational and cultural institutions, theaters, cultural centers, and folk dance groups established in the HAR played a vital role in the preservation of the archaic Székely Hungarian identity, albeit modified to suit socialist modernization. The greenhouse of the HAR provided the Székely Hungarians with a new identity discourse that was based only formally on official communist ideology and was rooted primarily in the egalitarian social outlook and Hungarian folk culture.[18]

During the early years of this period, Stalin successfully manipulated the national pride and territorial demands of the peoples of Eastern Europe in order to establish a new folk culture that was "national in form and socialist in content."[19] The Stalinist cultural revolution included the radical rewriting of the past as well. Historians were assigned the duty of researching and glorifying folk heroes and social and historical events such as the medieval peasant uprisings, the nineteenth-century emancipation of the serfs, and the development of workers' and socialist movements. National and religious traditions could be incorporated into the new historical narrative only if they were compatible with the principle of Slavic brotherhood and the paradigm of social progress. The Marxist concept of class conflict eliminated nationalism as the key factor sustaining the formation and development of Eastern European nations. The new official historiography portrayed the wars and political movements of all ages as the struggle of the proletarian- and peasant-led progressive internationalist spirit.

The communist systems of Eastern Europe adopted differentiated religious policies resembling those of Stalin toward the Russian Orthodox Church during the Second World War. Although the ultimate objective of these policies remained the establishment of secularized societies, Soviet experience showed that the radical suppression of religion demanded not only an enormous amount of time and energy but the cooperation of the masses as well. Eastern European states attempted to reach accord with the churches, particularly the Eastern Orthodox Church, to which the large majority of Romanians and Bulgarians and around half the population of Yugoslavia belonged, and the various Protestant denominations, to which many citizens of Estonia, Lithuania, the German Democratic Republic, Czechoslovakia, Hungary, and Romania belonged. The Protestant churches had maintained a strongly national character since the time of the Lutheran reforms, even if they were tightly connected to the West. The autocephalous Eastern Orthodox churches in Romania and Bulgaria played the traditional role of harmonizing the interests of the historical-cultural religion and the state on the basis of the premise that all political systems represent the reflection of God's will, and in Yugoslavia Eastern Orthodox priests fought among the partisans.[20] Patriarch of the Romanian Orthodox Church Justinian Marina utilized his authority as head of the church to promote the political integration of the Orthodox world. Beginning in 1948, the Romanian Orthodox Church hierarchy cooperated with communist state organizations in their ruthless dissolution of the Romanian Greek Catholic Church. This act brought an end to the schism that had occurred at the end of the seventeenth century and entailed the persecution of the Romanian Greek Catholic Church's priests and monks as well as a million and a half congregants.[21] The Eastern Orthodox Church supported the communist "struggle for peace" movements throughout the Eastern Bloc as well as the 1950 Stockholm Appeal and subsequent anti-nuclear campaigns. The Eastern Orthodox Church leadership played an active role in monitoring and neutralizing anti-communist political exiles.

The Muslim community in Yugoslavia was a special case. Despite the guarantee of religious freedom in the 1946 Yugoslav Constitution, in that same year communist officials banned Islamic courts, closed schools that taught the Quran and the foundations of Islam, and abolished Sufi meeting and prayer houses; in 1952 they banned the dervish orders. Underground Muslim publishing houses functioned in violation of a law banning the publication of Islamic texts that remained in effect until 1964. The Yugoslav state permitted only one Islamic association to operate under its strict oversight. The state of Muslim religious, ethnic, and national identity within Yugoslavia remained unresolved in the Socialist Republic of Bosnia and Herzegovina, even though the communist system in the country claimed that that Muslims "had not yet decided on their identity" and gradually classified them as either Serbs or Croats.[22]

The Roman Catholic Church was subjected to the greatest degree of persecution among the major religious denominations in the Soviet Bloc. All communist states in Eastern Europe repudiated agreements concluded with the Vatican during the interwar period and prohibited the operation of Roman Catholic schools, organizations, and newspapers. The Vatican responded to this persecution by excommunicating Roman Catholic officials and parishioners who supported communism.

In Hungary, where Roman Catholics constituted two-thirds of the population, beginning in 1945 the leader of the Roman Catholic Church in Hungary—archbishop of Esztergom József Mindszenty—voiced strong criticism not only of the nationalization of the denomination's property and the closure of its schools but also of the new social and political system being built in the country. Mindszenty was arrested in late 1948 and condemned to life in prison on charges of anti-state conspiracy the following year.[23] The persecution of Roman Catholics in Hungary continued with the closing of monasteries, the dissolution of monastic orders, the prohibition of all public pastoral activity, and the arrest of several hundred priests and communicants.

Although Archbishop Josef Beran of Prague had initially adopted a conciliatory stance toward the communist system in Czechoslovakia, the political campaign against the Roman Catholic Church was even more intensive in that country than it was in Hungary. Beran was arrested in June 1949 and forced to remain silent until 1963. Communist authorities closed Catholic seminaries, priests and monks were discharged, and many of them interned in labor camps. Czechoslovak communists attempted to intimidate Roman Catholic officials, initiating political trials against the bishops Ján Vojtaššák and Michal Buzalka. The Slovak Greek Catholic Church was dissolved and its adherents forced to join the Orthodox Church of Czechoslovakia. Roman Catholics in Czechoslovakia had great difficulty coping with the prohibition of their faith, particularly in Slovakia, where church traditions were stronger.

The persecution of the Roman Catholic Church assumed an ethno-national dimension in Romania, where the more than 1.5 million Catholics belonged to several ethnicities.[24] Hungarian bishop of Alba Iulia Áron Márton was arrested in 1949 and condemned to prison two years later after being found guilty of participation in an anti-state conspiracy. Whereas in Czechoslovakia and—to an even greater degree—Romania the communist dictatorship attempted to create a split within the leadership of the Catholic Church (an excommunicated priest founded the Catholic Action Committee in Romania in April 1950 to serve as an organizational vehicle for the country's national Catholic movement), in Poland the Communist Party adopted a dual policy toward the church.[25] On the one hand, the Polish United Workers' Party orchestrated the foundation of the pro-communist Catholic PAX Association and ordered the arrest of hundreds of priests and monks regarded as enemies of the new system. On the other hand, authorities concluded an agreement—which the Vatican opposed—with Warsaw's Archbishop Stefan Wyszyński. The communist government not only permitted seminaries and monasteries to remain open and allowed Catholic newspapers to continue publication but also provided state funding to Roman Catholic schools and accorded limited autonomy to church organizations in exchange for Catholic support for the communist peace policy. The 1950 pact allowed the church the freedom to operate without impediment in many other domains, such as higher education (e.g., Catholic University of Lublin). The Bierut regime was furthermore able to take advantage of the controversy surrounding the German episcopate located on the territory that had been transferred from Germany to Poland following the Second World War. Contrary to the agreement that had been concluded in Hungary in August 1950, which only a few Hungarian bishops had signed, the Polish agreement represented a certain compromise with the entire Roman Catholic world, guaranteeing a large degree of religious freedom, which Catholics rapidly exploited.

Planned Economy and Rearmament

The Classical System: Industrialization and the Collectivization of Agriculture

The economies of Eastern Europe underwent a radical change in the autumn of 1947. In a period of just a few years, the preponderance of the state sector in the countries of Eastern Europe went on to transcend that which had prevailed in the region in the prewar period given the application of the principle of collective guilt on the former elites and the ideological transformation of previous social structures. By 1950, communist authorities nationalized 90 percent of nonagricultural production units throughout most of Eastern Europe.[26] The German Democratic Republic (GDR), where Stalinist political and economic policies were introduced later than elsewhere in the region, was the only exception: until the middle of the 1950s, the state sector constituted only 75 percent of the country's economy.[27]

The reorganization of the economy in multiyear cycles, industrialization, the collectivization of agriculture, and accelerated urbanization became accepted practices in the Soviet Union during the 1930s. The exceptionally ambitious Five-Year Plans launched in Czechoslovakia and Bulgaria in 1949, in Poland and Hungary in 1950, and in Romania and Albania in 1951 focused on development of heavy industry, particularly the iron and steel industries, and required the establishment of new interministerial organizations based on the model of the Soviet State Planning Committee (Gosplan).[28] In January 1949, Stalin initiated the establishment of an international organization called the Council for Mutual Economic Assistance (CMEA), which would promote the economic development of Eastern Europe, facilitate economic coordination between the states of the region and the Soviet Union, and improve the Soviet trade balance. The council was also intended to provide Eastern Europe with a counterpart to the Organization for European Economic Cooperation that had been established in 1948 to administer the Marshall Plan in Western Europe. The CMEA convened three council sessions in its first two years of operation before entering a state of hibernation. Meanwhile, the Western embargos conducted through the Coordinating Committee for Multilateral Export Controls mechanism caused serious problems for the communist planned economies, which regulated the trade and licensing of thousands of products within the commercial domain of the Soviet Bloc.[29]

Official data seem to suggest that the first Five-Year Plans in the states of Eastern Europe were quantitatively successful: in the period 1951–1955, gross national product (GNP) grew annually at a rate between 12 percent and 14 percent in the German Democratic Republic, Romania, and Bulgaria; between 8 percent and 9 percent in Poland and Czechoslovakia; and just less than 6 percent in Hungary.[30] The new planned economies functioned as closed, segmented, unilateral command systems that were controlled entirely from above. The external economy was separated from the internal economy and placed under the direction of a small number of trade companies that operated under the immediate authority of the foreign trade ministry of each country. The volume of trade between Eastern and Western Europe decreased significantly as a result of the intensification of ideological conflict between the Soviet Union and its former Western allies beginning in 1948. From 1948 until 1951, the states of Eastern Europe recorded declines in the range of 20 percent in trade with the West—with the exception of Czechoslovakia, which in 1950 still generated only about half of its annual trade volume with fellow CMEA members. In the years following the Second World War, the Soviet Union utilized its satellite states as a source of raw materials both through bilateral trade agreements—in the cases of Hungary, Romania, and Bulgaria—and through joint ventures. Warren G. Nutter demonstrated in his 1962 book *The Growth of Industrial Production in the Soviet Union* that Eastern European satellite states sustained significant economic losses in their bilateral trade with the Soviet Union during this period.[31] The amount of financial benefit that the Soviet Union derived through its exploitation of Eastern Europe was greater than the amount of aid that the United States provided to the states of Western Europe through the Marshall Plan. The newly established heavy industry in Poland and Hungary operated at a loss to furnish the Soviet market with its products, and in Czechoslovakia ideology triumphed over economic rationality: the Škoda Works—the most productive and technologically innovative company in all of Eastern Europe—was for years compelled to suspend its assembly of motor vehicles produced for private consumption.[32]

Thus, the "classic" socialist economic system, to use János Kornai's description of the planned economic model, came into being with numerous inherent structural dysfunctions, which neither external factors such as the Cold War–dictated need for economic self-sufficiency nor internal factors such as centralization pressure managed to resolve.[33] Implementation of the New Economic Policy caused particularly significant damage to the Eastern European agricultural sector that employed about half of the region's population. The land reforms that took place in the states of Eastern Europe following the Second World War—with the exception of Bulgaria, where land reform had been carried out shortly after the First World War—resulted in the breakup of large estates and the creation of a new smallholder class composed of former day laborers and tenant farmers. The illusion of economic and social security quickly faded in rural areas of Eastern Europe, partially as a result of the 1946–1947 famine. Following Yugoslavia's lead, the newly ascendant Eastern European communist parties initiated the process of collectivizing agriculture. Official propaganda vilified the kulaks, that is, the prosperous peasants. In the spring of 1949, communist authorities launched an offensive against traditional peasant society. However, in the face of mass resistance they were forced to temporarily decrease the number of such quasi-military actions, which entailed surrounding designated villages with police and publically denouncing and beating kulaks and their family members, or at the very least, subjecting them to official registration and discriminatory taxes.[34]

Millions of Eastern Europeans left the agricultural sector, but they encountered significant difficulties after fleeing from rural areas in search of economic opportunity. Large cities in Eastern Europe constituted "closed zones" in which those who desired to become residents were required to obtain special permission from local authorities. Because housing programs had not yet been launched in Eastern Europe, the new inhabitants of cities in the region, mostly young workers, frequently found accommodations in overcrowded barracks or dormitories that lacked bathrooms. The process of urbanization resulted in decreasing living standards among residents of both cities and the countryside. Members of rural society confronted not only the long-standing afflictions of infant mortality and illiteracy but also new problems such as malnutrition, general persecution, and stress related to collectivization.[35] The communist dictatorships established an extraordinarily narrow normative framework, and the process of compulsory collectivization launched in March 1949 delivered the most severe shock to Eastern European peasant society. The grassroots peasant resistance and the popularity of pilgrimages reflected the array of visionary religious beliefs with which Eastern European rural societies attempted to cope with the cultural crisis generated by the state-run attack on the traditional values of the rural communities.[36]

Although the opening phase of agricultural collectivization produced a great deal of personal tragedy in Eastern Europe, the use of state coercive force in the region remained "below the level" of that which Soviet authorities had employed during the collectivization of agricultural in the Soviet Union during the 1930s. Scholarly literature later attributed the smaller degree of state violence during the collectivization process in Eastern Europe to the use of "cautious and refined" methods.[37] Authorities in Hungary and Romania initially attempted to introduce the Stalinist kolkhoz system in which those who joined collective farms surrendered not only their land but their agricultural animals and implements as well. However, in 1952 Romanian officials were compelled to institute a new cooperative system in which only land and labor were communal. In Czechoslovakia, however, collectivization accelerated in its own extreme form precisely during the months preceding Stalin's death in March 1953. In that year, the percentage of all arable land under common ownership in the various states of Eastern Europe was 62 percent in Bulgaria, 48 percent in Czechoslovakia, 37 percent in Hungary, 24 percent in Yugoslavia, 21 percent in Romania, and 17 percent in Poland and in East Germany.[38]

The level of agricultural production, which had always been relatively meager in Central and Eastern Europe—particularly in the Balkans—dropped even lower as a result of insufficient agricultural investment in seeds, fertilizer, tools, and machinery. Whereas heavy industry and construction consumed two-thirds of state investments made in Eastern Europe during this period, only a negligible part of public funding in the region was allocated to the agricultural sector.[39]

Preparation for War and Economic Collapse

The reorganization of Eastern Europe's system of production offers only a partial explanation of the economic decline that took place within the Soviet Bloc between 1950 and 1952. Only Stalin's death prevented this general downturn from producing grave upheaval. The Tito-Stalin split and Yugoslavia's expulsion from Cominform in 1948 exacerbated the already-tense international situation. With the Berlin Blockade in 1948 and 1949 and the outbreak of the Korean War in 1950, the states of Eastern Europe found themselves engaged in a process of rearmament in preparation for a possible military conflict against the West and Yugoslavia. All of those who spoke at the third and final conference of Cominform in November 1949 alluded to the Yugoslav question as a military and security problem. The Communist Party of the Soviet Union's (CPSU) Central Committee Propaganda Department director Mikhail Suslov referred during his speech to an impending "Third World War" as the result of Tito's defiance.[40]

It has become possible only in the present era to gauge the precise long-term impact that the increasing preparation for war exercised on the economies and societies of Eastern Europe during the early years of one-party dictatorship. The development of military capacity presented the Eastern Bloc states bordering Yugoslavia that had been affiliated with the Axis powers during the Second World War—Hungary, Romania, and Bulgaria—with a predicament, as the 1947 Paris Peace Treaties had imposed strict limits on the sizes of their armies. The case of Hungary illustrates the scale of the problem. The number of enlisted soldiers and officers in the Hungarian army nearly tripled from 70,000 in 1948 to more than 211,000 in 1952. The Hungarian army had been assigned the duty of defending the southern frontier of the Soviet Bloc in the event of an attack along its sensitive 660-kilometer common border with Yugoslavia. State allocations related to the construction of the latter integrated system accounted for 22.5 percent of all investment funding stipulated in Hungary's first Five-Year Plan. This system underwent further development over the subsequent years, though remained nearly useless as a result of numerous planning errors and inefficient use of resources.[41]

Amid this atmosphere of general uncertainty and fear, Stalin convened a meeting of Eastern European party leaders and government defense ministers in Moscow in January 1951 to discuss military conditions within the Soviet Bloc. The precise outcome of this meeting is unclear because of an absence of irrefutable

documentation, although available evidence suggests that it may have been crucial to the subsequent economic and social development of bloc states.

According to Defense Minister Alexej Čepička of Czechoslovakia, Stalin
declared during the Moscow meeting that the Soviet Union would be capable
of maintaining its military superiority vis-à-vis the West for only three or four
more years; thus, it would be necessary that "the military potential of the Eastern
Bloc . . . be multiplied in such a way that all of Europe can be targeted once action
is initiated."[42]

Several scholars have expressed cautious views regarding the widely held notion of preventive war, claiming that Stalin referred to the inevitability of armed
conflict only in general terms as a means of warning the Soviet Union's Eastern
European allies that they had only a few years to conduct military preparations
for such an eventuality.[43] With regard to both the Soviet Union and its satellite
states, Geoffrey Roberts emphasizes the enormous scope of rearmament, which
he contends was the product of defensive considerations.[44] In contrast, others
have asserted that Stalin wanted to improve the offensive capacity of Soviet and
Eastern European military forces in preparation for the occupation of Western
Europe before the United States was able to increase its military strength in this
part of the Eurasian continent.[45]

Mátyás Rákosi mentioned the January 1951 meeting in his memoirs. Stalin's
idea greatly surprised Eastern European leaders. Defense Minister Konstantin
Rokossovsky of Poland, who, though of Polish origin, arrived in Warsaw in 1945
as a Soviet general, complained vociferously about the excessive volume of military development stipulated in Poland's Six-Year Plan. In response to this griev-
ance, Stalin told Rokossovsky that Poland would be exempted from satisfying the
military-investment targets specified in the country's plan if he could guarantee
that Europe would remain at peace until 1956, otherwise the Polish should "comply with the Soviet proposals to the best of their ability."[46]

The Soviet leader also requested during the meeting that Hungarian authorities evacuate the 140,000 people residing in a two-thousand-square-kilometer
border zone in a period of just a few days. Hungarian representatives barely managed to convince their Soviet counterparts that this would be impossible in such
a short period of time.[47] Although Rákosi's memoirs reflect the obvious motive
of self-preservation, they nevertheless provide a fairly accurate indication of the
dependence of Eastern European states on the Soviet Union during the 1950s and
of the key element that encumbered relations between them—the question of
scale: Soviet economic and military plans simply exceeded the production capacity of Eastern Bloc satellites. This economic overload resulted in a widening gap
between production and consumption, which was among the causes of social
unrest and political division within the ruling parties.

The Years of Mass Terror

Conditions in Eastern Europe between 1949 and 1953 were the product of a complex admixture of ideological force and social, ethnic, and religious repression. The political police represented the primary agent of mass terror in the region. In accordance with the model of the Soviet Ministry of State Security, powerful internal security forces monitored the activities of all citizens in Eastern Europe via expansive networks of paid informants and other sources of information. One must differentiate the political police that existed in the Soviet Bloc in the 1950s from Western-style secret services, including the direct predecessors of these newly established and fortified organizations of state violence. These political police forces operated under the immediate supervision and control of Soviet advisers who occupied important positions in the state administrative organs in the countries of Eastern Europe. The selection of personnel in these police forces was based on ideological and psychological factors rather than professional qualifications such as education, technical knowledge, and proficiency in foreign languages. The enemy had to be despised and eradicated in order to be defeated. During the early part of the communist era, state-security organizations in Poland, Hungary, and Romania engaged many minorities, particularly Jews, among their personnel to suppress the right-wing opponents of the newly established communist systems.

Such state-security recruits often had suffered personally from discrimination based on race, religion, and nationality and eagerly participated in the establishment of a system that promised to punish their former oppressors. Many Jews disavowed the religion of their ancestors and even made conscious attempts to strengthen their antipathy toward their rejected identity.[48] Memoirs and documentary sources show that political police forces often used Inquisition-like methods to humiliate class enemies and other presumed adversaries detained in their brutal prison systems. Moreover, these forces frequently operated without legal foundations and clear political supervision in the years following their establishment. The following sections describe five main types of repressive activity that took place in Sovietized Eastern Europe: the prosecution of accused "Titoists" as a means of eliminating pluralism within communist parties; the suppression of the Roman Catholic Church, neo-Protestant denominations, and Jehovah's Witnesses; the persecution of those who opposed the 1948 unification of workers' parties, primarily social democrats; the arrest and internal resettlement of various groups such as kulaks and members of the bourgeoisie; and preventive police action against "unproductive elements" such as prostitutes, beggars, black marketeers, and the chronically unemployed. Several scholars refer to the arbitrary intimidation and persecution of predominantly innocent citizens that took place throughout Eastern Europe during this period as "state terrorism."[49]

Interparty Purges

Eastern European communist parties emerged in the postwar period as the outgrowth of small underground movements that had operated with the backing of between 5 percent and 10 percent of the population—a minor degree of support that nevertheless exceeded that in the Soviet Union. All segments of society were represented in the communist parties of Eastern Europe, though workers and civil servants constituted a greater proportion of party members than peasants and intellectuals. According to the logic of the late Stalinist period, communist parties had been subjected to the work of enemy infiltrators. This suspicion was not completely unsubstantiated: the communist parties of Hungary and Romania had admitted tens of thousands of members who had formerly been active in far-right political organizations and were thus vulnerable to blackmail, whereas the Communist Party of Czechoslovakia permitted the enrollment of anti-communist social democrats. Obtaining a party membership booklet was also a recognized means of obtaining employment, housing, and public assistance throughout the Eastern Bloc.

Beginning in the spring of 1948, Eastern European communist parties conducted a review of membership based on past political activities and social background via so-called Central Control Commissions. The parties suspended recruitment to reduce membership and to revive their former revolutionary, vanguard character. By 1953, membership in Eastern Bloc communist parties had fallen by one-third from their prepurge levels, which parties did not regain and surpass until the early 1960s.[50] The next phase of the purges—those targeting members of the high-ranking party leadership—began with the expulsion of Yugoslavia from Cominform in the summer of 1948. These purges were intended to prevent the potential emergence of interparty opposition through the elimination of leaders classified as right-wing deviationists, Titoists, and nationalists. In Hungary, László Rajk—who during his stint as interior minister had orchestrated the persecution of presumed political enemies—was accused during a show trial broadcast on Hungarian Radio of leading a US-, Vatican- and Tito-planned conspiracy to overthrow the communist system in Hungary. Rajk's execution signaled the beginning of a large-scale purge that over the subsequent years would claim the lives of eighty communist and social-democratic leaders and several dozen military officers. This purge also entailed the arrest and internment in labor camps of intellectuals and other political officials such as Hungary's future leader, János Kádár, who had succeeded Rajk as interior minister.[51]

In Bulgaria, former Council of Ministers chair and economic official Traicho Kostov was the most prominent victim of the party purges. After being dismissed from his posts, Kostov was executed in December 1949 following a show trial that closely resembled what had taken place in Hungary earlier that year. Over the following four years, charges of sabotage were launched in Bulgaria against many functionaries, military officers, and engineers.[52]

The Tito-Stalin split was particularly damaging to the political and economic interests of Albania. The purges that took place in this country were more extensive than those that had occurred elsewhere in the Eastern Bloc. The ruthless Albanian interior minister Koçi Xoxe was removed from office and confronted with the typical charges of Titoism and covert collaboration with the imperialists. Xoxe was sentenced to death in June 1949 following a show trial that employed the same choreography as that used in the trials of Rajk, Kostov, and many others. Over the following years, the purges in Albania decimated party Central Committee members and parliamentary representatives.[53]

In Poland and Romania, the political police took action against officials who appeared to reject the implementation of radical social and economic policies and the adoption of Soviet cultural models. The charismatic justice minister Lucrețiu Pătrășcanu became the first and most notable victim of this campaign in Romania in April 1948. The leadership of the Romanian Workers' Party regarded Pătrășcanu's rejection of the party's Bolshevization and explicit support for the Romanian majority living in Transylvania as a violation of the principle of communist internationalism and of the rights that had been promised to the country's minority nationalities. After being held in custody for six years, Pătrășcanu—who refused to exercise self-criticism—was put on trial and executed in April 1954.[54]

In Poland, the scope of the purges reached the highest levels of political authority: in September 1948, the Central Committee of the Polish United Workers' Party dismissed First Secretary Władysław Gomułka on charges that the anti-Ukrainian policies he had earlier implemented as minister of recovered territories had constituted an act of right-wing deviationism. Soviet-supported Muscovite communist Bolesław Bierut succeeded Gomułka, whose removal from power led to the arrest of hundreds of his supporters and other functionaries within the PUWP. Gomułka was placed under arrest in August 1951 and not released from custody until 1954.[55] However, Polish authorities remained faithful to their established policies and did not put imprisoned party leaders on trial, as had occurred elsewhere in Eastern Europe. The attention of Poland's political police instead turned toward activists from the dissolved Polish Socialist Party, former military officers who had returned from exile in the West, and armed groups resisting agricultural collectivization. Between 1945 and 1954, the Commission for the Struggle against Economic Abuse and Sabotage ordered the internment and confinement in forced-labor camps of around 84,000 Polish citizens.[56]

Finally, the purges that took place in Czechoslovakia were connected to developments in the 1949 Rajk trial in Hungary. Communist authorities in Prague and Bratislava identified those who would play the role of the Czechoslovak Rajk as "Slovak nationalists" such as Foreign Minister Vladimír Clementis, Slovak National Council President Gustáv Husák, "Trotskyites," and officials accused of covertly seeking alliance with the West. In 1952, indictments based on coerced confessions that transformed allegations into actual crimes were lodged against the Communist Party of Czechoslovakia's general secretary Rudolf Slánský and thirteen other high-ranking party and government officials, most of whom were sentenced to death and executed. The fact that eleven of these fourteen officials, including Slánský, were of Jewish origin received strong emphasis during their show trial as a result of the official anti-Semitism that emerged during the late Stalinist period.[57]

Following the outbreak of the Cold War, two new terms emerged in Soviet Bloc propaganda that carried anti-Semitic connotations: *Zionism* and *cosmopolitanism*. These terms were used to describe primarily Jewish attitudes and behavior that were deemed incompatible with the principle of socialist patriotism. The character of anti-Zionist campaigns that took place in the Eastern Bloc closely resembled that of anti-Semitic propaganda conducted in Eastern Europe during the interwar period and accurately reflected both the popular anti-Semitism that permeated the societies of the region and the powerful anti-Semitic impulse that emanated from the Soviet Union following Stalin's dissolution of the Jewish Anti-Fascist Committee in 1948.

The Soviet Union and its Eastern European allies had, in fact, adopted a flexible policy toward Jews following the Second World War—the Soviet Union was the first country to accord diplomatic recognition to Israel following its foundation in May 1948. However, beginning with Stalin's anti-Semitic campaign, communist authorities in Poland, Hungary, Romania, and Bulgaria permitted and sometimes even encouraged tens of thousands of members of Zionist organizations to emigrate to the new Jewish homeland.[58]

The anti-Semitic campaign in the Soviet Union became more intense following the uncovering of an alleged conspiracy of primarily Jewish physicians to assassinate Soviet leaders in what became known as the Doctor's Plot. Some authors claim that just before his death in March 1953, Stalin was planning to implement severe anti-Semitic measures including the deportation of all Jews from Moscow and Leningrad to Siberia.[59] According to Jonathan Brent and Vladimir Naumov, the paranoid Soviet dictator's charge that Jewish physicians were trying to kill Soviet leaders constituted a natural component of his consciously developed conspiratorial system.[60] These anti-Semitic purges undermined the position of CPSU Politburo member Lavrenti Beria, the former People's Commissariat for Internal Affairs director who was responsible for the appointment of officials to lead the security organizations of Sovietized Europe.

The Soviet anti-Zionist campaign spread to Romania, where Ana Pauker was dismissed from the Romanian Workers' Party Central Committee in May 1952 and removed from her position as foreign minister in July of the same year before being arrested in February 1953. Pauker's downfall triggered the arrest of several hundred other party and government officials, particularly those regarded as part of Jewish interconnections in the ministries of foreign affairs, foreign trade, and finance as well as in cadre departments and propaganda organs.[61] As Robert Levy demonstrated in his biography of Pauker, the "Iron Lady" of Romania—who was the atheist daughter of an Orthodox rabbi—had committed the cardinal sin of using every possible means to help fellow Romanian Jews emigrate to Israel.

In Hungary, Jews continued to fill many of the most powerful positions within the Hungarian Workers' Party despite Stalin's warning that the party leadership be nationalized. However, the anti-Semitic purges began in Hungary as well with the arrest and imprisonment of State Protection Authority chief Gábor Péter and other high-ranking Jewish officials in the country's political police.[62] Stalin's sudden death put an end to these purges and resulted in the release or transfer to house arrest of imprisoned political-police officials. Although anti-Semitism subsequently disappeared from official propaganda, the relationship remained tense between the Soviet-type political system in Hungary and the relatively small number of Jews who lived in the country following the wartime genocide and the postwar emigration to Israel and the West. According to a World Jewish Congress report published in July 1955, Hungary's communist governments had destroyed the traditional structure of the Hungarian Jewish community. The report stated that Jews in Hungary had suffered "greater material impoverishment than other segments of society" as a result of their systematic exclusion from the trade and small-scale industrial sectors in which they had traditionally been active.[63]

Mass Repression: The Eastern European Gulag System

The physical violence that various state agencies directed against ordinary citizens in Sovietized Eastern Europe reached unprecedented proportions for a time of peace during the late Stalinist era. Until the middle of the 1950s, the newly established communist systems in the region encountered strong resistance—both active in the form of armed opposition and sabotage and passive in the form of refusal to cooperate and expression of criticism. The number of Eastern Europeans placed under arrest or administrative detention from 1948 to 1953 is unknown, although it is estimated to be in the range of 1 million. The number of those who were executed or who died in prisons or labor camps during this period is likely in the tens of thousands. In addition, more than a million prisoners of war and anti-communist Polish, Ukrainian, and Romanian partisans disappeared in the Soviet Union. Anti-communism constituted the sole common

internal purge

ideological platform of armed resistance, which was composed primarily of former military officers and peasants who had taken refuge in the mountains and had long hoped for the arrival of Western liberation forces.[64]

In Romania, special large-scale military operations carried out as a means of strengthening internal security and social prophylaxis represented a feature of mass terror during the early 1950s. Extraordinary security measures had been implemented in Romania before this time as well, such as the deportation of 150,000 prisoners of war to the Soviet Union after August 1944, the expulsion of Romanian citizens of German nationality to the Soviet Union in January 1945, and the internment of 90,000 people in labor camps established in July 1945. The authority of the regime led by Gheorghiu-Dej nevertheless remained weak in many parts of Romania, particularly in rural areas, where the launch of agricultural collectivization resulted in the first special military operations conducted in the country during the communist period. In February 1949, Romanian Workers' Party (RWP) officials initiated a campaign to "liquidate the vestiges of the great estates." During a single night in early March 1949, communist authorities in Romania seized the final economically viable plots of independently owned agricultural land from nearly 8,000 farmers, confiscated their movable and immovable property, and evicted them from their homes.[65] The Council of Ministers designated new dwellings for these evicted farmers in a decree that was validated retroactively via secret resolution in October 1950. Many of those peasants who actively resisted collectivization were subjected to physical abuse, while 2,000 others were deported to desolate parts of the region of Dobruja in eastern Romania.

The fate of political prisoners forced to build the Danube–Black Sea Canal was even more tragic. Several tens of thousands of prisoners participated in construction of this immense, Soviet-instigated canal from the start of the project in 1949 until its suspension in 1953, during which time most of them lived in unheated barracks. The precise number of political prisoners who died while building the Danube–Black Sea Canal during this period has not yet been determined, although it is likely in the several thousands.

The largest punitive-type security measure in the history of postwar Eastern Europe began with an operation, presumably orchestrated in Moscow, late on June 18 and into the early morning on June 19, 1951, to evacuate "unreliable elements" from a twenty-five-kilometer-wide zone along Romania's border with Yugoslavia. This operation resulted in the expulsion of 44,000 residents whose only transgression was that they were of German, Hungarian, Serbian, or Macedonian nationality, belonged to the Aromanian ethnic group, had fled to the area from Soviet-controlled northern Bukovina or Bessarabia, originated from prosperous families, or were former merchants or gendarmerie officers. These presumed enemies were deported to the Bărăgan Plain east of Bucharest, where they were forced to build their own houses and public buildings in newly established villages before the onset of winter. Mortality was extremely high among the people deported from the Romanian-Yugoslav border zone—1,700 died in the year 1956 alone—as a result of inadequate supplies of food and drinking water and an absence of medical facilities. However, the declining population of deportees did not represent a long-term problem: authorities forced newly released prisoners classified as continuing threats to state security to move to the new villages on the Bărăgan Plain.[66]

Following the expulsion of residents from the Romanian-Yugoslav border zone, communist officials initiated another mass deportation in May 1952, issuing a decree ordering the removal of "class aliens" from overcrowded cities. By 1953, more than 39,000 people—merchants, civil servants, police officers, and soldiers—were evicted from their urban homes, including 16,000 from Bucharest alone.

An ad hoc Interior Ministry committee convened in Bucharest once a week to determine the identities of undesirable citizens who would be required to perform between six months and five years of forced labor. Authorities finally stopped the deportations in September 1953. In addition to the more than 80,000 people subjected to internal deportation in Romania, around 64,000 people had been imprisoned for political offenses and 22,000 placed under administrative detention. The Romanian terror mechanism maintained no pretense of bureaucratic formality during procedures launched against presumed enemies of the state. According to a secret inquiry conducted for the Romanian Communist Party Central Committee, more than 100,000 peasants had been imprisoned in Romania in the early 1950s.[67] Political inmates were confined at special locations, and many of them were forced to undergo the Soviet educational theorist Anton Makarenko's method of brutal psychological reeducation at prisons in Pitești and two other sites, as well as at Danube–Black Sea Canal labor camps. This was done in an effort to obliterate the former identities of the young suspected right-wing extremists ("total psychological exposure") as the first step toward their adaptation to the desired new ideology ("metamorphosis"). This system of reeducation was abruptly discontinued in the autumn of 1952, and some of the guards at the prisons where it was utilized were brought to trial and condemned to death. Many of those who had been exposed to the experiment either committed suicide or became insane following their release from prison.[68]

Although the magnitude of political repression was not as great in Hungary as it was in Romania during the early 1950s, it nevertheless tested the tolerance of the former country's population to a greater degree. As a consequence of Soviet war plans against Titoist Yugoslavia, authorities in Hungary conducted special operations on June 22 and 23, 1950, that resulted in the deportation of nearly 2,500 citizens of Serbian or Croatian nationality from the Hungarian-Yugoslav border zone to sparsely populated regions of the country. During the summer of 1951, a further 7,000 families, primarily those of former military officers, government ministers, aristocrats, and industrialists, were expelled from Budapest to various locations on the Great Hungarian Plain, and their property was seized and distributed among Hungarian Workers' Party functionaries.[69] The collectivization of agriculture and the anti-kulak campaign in Hungary generated a great deal of violence and produced an immense number of arrests, which resulted in 400,000 administrative judgments and 24,000 penal sentences. Courts dispensed particularly harsh punishments in cases involving peasants, who could be condemned to serve several years in labor camps if they were found guilty of economic sabotage for having illegally slaughtered their farm animals. Around 1,500 prisoners performed forced labor at the most notorious of these camps, located near the village of Recsk in northern Hungary. In the years following the 1949 Rajk trial, Hungarian Workers' Party (HWP) authorities staged show trials involving former military officers and social democrats as well as "national" communists. Among the latter, HWP General Secretary Rákosi and fellow Muscovite party officials focused particular attention on prosecution of János Kádár and Gyula Kállai, charging them with betraying communist ideals and cooperating with the Horthy-era political police.[70]

In Czechoslovakia, political repression weighed most heavily on the country's German and Hungarian minorities between 1945 and 1948, before shifting to Czech and Slovak internal enemies following the communist takeover in February 1948. Other than the previously described Slánský case, the most prominent political trial in Czechoslovakia during this period involved president of the Council of Czechoslovak Women Milada Horávková, the wartime anti-German resistance leader who relinquished her seat in the Constituent National Assembly to protest the communist takeover in 1948. Horávková was arrested the following year and charged with espionage and conspiracy against the communist system in a 1950 show trial that resulted in her execution. Between 1948 and 1954, people's courts in Czechoslovakia convicted nearly 90,600 people, primarily those from Roman Catholic, conservative, and rural backgrounds. The number of prisoners interned at labor camps jumped from around 13,000 in 1949 to nearly double that number in 1950. Several tens of thousands more people were conscripted into military technical battalions and labor brigades performing particularly dangerous duties.[71]

Police repression was apparently less pervasive and severe in Bulgaria and, especially, Poland, where former party members were the primary targets of Stalinist terror.[72] Although violent peasant rebellions took place in both Bulgaria and Poland during the initial phase of agricultural collectivization in 1949 and 1950, no mass expulsions or internal deportations occurred in those countries. The relatively moderate degree of persecution in Poland and Bulgaria during this period was partially because political repression had peaked in these states with the effort of their people's-front governments to eliminate existing and potential enemies of communism in the years 1944–1947.

In Albania, the magnitude of internal political repression was extremely severe considering an overall population of only 1.2 million. According to figures recently released by the Institute for the Integration of the Former Politically Persecuted, about 6,000 people were executed with or without trial during the communist regime. A total of 18,000 people were imprisoned for political reasons and some 30,000 sent to internment camps within the country.[73] State violence against internal enemies was also linked to the geopolitical difficulties that the country's communist government confronted after 1948. Albania maintained hostile relations with both of its neighboring states, Yugoslavia and Greece, and thus became the weak link in the Soviet Union's Eastern European security system following the Tito-Stalin split. Between 1949 and 1952, the Western powers attempted on several occasions to infiltrate guerilla fighters loyal to the exiled King Zog. The governments of Italy and Greece authorized the establishment of military camps at which operatives were trained to foment a military uprising aimed at overthrowing the Hoxha administration. However, using information from the KGB double agent Kim Philby, the Albanian partisan network was easily exposed, enabling local communist authorities to arrest and execute three hundred guerillas and several thousand citizens accused of cooperating with them.[74]

Contradictions of the Post-Stalin Thaw

Reactions to Stalin's Death

The death of Joseph Stalin on March 5, 1953, quickly produced significant changes in Eastern Europe. Following his death, the previously exalted and irreproachable Soviet leader became the object of critical revision among high-ranking CPSU officials. The catastrophic state of the Soviet economy and the enormous number of prisoners working in Gulag labor camps, which at the time of Stalin's death stood at around 2.5 million people, were indicative of an empire that had won the war though was losing the peace. As Tony Judt noted, the "colonial relationship" that characterized the connection between the Soviet Union and its Eastern European satellite states had begun to change, although it nevertheless retained the aspect of transmitting the economic and social deficits of the center to the periphery.[75]

The signs of profound crisis began to surface in the Soviet Union in the weeks following Stalin's death. The newly established collective leadership composed of new CPSU first secretary Nikita Khrushchev, Council of Ministers chair Georgiy Malenkov, and political-police leader Lavrenti Beria launched an investigation of the crimes that Soviet authorities had committed during the final years of Stalin's rule. Beria himself announced that the charges on which the alleged Doctor's Plot had been based were fraudulent and ordered the release of 1 million people imprisoned for crimes against public order, which, paradoxically, led to the disruption of the system of penal confinement and severe prison riots.[76]

Both ordinary citizens and communist leaders in the states of Eastern Europe attempted to determine the implications of the political transformation and internal power struggle that had begun to take place in the Soviet Union following Stalin's death. Klement Gottwald, general secretary of the Communist Party of Czechoslovakia, died just a few days after attending the former Soviet dictator's funeral in Moscow. Gottwald's successor, Antonín Novotný, advocated maintaining the orthodox Stalinist policies that CPC had pursued since taking power in Czechoslovakia. However, on May 30, 1953, Novotný announced the introduction of financial reform that would have exercised a negative economic impact on both the middle and working classes. A spontaneous strike at the Škoda plant in Plzeň quickly spread to other industrial complexes. The Czechoslovak government deployed tanks and troops armed with heavy weaponry to suppress the strikes and subsequent demonstrations. In Moscow, Beria and Malenkov followed the events in Czechoslovakia with considerable dismay, concluding that Soviet authorities had underestimated the extent of political dissatisfaction among citizens of the country. The three-day period of upheaval resulted in several dozen deaths and around 2,000 prison convictions.[77] Earlier in May 1953, workers at a tobacco factory in Plovdiv, Bulgaria, had also gone on strike, signaling that labor unrest in Eastern Europe was not confined to Czechoslovakia.[78]

Among all the countries of the Soviet Bloc, the process of destalinization caused the greatest degree of political turmoil in the German Democratic Republic and Hungary.

At Stalin's urging, the Socialist Unity Party of Germany decided in July 1952 to launch an initiative for the "systematic implementation of socialism," the primary objective of which was to raise the GDR's industrial and agricultural production. At the same time, the communist leadership of East Germany, fearing a possible armed conflict with the West, increased state allocations to the military-defense sector, which served to accelerate existing declines in living standards in the country, thus prompting around 300,000 citizens of the GDR, primarily young people and members of the intelligentsia, to emigrate to West Germany.

On June 16, 1953, construction workers went on strike in East Berlin to protest a rise in production quotas scheduled to come into effect at the end of that month. The unrest in East Berlin spread quickly, eventually involving nearly a half million workers, who attacked Socialist Unity Party buildings and, in some instances, killed communist functionaries and police informers.[79] Soviet occupying forces were compelled to play the primary role in military operations to quell the rebellion, which claimed at least 125 lives. In response to the June 1953 uprising, East German communist officials made several economic and social concessions, which, along with harmonized repayment of war reparations to the Soviet Union, resulted in a significant rise in wages and labor productivity over the subsequent years.[80]

In Hungary, the opportunity for political change emerged in the early summer of 1953: on June 13, Hungarian Workers' Party leaders arrived to Moscow for a three-day consultation with their CPSU counterparts during which Beria and Malenkov severely criticized HWP General Secretary Rákosi for pursuing flawed economic policies and utilizing excessive state force in rural Hungary to expedite the process of agricultural collectivization. Although Soviet officials permitted Rákosi to retain his leadership over the Hungarian Workers' Party, they forced him to cede his position as head of government (Council of Ministers chair) to Imre Nagy, the popular former agricultural minister whose personal qualities and genuine "Hungarian" origin (peasant, Reformed) CPSU leaders preferred to those of Rákosi, whom Beria accused of striving to become the "Jewish king of Hungary."[81] Mark Kramer emphasizes that the display of unity among Soviet leaders during these consultations with Rákosi and other HWP officials concealed the fact that by this time Khrushchev and Malenkov had already begun to conspire against Beria, whose arrest on June 26, 1953, took place amid an atmosphere of political crisis throughout Eastern Europe and diplomatic opening vis-à-vis the West (the armistice ending the Korean War was signed just over one month later).[82]

The arrest and execution of Beria, who had been an unofficial supporter of comprehensive political reform in the spring of 1953, circumscribed the room for maneuver of the Nagy government. During his eighteen months as Council of Ministers chair, Nagy was unable to implement his reform program that had aroused expectations of liberalization and improved living standards among the citizens of Hungary. The Nagy government's reforms, which included the moderation of police repression, the reallocation of state funding for the military industry toward other industrial sectors, and the dissolution of agricultural cooperatives, resulted in the emergence of conflict between two distinct factions within the Hungarian Workers' Party: the broadly supported Nagy-led reformists and the Rákosi-led Stalinists. At the recommendation of the Soviet ambassador to Hungary Yuri Andropov, the CPSU leaders shifted their support back to the Stalinist faction of the Hungarian Workers' Party. By the autumn of 1954, Nagy faced increasing popular unrest. His government's release of 15,000 political prisoners revealed the true extent of the crimes and illegalities that the communists had committed during their first five years in power. At around this same time, the police used force to suppress mass demonstrations held in working-class districts of Budapest to protest the decision of communist authorities to evict the large number of squatters who had been compelled to take up unlawful residence in the rapidly growing capital city partially as the result of the total lack of new government-built housing. According to János M. Rainer, these demonstrations reflected an irreversible transformation in public sentiment vis-à-vis the single-party state: the citizens of Hungary no longer feared communist authorities, while the country's intelligentsia had overcome its former ideological-loyalty complex and demanded the freedom to express critical opinions.[83]

Stalin's death did not produce a major change in the course of politics in Romania. After the general secretary Gheorghe Gheorghiu-Dej of the Romanian Workers' Party removed RWP Muscovite-faction leaders from power in 1952, he announced a general amnesty that resulted in the pardoning of 525,000 people convicted of crimes against public order and the release of 15,000 political prisoners. Before the plenary meeting of the RWP Central Committee, Gheorghiu-Dej promised to reduce the proportion of state investment allocated to the industrial sector, though refused to introduce reform resembling that of the Nagy government in Hungary on the grounds that the political distortions had already been corrected in Romania. Gheorghiu-Dej subsequently initiated the process of destalinization without altering the ideological foundations of the communist system, dissolving the Soviet-Romanian joint ventures (SovRoms) that controlled Romania's petroleum and mineral industries, suspending construction of the Danube–Black Sea Canal, and reducing compulsory delivery quotas for all agricultural products, with the exception of milk and meat. In August 1955, Gheorghiu-Dej asked CPSU First Secretary Khrushchev to withdraw all Soviet troops from Romania on the grounds that the conclusion of the Austrian State Treaty earlier that year had made their presence in the country unnecessary. Khrushchev agreed to Gheorghiu-Dej's unusually assertive request, concluding that the withdrawal of Soviet troops from Romania would contribute to the broad international détente that had begun following Stalin's death.[84]

In Poland, Beria's downfall had led to a temporary increase in police repression, which culminated in the September 26, 1953, arrest of Archbishop Wyszyński.[85] However, only one year after the arrest, the Polish section of Radio Free Europe broadcast sensational reports regarding the operations and criminal conduct of Poland's security services based on CIA interrogations of former high-ranking Ministry of Public Security official Józef Światło, who had defected to the US military mission in West Berlin. The scandal prompted the authorities to undertake a reorganization of security services.[86]

Soviet-Yugoslav Reconciliation and the Warsaw Pact Treaty

Stalin's death forced both the Soviet Union and the Western powers to reconsider their mutual relations. The end of the Korean War significantly decreased the prospect of armed conflict between the West and the East and created the possibility of reestablishing limited commercial and cultural contacts between capitalist and communist states. The July 1955 Geneva Summit at which government leaders from the United States, the United Kingdom, France, and the Soviet Union met to discuss disarmament and other means of assuaging Cold War antagonism was the initial manifestation of global détente. Although the summit produced no agreements, it did signify the beginning of a fleeting new era in international relations. Meanwhile, Italy and Yugoslavia resolved their dispute regarding the Free Territory of Trieste via the 1954 London Memorandum, which granted Italy the right to exercise sovereignty over the city of Trieste and the northern part of the territory (Zone A).[87]

As the states of Western Europe were building greater political and economic unity, Khrushchev was forced to confront the fact that after 1948 the Soviet Union had failed to achieve integration within the Eastern Bloc and that the economic embargo and ideological pressure on Yugoslavia had not produced their intended results. Soviet officials therefore began to secretly prepare for rapprochement with Yugoslavia, and Khrushchev paid an official visit to Belgrade on May 26, 1955, to acknowledge the mistakes of the Soviet Union and, implicitly, the legitimacy of the Yugoslav path to socialism. In fact, Tito had long regarded political and economic development as a means of ideological counterattack against the Soviet Union and its allies. Tito's development strategy was based on the repudiation of the planned economy via workers' self-management, the reduction of bureaucracy through workers' councils, and the conversion of state property into social property. In 1953, Tito abandoned agricultural collectivization, thereby preempting the self-criticism of Eastern European communist leaders. During this same year, Yugoslavia adopted a new constitution that established the Council of Producers, composed of representatives elected by workers from the various economic sectors. According to John R. Lampe, however, the decentralization stipulated in the 1953 Yugoslav constitution remained largely unimplemented because of a lack of executive resolutions.[88]

In external terms, Yugoslavia was able to exploit its sovereignty in order to establish a complex and continually expanding network of foreign relations. After signing in 1953 an agreement called the Balkan Pact along with Greece and Turkey, which transformed Yugoslavia into a derivative component of the Western defensive system, in 1955 Tito played a significant role in promoting the establishment of a transnational movement of non-aligned countries led by President Sukarno of Indonesia and President Nasser of Egypt. However, the limit of Tito's ideological flexibility soon manifested: in 1954, the Yugoslav leader had his former political ally Milovan Djilas expelled from the League of Communists of Yugoslavia Central Committee and placed under arrest as punishment for his publication of a series of articles in the official party daily *Borba* that expressed criticism of the country's communist system. These articles served as the basis for Djilas's book *Nova Klasa* (The New Class), which was published in the United States and several Western European countries in 1957. In this book, Djilas scornfully characterized Eastern European communism as inegalitarian "state capitalism," claiming that the oligarchy of party bureaucrats who derived significant material benefit from their position had created a "new class."[89]

The partial reconciliation between the Soviet Union and Yugoslavia produced political repercussions throughout the Eastern Bloc, notably Hungary. In February 1955, Georgiy Malenkov—the sole high-ranking Soviet official who supported nuclear disarmament and the increase of internal consumption—was removed from power. As a result, in April 1955 Rákosi protégé András Hegedüs was appointed to serve as Council of Ministers chair in place of Imre Nagy, who was expelled from the Hungarian Workers' Party at the end of the year. Despite the repressive measures that the resurgent Stalinist leadership utilized to reassert its authority, Nagy retained the active support of most Hungarian intellectuals, who acting together with dissatisfied university students sparked the outbreak of popular revolt just a few months later.

Several events took place during the second half of the 1950s that served to accelerate the military integration of the socialist bloc. On May 9, 1955, the Federal Republic of Germany joined the North Atlantic Treaty Organization (NATO). A few days later, eight Eastern European countries signed the Warsaw Pact collective-defense treaty, which member states regarded as a symmetrical counterpart to NATO, and an internationally guaranteed state treaty reinstated the national sovereignty of Austria, declared the country's permanent neutrality, and entailed the withdrawal of all Soviet, US, British, and French forces from their Austrian zones of occupation.[90] These events established a new diplomatic and military balance and consolidated the division of Europe into spheres of influence. However, neither the Warsaw Pact nor CMEA, which had become active again after a pause of nearly five years, maintained long-term strategic perspectives. The Soviets initially attempted to utilize the Warsaw Pact as a means of demilitarizing the Cold War, but the operations of CMEA suffered from the inconvertibility of Eastern European currencies and the lack of effective specialization among member states. Khrushchev understood the necessity of peaceful competition with the West, although he remained loyal to the Stalinist *nomenklatura*. According to Mark Pittaway, in the middle of the 1950s "the foundations of communist authority were almost invisible everywhere."[91] The political impact of the Twentieth Congress of the Communist Party of the Soviet Union in February 1956 contributed further to the difficulties of establishing totalitarian-based unity in the Eastern Bloc.

Notes

1. For a conceptual introduction to the Sovietization of Eastern Europe, see Apor, Apor, and Rees, *Sovietization of Eastern Europe*, 1–27.
2. This term originally applied to the Soviet republics. Zaslavasky, *Dopo l'Unione Sovietica*, 21.
3. Hoffmann, *Stalinist Values.*
4. Fowkes, *L'Europa orientale dal 1945 al 1970*, 79.
5. Apor, Behrends, Jones, and Rees, *Leader Cult in Communist Dictatorships.*
6. Zhdanov, "Soviet Literature."
7. Connelly, *Captive University.*
8. For a general introduction, see Crowley and Reid, *Socialist Spaces.*
9. Horváth, *Stalinism Reloaded.*
10. Puddington, *Broadcasting Freedom.*
11. The word *korenizatsiya* emerged in the 1920s. It is derived from the term *korennoye naseleniye,* or "root population," used to describe "indigenous" nationalities.
12. Martin, *Affirmative Action Empire*, 460–461.
13. Slezkine, "USSR as a Communal Apartment," 318.
14. Stalin, "Marxism and the National Question," 60–61.
15. Popély, *A (cseh)szlovákiai magyarság*, 290.
16. Olti and Nagy, *Érdekképviselet vagy pártpolitika*, 17–100.
17. Andreescu, Nastasă, and Varga, *Maghiarii din România*; Hunyadi, *State and Minority in Transylvania*, 329–427.
18. Bottoni, *Stalin's Legacy.*
19. Mevius, "Reappraising Communism and Nationalism," 377–400.
20. Leuştean, *Orthodoxy and the Cold War,* 23.
21. Vasile, *Între Vatican şi Kremlin.*
22. Noel Malcolm, *Storia della Bosnia*, 264.
23. Balogh, *Mindszenty József I-II.*
24. Bozgan, *Cronica unui eşec previzibil.*
25. Leuştean, *Orthodoxy and the Cold War*, 97.
26. Berend, *Storia economica*, 173.
27. Connelly, "Paradox of East German Communism," 179–180.
28. Berend, *Storia economica dell'Europa*, 178–179.
29. Van Brabant, *Economic Integration*, 17.
30. Berend, *Storia economica dell'Europa*, 190–191.
31. Graziosi, *L'URSS dal trionfo al degrado*, 27.
32. Fava, *Storia di una fabbrica socialista.*
33. Kornai, *Overcentralization in Economic Administration.*
34. For the collectivization process in Romania, see Iordachi and Dobrincu, *Transforming Peasants, Property and Power.*
35. Zubkova, *Russia after the War.*
36. From an anthropological perspective, see Gagyi, *A krízis éve.*
37. Bideleux and Jeffries, *History of Eastern Europe*, 528–529.
38. Völgyes, *Politics in Eastern Europe*, 76.
39. Berend, *Storia economica dell'Europa*, 279.
40. See Procacci, *Cominform*, 665; Banac, *With Stalin against Tito*, 131.
41. Okváth, *Bástya a béke frontján*, 119.

42. Kaplan, *Dans les archives*, 164–165.
43. Mastny, *Il dittatore insicuro*, 149.
44. Roberts, *Stalin's Wars*, 361–362.
45. Holloway, *Stalin and the Bomb*, 288.
46. Rákosi, *Visszaemlékezések*, 861.
47. Ibid., 864.
48. With regard to the myth equating Jews with communists, see Gerrits, *Myth of Jewish Communism*, 130–190.
49. Oprea, *Bastionul cruzimii*, 10.
50. Crampton, *Eastern Europe*, 262–263.
51. Romsics, *Hungary in the Twentieth Century*, 272–273.
52. Courtois, *Il libro nero del comunismo europeo*, 268.
53. Hodos, *Show Trials*, 10.
54. Tismăneanu, *Stalinism for All Seasons*, 110–120.
55. Rothschild, *Return to Diversity*, 148.
56. Courtois, *Il libro nero del comunismo europeo*, 356–357.
57. Clementi, *Cecoslovacchia*, 145–153.
58. Wasserstein, *Vanishing Diaspora*, esp. chapter 2.
59. Graziosi, *L'URSS dal trionfo al degrado*, 133–135.
60. Brent and Naumov, *Stalin's Last Crime*, 333.
61. Levy, *Ana Pauker*, 194–220.
62. Borhi, *Hungary in the Cold War*, 210.
63. The National Archives, London, Foreign Office, fond 371, file 116143 (Hungary, Political Correspondence 1955).
64. For the social context of anti-communist resistance, see Dobrincu, "Historicizing a Highly Disputed Theme," 305–344.
65. Oprea, *Banalitatea răului*, 114–115.
66. Milin and Stepanov, *Golgota Bărăganului*, 22.
67. Bottoni, *Transilvania rossa*, 56–58.
68. Stănescu, *The Reeducation Trials*.
69. Bank, Palasik, and Gyarmati, *"Állami titok."*
70. Papo, *L'Ungheria contemporanea*, 98.
71. Clementi, *Cecoslovacchia*, 139–146.
72. Kemp-Welch, *Poland under Communism*, 42–43.
73. Figures provided by Bilal Kula: http://www.dailysabah.com/balkans/2016/05/26/albania-recalls-atrocities-inside-communist-era-prison.
74. Pearson, *Albania as Dictatorship and Democracy*, 393–450.
75. Judt, *Postwar*, 167.
76. Craveri, *Resistenza nel Gulag*.
77. Ostermann, *Uprising in East Germany*, 111–127.
78. Ibid., 86–89.
79. Ibid., 164.
80. Fowkes, *L'Europa orientale*, 94.
81. Borhi, *Hungary in the Cold War*, 231.
82. Kramer, "Early Post-Stalin Succession Struggle," 3–55.
83. Rainer, *Imre Nagy*, 74–81.
84. Scurtu, *România*, 43–44.
85. Rothschild, *Return to Diversity*, 86.

86. Kramer, "Early Post-Stalin Succession Struggle," 48; Gluchowski, "The Defection of Josef Swiatlo."

87. Cattaruzza, *L'Italia e il confine orientale*, 312–326.

88. Lampe, *Yugoslavia as History*, 260–261.

89. Djilas, *New Class*.

90. Mastny and Byrne, *Cardboard Castle?*, 2–6.

91. Pittaway, *Eastern Europe*, 121.

Chapter 3

Political Crises and Social Consolidation (1956–1972)

Poland and Hungary—1956

The Impact of the CPSU Twentieth Congress and the "Polish October"

On February 25, 1956, Communist Party of the Soviet Union First Secretary Nikita Khrushchev delivered an unscheduled, several-hours-long speech at the CPSU's Twentieth Congress during which he detailed the crimes of the Stalinist era. Khrushchev's confession shocked the delegates attending the party congress and undermined the previously unquestionable faith in Stalinist-type socialism, thus provoking deep political crisis throughout the Soviet Bloc. Cominform was dissolved in April 1956 as a result of the rapprochement between the Soviet Union and Yugoslavia the previous year. In Poland and Hungary, Khrushchev's recognition of the mistakes and misdeeds committed during the Stalinist era served to strengthen the domestic proponents of reform and to weaken the legitimacy of the political forces in power. Details surrounding Khrushchev's secret speech at the Twentieth Congress of the CPSU were publicized in Poland shortly following the sudden death in Moscow of Polish United Workers' Party general secretary Bolesław Bierut.[1] The public debate in Poland generated a reformist-conservative split within the PUWP that new party first secretary Edward Ochab attempted to mediate. As a result of the political thaw, censorship was relaxed, the *Sejm* (parliament) regained some of the political functions it had lost following the communist takeover, and the increasingly popular former Polish United Workers' Party leader Władysław Gomułka was permitted to rejoin the PUWP. One may agree with Joseph Rothschild that "the thrust of Polish society's moral and ideological groping in the spring of 1956 was not so much for an anti-Communist system as toward a combination of humane Marxism with nationalistic idealism, implemented through real policy reforms."[2]

The popular uprising that took place in Poznań during the final three days of June 1956 shattered the illusion of controlled liberalization that was part of Gomułka's program. The events began with a strike among workers at the city's Joseph Stalin Metal Works on June 28 and quickly grew into massive demonstrations. Polish security and military forces intervened with Soviet assistance, killing seventy-four and wounding more than five hundred in the process.

On July 18, 1956, the PUWP Central Committee determined in its official appraisal of the events in Poznań that a distinction must be made between the activity of "a few provocateurs" and that of the "honorable masses" who had demanded an improvement in working conditions and the dismissal of compromised political leaders. The participation of more than a million people in the traditional pilgrimage to venerate the Black Madonna of Częstochowa in August 1956 showed the widespread dissatisfaction among the citizens of Poland.

In September 1956, the conservative Muscovite faction of the Polish United Workers' Party announced a series of symbolic concessions: the appointment of Gomułka to the PUWP Central Committee, the release from house arrest of archbishop of Warsaw Stefan Wyszyński, a 50 percent rise in wages, and the removal of several Jewish party and government officials. The public mood underwent fast radicalization in the autumn of 1956. People openly voiced their antipathy toward the communist system and rejection of Poland's dependence on the Soviet Union at demonstrations and assemblies held with increasing frequency. At a plenary session convened in Warsaw on October 19, the PUWP Central Committee approved Gomułka's appointment to the body before abruptly suspending the meeting after news emerged that a high-ranking Soviet delegation had arrived to the city with the objective of preventing a change in the party leadership. Dramatic negotiations between Soviet and Polish officials resulted in a compromise agreement. The Soviets assented to Gomułka's political return and to withdraw military forces that were prepared to intervene in Poland; in exchange, the Polish pledged to remain in the Warsaw Pact and the Soviet Bloc.[3] On October 24, 1956, Gomułka asked the huge crowds of people in Warsaw celebrating him as a national hero to cease all demonstrations and go back to work.

Poland's communist leaders made three major political compromises that brought the Polish October to a peaceful end: first, they returned some collectivized agricultural land to private ownership, thereby making the survival of the smallholding peasantry possible; second, they forced Defense Minister Konstantin Rokossovsky to resign and persuaded the Soviets to relinquish their supervision over the Polish armed forces and to recall all their military advisers to the Soviet Union; and third, they strengthened the modus vivendi with the Roman Catholic Church, an arrangement that had included the release of Archbishop Wyszyński from house arrest the previous month. The political conflict and animosity that had manifested themselves in the October demonstrations were channeled into a program of regulated liberalization. The parliamentary elections held on January 20, 1957, produced a limited degree of political pluralism, with the inclusion of Catholic and independent candidates.[4] The Gomułka thaw proved ephemeral: the PUPW's "revisionist" (i.e., liberal) faction soon came under renewed attack, thus significantly narrowing the permitted degree of autonomy within Polish society. The PUWP expelled nearly 30,000 members in 1957 and 1958 while party and trade-union officials intensified their struggle to curtail the authority of workers' councils. However, despite this transitory deceleration in the process of destalinization, scholars argue that the self-organization of Polish civil society, also called the "horizontal relationship of civil society with itself," was possible only in an authoritarian regime, not a totalitarian one.[5]

Crisis and Revolution in Hungary

The demonstrations in Poland had an impact on the political climate in Hungary, although the 1956 revolution was primarily the consequence of an internal political struggle that had been taking place in the country since 1953. Former head of government Imre Nagy and his pro-reform allies regained their previous political momentum as a result of the Twentieth Party Congress of the CPSU and the support of the opposition intelligentsia. On June 27, 1956, the Petőfi Circle, a pro-reform intellectual organization that had formed the previous year, held an assembly to discuss press freedom in Hungary. Speakers openly denounced Rákosi's political and economic policies during the meeting, which transformed into an unauthorized demonstration. Rákosi, whom Soviet officials had begun to regard as a political liability, was forced to resign from his position at the head of the Hungarian Workers' Party (HWP) and go into exile in the Soviet Union.[6]

However, HWP leaders committed a grave political error that cast doubt on their political motives when they named the hard-liner Ernő Gerő to succeed Rákosi as party general secretary. Whereas in Poland political concessions and the popularity of the new leader had validated the changes that had taken place, in Hungary the appointment of one Stalinist to replace another served merely to provoke greater unrest. This discontent had two primary aspects: an emotionally fueled national aspect based on the presence of Soviet troops in Hungary and the Soviet exploitation of the country's economy, and a social-economic aspect based on the sharp decline in the living standards during the first years of communism, especially until 1953.

International conditions also contributed to the continuing uncertainty in Hungary. Many Hungarians supported the demonstrations in Poland, regarded the de facto reincorporation of Yugoslavia into the communist movement as a promising sign of political tolerance, and—mistakenly—interpreted the signing of the Austrian State Treaty, the withdrawal of Soviet troops from Austria, and

Hungary's admission to the United Nations as precursors of change. The symbolic actions of NATO, such as the launch of balloons carrying anti-communist
leaflets into Eastern Bloc countries, and references in the international press to
the liberation of the "captive nations" served to reinforce these unfounded expectations. Archival sources show that official US policy toward Eastern Europe
was much more cautious: in July 1956, the National Security Council excluded
the possibility of mass revolution in the region and recommended that the Eisen-
hower Administration provide Eastern European opposition groups with support that would not precipitate radical change.[7] In the meantime, the increasingly
chaotic situation in Hungary alarmed Soviet ambassador Yuri Andropov, who
maintained a broad network of informants within the dogmatic wing of HWP.[8]

Discontent and both internal and external tension culminated within the
ranks of the Hungarian Workers' Party. On October 6, tens of thousands of people, including HWP leaders, attended the official reburial of former prime minister László Rajk and his associates who had been executed in 1949 on fabricated
charges of conspiracy. Unrest grew among students at the Budapest Technical
University and the University of Szeged in southern Hungary as a result of the
events in Poland. On October 22, students convened a public assembly in Budapest at which they issued a series of demands—which included the holding of free
elections, the withdrawal of Soviet troops from Hungary, an increase in wages and
scholarships, and the reinstatement of the country's traditional Kossuth Coat of
Arms in place of the red-starred "Rákosi Coat of Arms" introduced in 1949—and
announced that they would stage a demonstration the following day to express
solidarity with the people of Poland. HWP General Secretary Gerő responded
indecisively to the unrest in Budapest, reversing the party's initial decision to ban
the October 23 demonstration, which drew thousands of participants—students,
workers, civil servants, and others.

Armed conflict erupted in Budapest on the evening of October 23, 1956, following a massive demonstration outside Hungary's parliament. Imre Nagy—
whom the HWP leadership had asked to rejoin the government in order to
alleviate the political crisis—spoke to the demonstrators, who, taking courage
from the withdrawal of police, rejected the former head of government's call for
them to disperse peacefully with the promise that the reforms he had initiated in
1953 would be continued. Already before Nagy's ineffectual speech, demonstrators had overturned the gigantic statue of Stalin on a square a few kilometers away
from the parliament. The first shots were fired at the Hungarian Radio headquarters, where demonstrators had gathered to demand the broadcast of the student
demands but instead heard a provocative radio address from Gerő in which he
portrayed the party leadership as the guardian of reform and the demonstrations
as a nationalist-chauvinist (i.e., right-wing and anti-Soviet) provocation. On the
morning of October 24, Hungarian Radio announced the appointment of Nagy

as Council of Ministers chair in place of András Hegedüs, the imposition of martial law, and the cooperation of the Soviet military—at the request of the government—in operations to subdue "counterrevolutionary bandits." The concurrent announcement of these measures prompted many Hungarians to mistakenly conclude that Nagy himself had requested the intervention of Soviet military forces to quell the uprising.[9] HWP officials ordered all Hungarian People's Army personnel to remain in their barracks. Only a few Hungarian military officers followed the lead of Colonel Pál Maléter, who on October 28 ordered the units under his command to fight on the side of the revolutionaries.

Hungary's state apparatus collapsed with stunning speed after the outbreak of the revolution. Budapest entered a state of undeclared war in which the State Protection Authority (the political police) waged a merciless campaign with the help of Soviet military forces against armed revolutionary groups composed of an estimated 10,000 to 15,000 civilians and former soldiers. On October 25, an estimated two hundred civilians were killed in a fusillade at parliament in Budapest, and demonstrators were massacred in Miskolc, Mosonmagyaróvár, and other locations in Hungary. Insurgents lynched several political police officers and communist functionaries after capturing the Budapest headquarters of the Hungarian Workers' Party on October 30. Revolutionary councils formed in most centers of local administration, where the revolution had assumed a more peaceful, negotiated character. Communists whom the local population regarded as decent people were often granted membership in the revolutionary councils.[10]

The disparity that existed in the attitudes of the various participants in the revolution—armed civilians, workers, former soldiers, and reform communists—toward the socialist and multiparty systems undermined the strength of the unplanned uprising. The revolutionary government of Prime Minister Imre Nagy inherited chaotic conditions and failed to gain the confidence of the executive apparatus. János M. Rainer maintains that Nagy, himself a communist functionary who had spent fifteen years in the Soviet Union, came to fully identify with the scope of the anti-Soviet revolt only at the beginning of November, after the treachery of the Soviet Union had become completely obvious to him.[11]

On October 25, the HWP appointed János Kádár to serve as party general secretary in place of the unpopular Ernő Gerő. Three days later, Nagy announced the formation of a national government that supported some of the demands of the revolutionaries, such as the withdrawal of Soviet troops from Budapest, the conclusion of a cease-fire agreement, the dissolution of the State Protection Authority, the establishment of a new police force composed of insurgents, and amnesty for all those who had participated in the uprising.

The change in the direction of the revolution that occurred in the final days of October forced the Soviets to make decisions regarding the future of Hungary. On October 30, Prime Minister Nagy, under popular pressure, formed a new government including parties that had been active in Hungary during the three-year transitional period from the end of the Second World War until the communist takeover and voiced support for the organization of a National Guard composed of members of the armed insurgent groups. Senior Soviet officials Anastas Mikoyan and Mikhail Suslov approved the initial measures of the new Nagy government and encouraged the reconstitution of the Hungarian Workers' Party in the form of the János Kádár–led Hungarian Socialist Workers' Party (HSWP). Meanwhile, Soviet leaders, who at a meeting on October 30 had expressed support for the reforms of the "Hungarian Gomułka," a few hours later revised their position regarding the withdrawal of Soviet troops from Hungary, for a variety of reasons. The open manifestation of solidarity with the Hungarian uprising in Poland and Yugoslavia and a pro-revolution demonstration among university students in the western Romanian city of Timișoara on October 30 played a role in the policy change. Unrest spread during this period among Hungarians living in other locations in Romania and southern Slovakia, prompting authorities to seal the borders with Hungary, impose curfews, and tighten press censorship.[12]

However, it was the outbreak of the Suez Crisis that exercised a decisive impact on the Soviet stance toward the fate of the revolution. On October 29, Israeli military forces attacked the Gaza Strip and the Sinai Peninsula, and two days later Anglo-French air forces initiated a bombing campaign against Egypt to regain Western control over the Suez Canal and overthrow the government of the country's pro-Soviet President Gamal Abdel Nasser. CPSU First Secretary Khrushchev regarded the second Soviet military intervention to suppress the Hungarian uprising as a means of demonstrating the resolve of the Soviet Union to defend its European zone of influence.[13] As Soviet armed forces entered Hungary and placed Budapest under military blockade, Khrushchev conducted a political tour of Eastern Europe to personally inform the leaders of various states in the region of the invasion. Until the second military intervention Western leaders voiced no protest of the Soviet invasion of Hungary. US Secretary of State John Foster Dulles declared that he did not regard the Soviet-occupied states of Eastern Europe as potential allies. Neither political leaders nor military intelligence in the United States urged intervention in the Hungarian conflict, lacking both the will and the means to do so. The US initiative to place the Hungarian issue on the agenda of the UN Security Council represented a mere tactical concession intended to appease domestic demands for decisive action in support of the Hungarian uprising rather than a genuine threat to Soviet interests.[14]

On November 1, Prime Minister Nagy was informed that the Soviets were secretly preparing a new armed invasion. In response, he announced Hungary's withdrawal from the Warsaw Pact and military neutrality, in the hopes of gaining international support. On that same day, János Kádár disappeared and went voluntarily to the Soviet embassy in Budapest, from where he was taken to a nearby military airfield and flown to Moscow.[15] Khrushchev, in fact, appointed Kádár to serve as the leader of the new system to be established in Hungary on November 2, just before his previously mentioned meetings with Gomułka, Tito, and officials from Czechoslovakia, Romania, and Bulgaria. The first days of November were ones of improbable calm in Hungary. The old and new parties increased their activity and Nagy reshuffled his cabinet for the last time on November 3, the eve of the second Soviet intervention. This pluralist government included several members of the reconstituted parties and respected intellectuals like the political scientist and sociologist István Bibó. Also on November 3, Hungarian Radio broadcast a strongly anti-communist speech from the archbishop of Esztergom József Mindszenty, who, along with other political prisoners, had been released from prison at the end of October. The chief of the Catholic Church in Hungary demanded dismissal of compromised communist leaders and the restitution of confiscated properties and schools. Some later voiced the opinion that Cardinal Mindszenty's speech had damaged the reputation of the Nagy administration. In fact, the political message of Mindszenty's speech was intentionally distorted by the Kádár regime's propaganda in an attempt to denigrate him.[16]

The second Soviet intervention made any political negotiations impossible and curtailed the Nagy government's scope of action. The Soviet invasion launched on November 4, code-named Operation Whirlwind, quelled the armed opposition of the few Hungarian military units fighting in support of the civilian revolutionaries. Prime Minister Nagy had taken refuge at the embassy of Yugoslavia in Budapest with other members of his government, paradoxically after broadcasting a speech on Free Radio Kossuth urging Hungarians to resist the Soviet invasion. A few weeks later, Soviet special forces arrested Nagy and his associates despite their diplomatic immunity, transporting them to Romania, where they were held captive on the shores of Lake Snagov, just north of Bucharest, before being returned to Hungary to face trial.

On November 7, Kádár and other members of the newly formed "revolutionary worker-peasant" government arrived in Budapest under Soviet military escort to begin the process of rebuilding the communist power structure. During three weeks of armed conflict, around 2,500 people had been killed fighting on the side of the revolution and a further 10,000 people wounded. Most of these casualties were of working-class origin, and around half were younger than thirty years old. Soviet armed forces suffered 720 dead and 1,500 wounded or missing.[17] By the time authorities closed the country's western borders in December 1956, nearly 200,000 citizens had taken refuge in Austria and Yugoslavia. As a result of the peaceful resistance of the workers' councils, the new Kádár-led communist government was unable to stabilize its hold on power for several months following the revolution. Post-revolution political consolidation began only in the spring of 1957, with the intensification of reprisals against those accused of committing crimes at the time of the "October counterrevolution."

During the Kádár era, the 1956 revolution was a highly sensitive issue in Hungarian public discourse. Officials portrayed the uprising as a foreign-supported counterrevolution until the 1970s, when the Kádár government began to focus on expunging the memory of the revolution from the collective memory of the country's citizens in the hope of producing a type of guided amnesia. In doing this, the communist authorities could rely not only on the complicity of a substantial part of the Western European left but also on the remunerated help of authors like David Irving, who has gained notoriety as a Holocaust denier and depicted the 1956 Hungarian uprising as an anti-Jewish revolt in a book written following an extended official visit to Hungary during which Hungarian authorities provided him with documentary sources.[18] Only after 1989 did the revolution become the subject of social memory and historical debate. Current scholarship mostly agrees that those who participated in the 1956 Hungarian Revolution maintained the common objective of regaining national independence, though supported the introduction of a broad range of political systems—from anti-Stalinist socialism to free-market democracy—in place of the Soviet-style communism of the prerevolutionary period.

The failure of the revolution resulted in profound social reordering and long-term collective psychological crisis in Hungary. The official propaganda attempted to instill in the minds of Hungarian citizens the notion that resistance to the system is futile—that leading a normal life is more important than engaging in heroic deeds. For decades, the officially denigrated revolution could be honored only privately in Hungary. The secret memory of the revolution was transmitted from generation to generation, even among Hungarians living in exile.[19] The alternative memory of the revolution was therefore deprived of much of its original social base in Hungary and became the contended legacy of small groups of intellectuals.

Continuity and Change during the Khrushchev Era

The 1956 Hungarian Revolution is often regarded as an indication of general crisis within the Soviet Bloc. According to commonsense opinion, the revolution represented "the first nail in the coffin of communism." However, when examined from a long-term perspective, the significance of the Twentieth Party Congress of the CPSU, the Polish October, and the 1956 Hungarian Revolution becomes subject to critical reassessment. As Mark Kramer puts it, the Soviet suppression of the revolution did not contribute to the crisis that emerged in Eastern Europe during the 1970s and 1980s but served to reunite the previously factious communist states of the region, thus enabling the Soviet Bloc to survive for three more decades.[20] The Soviet Bloc endured the 1956 crisis and started implementing growth policies that were still based on the development of heavy industry but placed greater emphasis on satisfying the fundamental needs of the population.

The suppression of the Hungarian uprising also showed the growing degree of interdependence between the two blocs, as it contributed to accelerate the negotiations that led in 1957 to the Treaty of Rome, establishing the European Economic Community. The restrained response of the United States to the crises in Poland and Hungary in 1956 signaled the leading Western power's acknowledgment of the Soviet Union's policy with regard to the Cold War balance of power in Europe.

Examined from an inside perspective, Khrushchev's policies appear to be a tempestuous series of improvised and often failed initiatives. The events at the Twentieth Congress and the subsequent failed palace revolution to depose Khrushchev in June 1957 profoundly agitated the party apparatus. Only the forceful intervention of Defense Minister Georgy Zhukov foiled the conservative attempt to overthrow Khrushchev and provided the CPSU leader with the opportunity to initiate a second round of reforms, particularly in the ideological domain.[21] Khrushchev permitted writers, artists, scientists, and regular citizens to maintain contacts with foreigners, encouraged the revival of artistic styles and movements that had been prohibited during the Stalinist period (at least until he publically attacked nonconformist art and closed down an exhibition of avant-garde paintings in 1962), and authorized the publication of Aleksandr Solzhenitsyn's novel of enormous impact depicting Stalinist repression in a Soviet labor camp, *One Day in the Life of Ivan Denisovich*.

From 1958 the same Khrushchev conducted an ideological-social offensive— which Andrea Graziosi refers to as the "small leap forward"—that was based on a less radical but equally assertive version of the Maoist model.[22] Soviet authorities placed renewed emphasis on ideology, condemning revisionism and persecuting early dissident intellectuals, and intensified the struggle against religion, closing and demolishing churches and monasteries, arresting ecclesiastical officials, intimidating worshipers, and disseminating atheist and evolutionist propaganda in schools and workplaces. During this period the state escalated its intervention in the most intimate spheres of the private lives of Soviet citizens, transforming rites of passage such as births, marriages, and funerals into civil, emphatically nonreligious, ceremonies.

The Eastern Orthodox Church, which had by the end of the Second World War become integrated into the Soviet system, again became the focus of official attacks aimed at further reducing its social influence. However, the patriarch of Moscow continued to play an important legitimizing role in Soviet foreign propaganda, and the start of ecumenical dialogue with the Vatican served to enhance the political significance of the state-controlled church.[23] According to

```

Andrea Riccardi, one of Khrushchev's objectives was to restore the ideological primacy of "Leninism"—that is, modernizing Bolshevism cleansed of its Stalinist excesses—as a means of providing the Soviet Union with a means of responding effectively to the West's strategy of détente.[24]

The Soviet reinterpretation of Russian nationalism represented the next theme that forced Khrushchev to confront the Soviet Union's Stalinist legacy. In 1954, Khrushchev thus had provoked the indignation of Russian intellectuals upon the arbitrary transfer of the mostly Russian-inhabited Crimean Peninsula from the Russian Soviet Federative Socialist Republic to the Ukrainian Soviet Socialist Republic. In 1958, the CPSU first secretary instigated educational reform that greatly curtailed the use of minority languages in Soviet schools. One of the stated objectives of this initiative was to "reduce the distance between school and work." However, another clear goal of this Khrushchev-inspired reform was to eliminate the use of non-Russian languages in schools located in republics of the Soviet Union where Russians constituted a minority of the population. The measure also served to heighten the role of the Russian language as a lingua franca in all spheres of activity and to strengthen the ideology of self-identification with the ethnically neutral "Soviet people" rather than with a specific nationality. Khrushchev's program of peaceful Russification triggered a wave of protest in the Ukrainian Soviet Socialist Republic and other Soviet republics in the Baltic region, the Caucasus, and Central Asia.[25] During the 1960s, the Soviet practice of cultural integration inspired support among Eastern Europeans for the notion of unified national identity ("the socialist nation"), which national minorities regarded as an infringement of their rights.[26]

Khrushchev's foreign policy was contradictory and confused. The Soviet leader showed considerable foresight when he abandoned the nearly exclusive focus on Europe that had characterized the Stalinist period and initiated the expansion of Soviet imperial power into the decolonizing states of Asia and Africa. Following the crises of 1956, the Soviet Union managed to incorporate many of the latter states into the "progress and peace camp" and to solidify Soviet influence in the name of economic and technological competition with the West. However, the CPSU first secretary engaged in several unsuccessful maneuvers that stood in stark contrast to his spectacular overtures toward the West. Khrushchev's effort to settle the status of Berlin through the conclusion of a peace treaty resulted in a diplomatic conflict. This prompted the leadership of the German Democratic Republic to begin construction on August 13, 1961, of a fortified barrier to serve as a means of "anti-fascist defense" and to stop the mass exodus from the country that had pushed 3 million East German citizens to the West in a period of just ten years. The Berlin Wall, which bisected the city until November 1989, became the supreme symbol of Europe's division and the extremely limited freedom of movement among the citizens of East Berlin.[27] In October 1962, Khrushchev attempted
```

to gauge the US response to the broadening of Soviet influence in Cuba, thus provoking a severe diplomatic-military crisis. The forceful response of US political and military leaders to the Soviet maneuver and the threat of nuclear war forced Khrushchev to order the removal of the missiles from Cuba. Conflicts within the international communist movement compounded the impact of these humiliating failures of Soviet foreign policy: leaders of the Communist Party of China, which had for years maintained tense relations with the CPSU, accused Khrushchev of revisionism and defeatism.

Khrushchev's domestic positions also weakened in the early 1960s. His belief that the Soviet Union's level of economic development could surpass that of the United States within twenty years seemed to be illusory under the prevailing conditions. Soviet developmental strategy continued to place a priority on increasing industrial production, particularly within the military sector. Meanwhile, Khrushchev's ambitious virgin lands campaign to boost Soviet agricultural production ended in ignominious failure. Two years of drought in 1962 and 1963 forced the Soviet Union and other Eastern Bloc countries to import an enormous quantity of grain from the West. Ideological restrictions and continuous campaigns intended to eliminate corruption and crimes against property resulted in widespread social repression. These factors generated a broad coalition of interests that stood to benefit from Khrushchev's removal from power. The leader of this front was Leonid Brezhnev, who managed to supplant Khrushchev as leader of the Communist Party of the Soviet Union in October 1964.

Repression and Consolidation (1956–1967)

The Soviet Bloc between Unity and Crisis

The developmental paths of communist states in Eastern Europe began to diverge in the decade after the crises of 1956 in both economic and cultural terms, as well as with regard to their relations with the West. The resistance of rural society to the communist system came to a permanent end during this period, and states that had previously possessed an enormous supply of peasant labor were subjected to modernization procedures. The state regulated the increasingly complex personal needs related to housing, work, education, and leisure for the massive number of people moving from rural areas to cities.[28] The monolithic international communist movement of the Stalinist era evolved into a multipolar, complex system in which the internal dialectic generated conflict despite its relative independence from the Soviet Union.[29]

Debunking the Cold War–inherited frameworks about the purely totalitarian character of these societies, new historiographical approaches regard the late Soviet-type state as a heterogeneous complex of agencies and individual actors, with mixed and at times contradicting interests. In Hungary, seminal research by the political scientist Ervin Csizmadia about the Kádár regime's slow transformation into a discursive dictatorship has stimulated further research about "soft violence" and accommodation mechanisms between the party state and society.[30] Michal Kopeček and Michal Pullmann put forward concepts like civilized violence and routinization of the ideological while analyzing the shift that occurred from physical violence to more sophisticated population control in Czechoslovakia. Comparing the social penetration of the communist regime under Stalin and Brezhnev, Jörg Baberowski pointed out how much the growing "reliability of expectations" helped the internal consolidation of the Soviet Union during the Brezhnev era.[31]

After 1957, the Eastern Bloc communist elite attained a genuinely transnational and cohesive character despite the frequently incompatible political and economic interests of its members. Until the early 1980s, the high-ranking communist leadership of Eastern Bloc countries enjoyed an unprecedented degree of personal stability, with the exception of Poland.

In Hungary, consolidation of the Kádár regime resulted in broad reprisals against both those who had participated in the revolution as well as members of the latent opposition—former military officers and gendarmes, priests, and aristocrats. During the mass repression that took place until the proclamation of a general amnesty in March 1963, people's courts in Hungary pronounced 229 death sentences and 20,000 prison sentences. Another 13,000 people suffered administrative internment. Revolutionary political and military leaders Imre Nagy and Pál Maléter were executed on June 16, 1958, in accordance with the will of Kádár. The Kádár regime attempted for many years to establish its legitimacy within a largely hostile Hungarian domestic environment. From 1958 to 1961, the regime implemented the second phase of agricultural collectivization, which resulted in the incorporation of 92 percent of the arable land in Hungary into state farms or agricultural cooperatives. József Ö. Kovács contends that this phase of collectivization entailed a greater degree of physical violence than previously recorded in scholarly literature.[32] The Hungarian Socialist Workers' Party (HSWP) nevertheless pursued more prudent and flexible agricultural policies than its prerevolution predecessor, permitting the peasants who constituted one-third of Hungary's economically active population to grow produce and raise livestock for private use on the land surrounding their houses and making them eligible to receive social assistance and pensions.[33]

Speaking at the congress of the Patriotic People's Front in December 1961, HSWP General Secretary Kádár declared that "those who are not against us are with us," thus inverting Rákosi's notorious assertion that "whoever is not with us is against us."[34] This new motto served as a reflection of the controlled thaw that had begun in Hungary. By the time of the Eighth Congress of the Hungarian Socialist Workers' Party in 1962, the HSWP's membership had increased to

500,000 people—or around 5 percent of Hungary's total population. During the congress, Kádár announced that the foundations of socialism had been laid in Hungary. Hungarian society, tired of war and violent changes of regime, had by the early 1960s become prepared to accept the notion of building a type of social-ism that was less dogmatic, more moderate in scope, and accepting of all those who did not actively reject its political legitimacy. Average Hungarians simply wanted to live normal lives with their families without the everyday state inter-ference and intimidation. The stable price of bread became the primary symbol of accountable everyday life during the Kádár era among the working class. The support for the HSWP gained traction among the intellectuals amid the clever implementation of a cultural policy whose aim was to include the best authors into a new national pantheon, and which categorized literary works, films, and fine arts as supported, tolerated, or prohibited. The latter was applied to only a tiny minority of authors, for most self-censored or practiced "self-control," to borrow the words of György Aczél, the man responsible for cultural policies from 1956 to the late 1980s.[35]

Only the intractability of the nationality question caused the Kádár regime a bit of an ideological headache. In 1958 the party launched a vehement campaign to eliminate the remnants of petty bourgeois nationalism, which had been declared the enemy of socialist patriotism. Until the end of the 1960s, the status of Hun-garian minorities—an issue with which intellectuals associated with the populist orientation and ordinary citizens with relatives living in neighboring countries were familiar—officially was a taboo theme. The Kádár regime's cultural policy nevertheless subsequently transformed into an interesting amalgam of both loy-alty toward the Soviet Union and values and elements of national culture that were less sensitive to political manipulation and nationalist demands (e.g., folk music, choral singing, support for monuments, landscape conservation).[36] On September 15, 1964, the Hungarian government obtained what the propaganda of the Kádár regime long portrayed as one of its greatest successes: the signing of a partial agreement with the Vatican—the first such accord between the Vati-can and a communist country, one that strengthened the dialogue between the pope and Eastern European communist authorities that had begun during the papacy of John XXIII.[37] The only issue that remained unsettled was that of Car-dinal Mindszenty, the increasingly awkward guest at the embassy of the United States in Budapest. The agreement, the text of which remained secret for decades, made it possible for the Vatican to appoint a new loyal archbishop. For Moscow, Hungary became the positive example among socialist countries of relations be-tween the state and the church. To preserve good relations with the Hungarian state, Vatican diplomats decided not to attribute particular significance to the continued harassment of religious people and the new wave of arrests in 1965, just a few months following the conclusion of the agreement.[38]

In Romania, the Gheorghiu-Dej regime exploited the tensions that had arisen within the Hungarian population of Transylvania as a result of the 1956 Hungarian Revolution to silence its political opponents as well as the social groups that had shown the greatest resistance to socialism—the peasantry and the urban petty bourgeoisie. According to a later report, almost 30,000 people were arrested in Romania for alleged political transgressions (from high treason to illegal border crossing and causing damage to the national economy) between 1956 and 1963. Detailed information regarding those cases that reached the judicial stage is available only for the period from January 1957 to July 1959, when almost 10,000 convictions were pronounced. It should be noted that although only approximately a minority of those convicted in Romania for political offenses were of Hungarian nationality, the most severe penalties were imposed in the course of around twenty trials against supposed Hungarian nationalists that took place during this period.[39]

Prisons became overcrowded following the wave of arrests that began in early 1957, resulting in frequent epidemics and increased mortality. To avoid uprisings, in 1958 Romanian authorities transferred several thousand political prisoners to labor camps located in the marshlands of the Danube delta, where they were kept in inhumane conditions until 1964. The convicts were not permitted to maintain contact of any kind with their family members and relatives, who did not even know if they were still alive. Deaths were frequently not registered or were reported to next of kin only years later. The post-1956 judicial reprisals performed the dual function of determining individual culpability and, to an increasing degree, intimidating entire national, religious, or village communities. The birth and subsequent strengthening of the Ceauşescu-era power structure was one of the long-term reprisals launched in Romania in connection to the Hungarian counterrevolution. However, the medium-term objectives of the post-1956 repression differed in the two countries: whereas in Romania the notion of gradually liberalizing the consolidated system was not even considered at the beginning of the 1960s, in Hungary the totalitarian state initiated a new state-building process following the revolution that simultaneously responded to challenges from both below and above.[40]

Beginning in the late 1950s, the Romanian government began to implement minority policies that represented a complete break with those of the previous decade. In 1959, Gheorghiu-Dej and Nicolae Ceauşescu, who had become the second most powerful official in the Romanian regime, unified the Hungarian- and Romanian-language universities in the city of Cluj despite objections from the communist elite of Hungarian nationality. The result of this measure, which had been inspired by changes made to the system of education in the Soviet Union, was the establishment of a formally bilingual though in fact Romanian-dominated new structure. In the school year 1959–1960, the Romanianization campaign merged

Hungarian- and German-language schools into exclusively Romanian-language institutes, and in December 1960, the borders of the Hungarian Autonomous Region were redrawn to include regions in which the majority of the population was Romanian. The reorganization of the Hungarian Autonomous Region led to the de facto elimination of territorial and administrative autonomy in the Székely Land of Transylvania. The struggle against the alleged cultural separatism of minorities represented the ideological point of departure for the national-communist turning point that occurred following Ceaușescu's rise to power in 1965.[41] Hungarians, and especially Jews, were removed from sensitive positions within the state apparatus (e.g., economy, political police, cultural institutions) as a result of the large-scale purge of personnel that took place in the late 1950s and the 1960s. In January 1958, the government reopened the channel of Jewish emigration and came to an agreement via treaty with Israel. Over the following seven years, more than 100,000 Romanian Jews left Romania and moved to Israel, while many emigrated to the United States and Western Europe. The exodus of Jews from Romania was not a spontaneous process. Authorities had created a hostile environment for Jews (e.g., press attacks, workplace intimidation, administrative sanctions, criminal trials) intended to induce a change in the composition of the cultural and professional elite.[42]

Gheorghiu-Dej's foreign policy also became more assertive, designed to increase Romania's autonomy within the Soviet Bloc. In May 1958, Khrushchev announced the withdrawal of the Soviet troops stationed in Romania, which was regarded as reliable and easily defendable in the event of attack, as well as the removal of a total of 84,000 Soviet troops from Poland, the German Democratic Republic, and Hungary. China withdrew troops from North Korea at the same time, although the Soviet measure did not inspire NATO to decrease the size of its military forces in Western Europe. However, the withdrawal of Soviet troops from Romania, which many analysts have regarded as a precondition to the country's pro-independence policy, did not signify total liberation. Dennis Deletant points out that the Soviets continued to maintain air and naval bases on Romanian territory and stationed combat-ready troops in the Moldavian Soviet Socialist Republic, in the territory beyond the Prut and in the southern part of the Ukrainian Soviet Socialist Republic.[43] Gheorghiu-Dej skillfully portrayed the Soviet concession as the result of the autonomy of Romanian foreign policy. In 1964, the Romanian Workers' Party issued its so-called April Theses rejecting Soviet supremacy and demanding equal rights for all communist parties, thus causing a serious crisis in relations between Romania and the Soviet Union. However, the ideological conflict between Romania and the Soviet Union was actually based on economic and strategic factors, and therefore did not lead to a permanent break between the two countries. Romania continued its two-faced policies following the death of Gheorghiu-Dej and the appointment of Nicolae

Ceaușescu to serve as party general secretary in March 1965, engaging in limited cooperation within the Soviet Bloc and increasing its activity involving the West and the developed countries.

Whereas the signs of thaw were hardly visible in terms of domestic policy until the middle of the 1960s and state-security oversight had, in fact, increased, a spectacular opening to the West took place in the domain of foreign policy.[44] Romania became the first socialist country to normalize its diplomatic and trade relations with the United States and West Germany. Romania was, furthermore, the only country in the Eastern Bloc not to sever diplomatic relations with Israel following its defeat of a Soviet-supported Arab coalition composed of Egypt, Syria, and Jordan in the Six-Day War in June 1967. This foresight was based to a significant degree on economic factors: Radu Ioanid estimates that the Romanian state generated annual profit of US$100 million through the sale of its own citizens to Israel and West Germany.[45]

The Twentieth Congress of the CPSU exercised a profound effect on the domestic political situation in Bulgaria. Before the Bulgarian Communist Party's plenary meeting in April 1956, General Secretary Todor Zhivkov forced Prime Minister Vulko Chervenkov to resign, thus consolidating his personal power. However, the effects of the 1956 Hungarian Revolution frustrated all attempts to liberalize the system. Political repression reached its pinnacle in Bulgaria in the years 1957–1958 and did not begin to decrease perceptibly until the proclamation of a general amnesty in 1964, which resulted in the release of several thousand political prisoners. Many of the latter had been subjected to "work-therapy re-education" while interned at a camp near the stone quarries of Lovech.[46] During those years, Bulgarian political leaders pursued an economic strategy that was based on the policies of the Soviet Union. The collectivization of agriculture proceeded at a rapid pace in Bulgaria, though decrees authorizing the retention of dwarf holdings and livestock moderated this process, which was necessary since half the total supply of meat and milk in the country was produced on privately held land of that type. Within Bulgaria's still-rudimentary industrial sector, the modernization program launched as part of the Third Five-Year Plan in early 1958 focused on the food industry and durable goods. Following a visit to China, Bulgarian Communist Party (BCP) leaders decided to adopt some of the policies of the Chinese "Great Leap Forward," which led to the radical revision of the Third Five-Year Plan and an increase in conflict within the party leadership, as well as the triumph of the Soviet-supported party general secretary Zhivkov over Politburo member and prime minister Anton Yugov in 1962.[47]

The nationality question reemerged in Bulgaria at the instigation of the Soviet Union beginning in the second half of the 1950s. Bulgaria's 1956 census recorded nearly 200,000 Macedonians, most of them living near the border of the present-day Republic of Macedonia. After the government revived the policy of cultural assimilation of the interwar era in an attempt to induce these Macedonians to declare themselves Bulgarians, relations with Yugoslavia deteriorated and tensions grew among the local population. At the time of the subsequent census, just 8,000 citizens of Bulgaria declared their Macedonian nationality.[48] The ethnic policy change entailed even more serious consequences for Bulgaria's Muslim population, which numbered around 750,000 people (Turks of southern Dobruja, Pomaks and Bulgarians, and Roma who had converted to Islam). At its plenary meeting in 1958, the BCP decided to transform Turkish-language schools into bilingual schools, which subsequently became totally Bulgarianized, and increasing restrictions were issued in the religious and cultural life of that community. In 1964, Bulgarian officials banned the use of the Turkish language in all schools in Bulgaria and enacted measures to Bulgarianize the Pomaks, which only the vigorous opposition of the affected population managed to prevent. Bulgaria's relations with Turkey, already tense because of the Cold War, became even worse. At the urging of the Soviet Union, Bulgaria signed an agreement with Turkey in 1968 that, in addition to normalizing diplomatic relations and facilitating bilateral trade, enabled 130,000 more Bulgarian citizens to emigrate to Turkey.[49]

The contradictions, openings, and closures of the Khrushchev era exercised a significant influence on the political development of Poland, Czechoslovakia, and, to the greatest degree, East Germany. Gomułka very quickly caused disappointment among those who had placed hope in him. The suspension of economic reforms at the beginning of the 1960s resulted in open conflict between the authorities and "revisionist" philosophers who defied dogmatic Marxism and questioned the leading role of the party. The leading figure among these philosophers was Leszek Kołakowski, whose 1957 essay "Responsibility and History" represented the most powerful intellectual embodiment of the Polish October.[50]

Polish authorities responded to the social discontent that had risen to the surface by placing increased emphasis on nationalist propaganda, particularly vis-à-vis West Germany, which had not recognized the Oder-Neisse line. Moreover, beginning in 1964 the faction of cadres within the Polish United Workers' Party under the leadership of Interior Minister Mierczysław Moczar that was of working-class origin and nurtured memories of the partisan past began to strengthen. Three years later, the Six-Day War served as an excellent pretext to conduct the long-desired clampdown on Jewish intellectuals. Newspaper articles containing anti-Jewish allusions and other manifestations of anti-Semitism increased significantly in Poland over the months following the brief 1967 Arab-Israeli War. With Gomułka's support, Moczar did not hesitate to exploit the student unrest of 1968 to launch an anti-Zionist campaign and to suppress the liberal faction within the PUWP. These actions forced most of the remaining Jews in Poland to renounce their Polish citizenship and leave the country. Many of Poland's most prominent intellectuals, including Kołakowski, were among those who were compelled to join this exodus.[51]

Political leaders in Czechoslovakia failed to take advantage of the opportunity to launch reforms in 1956. Contrary to the case in Poland and Hungary, where party leaders had attempted at various times and with disparate means to respond to the challenges posed in the streets, the Novotný regime in Czechoslovakia was not forced to conduct a reassessment of the Stalinist period.[52] Public demonstrations expressing solidarity with the revolution in Hungary took place in the Hungarian-inhabited regions of southern Slovakia in 1956. Although some of these incidents resulted in arrests and imprisonments, they did not pose a significant threat to the political stability of the Novotný regime. Preceding its Eastern Bloc peers by a few years, the Novotný regime adopted a new constitution in 1960 that was based on an alliance of workers, peasants, and intellectuals and defined Czechoslovakia as a "socialist state."

The decrease of Slovak autonomy and the Novotný-urged centralization of bureaucracy represented more important measures from a political perspective. The powerless Slovak National Council assumed the role of the dissolved Slovak section of the government.[53] The purge of Slovak intellectuals generated some nationality-based opposition in the 1960s. The pro-reform Alexander Dubček was appointed to the Communist Party of Czechoslovakia Presidium in 1962 and one year later overcame Prague-favored rivals to become the general secretary of the party's Slovak section. Dubček's rise was attended by a cautious cultural liberalization, among the initial signs of which were the 1963 rehabilitation of Franz Kafka and the 1966 release of the Jiří Menzel–directed film *Closely Watched Trains*, which won the Academy Award for Best Foreign Language Film the following year. Czechoslovak historiography referred to this cultural ferment as *předjaro*, or "early spring."[54]

Economic policy in Czechoslovakia, in contrast, was characterized by total rigidity. The collectivization of agriculture proceeded systematically, without concessions. The country's 1960–1965 Five-Year Plan, which called for a significant increase in the production of agricultural goods, failed because of adverse climate conditions and, mostly, organizational flaws. Heavy industry suffered from operational inefficiencies connected to centralized planning, although the rationalization plan adopted in 1958 did not affect this sector. In the years 1962–1963, Czechoslovakia—the most industrialized and economically developed member of the Eastern Bloc—recorded a nominal decrease in gross domestic product and a strongly negative trade balance, thus forcing the country to go into debt in order to ensure that its citizens would have access to a sufficient supply of basic consumer goods.

In the German Democratic Republic, the power structure of the communist system underwent consolidation in the decade before 1968, particularly following the construction of the Berlin Wall in 1961. The GDR suffered a crisis of legitimacy in the 1950s. The steady flight of citizens from the German Democratic Republic to the Federal Republic of Germany (FRG) was the primary cause of internal crisis, whereas the unwillingness of the FRG, which regarded itself as the only legitimate German state, to recognize the GDR represented the main source of external crisis.

Stabilization of the East German state constituted the cornerstone of Ulbricht-regime policy during the 1960s, although mutual diplomatic recognition between the GDR and the FRG did not take place until the *Ostpolitik* of West German chancellor Willy Brandt came to fruition in 1972. Mary Fulbrook refers to the stabilization of the East German state as "normalization," which in the 1960s and 1970s represented the transition to the inclusive totalitarianism that East Germans had endured and come to accept.[55] In spite of the economic crisis that afflicted the German Democratic Republic at the end of the 1960s—one that led to Erich Honecker's rise to power in place of the aging Ulbricht—the decade offered the possibility of modernization and moderate prosperity to the conflict-fatigued population of the GDR. In 1970, more than 70 percent of East Germans owned a television, a refrigerator, and a washing machine—a higher percentage than in any other socialist country.[56] At the same time, the East German regime became entrenched in a condition of inaction and rigidity. The Stasi political police worked in close symbiosis with Soviet authorities, thereby becoming the strongest and most effective organization of repression in the Eastern Bloc.[57]

Socialism Outside the Bloc: Yugoslavia and Albania

The 1956 Hungarian Revolution and Yugoslavia's heterodox policies in the 1960s challenged the unity of the socialist bloc that had formed around the Soviet Union. The deterioration in relations between the Communist Party of the Soviet Union and the Communist Party of China signified the permanent dissolution of interbloc unity. The Sino-Soviet split was based on ideological, strategic issues (the Soviet Union did not support China in its conflict with India) and economic contingencies. In 1960 the Soviets recalled their advisers from China. In 1961 the Chinese characterized Soviet leaders as "revisionist traitors," while the Soviets referred to Chairman Mao and his European supporters as "adventurers" and "nationalists." In March 1969 the conflict between the two largest communist countries led to armed confrontation along the Ussuri River on the Chinese-Soviet border. Tito's refusal to take the side of the Soviet Union in the Sino-Soviet conflict put an end to the rapprochement between Moscow and Belgrade. At the beginning of the 1960s, Khrushchev repeatedly attempted to draw Yugoslavia back toward the Soviet Bloc, and over the following decades, relations between Moscow and Belgrade stabilized at an acceptable level of economic cooperation and more limited mutual political support. The Yugoslav model inspired envy among other Eastern European countries at the socioeconomic level. A series of decrees enacted between 1957 and 1965 established the foundations for genuine decentralization following the dismantling of Soviet-type hierarchical structures and the introduction of elected committees operating on the basis of worker self-management and workers' councils that formulated labor plans in enterprises, determined the amount of profit to be put back into companies, and regulated wage differentials according to productivity. Control over bureaucratic apparatuses (with a few significant exceptions, such as the Defense Ministry) was placed under the authority of the republic, and the management of enterprises was granted the freedom to determine the distribution of profit. State supervision was limited to defense-related sectors, infrastructural investments, regional development, scientific research, foreign trade, and wage policy related to foreign-currency exchange.[58]

The 1963 Yugoslav Constitution was not by mere chance referred to as the constitution of self-management. In 1965, the reform launched at the initiative of the Tito regime's chief theoretician Edvard Kardelj served to eliminate most price controls, to strengthen self-management autonomy at every level of the economy and within all production sectors, and, most important, to withdraw state support for factories and workshops that recorded inadequate productivity. This reform was the subject of sharp criticism from the left. Argentine revolutionary Ernesto "Che" Guevara articulated his negative opinion during a visit to Yugoslavia in the summer of 1959, asserting that it represented "managerial capitalism with the socialist distribution of profits."[59]

Yugoslavia underwent contradiction-filled economic development in the 1960s. Per capita wages rose to a significant degree in Yugoslavia during the decade, primarily in the developed republics and regions of the country (Slovenia, Croatia, and northern and central Serbia). For reform-minded economic experts like the Hungarian Rezső Nyers, Yugoslavia represented an example to be emulated. The economy of Yugoslavia already contained a significant number of market elements and the country was a member of the International Monetary Fund and the World Bank. Yugoslavia's stock of foreign currency increased during the period as a result of developing tourism, primarily to the Adriatic coast of Croatia. In 1967, Yugoslavia eliminated visa requirements for citizens of both capitalist and communist countries, granting entry to all those who wished to visit the country. Remittances from Yugoslav guest workers in Western Europe grew substantially after an agreement between Yugoslavia and the Federal Republic of Germany enabled a large number of Yugoslav citizens (1 million according the Yugoslavia's 1971 census) to legally live and work in the FRG.[60] However, Titoist Yugoslavia could provide its citizens with an adequate supply of durable consumer goods only through Western imports and with considerable support from the United States.

Moreover, Yugoslavia's intensive contacts with Western societies resulted in new problems that were unknown elsewhere. Mass unemployment, high inflation, and the introduction of free-market elements to the controlled economy heightened ideological conflict within the League of Communists of Yugoslavia and brought ethnic tensions to the surface beginning in the middle of the 1960s. The forced resignation of the feared ideological hard-liner Aleksandar Ranković, from his position as head of the political police in 1966 on charges of plotting against Tito, caused widespread surprise in Yugoslavia. Ranković had engaged in vehement arguments with President Tito and Edvard Kardelj regarding the pace of economic reform. To many Yugoslavs, particularly Slovenes, Croats, and Kosovars, Ranković represented an embodiment of the Serbian party elite that opposed nationality rights. An investigation following Ranković's resignation revealed that thousands of Croats and Kosovo Albanians had been registered as potential enemies of the state on ethnic grounds.[61]

Rapid liberalization attended the reorganization of the internal-security apparatus. Moreover, the expansion of the opportunity to travel abroad occurred at the same time as the student protests in Western Europe, thus placing young Yugoslavs in a position to gain greater exposure to the upheaval than other Eastern Europeans. In July 1968, several thousand students went on strike in Belgrade and subsequently in Ljubljana and Zagreb. The police conducted surveillance on the participants in the strikes, although they were ordered to avoid physical contact with them and to intervene only to prevent street clashes.[62] Purges conducted at universities and within the intelligentsia in 1971 and 1972 served to reverse the political opening that had taken place.

Croatian demands were based partially on economic considerations (specifically, to keep half of all revenue derived from tourism to the republic in place of the centrally stipulated 7 percent) and partially on cultural factors related to national identity. In 1967, a group of linguists issued the Declaration on the Status and Name of the Croatian Literary Language, in which they requested greater protection for the Croatian language, while the student protestors demanded the right to use pre–Second World War national symbols and to sing banned nationalist songs in public. An increasing number of opposition intellectuals, pro-Ustaše nationalists—some of whom were party cadres—and university students participated in the Maspok, or "mass movement," which coalesced around the periodical *Matica hrvatska*. During the Croatian spring of 1971, members of the opposition demanded recognition of the homogeneous ethnic and linguistic conditions within the Socialist Republic of Croatia and even requested that the United Nations grant the republic a separate mandate within the organization. The radicalization of the Maspok movement elicited protests among Serbs. Worried by the potential impact of the Croatian demands, Tito suppressed the mass movement through intimidation, purges of the leadership group, and the arrest of Maspok leaders, including the former Partisan and military historian and future president of Croatia Franjo Tuđman. Although the 1972 "normalization" succeeded in reducing political tension in Yugoslavia, it failed to alleviate suppressed anger and to settle unresolved political issues, which the country's 1974 constitution likewise failed to address.[63]

In Kosovo, in November 1968 members of the Albanian majority population engaged in violent protests to voice their demands for greater autonomy vis-à-vis Serbia and greater cultural contacts with Albania. The conflict was settled with partial success: Kosovo-Metohija became the autonomous province of Kosovo, under the eighteenth amendment to Yugoslavia's constitution, and a constituent element of the federation. Kosovo gained its own constitution (instead of statutes) and the right for its regional assembly to pass laws equal to those of a Yugoslav republic. These concessions did not elevate Kosovo to the status of republic, which would have provided the province with the same degree of autonomy as Serbia. However, they did authorize the public display of Albanian national symbols and the operation of a bilingual university in the provincial capital of Pristina that during the 1970s played a fundamental role in the propagation of Albanian political consciousness. The Albanian elite gained more proportional representation within local administration, receiving more than one-third of economic-development support granted to the republic through central funds (to which the most developed republics contributed in accordance with the principle of subsidiarity). Following these changes, Yugoslavia's Albanian population began gravitating toward Kosovo, while Slavs and Serbs in particular started moving out of the province.[64]

During the 1950s, Albania depended totally on the political, military, and economic support of the Soviet Union, which had not failed to notice the strategic importance of the small Balkan state located between Yugoslavia and Greece. Following the anti-Tito purges, the personal power of Enver Hoxha solidified the internal stability of the Communist Party. However, following its reconciliation with Yugoslavia, the Soviet Union lost its interest in Albania, the economic capacity of which was negligible. Tension between the Soviet Union and Albania emerged following the Twentieth Congress of the CPSU. Khrushchev's censure of Stalinism at the congress angered and alarmed Albanian leaders, who were also wary of the subsequent rapprochement between the Soviet Union and Yugoslavia and the spread of concepts regarding peaceful coexistence and divergent national paths toward socialism. The leadership of Albania reacted to these perceived threats by strengthening the classic version of the Stalinist system.[65] The collectivization of agriculture was implemented in Albania over a period of just a few years, from 1957 to 1961. Albanian leaders also considered the Khrushchev-supported CMEA integration plan to represent a serious danger for Albania because it relegated the country to the periphery of Eastern Bloc economic development.

They thus decided to build new mining and industrial complexes that would be capable of accommodating new generations of workers.

Albania's relations with China began to strengthen conspicuously in 1960, which first led to public conflict between Soviet and Albanian officials at the Third Congress of the Romanian Workers' Party. The split between Albania and the Soviet Union took place during a meeting of eighty-one communist parties in Moscow in November 1960 at which the Albanian-supported Chinese delegation launched a sharp attack against Soviet supremacy. In response, the Soviet Union severed diplomatic relations with Albania, withdrew its advisers, and suspended its economic-assistance programs with the country. In 1962, Albania recalled its representatives from the Council of Mutual Economic Assistance and the Warsaw Pact, from which it withdrew officially in 1968.[66] Hoxha subsequently turned toward China, with which Albania's foreign trade increased by 46 percent in 1964. One of the most distressing consequences of the Albanian leadership's support for the policies of Maoist Cultural Revolution was its anti-religious campaign (Albania was traditionally a religiously diverse country in which the Muslim majority lived peacefully with Eastern Orthodox and Roman Catholic minorities). The anti-religious campaign reached its height in November 1967, when the Albanian parliament declared Albania to be the first atheist state in the world. Neither the constitution nor the criminal code recognized any religion, and both sanctioned the death penalty (which was generally reduced to imprisonment) for those caught engaging in religious rites or participating in religious events. All mosques and churches in Albania were either destroyed or converted into schools, cinemas, or shops. Many hundreds of buildings of inestimable worth fell victim to this senseless campaign of persecution.[67]

The Successes and Failures of "Existing Socialism"

Economic and Military Integration

Under Khrushchev's leadership, the Soviet Union began to strengthen economic cooperation. In the 1960s, the Council of Mutual Economic Assistance participated as an international organization in the operations of the United Nations, and each member state represented itself in the body that coordinated the activity of the CMEA's multinational technical apparatus in Moscow. In 1962 the CMEA established its supreme decision-making body, the Executive Committee, formed new permanent committees, and reorganized its Secretariat to increase institutional centralization and harmonize economic planning. The mottos of Khrushchev's economic specialists were "specialization" and "complementarity." Eastern Europe was divided into two macroregions: the more developed northern sector (the German Democratic Republic, Poland, and Czechoslovakia), where industrial investments were concentrated, and the less developed southern sector (Romania, Bulgaria, and Albania), where agriculture, the food industry, and light industry received emphasis. Hungary occupied an intermediary position between the two areas.

Following an intense debate at its Fifteenth Council Session in 1962, the Council for Mutual Economic Assistance adopted its Basic Principles of the International Socialist Division of Labor. Romanian party leaders reacted negatively to the organization's plan to transform Romania into the breadbasket of Eastern Europe, a stance that was fully compatible with the country's new nationalist course. In February 1964, Soviet officials introduced the so-called Valev Plan, which proposed the establishment of Soviet, Romanian, and Bulgarian developmental regions around the Black Sea. Although Romania did not withdraw from the CMEA, both Gheorghiu-Dej and his successor, Nicolae Ceauşescu, chose on a case-by-case basis when and how to participate in the organization's economic plans and implemented policies to increase self-sufficiency and accelerate the process of industrialization. In 1960, Romania conducted 66 percent of its foreign trade with CMEA member states; two decades later, Romania conducted only 35 percent of its foreign trade with fellow CMEA members and more than 40 percent of it with developed capitalist countries.[68]

Aside from difficulties arising from the recalcitrance of Romania and Albania, the CMEA's greatest problems were connected to the organization's hybrid nature, which forced participating member states to make frequent changes of course and economically irrational decisions based on established ideological patterns and variable power constellations. Council of Mutual Economic Assistance member states—which assiduously preserved their own economic-planning capacity while at the same time attempting to broaden the consensual basis of various systems—rejected all measures aimed at transforming the CMEA into a genuinely supranational planning organization. CMEA member-state national currencies, the official exchange rates of which fluctuated in a range well below genuine gold- and US dollar–based exchange rates, for many years remained inconvertible between themselves and with the Soviet ruble. The virtually convertible ruble was established only following the foundation of the International Bank for Economic Cooperation in Moscow in 1963, to simplify compensation between debt and credit. Bilateralism, in any case, remained a component of commerce between CMEA member states, and the proportion of regulated trade conducted through the clearing system (or with compensation mechanisms) never reached the desired level. As Marie Lavigne has emphasized, Eastern Europe came to occupy an advantageous position in terms of CMEA-level specialization compared to that of the Soviet Union, which provided states in the region with inexpensive oil, gas, coal, iron, and other raw materials. In exchange, Eastern Bloc countries exported large quantities of machine-industry products to the Soviet Union at low fixed prices. With regard to the mining industry, one can speak of nothing less than planned losses—an economic absurdity that reduced the total expenditures of the planned economy.[69]

Despite all its innate flaws, the CMEA became the flywheel of integration during the second half of the 1960s. The Friendship Pipeline (Nefteprovod Druzhba) built between 1959 and 1964 provided East Germany, Poland (the northern branch), Czechoslovakia, and Hungary (the southern branch) with Soviet petroleum extracted in Siberia. Between 1966 and 1970, the construction of transcontinental gas pipelines and the linkage of power lines as well as road and railway developments contributed to the strengthening of the Soviet Bloc's economic network and the (re)integration of Eastern Europe into the world economy. In 1969, CMEA issued its total integration program, which organizational member states adopted two years later. In 1971, CMEA founded the International Investment Bank (IIB) to provide financing to international projects through the provision of medium- and long-term loans. However, the total value of bank-financed projects remained extremely low. Construction between 1973 and 1978 of the Orenburg gas complex and pipeline, which today serves as in indispensable conduit for the transport of gas to continental Europe, was the only major project in which the IIB participated. However, even in this case Western creditors—which provided CMEA member states with nearly $3 billion in loans—played the most important role in financing the project.[70]

Military cooperation represented the other motor of socialist integration. Khrushchev had initiated the establishment of the Warsaw Pact to serve as a vehicle for bringing the Cold War to an end through the exertion of pressure on the West. After this failed to produce its intended results, Khrushchev came up with a new, suggestive ideological construct (the conquest of outer space in competition with the United States) and attempted with little success to display Soviet power in the diplomatic and military domain.

Soviet leaders expected Warsaw Pact member states to significantly increase military expenditures and, if necessary, to place their economies on a wartime footing. According to Vojtech Mastny and Malcolm Byrne, the Warsaw Pact at this time replaced its previous defensive military strategy with an offensive approach along both the primary, northern front (West Germany, East Germany, Czechoslovakia, and Poland) as well as the secondary, southern front (Austria, Italy, Greece, Turkey, Hungary, and Bulgaria).[71]

Warsaw Pact military plans called for ground forces to launch a rapid counterattack of Western Europe via West Germany and northern Italy in the event of Western threat or attack. The nearly 400,000 Soviet troops stationed in East Germany and 100,000 Soviet troops stationed in Hungary would support these ground forces in the counterattack along with liaison units from Poland and short- and medium-range missiles. These missiles would be fired at cities in northern Italy from Soviet bases in Hungary and at West Germany from bases in East Germany and Czechoslovakia.[72] The "war games" of the 1960s burdened the budgets of the smaller allies of the Soviet Union to such a degree that they managed to partially liberate themselves from this framework of specialization only in the course of the following decade to focus on development of their own military industries, which conducted much of its trade in US dollars with buyers from the Middle East.[73]

The process of military integration did not always proceed smoothly. Until 1964, the organizational structure of the Warsaw Pact's unified command was very rudimentary, although even after this year Soviet military doctrine frequently clashed with the caution of member states that were concerned about maintaining their political stability. Contrary to the case in the period before Stalin's death, the resistance of these allied states was enough to obstruct Soviet military initiatives. Albania began to distance itself from the Warsaw Pact following the Sino-Soviet split, while the loyalty of Romania had also become increasingly tenuous: in October 1963, the pro-West foreign minister of Romania, Corneliu Mănescu, confidentially informed US officials that the country would remain neutral in the event of an East-West armed conflict.[74] Over the subsequent decades, Romania participated only occasionally in Warsaw Pact military exercises (sometimes as an observer) and meetings of the organization's primary decision-making body, the Political Consultative Committee.[75]

Cooperation between the various secret services and political police forces within the Soviet Bloc represented a unique aspect of interbloc relations beginning in the 1950s. Contacts between such organizations were initially conducted via Soviet advisers (or individuals connected to Soviet security services) stationed in Eastern Europe, although direct organizational links were established after 1956. Although Soviet-type state-security institutions remained under Moscow's control in terms of their organizational structure and ideological objectives, Eastern European states attempted to interconnect their own systems to strengthen operative cooperation and the horizontal exchange of information. This proved an extremely difficult task given the unwritten rule of noninterference in the internal affairs of other states within the socialist bloc.

Although the acquisition of nondiplomatic internal information was forbidden even under "fraternal" conditions, intelligence and counterintelligence organizations of most Eastern Bloc countries—particularly those of Romania—increasingly acted according to the traditional motive of enhancing the security of the nation state. The need for organized cooperation first emerged in the spring of 1956. Radio connections were first established in 1957 between the state-security organs of East Germany, Czechoslovakia, Hungary, and Romania. Numerous bilateral agreements were signed between the Soviet Union and the Warsaw Pact countries, with the exception of Romania in the early 1960s.[76]

The relationship between the state security organizations of Romania and the hard-line German Democratic Republic were particularly interesting. Cooperation between the interior ministries of Romania and the GDR started strongly in the second half of the 1950s. Romanian state-security organizations maintained an operative group at Romania's embassy in East Berlin to monitor (and sometimes even kidnap and repatriate) Romanian exiles living in West Berlin. However, the "declaration of independence" in April 1964 represented a turning point in Romania's state-security relations with other Eastern Bloc states. KGB advisers left Bucharest following the Romanian Workers' Party (RWP) declaration, and until 1989 Romania was the only Warsaw Pact member state that lacked systematic intelligence contacts with other countries in the socialist bloc and in which the Soviets did not exercise direct control over internal state-security organs. In fact, beginning in the 1970s, East Germany regarded Romania as a potential enemy because of the cordial relations it had established with West Germany.[77]

Beginning in the second half of the 1960s, Warsaw Pact member states made coordinated attempts to weaken the moral influence of the Vatican in Eastern Europe and to guide the pro-Western conservative theological and social outlook in the direction of ideological neutrality, which made no distinction between capitalism and socialism. To achieve these objectives, the security organs of Soviet Bloc countries cooperated in espionage activities aimed primarily at the United States, West Germany, the Vatican, and "reactionary" communist-exile groups. Hungary's state-security organizations recorded particular success in gaining intelligence from within the Vatican in the 1970s.[78] Eastern European intelligence services regularly exchanged personal data and operative information regarding foreign ecclesiastical officials. Hungarian diplomats and/or intelligence officials established intensive bilateral relations with their Polish and East German counterparts stationed in Rome. Many Warsaw Pact member states that maintained little direct contact with the Vatican, including the Soviet Union, Czechoslovakia, and Bulgaria, turned to Hungary and later Poland for intelligence regarding the Vatican.[79] In 1977, the member states of the Warsaw Pact, with the exception of Romania, established a unified, Moscow-based military database that by the 1980s contained information regarding nearly 200,000 citizens suspected of anti-socialist activity.[80]

Modernization Debates and System-Correction Proposals

The Soviet Union and the countries of Eastern Europe undertook full economic competition with the West from the late 1950s until the early 1970s. In the opinion of Stefano Bianchini, this period "represented a dynamic historical upturn in which an economically modern, transnational model began to emerge that diverged from conditions established in the West."[81] Economic-reform measures implemented in the Eastern Bloc (and to a much lesser degree in the Soviet Union as well) were based on the premise that the centralized planned economy stifles technological innovation and inhibits both cooperation and competition. Theoretical debates surrounding the planned economy extended back to criticisms that Hungarian-born economist and ideologue Eugen Varga articulated in the 1930s and 1940s, when he served as the director of the Soviet Academy of Sciences Institute of World Economy and International Affairs. Varga was forced to exercise humiliating self-criticism for "falling under the influence of bourgeois cosmopolitanism" after acknowledging in a 1946 study that capitalism had not entered a period of final crisis as Lenin had predicted it would, but until his death in 1964 he continued to exert a considerable authority over young economists studying in Moscow. Iván T. Berend asserts that the reintroduction of the notion of market processes to public thought in Hungary played a central role in the formulation of criticism toward the logic of the communist system. Under pressure from the workers' councils that formed after the 1956 revolution, the Hungarian Socialist Workers' Party began to develop a new economic system that would be capable of preventing the renewed emergence of social discontent.[82] This effort was associated with Hungary's increasing indebtedness to non-CMEA countries, which surpassed $4 million in 1963 and represented more than half the value of all Hungarian exports.[83]

On September 9, 1962, senior Soviet economist Evsei Liberman published an article in *Pravda* titled "Plan, Benefit and Prisms" in which he advocated curbing centralized economic planning and, rehabilitating the notion of profit, increasing the decision-making autonomy of companies. In 1963, the German Democratic Republic became the first country in the Eastern Bloc to adopt the Liberman-proposed version of the planned economy. However, the failure of this system to produce its intended results compelled the Socialist Unity Party of Germany to gradually reinstitute the former centralized-planning mechanism during the years 1968–1970 and to allocate increased state support for the development of industrial sectors with high technological potential (e.g., the chemical industry, electronics, precision optics). The first attempt at comprehensive economic liberalization took place after the 1963 recession, which was particularly severe in heavily industrialized Czechoslovakia and put an end to the illusion of the extensive economic model based on essentially unlimited manpower.[84]

Corrective reform was launched in the Soviet Union in September 1965, one year after the removal of Khrushchev from power and the rise of a new leadership group led by CPSU General Secretary Leonid Brezhnev that was much more sensitive to the issue of economic efficiency. The Council of Ministers Chairman Alexei Kosygin—initiated reforms increased the autonomy of enterprises and touched upon the fundamental coordinates of the planned economic system—economically irrational production costs, the calculation of consumer prices and the general production index, which obscured the connection between prices and the added value of products.[85]

Most Eastern European countries implemented changes to their economic policies during the second half of the 1960s. Poland and Bulgaria carried out moderate reforms according to the Soviet model, while Romania pursued an independent industrialization policy that went against the general direction of development within the CMEA organization. The development of heavy industry that took place in Romania during the years 1967–1971, although conducted in rigid adherence to the principles of the planned economy, corresponded to the country's opening toward Western markets and international financial organizations. In 1966 Romanian and French officials signed an agreement that resulted in the production of Renault-licensed Dacia passenger vehicles in Romania beginning two years later, which contributed significantly to the country's motorization. In the early 1970s, Romania became the first country in Eastern Europe to join the General Agreements on Tariffs and Trade as well as the International Monetary Fund and the World Bank, and it also signed numerous bilateral cooperative agreements with Western companies concerning the import of technology and modern machinery.

Hungary devised its economic-reform plan, known as the New Economic Mechanism (NEM), in May 1966, although the reform was not launched until 1968. The NEM represented the introduction of "socialist market-economy" even though it lacked fundamental elements of capitalism, such as a banking system that was capable of providing investment resources and an integrated state-budgetary system. The NEM removed state ownership over the means of production and the central role of the planned economic mechanism in the allocation of financial resources. It furnished enterprises with a certain degree of autonomy in setting wages and prices according to the profit principle, permitted workers to participate in the determination production goals and investments, and granted small-scale production units and agricultural cooperatives greater freedom to engage in direct barter transactions. Hungary's agricultural and livestock cooperatives for decades generated the most significant share of Hungarian exports to Western markets.[86]

The New Economic Mechanism was initially successful: Hungary's economy grew by 4.5 percent in 1968 and by more than 6 percent in 1969 at the same time that its balance of payments came into equilibrium. However, the process of reform produced increasing antipathy among industrial managers and trade-union directors, whom conservative officials within the Hungarian Socialist Workers' Party supported. Moreover, party leaders from the Soviet Union, East Germany, and Czechoslovakia, which had undertaken the process of normalization following the suppression of the Prague Spring, rejected the introduction of market processes. Thus in 1972, the workers' wing of the Hungarian Socialist Workers' Party, led by Central Committee secretary and former interior minister Béla Biszku, managed to stifle the NEM with strong Soviet support. The failure of the New Economic Mechanism for a short time jeopardized the position of HSWP General Secretary János Kádár, although Brezhnev's eventual support for the longtime party leader as part of a compromise settlement of the economic-reform issue allowed him to remain in power.

Over the long term and despite any setbacks, the New Economic Mechanism resulted in decreased party control over the economy and the transfer of economic-management operations to a broad range of technocrats (company directors, economists, and engineers). Hungary's transformed economic system required socialist managers to possess economic and financial expertise (which ten years previous would have been unimaginable) and offered them a certain degree of authority to make independent decisions. This resulted in the formation of a new stratum within the Hungarian Socialist Workers' Party apparatus that was based on professional competence and technical knowledge rather than pure ideological fidelity. According to Nigel Swain, the New Economic Mechanism, though only partially implemented and on several occasions subordinated to external ideological dictates that lacked any economic rationality (1972–1973, 1985–1986), rescued Hungary from economic collapse, whereas in Poland the absence of a social-democratic or "third road" reform placed the country on the path to economic ruin.[87] Ignác Romsics, however, contends that the NEM's success was relative when examined in the comparative context of economic growth in the Soviet Bloc.[88]

The economic reforms attempted in Eastern Europe, which though bold were still compatible with the principles of the planned economy, served only to deepen the inequalities of the classical system.[89] By the eve of the first oil crisis in 1973, the countries of Eastern Europe had become reintegrated into the global economic system, albeit in a semiperipheral position and under circumstances that made them dependent on production cycles. By this time, hard-currency exports had grown to constitute a significant portion of the gross national product generated in Eastern European states, including nearly half of gross domestic product in Hungary and between 20 percent and 25 percent of gross domestic product in Poland, Yugoslavia, and Romania. Although the economic difficulties that emerged throughout Eastern Europe in the 1970s were partially the result of external factors such as the oil crisis, the stagnation of Western economies, and the devaluation of the US dollar, they were primarily the consequence of the exhaustion of the natural and human resources required for heavy-industry based extensive economic development.

The Last Utopia: The Czechoslovak 1968

The "Prague Spring"

A cautious process of destalinization began in Czechoslovakia in 1963 that served to highlight the contradiction between the enthusiasm of intellectuals and the immobility of politics. Kieran Williams has identified several factors that contributed to the intensification of the struggle between reformers and conservatives in Czechoslovakia: the Ota Šik–devised economic policy to spur growth through decentralization launched in 1965; the opposition of the conservative wing of the Communist Party of Czechoslovakia to economic reform; the increasing tension between Czechs and Slovaks, who accused party and government officials of neglecting Slovak economic and cultural interests; and the legitimacy crisis of veteran communists and those who had benefited from previous political purges, whom Czechoslovak society regarded as a highly incompetent elite selected on the basis of position and loyalty. Although the decision, initially under pressure from the intelligentsia, in the autumn of 1967 to liberalize the system was based on broad consensus within the party leadership, it nevertheless represented a strategic choice to implement radical reforms intended to introduce "socialism with a human face."[90]

Czechoslovak liberal intellectuals and party reformers achieved their greatest success on January 5, 1968, when they forced the inflexible Antonín Novotný to resign from his post as party first secretary with Soviet approval in favor of Alexander Dubček, who immediately initiated the process of cultural and political liberalization. The Dubček program, which was based on Marxist socialism, did not intend to transcend Soviet-established boundaries. However, the concessions contained in Dubček's policies were significantly greater than those of Imre Nagy in 1953 and of Władysław Gomułka in 1956. They included such measures as the elimination of prior censorship and the significant restriction of the prerogatives of state-security services, including the authority to conduct surveillance on citizens. Although Dubček did not question the leading role of the party, the liberalization program that he launched did exercise a revitalizing effect on the mood of society. Pro-reform officials in Hungary and Yugoslavia looked upon the liberal economic and political changes taking place in Czechoslovakia with sympathy, while party leaders in Romania, who were proceeding down a national-communist path, also approved of them as a result of their anti-Soviet, pro-independence tendencies.[91] However, Dubček's reforms caused alarm in the Soviet Union and, to an even greater degree, Poland and the German Democratic Republic, whose party leaders soon decided that it had become necessary to initiate the suppression of "hostile and anti-socialist influences." Eastern European communist leaders attending an extraordinary summit meeting that Brezhnev had convened in Dresden on March 23, 1968, launched a harsh verbal attack against Czechoslovak delegates. The only delegations that did not fully participate in the castigation of their Czechoslovak counterparts at the summit meeting were those from Romania and Hungary, the latter of which knew that the fate of Hungarian economic reform depended on the success of Dubček's liberalization program.[92] The criticism of Czechoslovak reforms articulated in Dresden did not deter Dubček, who on April 5, 1968, announced his action program, which portrayed the Communist Party of Czechoslovakia as the vehicle for renewal and proclaimed equality between Czechs and Slovaks.

High-ranking Soviet leaders were divided in their proposed response to the events in Czechoslovakia in 1968, just as they had been with regard to Hungary in 1956: while KGB director Yuri Andropov and chairman of the Presidium of the Supreme Soviet Nikolai Podgorny advocated military intervention, Leonid Brezhnev and party Secretariat and Politburo member Mikhail Suslov hoped to find a compromise solution. In April 1968 the Soviet Politburo authorized Soviet armed forces stationed in Eastern Europe to formulate attack plans. Soviet officials feared that the triumph of the radical reforms in Czechoslovakia could undermine the stability of the socialist camp and push the country in the direction of Yugoslav-type neutrality. Soviet and Polish military forces held exercises near the Czechoslovak border in May and continued to conduct war games in June. Czechoslovak military leaders knew nothing about the details of these actions, the objectives of which were purely tactical—to permit invading forces to reach as far into Czechoslovak territory as possible and to ensure the "honorable" members of the party and military that the objective of the Soviet-led intervention was merely to reinstate the status quo ante.[93]

The publication in Czechoslovakia of the "Two Thousand Words" manifesto on June 27, 1968, prompted a change in the Soviet stance toward the events taking place in the country. The manifesto's call for the removal of Novotný and his allies from positions of power, the support of Dubček's reforms through strikes, and the assertion of the civil right to engage in passive resistance, boycotts, and acts of sabotage in the event of invasion prompted the Soviet leadership to conclude that military intervention in Czechoslovakia was necessary. The efforts of Brezhnev to persuade Czechoslovak officials to reject the heresy of the Dubček reforms failed, and his Eastern European allies, notably Walter Ulbricht of East Germany and Władysław Gomułka of Poland, began to place increasing pressure on him to choose the option of military intervention. Soviet leaders finally approved the extraordinary measure of invading a fellow Warsaw Pact state at meetings held on late July, ordering that the intervention to be initiated within one month.

Negotiations held on July 29, 1968, in a village near the Czechoslovak-Soviet border led to an agreement that Warsaw Pact member states, with the exception of Romania, signed in Bratislava five days later. This agreement proclaimed the fraternal cooperation of socialist states in the struggle against imperialism. However, Dubček and Brezhnev interpreted the agreement differently: whereas the former regarded it as Soviet acknowledgment of the demands of the Prague Spring, the latter saw it as a means of deterring the Czechoslovak leader from further pursuit of his reforms. The Communist Party of Czechoslovakia convened an extraordinary congress in September to articulate a response to Soviet objections to the Dubček program and to reconfirm their commitment to liberal course. Meanwhile, military preparations for the invasion of Czechoslovakia had begun: reservists were called up in the Soviet Union and other Warsaw Pact states that intended to participate in the intervention and shipments of fuel destined for Czechoslovakia were diverted to East Germany in order to impede possible Czechoslovak military resistance.

On August 18, Soviet leaders informed officials in allied states of their intention to invade Czechoslovakia. At a Warsaw Pact summit meeting held before the military intervention, Brezhnev read a letter from five dogmatic representatives of the CPC describing the counterrevolutionary situation in the country and the anti-Soviet chauvinism that prevailed within the CPC. This letter, the publication of which Russian President Boris Yeltsin made possible in the 1990s, reveals that the pro-Soviet faction of the CPC in 1968 was much stronger and more confident than those within the Hungarian Workers' Party and the Polish United Workers' Party in 1956.

Soviet Military Intervention and "Normalization" in Czechoslovakia

On the night of August 20 and into the morning of August 21, 1968, a Warsaw Pact force that included an estimated 350,000 Soviet troops; 80,000 Polish, Hungarian, and Bulgarian troops; and an East German liaison unit invaded Czechoslovakia from three directions. The invasion encountered only sporadic military resistance and officially resulted in the death of 108 people, primarily civilians.[94] Early on the morning of August 21, Warsaw Pact forces invading Czechoslovakia took control of road and telecommunications networks, public buildings, and Communist Party offices, while Soviet special forces attempted to arrest Dubček and other high-ranking political officials.

Operation Danube was a military success, although the Soviet Union and the other participating countries paid a high political price for their invasion of Czechoslovakia. International protest of the Soviet-led invasion was immediate and vehement: not only Western anti-communist and social-democratic political officials raised their voices against the intervention as in 1956, but the communist leaders of Italy and of countries such as Finland, China, Albania, Yugoslavia, and Romania did as well—the latter as a full member of both the CMEA and the Warsaw Pact. The Soviets reacted sternly to Ceaușescu's public criticism: Soviet and Romanian troops stood face-to-face along the common border between the Soviet Union and Romania for weeks following the invasion, which resulted in mutual provocations and minor armed incidents.[95]

The political restoration—which was euphemistically referred to as normalization—that took place in Czechoslovakia following the Soviet-led invasion was an extremely complex process. President of Czechoslovakia Ludvík Svoboda refused to approve the appointment of the new, Soviet-endorsed government, while delegates at the Fourteenth Congress of the CPC, which convened illegally on the grounds of a factory, expelled conservatives from the party's governing bodies and approved the continuation of reform. These measures did not, however, prevent the implementation of Soviet plans. In the days following the invasion, Dubček and other Czechoslovak leaders were transported to Moscow, where following negotiations with Soviet officials they signed a deal that apparently permitted them to remain in power and called for the withdrawal of Warsaw Pact military forces from Czechoslovakia in exchange for their promise to halt reforms. Although Dubček and his associates had agreed to implement the Soviet-devised program of normalization, Czechoslovak society continued to resist this process. Workers' councils called strikes that paralyzed industrial production, and students launched protests against government authorities that were similar to those of their peers in Western Europe. Meanwhile, more than 70,000 citizens of Czechoslovakia fled to the West, including prominent economist Ota Šik and journalist Jiří Pelikán, who eventually became an Italian Socialist Party member of the European Parliament.[96] On January 16, 1969, Charles University student Jan Palach protested the Soviet intervention to suppress the Czechoslovak reforms through self-immolation on Wenceslas Square in Prague, thereby becoming a symbol of the Prague Spring. Several young people conducted similar acts of self-immolation over the subsequent months, in Czechoslovakia as well as in Poland, Hungary, and Romania.

The second phase of normalization began in Czechoslovakia during the spring of 1969 after members of a large crowd—likely provocateurs—celebrating Czechoslovakia's victory over the Soviet Union in the World Ice Hockey Championships ransacked Soviet diplomatic offices in Prague. Soviet officials claimed that the so-called hockey riots proved that Dubček was unable to maintain public order; under this pretext, they forced Dubček to resign from his post at the head of the Communist Party of Czechoslovakia in favor of Gustáv Husák, a relatively minor-ranking Slovak political official. Husák, like Kádár, had not been associated with the repression of the Stalinist era and, in fact, had been the subject of a show trial on charges of bourgeois nationalism. Dubček was dismissed from all of his positions of power following the outbreak in September 1969 of demonstrations marking the one-year anniversary of the Soviet-led invasion. After briefly serving as ambassador to Turkey, Dubček moved back to Slovakia, where he was expelled from the party and performed manual labor under police supervision as an employee of the forestry service until the collapse of the communist regime.[97]

Purges took place at all levels of Czechoslovak society between 1969 and 1971. Courts in the country pronounced 47,877 guilty verdicts for political offenses during this period.[98] More than 300,000 people were expelled from the Communist Party of Czechoslovakia, almost one-third of its members, while others voluntarily left the party in protest. Workplace sanctions and various forms of harassment of those who protested the suppression of the Prague Spring represented a common form of punishment: ideological committees could force employees to exercise self-criticism or to resign from their jobs at any time. The purges were particularly extensive within the intelligentsia: two-thirds of the members of the Writers' Federation were expelled from the organization, while nine hundred university professors were dismissed and twenty-one university research institutes were closed.

Meanwhile, the Husák regime attempted to regain the support of the working class, particularly in Slovakia, where the political purges had been less severe. To achieve this objective, Husák implemented a so-called wage-equalization policy that was beneficial to workers and detrimental to intellectuals and those engaged in white collar occupations. The administrative system also underwent an important change: on January 1, 1969, Czechoslovakia was transformed into a federal socialist republic in which Slovakia—from this time on known as the Slovak Socialist Republic—regained the territorial autonomy it had lost in 1960. Moreover, the transformation led to the establishment of the Slovak National Council and a Slovak government possessing broad administrative authority. Although attempts were later made to recentralize the system, the Slovak cultural and political elite profited greatly from the opportunities for professional advancement offered within the framework of normalization.[99]

The crushing of the Prague Spring put forward the formalization of the so-called Brezhnev doctrine, proclaiming limited sovereignty for Eastern Bloc states. During a speech at the Polish United Workers' Party congress in November 1968, Brezhnev declared that any attempt at capitalist restoration in an Eastern Bloc country represented a threat to the entire socialist camp that could legitimately be addressed through both political and military means.[100] The crushing of both the 1956 Hungarian Revolution and the 1968 Prague Spring demonstrated that the countries of Eastern Europe were unable to change the balance of power that had emerged in the region following the Second World War without the preventive approval of the Soviet Union. The general conviction among the inhabitants of Eastern Europe that any effort to transform the foundations of the socialist

system was futile in the era of Cold War and Soviet hegemony promoted antipathy toward political participation. Hungarian Marxist philosopher György
Lukács told one of his friends shortly before his death that the events in Czechoslovakia had likely "condemned the experiment begun in 1917 to failure."[101]

Twenty Years of State Socialism: An Appraisal

Eastern Europe underwent an astonishing economic, social, and cultural transformation in the twenty-five years after the Second World War. Angus Maddison
has calculated that the gross domestic product of Soviet Bloc states rose 3.9 percent per year between 1945 and 1971—one of the highest such rates ever recorded.
Even taking into account the distortion of Soviet data regarding production and
economic growth, it is clear that the economic disparities between Eastern Europe and Western Europe declined considerably in the 1950s and 1960s. In 1948,
per capita income in the states of Eastern Europe was between 30 percent and
35 percent of that in the United Kingdom, whereas twenty years later it had risen
to between 36 percent (Romania and Albania) and 74 percent (East Germany and
Czechoslovakia) of that in the United Kingdom.[102]

Eastern Europe recorded particularly strong GDP growth in the second half
of the 1950s and, as a result of economic reforms, during the years 1966–1970. The
region's traditionally agricultural countries developed significant industrial sectors during the 1950s and 1960s, particularly the iron, steel, and chemical industries. By 1970, the number of people employed in the agricultural sector dropped
to below 20 percent of the total workforce in the German Democratic Republic
and Czechoslovakia, to less than a third of the total workforce in Poland and
Hungary, and to less than half of the total workforce in Romania and Bulgaria.
Industrial production generated between 45 percent and 55 percent of the GDP
in the countries of Eastern Europe; the agricultural sector produced only 20 percent.[103] Millions of Eastern European farmers migrated to cities either because
the collectivization of agriculture had destroyed their means of subsistence or
to take advantage of the benefits of urban life. Enormous residential districts
were established on the peripheries of cities (until the 1960s, residential buildings were made of brick and were five or six floors high, but beginning in the
1970s they were made of prefabricated reinforced-concrete panels and were typically between nine and eleven floors high). Although the newly built neighbor-
hoods in communist Eastern Europe were regarded as colorless and unappealing
in the West, they provided millions of former farmers and agricultural laborers
who had never previously seen a flush toilet or lived separately from their animals with the opportunity for social advancement. Raynar Banham notes that
the quadrangular forms and reinforced concrete of brutalist architecture were
used extensively throughout Europe—both Western and Eastern—following the

Second World War. In terms of appearance, the new housing developments built on the outskirts of large cities in France and Italy resembled their socialist real-ist counterparts in Eastern Europe much more closely than they did residential buildings located in the elegant inner cities of Western Europe.[104]

Reducing Eastern European societies to obedience required extensive su-pervision. Among the means of achieving this degree of social control were the introduction of systems to register all citizens, the criminalization of unemploy-ment and begging, emphasis on collective action, and the propagation of socialist culture via the mass media. At the same time, those countries that had undergone belated industrialization attempted to establish the minimal requirements neces-sary to ensure the successful functions of a modern society. All of the statistical indicators that sociologists and demographers use to appraise general conditions in a given country—life expectancy, infant mortality, dietary intake, illiteracy, the incidence of disease, and the availability of basic consumer goods—improved significantly in the countries of Eastern Europe from the 1950s to the 1970s. With the exception of the "déclassé" and politically stigmatized elements, almost all segments of society gained the opportunity for social mobility. Beginning in the 1960s, members of the former elite—major landowners and aristocrats—were again able to profit from their knowledge and education and regain a limited amount of social prestige and economic stability.[105]

The state maintained a complex system of social provision that furnished the needs of citizens from cradle to grave. Basic preventive health care was provided at schools and workplaces, and the increasing number of working women could place their children in free day-care facilities and preschools. The state organized every minute of the daily lives of people—even their leisure-time activities. Cul-tural centers, cinemas, and folklore groups were established in even the smallest settlements. The possibility for foreign tourism emerged with the increase in the number of passenger vehicles and the development of road networks in the 1960s. The introduction of travel visas for Westerners and the removal of restrictions on hosting them in private homes and other accommodations showed that authori-ties in communist states had finally realized that tourism represented a signifi-cant source of revenue (particularly in hard currencies) as well as an excellent opportunity to present the West with a positive and open image of the Soviet Bloc countries. However, for Eastern Europeans, private travel to Western countries remained strictly regulated until 1989.[106] Thus, until the transition to democracy, only a limited albeit growing number of Eastern Europeans were permitted to travel to the West.

Meanwhile, state-organized socialist tourism thrived behind the Iron Cur-tain, offering the citizens of Eastern Europe the chance to visit other Soviet Bloc countries with little difficulty. As those who have researched such tourism have remarked, the favored bloc destinations among other Eastern Europeans—the

Adriatic coast of Yugoslavia, the Black Sea coasts of Romania and Bulgaria, Lake Balaton in Hungary, the Tatra Mountains in Czechoslovakia, and the area around the town of Zakopane in southern Poland—became increasingly popular among Western Europeans as well. These locations also became common meeting places for families that had been divided as a result of the Cold War. In addition to their state-run tourist complexes of frequently questionable quality, these protocapitalist testing grounds featured an increasing number of privately owned restaurants and accommodations. These popular tourist destinations were nothing other than economic subsystems operating on unreported revenue at which bribery of supervisory authorities and employment of unregistered workers became commonplace.[107] The start of mass tourism in Eastern Europe represented the most visible sign of compromise between the socialist systems and the less collectivist-minded societies of the region.

The positive effects of socialist modernization must, however, be analyzed within a global context. Social and cultural indicators in Central and Western Europe as well as the Mediterranean region underwent improvement commensurate to that recorded in Eastern Europe. One may presume that the introduction of the Western-capitalist subsidy model (the welfare state) in the less developed countries of Eastern Europe such as Yugoslavia, Romania, Bulgaria, and Albania made it possible to achieve results that would have been at least comparable to those reached via socialist modernization. In the case of more developed Eastern European countries, particularly Czechoslovakia, the introduction of the planned economy impaired structures of production that were similar to those in Germany and Austria, thus leading to lower growth rates than those recorded in Western Europe.[108] The process of social leveling had very beneficial consequences in the most backward, mineral-poor Balkan states, while it prevented the countries of east-central Europe from preserving economic standards that used to be much closer to those in western Europe.

An analysis of some data has uncovered contradictions regarding planned development and its application to social and cultural phenomena. The cultural emancipation and professional advancement of women, for example, was based not only on the implementation of policies that served to promote equality, but on the temporary reduction in the social prestige and material returns of petty-bourgeois occupations such as those of teacher and physician. Moreover, the traditional male role in Eastern European society came into question with the spread of the dual-income family model. Many Eastern Europeans felt that the leveling of wages had deprived men of the attributes associated with the head of the family, while the large-scale employment of women had altered established gender roles. Family policy also traveled a difficult path in Eastern Europe. In comparison to Italy, for example, the countries of the region started from a much more liberal starting point. Civil marriage and divorce based on mutual consent had already become part of the legal system of the Austro-Hungarian monarchy before the First World War. However, the legality of abortion in Eastern Europe followed the fluctuations in the Soviet Union, where it was legalized in 1920, prohibited in 1936, and not decriminalized until Stalin's death. Following the establishment of communist systems in Eastern Europe after the Second World War, countries in the region adopted the restrictions on abortion imposed in the Soviet Union, banning the artificial termination of pregnancy until the second half of the 1950s. Birth control and sex education in schools were practically unknown throughout Eastern Europe until the 1980s—with the exception of the GDR, where sexuality and naturism were not regarded as taboos. The legalization of abortion in Romania in 1957 resulted in a sharp drop in the country's birth rate. In response to this decline in births, the Ceaușescu regime issued a degree recriminalizing abortion in October 1966. This decree prescribed severe penalties for both women who obtained an illegal abortion and physicians who performed them. Anthropologist Gail Kligman has estimated that 10,000 women died in Romania as the result of illegal abortions between 1966 and 1989.[109] Other Eastern European states, though they did not adopt the Romanian model, attempted to address the problem of population decline typically associated with urban and industrialized societies through the introduction of economic incentives (family and child-care subsidies) and the enactment of administrative measures to encourage families to have children. However, these policies did not produce their intended results: beginning in the 1960s, the number of births started to decline throughout Eastern Europe, inducing authorities to elaborate more effective family policies in the attempt to reverse the demographic trends.

Notes

1. Taubman, *Khrushchev*, 279–280. On the consequences of Khrushchev's speech, see also Graziosi, *L'URSS dal trionfo al degrado*, 191–207.

2. Rothschild, *Return to Diversity*, 151.

3. Kramer, "Soviet Union and the 1956 Crises in Hungary and Poland," 161–174.

4. Staar, "Elections in Communist Poland," 200–218.

5. Linz and Stepan, *Problems of Democratic Transition and Consolidation*, chapter 16. See also Staniszkis, *Poland's Self-Limiting Revolution*.

6. Granville, *First Domino*, 32–33.

7. Békés, Byrne, and Rainer, *1956 Hungarian Revolution*, 156.

8. On Andropov's activity as Soviet ambassador to Hungary, see Baráth, *Szovjet iratok Magyarországról*.

9. Borhi, *Hungary in the Cold War*, 244.

10. Szakolczai and Varga, *A vidék forradalma, 1956*, vols. 1–2.

11. Rainer, *Imre Nagy*, 100–117.

12. On Romania and Slovakia, see Sitariu, *Oaza de libertate*; Ivančiková and Simon, *Maďarská revolúciá 1956 a Slovensko*.

13. Békés, Byrne, and Rainer, *1956 Hungarian Revolution*, 307–310.

14. Gati, *Failed Illusions*, 200.

15. Gough, *Good Comrade*, 87–102.

16. Balogh, *Mindszenty József*, 1032–1046.

17. Györkei and Horváth, *Soviet Military Intervention in Hungary*, 187–188.

18. Irving, *Uprising!*. On the relationship between Irving and Hungarian communist authorities, see Mink, "David Irving and the 1956 Hungarian Revolution," 117–128.

19. Kőrösi and Molnár, *Carrying a Secret in My Heart*.

20. Mark Kramer's lecture "The World in 1989" during the conference "The Year 1989" at the Hungarian Academy of Sciences in Budapest on October 20, 2009. The argument is also developed in an interview Kramer released after the event, available at http://www.eurozine.com/gorbachevs-go-ahead/ (accessed March 26, 2017).

21. Graziosi, *L'URSS dal trionfo al degrado*, 215.

22. Ibid., 226.

23. The roots of the Soviet church policy turn are described in Roccucci, *Stalin e il patriarca*, 463–491.

24. Riccardi, *Il Vaticano e Mosca*, 206–207.

25. Graziosi, *L'URSS dal trionfo al degrado*, 227–229.

26. See King, *Minorities under Communism*.

27. Falanga, *Non si può dividere il cielo*.

28. Schöpflin, *Politics in Eastern Europe*, 134–135.

29. See Brzezinski, *Soviet Bloc*; Gati, *Bloc That Failed*.

30. Csizmadia, *Diskurzus és diktatúra*, 78. See also the research project, "Hatvanas évek Magyarországon" (The 1960s in Hungary), coordinated by the Institute of the 1956 Hungarian Revolution; Rainer, *"Hatvanas évek" Magyarországon*; and Rainer, *Bevezetés a kádárizmusba*. For an attempt at turning the study of state security files into social history, see Horváth, *Az ügynök arcai*, 7–37.

31. Baberowski, "Criticism as Crisis," 148–166.

32. Kovács, *A paraszti társadalom felszámolása*.

33. Varga, *Politikai, paraszti érdekérvényesítés és szövetkezetek*.

34. Gough, *Good Comrade*, 135.

35. For the literary policy of the Kádár regime, see Standeisky, *Gúzsba kötve*. On Aczél, the best account remains Révész, *Aczél és korunk*.

36. For the ideological construct of early Kádárism, see Kalmár, *Ennivaló és hozomány*.

37. A critical assessment of the 1964 agreement based on a wide range of new sources is found in Fejérdy, *Pressed by Double Loyalty*, 123–162. See also Szabó, *A Szentszék és a Magyar Népköztársaság kapcsolatai*.

38. The Vatican was more resolute with regard to Poland. Melloni, *L'altra Roma*, 352–357 and 368–371.

39. For the impact of the 1956 Hungarian Revolution in Romania, see Bottoni et al., *Az 1956-os forradalom és a romániai magyarság*.

40. Bottoni, *Transilvania rossa*, 171–196.

41. Verdery, *National Ideology under Socialism*.

42. Ioanid, *Ransom of the Jews*.

43. See www.php.isn.ethz.ch/collections/coll_romania/introduction.cfm?navinfo=15342.

44. Deletant, "Romania," 315.

45. Ioanid, *Ransom of the Jews*, 84–87, 120.

46. Courtois, *Il libro nero del comunismo*, 277–282.

47. Marceva, "Change of the Guard," 59–78 (part 1) and 36–57 (part 2).
48. Jelavich, *History of the Balkans*, 364–369.
49. Petkova, "Ethnic Turks in Bulgaria," 45–46. For the text of the 1968 Bulgarian-Turkish agreement, see www.untreaty.un.org/unts/I_60000/22/4/00042180.pdf. Accessed September 3, 2016.
50. The essay was first published in Poland (September 1957); an English translation is available in *East Europe*, February 1958, 18–21, and March 1958, 26–28.
51. Tonini, *Operazione Madagascar*, 242–269. On the 1968 anti-Semitic campaign in Poland, see Polonsky and Gluchowski, *1968*.
52. Blaive, *Une déstalinisasion manquée*.
53. Kirschbaum, *History of Slovakia*, 237.
54. Clementi, *Cecoslovacchia*, 177.
55. Fulbrook, *Power and Society in the GDR*, 1–30.
56. Fowkes, *L'Europa orientale dal 1945 al 1970*, 115.
57. An entangled introduction to operative activities and social penetration of Stasi is found in Gieseke, *History of the Stasi*.
58. Bianchini, *L'autogestione jugoslava*.
59. Yaffe, *Che Guevara*, 20.
60. Bianchini, *Le sfide della modernità*, 192–193.
61. Privitera, *Jugoslavia*, 103.
62. See Vučetić, "Violence against the Antiwar Demonstrations in Yugoslavia," 255–274.
63. Banac, "Political Change and National Diversity," 153–154. On the "Croatian Spring," see Irvine, "Croatian Spring and the Dissolution of Jugoslavia," 131–178.
64. Vickers, *Between Serb and Albanian*, 169–180.
65. Mëhilli, "Defying De-Stalinization: Albania's 1956," 4–56.
66. Jelavich, *History of the Balkans*, 378–384.
67. Tönnes, "Religious Persecution in Albania," 242–255.
68. Lavigne, *International Political Economy and Socialism*, 17.
69. Lavigne, *Socialist Economies of the Soviet Union and Europe*.
70. Zwass, *Council for Mutual Economic Assistance*, 68–69.
71. Mastny and Byrne, *Cardboard Castle?*, 18.
72. Uhl and Ivkin, "'Operation Atom': The Soviet Union's Stationing of Nuclear Missiles in the German Democratic Republic," 299–307.
73. Germuska, *Unified Military Industries of the Soviet Bloc*.
74. Garthoff, "When and Why Romania Distanced Itself from Warsaw Pact."
75. Deletant and Ionescu, *Romania and Warsaw Pact, 1955–89*.
76. Krahulcsán, "A magyar politikai rendőrség," 3–19.
77. Herbstritt and Olaru, *Stasi și Securitatea*.
78. Historical Archives of the Hungarian State Security, Budapest (Állambiztonsági Szolgálatok Történeti Levéltára), fond 3.2.5, file 0-8-552, vol. 13, fols. 159–173. The most active foreign agent working for Hungarian intelligence in Italy was the Vatican-accredited West German journalist who operated under the code name "Von Schiller."
79. Bottoni, "Special Relationship," 147–176.
80. Baczoni and Bikki: "Egyesített állambiztonsági adattár—a SZOUD," 217–225.
81. Bianchini, *Le sfide della modernità*, 231.
82. Berend, *Hungarian Economic Reforms*, 38.
83. Ibid., 114.
84. Bianchini, *Le sfide della modernità*, 178–181.

85. Graziosi, *L'URSS dal trionfo al degrado*, 306–311.

86. Berend, *Hungarian Economic Reforms*, 83, 111.

87. Swain, *Hungary*.

88. Romsics, "Economic Reforms in the Kádár Era," 69–79.

89. Berend, *From the Soviet Bloc to the European Union*, 23.

90. Williams, *Prague Spring and Its Aftermath*, 8–11.

91. Munteanu, "When the Levee Breaks," 43–61.

92. Békés, "'Prague Spring,'" 203–224.

93. Williams, *Prague Spring and Its Aftermath*, 116–117.

94. Ibid., 158.

95. Betea, *21 august 1968*.

96. Caccamo, *Jiři Pelikan*.

97. Kirschbaum, *History of Slovakia*, 245.

98. Clementi, *Cecoslovacchia*, 227.

99. Eyal, *Origins of Postcommunist Elites*, 51–53.

100. Ouimet, *Rise and the Fall of the Brezhnev Doctrine*, 66–69.

101. Pike, *Lukács and Brecht*, 189.

102. Fowkes, *L'Europa orientale dal 1945 al 1970*, 149.

103. Berend, *Storia economica dell'Europa nel XX secolo*, 195.

104. Judt, *Postwar*, 385–387.

105. Bauquet and Bocholier, *Le communisme et les élites en Europe Centrale*.

106. See Bencsik and Nagy, *A magyar úti okmányok története 1945–1989*.

107. See Borodziej, Kochanowski, and Puttkamer, *Schleichwege*; Kochanowski, "Pioneers of the Free Market Economy?" 196–220.

108. Pearce Hardt and Kaufman, *East-Central European Economies in Transition*, 17.

109. Kligman, *Politics of Duplicity*, 214.

Chapter 4

The Decline and Fall of the Soviet Bloc (1973–1991)

The Global Framework: From Détente to the "Second Cold War"

The dynamics of the Cold War underwent a profound change in the second half of the 1960s. The increasingly institutionalized and predictable conflict transformed the opposition of East against West into a competition that did not exclude the possibility of dialogue and cooperation. This change in perspective was originated by the elaboration of a more flexible Western policy toward the Soviet Bloc. At the time of the grand coalition between the Social Democratic Party and the Christian Democratic Union from 1966 to 1969, West Germany gradually adopted a policy of cautious dialogue with East Germany and other socialist countries called *Ostpolitik*. The new policy resulted in West Germany's establishment of diplomatic relations with the countries of the Eastern Bloc. During the pontificates of John XXIII (1958–1963) and Paul VI (1963–1978), the Vatican also initiated dialogue with the communist regimes of Eastern Europe. However, in spite of the partial agreements the Vatican concluded with Hungary and Yugoslavia, the Vatican did not achieve its primary goals of gaining diplomatic recognition from countries in Eastern Europe and restoring the freedom of religion in the region.[1]

West Germany's détente policy reached its zenith under the leadership of Chancellor Willy Brandt. In a treaty signed in Moscow on August 12, 1970, the Federal Republic of Germany officially recognized its border with Poland along the Oder-Neisse line, and the Soviet Union undertook the process of settling the status of the city of Berlin. The governments of West Germany and Poland concluded a separate agreement recognizing their common border in December 1970. Meanwhile, under the leadership of Erich Honecker, the German Democratic Republic (GDR) abandoned the illusion of a reunified, socialist Germany. "Divergent development" was the new motto that reflected the GDR's improving relations with the Western world. In December 1972, the GDR and the Federal Republic of Germany signed the basic agreement that determined the course of interstate relations between them until the end of the Cold War.[2] Berlin remained a divided city and a number of East German citizens were shot while trying to flee to West Germany over the wall surrounding the capital. However, the German Democratic Republic began to permit occasional visits with former citizens who had emigrated to the West, resumed communications with West Germany, and abolished restrictions on the reception of West German mass media. West German *Ostpolitik* was part of the global process of détente that culminated with the signing of the Helsinki Final Act at the end of the Conference on Security and Co-operation in Europe on August 1, 1975.[3] The agreement stipulated the following common objectives: refraining from the threat or use of force; the inviolability of frontiers; the territorial integrity of states; the peaceful settlement of disputes; nonintervention in internal affairs; respect for human rights and fundamental freedoms, including the freedoms of thought, conscience, religion, belief, and movement; and development of technical and scientific cooperation. For the United States, the signing of the Helsinki Final Act took place during a time of political uncertainty resulting from the Watergate scandal and the fall of Saigon. For the Soviet Union and its allies, the agreement signified the West's recognition of the division of Europe into two inviolable zones of influence, while it stipulations regarding human rights and the freedom of movement represented only symbolic concessions with which they would not be forced to comply.[4]

The international influence of the Soviet Bloc reached its peak in the first half of the 1970s. Socialism was spreading throughout developing countries in Latin America, Africa, and the Middle East, and the normalized regimes of Eastern Europe were able to take advantage of opportunities emerging from the increasingly interconnected and continually growing world economy. These regimes concluded agreements that made it possible for them to increase both the volume and the quality of trade products in Western markets (to which Eastern European countries exported foodstuffs) and Middle Eastern markets (to which they exported arms in exchange for oil derivatives). In this way, Eastern European countries were able to withdraw themselves from the framework of protected barter and raw-material exports conducted through intermediary companies associated with Western communist parties. In the economic domain, talks between the CMEA and the European Economic Community that the Soviet Union had initiated in 1972 continued for years without success: the two organizations recognized each other only following Gorbachev's rise to power in the middle of the 1980s.[5]

The boundaries of international détente began to emerge in the second half of the 1970s: the stipulations in the Helsinki Final Act regarding respect for human rights and fundamental freedoms, which the socialist countries of Eastern

Europe had initially downplayed, became a means for the West to assert its interests in the region. In 1974, the US Congress approved the Jackson-Vanik amendment to the Trade Act, which denied "most favored nation" status to countries that did not recognize the right of its citizens to emigrate. This made keeping the status of most favored nation from the United States difficult for the Soviet Union and its allies. Paradoxically, the West began to selectively attack Soviet Bloc economic interests just when Eastern European communist regimes began to abandon their practice of mass repression. Under President Jimmy Carter (1977–1981) and during President Ronald Reagan's first term in office (1981–1985), despite the attempts of the State Department in Washington to preserve formal dialogue, US foreign policy was no longer based on the raw political realism of President Richard Nixon (1969–1974) and his national security adviser, Henry Kissinger.[6] Although US foreign-policy officials such as the liberal Zbigniew Brzezinski, who served as national security adviser in the Carter Administration, and the neoconservatives Paul Wolfowitz and Richard Perle, both of whom served in the Reagan Administration, were divided on many issues, they were united in their committed anti-communism emphasizing respect for human rights in accordance with the Helsinki Final Act.[7]

The international political environment deteriorated perceptibly in the late 1970s, which led to a rise in East-West tensions that has been called the Second Cold War. The election of the archbishop of Kraków Karol Wojtyła to serve as pope in 1978, the Soviet invasion of Afghanistan and the anti-West revolutions in Iran and Nicaragua in 1979, the rise of the Solidarity Trade Union in Poland in 1980, and General Wojciech Jaruzelski's declaration of martial law in Poland the following year served to revive the hostile Cold War rhetoric and symbolism. The renewed confrontation between the capitalist and communist blocs prompted the Soviet Union and its allies to take measures aimed at destabilizing the West. The rise in ideological tensions represented a severe blow to Eastern European governments in spite of their stability and their location on the border of East-West conflict. Meanwhile, countries that had adopted the Soviet model were forced to confront a challenge from within the socialist camp: in 1978, newly appointed Chinese leader Deng Xiaoping announced reforms intended to create a system based on economic sustainability, political prestige, and social capitalism.

Political Stability, Economic Collapse

The Discreet Charm of Brezhnevian Grayness

The countries of Eastern Europe became the place of really existing socialism, a catchphrase popularized after the Prague Spring to counter to critiques of internal repression. According to the ideological formula set forth in the 1977 Soviet Constitution, the "developed socialist society" was proceeding in the direction of communism under the guidance of the communist party. The eighteen years of Brezhnev's leadership in the Soviet Union from 1964 to 1982 represented a period of cultural grayness in the Eastern Bloc that provided an accurate reflection of the CPSU general secretary's lack of personal charisma and political initiative. Along with the incapacity of local leaders to take decisive action and the lack of reforms dictated from above, the first signs of economic crisis in Eastern Europe prompted foreign observers to increasingly interpret the region's stability as a sign of stagnation, decadence, "moral depletion" (Gale Stokes), and "desolation" (Ernest Gellner).[8] After 1968, the legitimacy of existing socialism was based neither on the forced mobilization of society characteristic of the Stalinist period nor on the economic and cultural reform attempts of the late 1950s and 1960s, but on a mixture of moderate consumerism and feigned ideological compromise that often concealed contradictory personal opinions.[9] Party functionaries and leading economic and cultural authorities lived in luxury villas, spent their holidays abroad, drove expensive Western cars, wore brand-name clothing, and played tennis with others of suitable social status. The preferred leisure-time activity of the *nomenklatura* was hunting—the quintessential aristocratic sport that was inaccessible to regular civilians if for no other reason than they were prohibited from owning firearms. Participation in lavish hunting excursions and membership in one of the few hunting associations that existed in Eastern European countries were accurate gauges of the true influence of political officials.[10]

Moral-improvement campaigns came into increasing conflict with the private sphere, and by the 1970s many external symbols of prosperity had become accessible to millions of Eastern Europeans. Despite waiting periods of up to ten years, more than one-quarter of families in Eastern Europe—and nearly one-third of families in Poland and Czechoslovakia—owned a car. Eastern Europeans were not overburdened with work and were given much vacation time: in those places where it was not necessary to wait in line for goods in nearly empty shops, they often spent their weekends relaxing at small summer homes built gradually at locations far away from the noise of the city.[11] One of the greatest novelties of the Brezhnev era in Eastern Europe was precisely the lack of political excitement and the rediscovery of the family domain. Fellow citizens, aware of the futility of resistance, used the ideological crisis of communism and the partial relaxation of ideological prescriptions to establish a dignified human existence.

Some conscious Eastern European dissidents naturally opposed cultural conformism, the grotesque personality cults and nationalism of political leaders and official ideology that often concealed anti-Semitism. Opposition networks became stronger in Eastern Europe in the decade between the signing of the Helsinki Final Act and the rise of Mikhail Gorbachev to power in the Soviet Union. These networks, among them Charter 77 in Czechoslovakia and the "democratic opposition" in Hungary, engaged primarily in demonstrative and symbolic actions as part of intellectual movements. Dissidents gained publicity and exposure in the West as a result of their contacts with the foreign media and their knowledge of Western languages. The activity of opposition groups in Eastern Europe provided Western public opinion with intellectual and moral testimony refuting the notion that the communist system had gained broad social acceptance in the region. Opposition groups nevertheless remained politically weak. Authorities regarded them as a manageable phenomenon and were therefore satisfied with their containment rather than their total obliteration. Thus, the Polish opposition movement, which received renewed energy with the formation of the Committee for Social Self-Defense (Komitet Samoobrony Społecznej, or KOR) in 1977, represented an absolute exception. KOR activists provided workers with information on their rights, taught them how to organize strikes, defended them in criminal trials, and organized collection drives to help the families of political prisoners. The cooperation of Polish intellectuals and factory workers, who had until that time operated independently of one another, resulted in an unprecedented event: the formation of an independent trade union representing multiple segments of society—Solidarity (Solidarność).

Homeland-nationalist youth movements attracted large numbers of people in certain countries. However, it was much easier to disappear the young people who participated in these movements than it was the dissidents affiliated with the democratic opposition, since their spontaneous protests rarely attracted the attention of the international media. Unauthorized demonstrations and other alternative public events took place frequently in Hungary between 1972 and 1974 and in Poland during the 1980s, on traditional national holidays that the socialist system had either prohibited or trivialized—opposition groups sometimes found inspiration in the anniversaries of recent tragic events: until 1989, police in Czechoslovakia were put on alert on the August 21 anniversary of the 1968 Warsaw Pact invasion to suppress the Prague Spring and in Hungary on the October 23 anniversary of the 1956 Hungarian Revolution.[12] The suicide of a high school student precipitated enormous demonstrations rooted in nationalist, anti-Soviet sentiment and generational rebellion in Kaunas, second-largest city of Lithuania, on May 18 and 19, 1972.[13]

In the 1980s the West attributed much greater social influence and prestige to Eastern European opposition intellectuals and party dissidents than they actually possessed—an assertion that the electoral results would have confirmed following the collapse of the Soviet system. Emphasis on the fabricated contrast between civil society as a virtuous civilian community and the state as a foreign and hostile absolute evil represented a widespread shortcoming in the interpretation of Eastern European societies during the late communist era.[14] Stephen Kotkin contends that during the period of mature socialism in Eastern Europe, the frequently maligned state, in fact, represented the only organically functioning entity in the states of the region that was capable of social organization and regarded as legitimate. According to Kotkin, civil society remained an imagined category that cast a web of compromises and prerogatives prescribed by the party state over the citizenry.[15] Interdependence between political authority and society reached its apex during the final two decades of socialism. The grassroots opposition to communist regimes (peasant rebellions and spontaneous mass demonstrations) that manifested itself so frequently between 1945 and 1956 essentially disappeared in the 1970s and 1980s, when the majority of Eastern European society became resigned to the seeming permanence of socialism and enjoyed the benefits of the system—primarily social security.[16] According to Gail Kligman, Eastern European societies suffered from a collective "dissociative personality disorder" during this period, although the "structural mechanism of opposition" at the same time made it possible to develop personal adaptive strategies.[17] Many Eastern Europeans lived under the illusion that it was possible to separate formal public support for the existing system and private criticism of communism as a modern form of harmless *ius murmurandi*, the practice of grumbling about the government while posing no real threat to it.

Studying social expenditures during state socialism in Eastern Europe, Béla Tomka has come to a surprising conclusion: contrary to widespread belief, the Soviet Bloc countries spent a much smaller proportion of their per capita national income on social services than major Western European states. Thus communist systems "increased expenditures connected to the welfare state, primarily during periods of crisis for self-legitimacy purposes, though policies of the welfare state did not constitute their political priority."[18] In the Soviet-type redistributive state, modern technology and education coexisted with primitive, preindustrial labor and social organization. The state introduced social stratification that resembled the pyramid of closed social classes rather than the classes of a modern industrial society.[19] However, after learning how to live in the system, ordinary citizens held the monotonous dependability of existing socialism in even higher esteem than did the elite.[20] They could resolve many problems, from the admission of their children to universities to the acquisition of needed commodities, and even bribery of civil servants or via social networks. The Russian-language expression *blat* denotes the complex system of petty corruption that made it possible for Eastern Europeans to "oil" the slow wheels of bureaucracy through personal agreements and mutual favors.[21] At the same time, the grayness of the system increased feelings of confusion and doubt regarding the future, especially among young people. Stagnation and social security satisfied the expectations of those who had lived through the havoc of the Second World War, but not those of the baby boomers born between 1946 and 1953. Illusions regarding the possibility of changing the system vanished, thus prompting many young Eastern Europeans, even in the relatively open Hungary, to emigrate. The imitation of Western modes of behavior led to an exponential increase in forms of administratively or criminally punishable conduct among young Eastern Europeans, such as listening to rock or punk music, sexual promiscuousness, drug use, gang activity, and football hooliganism. A vast array of statistical data, including that regarding alcoholism, drug addiction, suicide, and violent crime, reflect deepening social crisis throughout Eastern Europe beginning in the late 1970s.[22] In the European regions of the Soviet Union, as well as Poland and Hungary, alcoholism and associated diseases afflicted a significant portion of the male population. Hungary had the world's highest suicide rate—an embarrassing statistic that was treated as a state secret in the German Democratic Republic beginning in the 1980s.[23]

Stagnation and Indebtedness

The year 1973 represented a watershed in the history of the Soviet Bloc. The victory of Israel over an Egypt- and Syria-led Arab coalition in the Yom Kippur War in October of that year induced the Organization of Petroleum Exporting Countries to stop exporting oil to the West. As a result of this measure, the price of oil on the global market jumped from three dollars a barrel to twelve dollars a barrel in under two months. This oil shock produced a world stagflation crisis in 1974, and then again following the Iranian Revolution during the years 1980–1982. Energy producers throughout the world profited greatly from the rise in the price of raw materials. However, the Soviet Union—which appeared to be the greatest beneficiary of the rise in energy prices—decided to export oil and gas to the countries of Eastern Europe at an artificially low price. Beginning in 1973, the Soviet Union supported the economies of Eastern Europe through direct assistance and the so-called socialist division of labor, which entailed the obligatory purchase of industrial and agricultural products from other Soviet Bloc states.[24]

The economies of Eastern Europe assumed a dual form: while most of the large companies in the region produced large quantities of technologically obsolete goods of modest quality for export to the Soviet Union and other CMEA member states, a growing number of enterprises began to manufacture products that were designed for sale in hard currency on global markets in competition with those made in the West. In addition to the inherent operational inefficiencies of production within the planned economic system, this growing competition with Western rivals represented the greatest challenge for the technologically underdeveloped economies of Eastern Europe.[25] The black list of goods that were strictly prohibited from export to the Soviet Union began to grow again in 1977 following a period of pause.[26] Industrially developed CMEA countries such as the Soviet Union, the German Democratic Republic, and Czechoslovakia were forced to acquire technology through the purchase of expensive licenses. The military industry represented the only sector of the Soviet Bloc economy that had become least partially digitalized. By the 1980s, the countries of Eastern Europe had fallen several decades behind those of the West in terms of their level of infrastructural and technological development.

The decline in exports to the West and to developing countries as a result of the Second Cold War caused Eastern Europe to slip into a serious economic crisis. Countries such as Hungary, Yugoslavia, and Romania either decreased moderately or stagnated beginning in the early 1980s. The most severe economic crisis during this period occurred in Poland, where gross domestic product declined 15 percent in the years 1981–1982.[27] Between the years 1973 and 1989, the planned economies grew 1.7 percent, compared to 2 percent in Western and Mediterranean countries. Per capita income decreased throughout Eastern Europe, with the exception of Yugoslavia, during this period, while the price scissors increased by six points in Czechoslovakia, seven points in the Soviet Union, and ten points in Poland.

To prevent the social consequences of the economic crisis, Eastern Bloc countries began to take steps to resolve their trade imbalances and to obtain loans, initially at low interest, on international financial markets. These loans also made it possible to temporarily preserve or even increase living standards. Aggregate net external debt in Eastern Europe grew from US$6 billion in 1970 to $79 billion in 1980 and $110 billion in 1990. Poland, Hungary, Yugoslavia, and Bulgaria accrued the greatest amount of debt in the region. This problem was less severe in the German Democratic Republic and Czechoslovakia, which conducted more conservative economic policies and maintained closer connections to Soviet heavy industry.

The debt spiral became increasingly unsustainable in the early 1980s. Western creditors withdrew their deposits from Hungarian banks in the spring of 1981, compelling the Kádár government to seek further loans from the International Monetary Fund, provided that Hungary accept austerity measures and step up economic reforms designed to build a system of market socialism.[28]

Romania, where the Ceaușescu regime had implemented severe austerity measures that led to a sharp decrease in living standards, was on the opposite end of the spectrum from the increasingly market-oriented Hungary in terms of economic policy. For nearly a decade, the Western financial organizations and private banks provided Romania with easy credit, which the Ceaușescu regime used to finance internal consumption and the industrialization program.[29] The economic situation grew increasingly severe beginning in 1979 as a result of the second oil shock. In September 1981 Romania unofficially asked to have the country's debt restructured. The World Bank approved a three-year, $1.2 billion loan to Romania, though required the country to decrease investment and consumption, devalue its currency, and implement a stability program to reform its banking system. It then suspended its disbursement after the Ceaușescu regime refused to implement the stipulated measures, but the World Bank agreed to release the credit in June 1982 after it approved the bank's recommended austerity program and agreed to partially acknowledge Romania's true financial situation.[30] Around 1984, while insiders of Soviet politics (and most probably the Romanian diplomats serving in Moscow, too) had already been familiarized with the name of Mikhail Gorbachev and Soviet policy making had started to elaborate exit strategies for the empire, Ceaușescu came to the bitter conclusion that Western betrayal, and not only the ill-conceived economic policies of his regime, had been responsible for the country's catastrophic situation. While Romania was repaying the sovereign debt of $12 billion that it had accrued over the previous twenty years, Ceaușescu started to prepare the country's withdrawal from international economic organizations.[31] The last International Monetary Fund (IMF) office memorandum issued on Romania in November 1989 stated that after the Romanian government had refused to sign the 1984 stand-by agreement, Bucharest had broken off all working relations with the fund and "pursued a policy of repaying all outstanding foreign debt." The IMF acknowledged that the policy was "accelerated in 1988 with early repayments to the International Bank for Reconstruction and Development, commercial banks, and the Fund." By March 1989, all foreign debts other than small short-term credits had been fully repaid. According to the IMF, this was feasible only through "strong export performance, with goods shifted from the domestic to foreign markets, and severe import compression."[32]

According to Cornel Ban, the rapid pace of loan repayment exercised a severely negative impact on the inhabitants of Romania: not only did the neo-Stalinist Ceaușescu regime base its social policy on the open use of force; it also promised social advancement for the masses as a means of maintaining its legitimacy. The drastic decline in living standards, the introduction of rationing, and the everyday power outages that occurred in Romania in the 1980s undermined the national legitimacy that the Ceaușescu regime had so carefully constructed.[33] Several analysts have also pinpointed the role and responsibility of Western governments and international organizations in Romania's economic crisis of the 1980s. The World Bank, for example, provided $200 million in support for an obsolete and irrational agricultural-modernization program implemented within the framework of Romania's 1981–1985 Five-Year Plan. The Western political and financial world thus unintentionally supported the absurd and destructive policies of the Ceaușescu regime, at least until his leadership could have been of some help on the global chessboard.

Finding Ways out of Existing Socialism

In the 1980s, the socialist countries were forced by the deepening economic crisis to pursue divergent individual survival strategies. The regimes of Romania and, to a lesser degree, Bulgaria, intensified social repression and exclusive nationalist rhetoric, whereas those of the German Democratic Republic and Czechoslovakia attempted to strengthen social unity based on the myth of egalitarianism and heighten ideological discipline. Poland and Hungary sought to reshape and later abandon the failed socialist developmental model. The crisis of legitimacy that arose in Yugoslavia following Tito's death in 1980 made it clear that the country's transnational elite was incapable of finding a solution to growing social and ethnic tensions. Albania remained isolated even following the death of Enver Hoxha in 1985.

The decline of Eastern Europe was closely connected to the twilight of the Soviet Union. Until Brezhnev's death in November 1982, the Soviet Union represented a restraining force moderating all attempts at reform in Eastern Europe. Brezhnev's successor, Yuri Andropov, had as longtime head of the KGB become more aware than anybody else of the true condition of the Soviet empire. However, Andropov's poor health and the opposition of the Soviet Union's strong anti-reform camp prevented any attempt to make changes to the system during the former KGB leader's short term as general secretary of the CPSU until his death in 1984.[34] The internal crisis that afflicted the Soviet state helps explain the weakness of its response to increasing centrifugal forces. Beginning in the 1980s, the Soviet Union no longer exercised total control over the states of Eastern Europe but had to satisfy itself with playing a coordinating role and, on occasion, taking action to stifle the nation-state aspirations of its allies in the region. In any event, Andrea Graziosi noted that even in the middle of the 1980s most analysts were unaware of the internal fragility of Soviet-type systems and were thus unable to foresee the impending collapse of the Soviet Union. Economist Igor Birman—who correctly estimated that the one-third of the total Soviet state budget was spent to maintain the military apparatus—was among the few Western analysts who did anticipate the collapse of the Soviet Union, as was the relentlessly anti-communist historian Richard Pipes.[35]

Poland: From Solidarity to Jaruzelski's Military Junta

Poland entered a period of prolonged social unrest following the economic and political crisis that took place in the country in 1968, when Gomułka let the genies of nationalism and anti-Semitism out of the bottle to put a quick end to the student demonstrations in Warsaw. The announced increase in the price of basic consumer goods in December 1970 caused internal tension to simmer once again in Poland. Workers at the Gdańsk Shipyard called a strike that spread to

Gdnyia, Elbląg, and Szczecin before the police and military suppressed them, killing forty-five people and wounding a thousand others. The technocrat Edward Gierek, who had firsthand experience of life in Western Europe, replaced the unpopular Gomułka as head of the Communist Party. Gierek long enjoyed the support of the Soviet leadership and during the first half of the 1970s had utilized international détente in order to modernize Poland's system of production, develop contacts with Western companies such as Italian car company Fiat, and rebuild social consensus with the help of international loans.[36]

Gierek managed to win the sympathy of many everyday Polish citizens by maintaining cordial relations with the Catholic Church, which was still under the leadership of the elderly Archbishop of Warsaw Stefan Wyszyński. Among the rising leaders of the Catholic Church in Poland at this time was the archbishop of Kraków Karol Wojtyła, who avoided open confrontation with the regime, though worked persistently to defend and strengthen church institutions. A 1975 Hungarian intelligence report described Wojtyła as the most dangerous of the papal candidates, for his rise "would have serious consequences with regard to world politics" and produce significant changes in Poland.[37]

Gierek furthermore encouraged personal consumption, built inexpensive housing, and finally forced into retirement former interior minister Mieczysław Moczar, who had been one of the architects of the "anti-cosmopolitan" campaign and the failed 1972 coup. Gierek's compromise-based legitimacy withstood the upheaval of the first oil crisis but came under pressure when Poland's increasing debt fully exposed the artificial nature of economic development based on heavy industry.

The sudden decision of the Polish government in June 1976 to raise the price of food products by 60 percent resulted in street clashes between angry citizens and police and attacks on Communist Party offices. The increased social embedment of the Polish opposition enabled it to begin building political organizations that were not dependent on the Communist Party. The mass support for the street demonstrations prompted previously active groups of opposition intellectuals to establish the Workers' Defense Committee (KOR) in the spirit of the Helsinki Final Act.[38] This initial attempt at social self-organization proved to be successful, resulting in the formation of additional opposition organizations, notably the Movement for Defense of Human and Civic Rights (Ruch Obrony Praw Człowieka i Obywatela, or ROPCiO), the first openly anti-communist, pro-independence organization to function in Poland after the Second World War. Critical Marxist intellectuals such as Adam Michnik and Jacek Kuroń opened up to the Roman Catholic world through these organizations.

Polish authorities regarded the election of Archbishop Wojtyła to succeed John Paul I as pope in October 1978 with a mixture of pride and uneasiness, while Soviet Bloc secret services began to intensively monitor the activities and examine the intentions of the new bishop of Rome. According to a Hungarian intelligence cable of early 1979, "Wojtyła, as Polish cardinal, did not agree with the eastern policy of Pope Paul VI. He believed that the Vatican made more essential compromises with certain socialist countries than would have been necessary. He objected to the fact that the Vatican negotiated directly—above the head of the episcopacy—with the state, thereby weakening the position of the national church. He had a serious role in the unwillingness of the Polish church to establish direct contacts with Hungarian church officials."[39]

The risk of destabilization appeared to be materializing when millions of Polish citizens greeted Pope John Paul II when he visited Poland in June 1979 in what marked the beginning of a moral revolution. One year later, strikes began at the Gdańsk Shipyard and spread throughout Poland. These strikes served to connect the opposition intelligentsia of Poland to the existing social unrest in the country. On August 31, 1980, Polish authorities were forced to sign a comprehensive agreement with the strikers, who were led by the electrician Lech Wałęsa. In this agreement, the Polish government acceded to popular economic demands, recognized the right to strike, promised to release those imprisoned for offenses committed during previous police actions, and provided the Catholic Church with greater ability to broadcast Sunday masses on the radio. Most significant, the agreement offered official recognition and legality to the Solidarity trade union, which became soon the most influential social and political organization in Poland, with 9 million registered members. In September 1980, Stanisław Kania, who supported regime self-criticism and continuing dialogue with Solidarity, replaced Gierek as the head of the communist party. According to Piotr Wandycz, the objective of Solidarity was not to seize power. The historical importance of Solidarity was that it did not emerge from any single political party and embodied a new type of politics based on dialogue and nonviolence resting on moral foundations that were close to those of Roman Catholicism.[40]

The Soviet leadership followed the events in Poland with increasing apprehension. In August 1980, the CPSU Politburo established a special committee under the leadership of Mikhail Suslov (and subsequently Yuri Andropov) to deal with Poland. In 1981, Soviet officials began to place increasing pressure on the Polish government to take various measures to annul the "endless concessions to counterrevolutionary forces."[41] The Soviet Union obtained support in this effort from other Eastern Bloc countries, which threatened to suspend support for a Polish economy that had already been paralyzed by the large number of strikes. The German Democratic Republic, Czechoslovakia, and Bulgaria decided to significantly reduce the amount of goods they exported to Poland at favorable prices, while Hungary and Romania, both of which were waging a continual struggle against insolvency, were reluctant to implement the demanded commercial retribution. The Soviet Union, however, felt compelled to provide Poland with economic support to prevent the West from drawing the country into its sphere of influence. Soviet officials feared that the upheaval in Poland might spill over into the German Democratic Republic, where the KGB had determined that nationalist and anti-Soviet sentiment could spread among the tens of thousands of citizens from Poland and other parts of Eastern Europe, including the Baltic area and Ukraine, who worked legally in the GDR.[42] In October 1981, General Wojciech Jaruzelski, who originated from a deeply religious noble family, was appointed to serve as first secretary of the Polish United Workers' Party after having become head of government in February of that year. On December 13, 1981, General Jaruzelski carried out a coup d'état with the support of the military and law-enforcement organizations. Jaruzelski's carefully prepared action surprised and paralyzed Poland's opposition forces. A total of 45 people were killed and around 1,200 wounded during the suppression of subsequent social resistance to the new military government, while thousands of trade-union activists and intellectuals were interned. The government declared martial law, which lasted until 1983, and banned Solidarity. Some leaders of the trade union, including Lech Wałęsa, were released from prison in 1982, while others remained in prison for several more years.

Jaruzelski's coup d'état, which the general later described as a lesser evil that was necessary to avert an impending Soviet intervention, put an end to democratic development in Poland for nearly a decade, though did not signify a return to classical communism. The Jaruzelski-led Military Council of National Salvation assumed executive powers in Poland, while the political authority of the Polish United Workers' Party declined to an absolute minimum. Solidarity continued to function illegally until 1989 with the support of diverse segments of Polish society and even some party functionaries. Political and mostly covert material support from the West also contributed to Solidarity's ability to continue functioning in spite of its official prohibition. The Jaruzelski regime attempted to stabilize financial and social conditions in Poland, although the standard of living decreased compared to that of previous decade. Although the military junta was unpopular, Polish society was exhausted from nearly ten years of continual conflict and therefore chose to tolerate its existence. The easing of requirements for obtaining an emigration visa prompted hundreds of thousands of Polish citizens to leave their homeland. To relieve the pressure of foreign debt, the Jaruzelski regime gained Poland's membership to the International Monetary Fund and the World Bank in the second half of the 1980s, thus launching the process of rapprochement with the West.

Stability and Unrest: East Germany, Czechoslovakia, Hungary

The 1970s and 1980s represented a period of relative calm in the most developed countries of the Soviet Bloc. In Czechoslovakia, a conservative, pro-Soviet oligarchy led the country even after December 1987, when Gustáv Husák relinquished leadership over the communist party to another apparatchik, Miloš Jakeš. The slogan of the Communist Party of Czechoslovakia elite at the time was the revealing "no surprises, no renewal."[43] Czechoslovak authorities conducted more responsible economic policies than those in the other countries of the Eastern Bloc during this period, avoiding the trap of accruing a large amount of debt and neglecting consumer needs in order to make investments in heavy industry—notably the high-capacity military sector. Czechoslovakia and East Germany were the only socialist countries in which the planned economic model retained some degree of ideological coherency until 1989. The silent coalition of civil servants, minor functionaries, and workers that existed in Czechoslovakia successfully prevented the domestic opposition from expanding its social base beyond intellectual and student circles in Prague and Brno. For more than a decade, former Dubček government Foreign Minister Jiří Hájek, writer Václav Havel, and other members of the Charter 77 group were the most prominent political dissidents in Czechoslovakia. Philosopher Jan Patočka served as the original spokesman for Charter 77, but he died of apoplexy following a police interrogation in March 1977. Havel, Patočka's successor, had spent a total of five years in prison for activities related to his struggle for intellectual and artistic freedom, particularly in the interest of rock and jazz music, which Czechoslovak communist authorities regarded as the manifestation of Western influences. Charter 77 did not present a direct challenge to communist authority, which in the disciplined, Husák-led police state seemed to be incontestable, choosing instead to provide the "powerless" masses with a paradigm of moral and ethical opposition to the cynicism of the communist regime. Michal Kopeček thoroughly described the activity of the Czechoslovak intellectual opposition as aimed "not to challenge authoritarian power, but to reconstitute the political community anew."[44] The "dissident legalism" of the opposition circles, as defined by Kopeček, implied a set of nonideological practices based on the post-Helsinki human rights doctrine. Stressing the importance of acting in conformity with the law—although it was clear that post-1968 socialist legalism was clearly permeated by authoritarian content—enabled the opposition to elaborate a political strategy for the public negotiation of civil rights.

Opposition in Slovakia to Husák's normalization was rooted in underground Catholic Church activity countering that of the pro-communist Pacem in Terris movement.[45] Small though influential opposition groups formed among the members of the Hungarian minority population living in Slovakia at around this same time. These groups voiced objection to both the assimilatory policies of the government of the Slovak Socialist Republic in Bratislava as well as to the construction of the Gabčíkovo-Nagymaros Dams spanning the Danube River between Czechoslovakia and Hungary. Opposition groups protested that the diversion of the river channel that would have been necessary to achieve the latter objective would have caused severe environmental damage. The arrest in November 1982 of one of the most prominent opponents of the proposed dams in Czechoslovakia, the Hungarian geologist and author Miklós Duray, caused an outcry both in the West and in Hungary.[46] In the 1980s, the issue of environmental protection was especially relevant in Slovakia, where many heavy-industrial centers had been built during of the post-1968 consolidation. The struggle to improve the quality of life in Slovakia united the region's Slovaks and Hungarians, who frequently found themselves in opposition to one another on cultural issues.

Until the second half of the 1980s, the political system in Hungary could not be qualified as structurally more liberal than that in Czechoslovakia, though it was informally much more permissive. The Hungarian communist leader János Kádár exploited to his domestic political advantage the portrayal of himself as a wise reformer that had taken root in the Western world. Under Kádár's leadership, Hungary managed to counterbalance the country's pro-Soviet foreign policy through a continual broadening of the relative autonomy it had attained in the economic and cultural spheres. The respect that Kádár had attained within the Eastern Bloc enabled him to foil the attempt of the Soviet-supported left wing of the Hungarian Socialist Workers' Party to remove him from power in the early 1970s. Although the Soviets permitted Kádár to retain his position as general secretary of the HSWP, they forced him to reconsider the boldest elements of his reforms. By the middle of the 1980s, Hungary's communist system had gained stability despite the deepening economic crisis as a result of the effort over the previous decade to build consensus through the formal integration of Hungarian society into the structure of power. This represented a significant achievement for a country in which several tens of thousands of citizens had taken up arms against Soviet communism. The consensus that had emerged in Hungary was based primarily on economic and social concessions. Hungarian communists had learned from the tragic events of October 1956 to treat the consumer ambitions of modern society as an interminable need and unavoidable evil. In 1978, Kádár returned to the path of reform in spite of Soviet opposition in order to relieve the deepening economic crisis in Hungary. These reforms reduced the tax imposed on retailers in order to stimulate private initiative, connected consumer prices to production costs, and authorized state enterprises to conduct trade with Western concerns.

By May 1982, however, the country teetered on the brink of default as a result of the financial mismanagement of the growing foreign debt and the economic assistance to be provided to Poland. In this dramatic context, a top-level decision was finally made to join the International Monetary Fund and the World Bank, to remain solvent and ensure that the country maintained an adequate reserve of hard currency. During the 1980s Hungary came under a sort of double control from the Soviet Union and the West, through international financial institutions that played a major, albeit discreet, role in Hungarian governance.[47] The disbursement of new loans was subject to austerity measures. Continual price increases, which were often hidden and not officially announced, and administrative measures designed to increase the flexibility of the labor market exercised a particularly significant impact on the lower strata of Hungarian society. These measures frequently resulted in the layoff of superfluous workers, thereby generating the previously nearly unknown phenomenon of unemployment. In 1984, the HSWP Central Committee adopted a resolution calling for the creation over the medium term of a mixed economy in which the cooperative movement and the growing private sector would exercise a reciprocal influence on each other. Three years later, the foundations of a monetary economy were laid in Hungary with the establishment of a two-level banking system. Commercial functions that had until this time been performed by the National Bank of Hungary were decentralized among newly established financial institutions in which foreign capital was linked with technocrats and local protocapitalists.[48]

In the 1980s, Hungary opened to the West more than any other country in the Soviet Bloc. The encouragement of personal consumption and initiative—the so-called second economy, that is, parallel economy—generated public support for the Kádár regime as well as pluralism in the economic and private sectors.[49] In his work regarding debated issues within the Hungarian intelligentsia during the Kádár era, Ervin Csizmadia shows that the explicitly pro-Western orientation of the majority of the elite in Hungary was not merely the product of opportunism but signified a natural means of breakout from the prevailing system. The idea that economic freedom rather than respect for human rights was the most important democratic attribute of the West to be emulated in Eastern Europe provided the main theme for debate among Hungarian intellectuals during this period. Pro-reform economists, young Hungarian Socialist Workers' Party technocrats, foreign-affairs specialists, and intellectuals within the democratic opposition all agreed that supranational political and economic integration represented Hungary's best opportunity to attain political stability and economic prosperity following the inevitable collapse of the Soviet-type system.[50]

The Kádár regime carefully monitored changes in public opinion, thus explaining the delicacy with which the apparently soft—though in terms of social consensus not in the least weak—Hungarian dictatorship handled opposition networks until the second half of the 1980s. Marxist philosophers from the Budapest school led the left-wing opposition in Hungary. Participants in the so-called flying university established in 1978 gathered at private residences to listen to lectures and debates regarding unconventional or explicitly forbidden themes, primarily the 1956 Hungarian Revolution. In 1981, samizdat *Beszélő* began publication, inspired by the flourishing Polish underground press.[51] Hungary's self-defined democratic opposition arose from a fusion of intellectual groups of the generations of the 1956 revolution and of the 1968 economic reform. Many of the youngest members of these loose groups were the descendants of bourgeois middle-class families or communist functionaries from Budapest. Hungary's state-security services quickly infiltrated opposition networks, which Kádár thought to be harmless even though they had been deemed important enough to keep under surveillance.

Neither did expression of the nationalist tradition represent a true political alternative. So-called populist writers moved even more comfortably within the coordinates of the existing system than did their "urban" counterparts, even though they challenged its historical and national legitimacy. These writers and their supporters demanded the greater presence of national values in public discourse, protested against the oppression of Hungarian minorities living in countries surrounding Hungary, and sought contacts with Hungarian émigrés living in the West. The political theorist István Bibó, who had spent years in prison in punishment for his political activities during the 1956 Hungarian Revolution and lived under strict police surveillance, was probably the only person whom both the populist and urban intellectuals respected and admired.

East Germany profited greatly from West Germany's *Ostpolitik*. During the final fifteen years of its existence, the second German state transformed into the most modern, urban, and educated society in the Eastern Bloc. As Mary Fulbrook has emphasized, East Germany's Erich Honecker–led regime was a participative dictatorship in which many ordinary citizens lived a pretty normal life without ever encountering any manifestation of oppressive authority such as restrictions on travel abroad.[52] An extremely high proportion of the East German population participated in trade-union activities and in regime-organized public life through membership in cultural and sports associations. Enthusiastic involvement in regime-organized activities might conceal frustration or family drama (one must only think only of the film *Good Bye Lenin!*, in which the character of the mother throws herself into the role of model citizen as a means of venting the painful defection of her husband to West Germany). It was possible for East Germans to integrate themselves into the structure of power to a certain point and even to criticize certain aspects of the regime.[53] The oppressive nature of the regime manifested itself in the ideological severity of the Socialist Unity Party of Germany and the operations of the Stasi, which in a country of 17 million citizens employed almost 100,000 full-time professional staff and 175,000 informants. Jens Gieseke believes that most East German citizens would likely be unable to state following candid self-examination that they never felt the veiled presence of state power and that this presence never determined the course of their actions. The attempt of East Germans to live an inconspicuous normal life can be interpreted as one of the symptoms of concealed political pressure. Gieseke maintains that taking into consideration traditional German social organization, the notion of participation during the Honecker era must be interpreted as a reproduction of old tradition of German political culture (*Untertänigkeit*, or "submissiveness"), which was perpetuated by the dictatorial rule in East Germany across the century.[54]

The rare signs of opposition in East Germany surfaced within the framework of closely monitored and controlled circles of debate. The Honecker regime expelled the popular singer Wolf Biermann from East Germany in November 1976 and over the subsequent five years expatriated several more intellectuals whom it had deemed troublesome.[55] The Lutheran Church, with which the majority of the East German population was affiliated, represented the only cultural counterweight and open critic of the regime in spite of the March 1978 agreement.

Beginning in the 1970s, the formulation of an alternative German identity represented one of the main political issues in East Germany. The Ninth Congress of the Socialist Unity Party of Germany held in May 1976 produced a resolution that contained an important change to the notion of the German Democratic Republic as a purely anti-fascist state, declaring the GDR to be the sole heritor of the traditions of the German-Prussian monarchy. In the 1980s, the East German regime began to build a patriotic cult surrounding historical figures who were unconnected to the workers' movement, such as Frederick the Great and Otto von Bismarck. The ennoblement of the Prussian tradition did not force the Honecker regime or citizens of the GDR to confront the recent past, which West Germany—labeled the heir of the Nazi system in East German propaganda— had already begun to do in a very candid and self-critical manner beginning in the 1960s.[56]

Until the 1980s, economic stability was a motor of social consensus in the German Democratic Republic. Following the reform attempts in the 1960s, East German industry—which had attained the highest degree of development in Eastern Europe—underwent restructuring that resulted in the establishment of large enterprises employing each tens of thousands of workers. The directors of each of these *Kombinat* were provided with almost total management authority, which temporarily improved the organization of production. Following the 1972 interstate agreement, "internal trade" with the Federal Republic of Germany resulted in not only the import of high-quality goods, large quantities of consumer products, and Western machinery and technology but also access to favorable credit and financing. In his analysis of the economic culture of the a system where money was equated with inequality, Jonathan R. Zatlin shows that the German Democratic Republic's increasing need for hard currency compelled the leaders of the GDR to make concessions enabling greater consumerism in the country. Beginning in 1974, goods that were regarded as luxury items in the Soviet Bloc could be purchased with Western currencies at a newly established network of

Intershop stores in East Germany. The leader of East Germany's Commercial Co-ordination Division (Bereich Kommerzielle Koordinierung), party functionary and economic specialist Alexander Schalck-Godolkowski, directed the activities of this unique economic-commercial structure in close cooperation with the interior ministry for nearly two decades. The Intershop network contributed $100 million to East Germany's state budget per year.[57] The Commercial Coordination Division, the operations of which remained secret throughout the communist period, sustained an enormous "gray"—in fact, explicitly illegal—economy in the GDR. During the final two decades of its existence, East Germany placed increasing economic emphasis on commercial joint ventures operating with Western companies in a questionably legal environment. Members of the East German elite acquired enormous sums of hard currency through industrial espionage, financial frauds committed in tax havens, and the illegal export of weapons to countries in the Middle East. Nevertheless, the German Democratic Republic managed to harmonize traditional puritanism with the new demands of the elite in a developed socialist society to a greater degree than any other country in Eastern Europe.

The Ethnic Question Comes to the Foreground: Romania, Yugoslavia, Bulgaria

The crisis of Soviet-type systems in the Balkans and the accelerating ideological depletion of the communist system led to an intensification of tension between nationalities (Yugoslavia) and increasing official discrimination toward ethnic and religious minorities (Romania and Bulgaria). As shown in the previous chapters of this book, nationality conflict represented a persistent problem in the socialist states of Eastern Europe and minority issues destabilized diplomatic relations between them on several occasions. Moreover, beginning in the 1970s, social relations and tensions were increasingly examined from an ethnic perspective in the Soviet Bloc. Yugoslavia fell into deep crisis with Tito's death in 1980, while the leaders of Romania and Bulgaria initiated policies directed at the forced assimilation of minorities to certify the utopia of the ethnically homogenous state.

In Romania, Ceaușescu abandoned his program of political and cultural liberalization (1968–1971) in favor of authoritarian and chauvinistic policies that assumed grotesque proportions in the 1980s. The "Stalinist for all seasons" Ceaușescu regime became a favorite of the West as a result of its verbal stand against the Soviet Union.[58] US officials long harbored the illusion that it might be possible to separate Romania from the Soviet Bloc and induce the country to withdraw from the Warsaw Pact. The first evidence of regressive authoritarianism and dynasty building in Romania occurred following Ceaușescu's official trips to China and North Korea in 1971. After returning from these visits, Ceaușescu issued his "July Theses," proclaiming the launch of a new political and cultural program based on revolutionary propaganda and the strengthening of the role of the party and the party apparatus. This program placed particular emphasis on patriotic education to promote the establishment of a unified socialist state.[59] Ceaușescu's wife, Elena, was elected to serve on the Political Executive Committee while the Romanian Communist Party leader assumed the duties of president and commander in chief of the armed forces. In the 1980s his children and brother became members of the RCP top leadership.[60] Manuela Marin argues that the historical significance of the cult around Ceaușescu goes beyond the folkloric aspects of the visual representation of the leader. The personalized and highly informal family power network that ran parallel to the existing formal hierarchy was the result of a complex relational process undergone between the leader and his constituency. While the object of the cult tried to maintain and consolidate power, his supporters perceived their cooptation into informal structures of power as a prerequisite to their promotion in the formal hierarchy of the party and state apparatus. The result of this duplication was the emergence of a hierarchical system of self-reproducing patronage.[61]

The deterioration of the economic situation in Romania during the second half of the 1970s and the growing foreign debt compelled the Ceaușescu regime to introduce its first austerity measures at the time of the second oil crisis in 1979 (gas rationing, the restriction of driving to even days for cars with even-numbered license plates and odd days for cars with odd-numbered license plates) and to impose an unprecedented program of austerity a few years later. The final years of the Ceaușescu era were characterized by general shortages of basic consumer goods, which citizens acquired either under the table, on the black market, or directly from producers in the countryside. Heating was limited at both private homes and workplaces, even during the cold winter months, and infant mortality doubled in the country in the period of just a few years.

The Ceaușescu regime pursued increasingly severe, albeit differentiated, policies toward Romania's national minorities. Already in the late 1950s, communist officials in Romania had begun to offer for sale citizens of Jewish and German (Saxon and Swabian) origin to Israel and West Germany, both of which were looking for skilled and grateful labor forces.[62] These secret transactions generated estimated revenue of several billion dollars for the state of Romania until the downfall of the Ceaușescu regime. Between 1990 and 1993 another hundred thousand people of German background left the country, resulting in the extinction of a centuries-old cultural community and social constituency.

The 1.7 million Hungarians living in Transylvania represented a greater challenge to the Romanian communist regime. On the one hand, Hungary was an official ally of Romania, thus excluding the possibility of such interstate migration;

and on the other hand, the removal of Hungarians from Transylvania would have established a dangerous precedent in terms of the several million Romanians living in the Soviet Union. Until 1989, officials from the Ceauşescu regime never spoke openly about the status of Bessarabia and the increasing plight of Romanians living in the Moldavian Soviet Socialist Republic, although issues surrounding the territories that Romania had lost to the Soviet Union represented a source of tension in bilateral relations.

The leadership of Romania maintained longtime flexible policies toward the Hungarians of Transylvania, who had successfully integrated into early Romanian society. However, after 1983, the Ceauşescu regime embraced a program of complete cultural liquidation and social disintegration. This change increased internal resistance and provoked international protest both in the West, where Ceauşescu's appeal was continually waning, and in the East. Relations between Hungary and Romania deteriorated steadily in spite of Soviet-instigated bilateral talks in Debrecen and Oradea in 1977 and in Arad in 1988. In Romania, the Transylvanian question transformed from a political matter to a cardinal security problem, while the issue of Hungarian refugees received the most international publicity. Until the mid-1980s, authorities in socialist Hungary maintained an ambivalent attitude toward Hungarian refugees arriving from Romania. While some Hungarian officials tolerated the refugees, others took strict measures against them, sometimes even deporting them back to Romania at the request of Romanian authorities. However, after Hungary signed the UN Convention Relating to the Status of Refugees in March 1989, the country admitted more than 30,000 Hungarian asylum seekers from Romania until the collapse of the Ceauşescu regime in December of that year.[63] The mass flight of Hungarians and disregard for fundamental human rights undermined the international legitimacy of the Ceauşescu regime. The Romanian communist regime went into self-isolation. In February 1988, the US government announced that it would withdraw most favored nation status from Romania to protest the Ceauşescu regime's human-rights violations.

The resilience of the Ceauşescu regime amid the vast political changes that were taking place in the Eastern Bloc may seem surprising. Many analysts have attributed the regime's hardiness to the brutality of Romania's police and state-security agencies. The Securitate indeed enjoyed a privileged standing both within the Romanian communist apparatus and among the state-security agencies operating in socialist states. In December 1964, Soviet officials yielded to Romanian pressure and withdrew the final KGB advisers from the country as well. However, in terms of method and mentality, the late Romanian communist state-security mechanism was based more closely on the Stalinist model than any other in Eastern Europe. Although Romanian dissidents were not confined in labor camps or executed following secret military trials during this period, state-security services subjected them to continual harassment, in several instances driving them to suicide. Meanwhile, the border guard and the workers' militia took brutal action against all of those who violated the written and unwritten rules of socialist coexistence—illegal border crossers, young men with long hair, rock music enthusiasts, jobless people, women who sought illegal abortions, and Western-radio listeners. Physical violence was an intrinsic element of the modus operandi of the Securitate, which the organization employed making greater use of psychological pressure and interference in the private lives of citizens as a means of coercion during the late Ceaușescu regime.[64] Moreover, the Securitate exercised a significant influence on the ideological orientation of the national-communist regime and utilized up-to-date methods of operative psychology in the course of its daily activities.[65] Police terror entailed daily corruption that citizens of Romania were forced to accept and which made it possible for many of them to survive the economic austerity measures. It is therefore worthwhile to examine the sources of the Ceaușescu regime's internal legitimacy if one wants to find an answer to the question of how it was able to endure for so long.

Unlike in most communist parties in Eastern Europe, internal conflict never took place between orthodox and liberal factions in the Romanian Communist Party and its predecessor, the Romanian Workers' Party. Those who were dissatisfied with Ceaușescu's personality cult did not attempt to modernize the system but contrived palace revolutions based on the models of the interwar political machinations that had occurred in Romania or the military putsch that had overthrown Marshal Antonescu in August 1944. The exceptions to these rules were scattered and ineffectual: in 1977 writer Paul Goma's expressed public support for Charter 77 and called on the Ceaușescu regime to respect the human rights of Romanian citizens, while in 1979 a worker from Ploiești, Vasile Paraschiv, collected thousands of signatures in support of a new, independent trade union. However, before the new union could be launched, the police arrested Paraschiv, who was forced to spend the subsequent years confined in a mental hospital, and initiated legal proceedings against many of the signatories, many of whom received long prison sentences. In the years 1981–1982, Hungarian intellectuals, including a group of high school teachers, published *Ellenpontok* (Counterpoints), the only samizdat that ever appeared in Romania. This short-lived illegal publication described the state oppression that manifested itself in every domain of life in Romania in the early 1980s as well as the increasing official discrimination against minority nationalities in the country during this period.[66] Cristina Petrescu finely analyzes the celebrated paradigm of "resistance through culture" during the last decades of Romanian communism. This intellectual practice originated from the work of the traditionalist philosopher Constantin Noica and represented the epitome of symbolic disagreement and lack of concrete political engagement. Resistance through culture was a tolerated form of spiritual dissent that did not comply with the concept that Western scholars had in mind when coining the term *dissident*, nor did it correspond to the definition the critical intellectuals of Central Europe and the Soviet Union adopted for themselves.[67]

The Ceaușescu regime attributed greater significance to workers' protests that voiced primarily economic rather than political demands. After 35,000 miners went on strike in the Jiu Valley in southern Transylvania in August 1977, and managed to take RCP negotiator Ilie Verdeț hostage, Ceaușescu was forced to go to the Jiu Valley to conduct face-to-face talks with the strikers. Although Ceaușescu made economic concessions to the miners in order to end the protest, subsequent legal and trade-union reprisals resulted in the dismissal of thousands of miners from their jobs and hundreds of criminal convictions.[68] A spontaneous workers' uprising involving several tens of thousands of people erupted in the city of Brașov in November 1987 but was quickly suppressed given the absence of mutual trust among participants and a lack of adequate communications. Until the eve of the events in Timișoara in December 1989, the old Hungarian proverb "The cornmeal porridge doesn't explode"—meaning that the people of Romania are not easily inspired to revolt—seemed to hold true.

The situation in Bulgaria was fundamentally different from that in Romania during the 1970s and 1980s. Beyond official rhetoric stating that Bulgaria and the Soviet Union acted "as one body, breathing through the same nostrils," the economic and political interests of the two countries were, in fact, compatible in many regards.[69] As other countries in the Eastern Bloc (Czechoslovakia in 1960 and Romania in 1965), the new constitution of Bulgaria, adopted in 1971, declared the country to be a developed socialist republic in which the communist party stood at the vanguard of society and state. Bulgaria did not reject Willy Brandt's *Ostpolitik* and strengthened bilateral relations with West Germany, while the predominantly Eastern Orthodox country made friendly gestures toward the Vatican, permitting a group of citizens to make a pilgrimage to the Vatican in 1975.

The family-based degeneration and megalomania of national communism that characterized Romania did not appear in Bulgaria during the thirty-five-year rule of Todor Zhivkov (1954–1989). According to Joseph Rothschild, the slow decline that took place in Bulgaria most resembled that of Hungary during the Kádár era, with the notable exception of the Zhivkov regime's strong mistrust of all attempts at systemic correction.[70] The establishment in Bulgaria beginning in the years 1969–1970 of enormous agro-industrial complexes that promoted mechanization and ensured adequate profit within the country's vital agricultural sector represented the only genuine reform implemented under Zhivkov's leadership. Tourism represented the other sector of preeminent importance in the otherwise traditional economy of Bulgaria: the country's Black Sea coast attracted a hundred thousand foreign tourists per year. As in Romania, the improvement of living standards in Bulgaria, coupled with the efficiency and severity of the Bulgarian secret service known as the Committee for State Security, prevented the emergence of an organized domestic opposition-movement, as the spectacular murder via poison-tipped umbrella of dissident writer Georgi Markov in 1978 demonstrated. Enrico Berlinguer, general secretary of the Italian Communist Party, was involved in a suspicious car accident while on an official visit to Sofia in the autumn of 1973. Despite the official silence surrounding this incident in Bulgaria and also Italy, diplomats from Hungary immediately remarked on the peculiarities surrounding Berlinguer's accident.[71] At that time, Berlinguer's call for a historic compromise between the Italian Communist Party and Italy's Christian Democracy party caused consternation in the Soviet Bloc states, and this might have stood behind the Bulgarian (and thus, Soviet) attempt to annihilate him.

The policies of the Zhivkov regime toward national and religious minorities—above all Muslim Turks—underwent nationalist regression similar to that of the Ceauşescu regime, thus resulting in discriminative cultural practices and increased assimilatory pressure. Ludmilla Zhivkova, the daughter of Todor Zhivkov, directed the Bulgarian Communist Party's cultural policies from the 1970s until her death amid suspicious circumstances in 1981. According to Vesselin Dimitrov, Zhivkova rejected Soviet-inspired communist orthodoxy and participated along with other members of the BCP Central Committee in a spiritual community called the White Fraternity that gravitated toward officially forbidden mysticism, including theosophy, certain Indian teachings, and astrology. Zhivkova steered effectively between opening toward the West and support for pre–Second World War cultural nationalism.[72]

Contrary to the case in Romania, where the deterioration of interstate relations with Hungary exercised only a minor impact on the lives of Hungarians living in Transylvania, the increasing tension between Bulgaria and Turkey constituted an element of greater interbloc conflict, thus leading to the wave of violence involving Bulgarian Turks. In August 1984, Bulgarian Turks carried out lethal bomb attacks at the railway station in Plovdiv and the airport in Varna with the support of the Turkish government, causing widespread panic among the citizens of Bulgaria. The Zhivkov regime decided to conduct the forced assimilation of Bulgaria's Turkish minority and launched a military-level offensive against the Turkish civilian population. On December 24, 1984, police established blockades around Turkish villages and subsequently forced their inhabitants to officially Bulgarianize their names. This action resulted in 300,000 instances of "consent" in a period of three weeks at a cost of strong social resistance and numerous violent episodes. Several thousand Turks who refused to cooperate were sent to forced-labor camps. The Zhivkov regime's assimilatory policy not only prohibited new Bulgarians from speaking Turkish but forbade them from wearing their traditional clothing and playing their folk music as well. Special units removed graves bearing Turkish inscriptions from cemeteries and changed the names of the deceased in local death records. Finally, access to health care and social services was restricted to those who declared themselves to be of Bulgarian nationality.[73] The brutal Bulgarianization campaign—officially known as Revival Process—was stopped amid widespread international protest and the emergence of new leadership in the Soviet Union.

The 1970s represented a period of contradiction in Yugoslavia. The normalization that began following the unrest in Slovenia, Croatia, and Kosovo resulted in a new start. The 1974 constitution transformed the country into a federal state that furnished its constituent republics with genuine autonomy and the governments of these republics with extensive legislative and executive powers. The new constitution also provided the two autonomous provinces in Serbia—Vojvodina and Kosovo—with potent local governments that until 1988 maintained the right to veto the cultural and administrative decisions of federal bodies.[74] The introduction of territorial militias in all six Yugoslav federal republics in 1970 was one of the most important reforms that took place as a result of this new constitutional phase. According to Stevan K. Pavlowitch, the political authority of the League of Communists of Yugoslavia proclaimed in the 1974 constitution actually represented the neo-feudalistic means of exercising power for eight state parties—one in each of the six constituent republics and the two autonomous provinces. Marshal Tito, the heirless absolute ruler, and the Yugoslav federal army, which was composed primarily of Serb, Bosnian Serb, and Montenegrin elements, remained the sole guarantors of Yugoslav national unity at the institutional level. This neo-feudal system nevertheless guaranteed broad compromise between central control and local autonomy for nearly a decade.[75] The deaths of Kardelj in 1979 and Tito in 1980 did not represent the inevitable beginning of the disintegration of Yugoslavia and the start of the Yugoslav wars of secession of the 1990s; however, they did result in economic difficulties and both the West as well as the Soviet Bloc lost their strategic interest in Yugoslavia. The absence of a charismatic leader produced a political crisis in Yugoslavia that the new system of authority based on rotational representation between the constituent republics proved unable to alleviate.[76]

The financial and economic situation deteriorated from the second half of the 1970s. The expansion of the prerogatives of employees and reduction of the authority of managers via the 1976 law regarding the operations of cooperatives resulted in disruptions within the system of production. Continual negotiations between workers and management served to reinforce phenomena already present within the Yugoslav economy such as undeclared employment and frequent strikes, euphemistically called "work suspensions," while local agreements produced unwarranted wage disparities both between and within republics. In the late 1970s, each Yugoslav republic was forced to take responsibility for its own balance of payments, while the federal government attempted to prevent republics from going into debt through the acquisition via export activity of hard currency needed for imports.

The coordination of the Yugoslav economic domain remained an unrealized goal: the amount of goods and services exchanged within individual republics rose from around 60 percent of all goods and services exchanged in 1970 to almost 70 percent of all goods and services exchanged in 1980. The divergent developmental paths of various Yugoslav republics reached their ultimate point: John R. Lampe refers to the crisis-management strategies that the relatively developed republics of Slovenia and Croatia employed in the 1980s as economic feudalism.[77]

Yugoslavia's high external debt forced the Yugoslav federal government to adopt unpopular austerity measures. Inflation rose to an annual rate of nearly 100 percent in the 1980s before jumping to 200 percent in 1989. The official unemployment rate varied from 1.7 percent in Slovenia to 25 percent in Bosnia and Herzegovina, 27 percent in both Montenegro and Macedonia, and 57 percent in Kosovo. Per capita income in Kosovo was 25 percent of that in Slovenia and around 40 percent of the federal average in spite of generous developmental funding to the autonomous province from the federal budget.[78]

The economic crisis in Yugoslavia served to politicize internal affairs and intensify nationality conflict. The increasing Serbo-centrism of the Yugoslav state undermined the pragmatic community of interests that had developed between Serbs and Slovenes during the interwar period and represented the foundation of Yugoslav political stability. The 1974 Yugoslav Constitution not only promoted the ambition of developed republics and provinces (Slovenia, Croatia, and Vojvodina) in which Serbs either constituted a minority or plurality of the population but recognized (Kosovo) and institutionalized (Bosnia and Herzegovina) the previously repudiated Albanian and Bosnian political identities. The frustration that the 1974 constitution aroused among Serbs became a destabilizing factor throughout Yugoslavia during the final years of the country's existence. The number of Albanians living in Kosovo grew sharply as a result of their high birth rate, while a great number of Serbs—particularly those who had arrived following the Second World War—emigrated from the autonomous province as a result of a sharp decline in their ethnic comfort. Moreover, the local party and state apparatus in Kosovo, including the police, came under Albanian control in the 1970s. As a result of these factors, the number of Serbs living in Kosovo fell from 27 percent of the total population in 1961 to 13.2 percent of the total population in 1981.[79] The number of Serbs also declined, though to a lesser degree, in Bosnia-Herzegovina, falling from 44 percent in 1948 to 32 percent in 1981.

Political and intellectual circles in Belgrade started claiming that the Titoist state, with active Slovenian and Croatian support, had purposely weakened

Serbia and the national self-identity of Serbs living in Croatia, Bosnia and Herzegovina, and Kosovo. In 1986, the Serbian Academy of Sciences and Arts published a lengthy memorandum on the "integrity and cultural situation" of the Serbian people, which first articulated the claim that all Serbs have the right to live in one state.[80] The Yugoslav federal government attempted to maintain the appearance of neutrality in order to negate strengthening radicalism at the republic level: both the future radical Serbian leader Vojislav Šešelj and Croatian head of government Franjo Tuđman were imprisoned for nationalist activities.

Bosniaks living in Bosnia and Herzegovina were permitted to define their nationality as "Muslim" following Yugoslavia's 1971 census. However, the government of the Socialist Republic of Bosnia and Herzegovina attempted to separate religion from nationality, though as a result of the Islamic revolution in Iran, Muslim religious leaders in Yugoslavia began to openly criticize the country's communist system. In April 1983, the future president of Bosnia and Herzegovina, Alija Izetbegović, and other Bosniaks were put on trial in Sarajevo on charges of "hostile activity proceeding from Muslim nationalism" and "the intention to establish an ethnically pure Bosnia and Herzegovina."[81] Ethnic particularism coalesced with the rise of a clannish political culture. The scandalous bankruptcy of the Agrokomerc food company in 1987 resulted in layoffs of several thousand workers, sparked numerous demonstrations, and exposed a vast system of corruption in which Bosniak leadership circles were heavily involved.[82]

Control over Kosovo slipped out of the hands of Yugoslav central authorities years previously, just a few months after Tito's death in 1980. In March 1981, students from the Albanian university in Pristina organized a series of demonstrations to demand that Kosovo be elevated to the status of republic and to protest high unemployment and economic underdevelopment in the autonomous province. These demonstrations transformed into genuine rebellion, which federal officials in Belgrade suppressed with military force that caused several deaths. This upheaval produced the most serious ethnic conflict in Kosovo since the end of the Second World War, thus accelerating the emigration of Serbs from the unruly province.[83]

The 1974 Yugoslav Constitution failed to resolve disputes regarding the borders between the constituent republics of Yugoslavia and the connected issue of the status of Serbs living outside the Socialist Republic of Serbia.[84] Every republic retained the right to self-determination and even to withdraw from the Yugoslav federation, although internal separatism and border disputes remained suppressed under the rule of Marshal Tito. However, following the death of the longtime leader of socialist Yugoslavia, the country that had become unified around his personality slipped into such a deep crisis that scenarios that had previously seemed unlikely became concrete threats.

The Demise of Communism (1988–1991)

Perestroika in the Soviet Union and Eastern Europe

On March 11, 1985, the fifty-four-year-old Mikhail Gorbachev was appointed to succeed Konstantin Chernenko as general secretary of the Communist Party of the Soviet Union. Gorbachev had greater education than most members of the party apparatus (he had earned degrees in both law and agricultural engineering) and had gained a realistic image of the state of affairs both internationally and within the Soviet Union. The new CPSU general secretary formulated ambitious plans for the Soviet Union which were composed of three coordinated elements: *uskoreniye* (acceleration), *perestroika* (restructuring), and *glasnost* (openness).[85] General Secretary Gorbachev and his pro-reform allies, whose relationship with Brezhnev-era party veterans was not free of conflict, initially focused on reviving the deteriorating Soviet economy. However, the Soviet Union's Twelfth Five-Year Plan launched in 1986 provided support to sectors of the economy that traditionally generated massive losses, notably military-oriented heavy industry, which consumed 30 percent of the state budget. According to Stephen Kotkin, this final, desperate, attempt to retain the established Soviet economic structure demonstrated the fundamental inability of the socialist economy to carry out reform.[86] The most important economic statistics, from those showing a rapid rise in foreign debt to those showing a significant decline in industrial and agricultural production, revealed that the Soviet economy was headed toward collapse. The Chernobyl nuclear power plant disaster in April 1986 caused thousands of deaths, exercised a destructive impact on the social psychology of many Soviet and East European citizens, and displayed to the entire world the inability of the Soviet state to handle the emergency.

Gorbachev's initiatives to liberalize cultural life generated expectations within the Soviet Union and were interpreted in the West as evidence of the new Soviet leadership's political opening, though they also resulted in conflict and uneasiness. Gorbachev also launched an anticorruption campaign based on measures already employed by Andropov. The main objective of this campaign, which took place primarily in non-Russian republics, was to weaken the dynastic structure of local communist parties and to reduce the corruption that permeated the grassroots apparatus. However, the inhabitants of republics in the Caucasus and Central Asia regarded Gorbachev's recentralization program to be aimed at the Russification and assimilation of minorities, thus leading to an increasing number of ethnic clashes. The pro-reform CPSU general secretary then initiated a campaign to combat alcoholism, which was causing increasingly severe social problems throughout the Soviet Union. This campaign criminalized drunkenness and resulted in the fining and imprisonment of several thousand Soviet citizens. Measures to curtail access to alcohol generated a growing black market for spirits that were frequently unfit for human consumption and resulted in a rise in alcoholism-related crime. Gorbachev's anti-alcoholism campaign, which was paradoxically based on the social objectives of the former nobility, harmed the personal interests of Soviet citizens to such a degree (the right to cheap vodka, for example) that it caused widespread popular alienation toward the new CPSU leadership.

The pro-reform image of Gorbachev and his associates that state propaganda so skillfully cultivated found much greater approval abroad than it did in the Soviet Union. The resumption of dialogue regarding disarmament and the withdrawal of Soviet troops from Afghanistan increased the Soviet leader's prestige in the Western world. However, Gorbachev's reforms served to heighten differences in political orientation within the Soviet sphere of interest.[87] The new course in the Soviet Union received broad political and intellectual support in Poland and Hungary. During official visits to these countries, Gorbachev endorsed Jaruzelski's policies and Hungarian reforms, particularly the modernization of the agricultural sector. Officials in the German Democratic Republic, Czechoslovakia, and Bulgaria confined themselves to appraisal of the new conditions, refusing to implement Soviet-urged measures connected to economic reform and cultural liberalization. The Ceauşescu regime simply ignored all Soviet recommendations and warnings.

In 1988, Soviet policy toward the states of Eastern Europe underwent the landmark transformation of renouncing the right to intervene in their internal affairs. Party officials endorsed this change of policy at the Nineteenth Conference of the CPSU held in 1988. Gorbachev reconfirmed this new noninterventionist policy during an address before the United Nations General Assembly several months later, in which the CPSU general secretary announced the unilateral withdrawal of Soviet troops and weaponry from Eastern Europe. Gorbachev's speech in New York represented the first time since the end of the Second World War that a Soviet leader had explicitly referred to the sovereignty of the Soviet Bloc countries and the freedom for them to choose their own social and economic systems.[88] Internal difficulties in the Soviet Union prompted Gorbachev to give free rein to the political changes that had begun to take form in Poland and Hungary.[89] The new Soviet receptiveness to revision of the socialist system in Eastern Europe not only led to the 1989 revolutions in the region, but contributed significantly to their largely peaceful and negotiated character.[90]

Internal developments in the Soviet Union also served to promote the gradual democratization of Eastern Europe: parliamentary elections held in March 1989 offered voters genuine choice between candidates for the first time since 1920, thus institutionalizing the already informally accepted notions of plurality and differences of opinion. However, the more permissive Soviet policy toward Central and Eastern Europe was not exclusively the result of the increasingly democratic inclinations of Gorbachev and his supporters, but of the domestic economic crisis that had emerged in the Soviet Union. Social and ethnic conflict spread uncontrollably throughout the Soviet Union in January 1989. Armed clashes occurred between Armenia and Azerbaijan over the disputed region of Nagorno-Karabakh. The Baltic republics strove to attain autonomy, while strikes among miners in the strategically important Donbass region of southeastern Ukraine clearly indicated the unsustainability of the situation.

The collapse of the external empire thus contributed to the deepening of the Soviet Union's internal crisis, which, in turn, gave rise to the unavoidable changes. In the economic domain, the mutual dependency that resulted from barter-based trade generated losses for all parties involved. The increasing independence of developed Eastern European countries severely undermined the legitimacy of Soviet authority.[91] While changes in the Soviet Union between 1985 and 1988 accelerated the crises afflicting Eastern European regimes, the collapse of communism in Soviet satellite states in 1989 was a major factor contributing to the subsequent collapse of the Soviet Union.

Negotiated Revolution, Guided Transformation: Poland, Hungary, and Bulgaria

The abrupt political transformation that took place in Eastern Europe during the years 1988–1990 caught Western political officials and analysts by surprise. A May 1988 CIA report asserted that resistance to Gorbachev-advocated reform in Eastern Europe was certain to continue for three to five more years, though the report also emphasized the unsustainability of the economic situation in the Soviet Union. The CIA report stated that factors of uncertainty could potentially increase in Eastern Europe as a consequence of perestroika, although it did not even consider the possibility that the Soviet Bloc might collapse entirely.[92]

The confrontation between weak regimes and even weaker oppositions in Poland and Hungary produced not revolution but gradual, negotiated change. The crucial year of transformation in both Poland and Hungary was 1988, when political and social upheaval shook both countries and the continuing validity of the Brezhnev doctrine entailed the possibility of Soviet military intervention to halt reform. Strikes paralyzed production in many factories in Poland from late May until the end of the summer, when Lech Wałęsa and Interior Minister Czesław Kiszczak agreed to initiate dialogue between the formally illegal Solidarity trade union and the government. The Soviets were informed of these provisional talks only following the decision of the Political Committee of the Polish United Workers' Party. Although Gorbachev worried about the speed of changes taking place in Poland, the Soviet leader understood that they were unavoidable and accepted them under the condition that he be informed of their technical aspects, such as the date and procedure of elections and Wałęsa's likely political role. Talks between the government of Poland and Solidarity began in February 1989 and concluded with the signing of an accord on April 4 of that year. The two sides had managed to come to agreement on several issues regarding the means of implementing the system change: the legalization of Solidarity; the introduction of a six-year presidential mandate, which the opposition deemed necessary in order to counterbalance the power of the Polish United Workers' Party; and the holding of semifree elections for the *Sejm* in which 65 percent of the seats would be reserved for PUWP candidates and of genuine multiparty elections for the newly created senate. The brutal suppression of the Tiananmen Square protests in Beijing on June 4, 1989, heightened the symbolic meaning of the historic elections held in Poland on that same date.[93]

Interpretation of the results of the elections in Poland is not a simple task. Western observers expressed wonder at the outcome of elections for the senate in which Solidarity won ninety-nine of one hundred seats. However, sociologist Jadwiga Staniszkis remarked that voter participation was a surprisingly low 62 percent and that turnout had been remarkably weak among the segments of the working class that had played a leading role in the 1980–1981 trade-union struggle.[94]

In August 1989, General Jaruzelski approved the appointment of the Roman Catholic intellectual and prominent representative of the Solidarity movement, Tadeusz Mazowiecki, to serve as prime minister. Poland thus became the first country in the Soviet Bloc to form a noncommunist government, which remained in power until January 1991. The Mazowiecki government adopted constitutional changes in December 1989 that transformed Poland into a *Rechtsstaat*, then supervised the dissolution of the internal political police and, over the course of the following year, initiated the withdrawal of Soviet troops from the country.

The institutional transition in Poland was apparently smooth, if compared to the revolutionary convulsions that had marked the political changes over the previous decades. However, Joachim von Puttkamer and Tom Junes recently made the case that widespread use of physical violence, social, and intergenerational conflicts marked the 1989 process to multiparty system.[95] The students' movement and the radical Catholic grassroots, who had played a pivotal role in the public opposition to the communist regime, felt betrayed by the roundtable talks and the failure of transitional justice. Younger activists soon began to complain about unfinished revolution and turned against Lech Wałęsa and the new political establishment.[96]

Resolving Poland's economic problems, which included inflation of nearly 600 percent and debt equaling 65 percent of gross domestic product, represented the greatest challenge to the new government. Prime Minister Mazowiecki relied on the counsel of the well-known economist Leszek Balcerowicz, who cooperated with a group of foreign advisors including young Harvard University professor Jeffrey Sachs. The Mazowiecki government introduced a package of economic and financial measures at the end of 1989. This "shock therapy"—which was based on neoliberal economic philosophy and had the support of international financial organizations—was meant to establish the foundations of a market economy in Poland as quickly as possible. The measures notably included the privatization of publically owned production units and the significant reduction of state expenditures on social programs and individual welfare. Analysts remain divided in their estimation of the success of the Mazowiecki government's shock therapy: while the Sachs-proposed debt cancellation enabled Poland to avoid insolvency and the country was able to generate economic growth again just a few years later, the decline in state subsidies caused a sharp rise in long-term unemployment—sometimes to even above 20 percent—in rural areas, particularly the underdeveloped eastern regions bordering Belarus and Ukraine.[97] Unemployment and inflation produced widespread disillusion toward the new free-market system among the citizens of Poland, while the communist *nomenklatura*, as in other countries of Eastern Europe, managed to transform its former political power into economic and financial power.

In Hungary, contrary to Poland, the transition from the planned economy to the market economy occurred before the introduction of the multiparty political system. In fact, it was prompted by the financial collapse of the late 1980s, when the foreign debt rose to an unsustainable level. A research paper recently published debunks the mainstream narrative that had made private overconsumption and social expenditures the main responsibility for the financial imbalance in Kádár's Hungary. The rapid growth of short-term foreign debt that occurred in 1986–1987 was apparently caused by a sequence of errors in the choice of the foreign currencies in which to contract the debt. This provoked exchange rate losses of almost ten billion dollars until 1989.[98]

According to Rudolf L. Tőkés, the Kádár compromise, which offered the citizens of Hungary a certain degree of economic security in exchange for their personal adaptation to the system, disintegrated during the second half of the 1980s because of the austerity policies required by the creditors and reluctantly implemented by the Hungarian authorities. It was precisely the cultural elite and socialist middle class that most vociferously supported the transformation of the communist system in the Gorbachev-indicated direction.[99] At the National Assembly elections held in 1985, the designation of multiple candidates was made possible under the pressure of the pro-reform faction of the Hungarian Socialist Workers' Party leadership, which regarded the use of the multiple-candidate system as an advance toward representation-based local self-administration, while the anti-reform faction regarded it as a concession that appeared to be significant, though actually entailed little risk.

The silent rebellion of the elites reached a turning point in 1987, when Marxist and liberal economists published an essay entitled "Social Contract" (*Társadalmi Szerződés*) in the still-illegal samizdat *Beszélő*, asserting that the crisis of the socialist system necessitated the rapid liberalization of the economy and strengthened the interdependence of the West and the East.[100] The authors of "Social Contract" stated the explicit conclusion that "Kádár must go" and that the proclaimed reform policies of the HSWP required new party leadership. Officials, economists, and those who opposed the existing system agreed that socialist integration was a burden that must be cast off as soon as possible. The technocrat and advocate of controlled transition Károly Grósz succeeded Kádár as general secretary of the Hungarian Socialist Workers' Party in May 1988.

In her landmark monograph of Hungary's role in the Soviet system, Melinda Kalmár pointed out that although the leadership of HSWP did take some steps toward political reforms, their new leaders hoped that the asynchrony between economic and political reforms could be maintained. Very different people like young technocrat prime minister Miklós Németh, popular secretary of the People's Front Imre Pozsgay, and new party secretary Grósz shared the hope that the economic stabilization program would bring some results, and the HSWP could emerge from the general crisis without having to introduce a real division of power. Until the spring of 1989, the ruling party did not elaborate any concrete scheme concerning the target of the political transition. Its leadership held the conviction that pluralism meant no more than a nominal division of power within the one-party system, and that transition could drive to a modern corporate system, where democratic elements would merge with authoritarian flavors.[101]

The duplicity of the regime is also reflected in its handling of alternative political activity. HSWP officials permitted the newly established opposition party, the Hungarian Democratic Forum and other social organizations to hold a large demonstration on June 27, 1988, against the Ceaușescu regime's planned destruction of villages in Transylvania, though prohibited public commemorations of the 1956 revolution on October 23 or of the execution of Imre Nagy on June 16. Meanwhile, the state security continued to monitor "suspicious elements" and engaged an increasing number of people involved in groups opposing the communist system as informants. The opposition meeting in the village of Monor in June 1985 represented the final time that populist and urban intellectuals, who had begun to openly question one another's historical, political, and moral legitimacy, engaged in common action. Following this meeting, the two most important political formations of the system-change era in Hungary—the Hungarian Democratic Forum associated with the populist intelligentsia and the urban Alliance of Free Democrats associated with the urban intelligentsia and middle class—grew out of the mutual ideological and cultural antagonism of these

two intellectual orientations. The compromising stance of the Catholic establishment narrowed the range of action of opposition-minded believers, while the absence of charismatic leaders and internal discord within the cultural elites served
to further undermine the already weak social legitimacy of the opposition.

Internal dissent erupted within the Hungarian Socialist Workers' Party at
the end of 1988, when the pro-reform economist Miklós Németh formed a new
government that remained in power until Hungary's first democratic elections
in April 1990. This government made it possible for the final one-party National
Assembly to approve important democratic reform measures, notably those
granting the right to strike and legalizing opposition movements. HSWP General Secretary Grósz attempted to impede the process of political change, on one
occasion even warning of the possibility of counterrevolutionary white terror,
though remained isolated in this endeavor. On January 28, 1989, State Minister
Imre Pozsgay referred in a radio interview to the 1956 revolution as a popular
uprising.[102] The fall of this final national taboo served to accelerate political reform. Roundtable negotiations based on the Polish consensual model began in
March 1989, while the right of the HSWP Central Committee and Political Committee to veto decisions of the government was abolished.[103]

National Assembly Chairman Mátyás Szűrös, who had previously served
as Hungary's ambassador to the Soviet Union, proclaimed the establishment of
the Hungarian Republic on October 23, 1989, while the major political parties
agreed to set up the Constitutional Court and hold elections during the spring of
1990. The only truly tense episode in Hungary during the transition year of 1989
was the arrival to the country of several tens of thousands of East German and
Czechoslovak "tourists" who intended to seek refuge in the West. This exodus
and the opening of the Hungarian-Austrian border severely undermined the social legitimacy of the GDR and, according to András Oplatka, accelerated to an
unimaginable degree the collapse not only of the East German regime but of the
entire Soviet Bloc.[104]

In Hungary, to an even greater degree than in Poland, the new capitalists of
the party *nomenklatura* turned their attention toward business opportunities on
the eve of the political transition.[105] In October 1988, the National Assembly of
Hungary approved the Company Law, which made the tumultuous "spontaneous
privatization" of the country's economy possible. State-owned companies were
artificially placed into bankruptcy and subsequently liquidated, while former
company managers privatized certain industrial units and sectors at a minimal
price. According to data from the State Audit Office, nearly five hundred companies were privatized in Hungary in 1989 and 1990 for a total price of around
100 billion forints (about $2 billion).[106] The increasing scandal surrounding the
rapid privatization of companies in Hungary divided the opposition: whereas
the populists demanded that the process be halted, liberals worried about the

departure of foreign investors and advocated its continuation. In November 1989, the economist János Kornai warned in an essay outlining the traditional reform-communist vision of market socialism against the foreseeable dangers associated with privatization. Kornai recommended in his essay the increase in the capacity of Hungary to attract capital and the introduction of a Western-type capitalist system in the country.[107] The reorganization of heavy industry resulting in the layoff of several hundred thousand workers had largely taken place and the legal environment and structure of the free-market economic transition had already been established long before Hungary's first democratic elections in the spring of 1990.

The political transition began in Bulgaria only during the second half of 1989, thus providing the country's opposition with little time to prepare for it. Beginning in 1985, Bulgaria had attempted to follow the Soviet path toward reform and the Bulgarian Communist Party leadership initiated all changes. The Bulgarian opposition coalesced around two poles on the social periphery: the Turkish-Muslim minority and the environmentalist intelligentsia. In a traditionally agricultural country like Bulgaria that had undergone an environmentally destructive process of industrialization, many political and social issues were tightly connected to ecology. In April 1989, members of the Bulgarian opposition had formed the independent Ecoglasnost organization, which on November 3, 1989—thus before the fall of the Berlin Wall—held a mass demonstration in Sofia that precipitated the transition to democracy in Bulgaria.

Official persecution of Bulgaria's Turkish minority resulted in the international stigmatization of the Zhivkov regime. In May 1989, Bulgaria—which, unlike Romania, had signed the UN Convention on Refugees—initiated the process of expelling Turks to Turkey through the out-of-the-blue liberalization of a passport policy targeting "persons with revived names" (i.e., the Turks and the Pomaks), which sparked rebellion in the northeastern region of the country. What followed in the summer of 1989 was the migration (officially named the Great Excursion) of 350,000 people to neighboring Turkey, many of whom left the country amid fear of new repression.[108] The humanitarian crisis caused by the refugees from Bulgaria to a NATO country stirred also security concerns in Moscow and played an important role in convincing Soviet leaders to transfer their support from longtime BCP General Secretary Zhivkov to younger and more flexible party officials associated with Foreign Minister Petar Mladenov.[109] However, the system change in Bulgaria was not part of the frequently cited domino effect that overturned communist regimes throughout Eastern Europe in 1989: the fall of the Berlin Wall on November 9 and the peaceful coup d'état that took place in Bulgaria the following day were unrelated.

The Soviets, in fact, planned and supervised the overthrow of Zhivkov on November 10, 1989. The role of opposition demonstrations remained purely symbolic until it became clear that the true objective of the changes that had occurred within Bulgaria's party-state was not the introduction of Western-style democracy, but the salvation of power. According to Guido Franzinetti, the fall of the Zhivkov regime represented "realization of that paradigm which would have liked to propagate the Gorbachev plan throughout all of Europe."[110] In Bulgaria and most other countries of Eastern Europe, the true political battles, which included attempts at restoration and destabilization, stirred up after rather than during the transition year of 1989.

Peaceful Revolution in Berlin and Prague

The downfall of communist regimes in East Germany and Czechoslovakia during the final two months of 1989 was the product of several common factors: the disintegration of leadership groups that were opposed to Gorbachev's reforms; social pressure; and finally, though not least important, the response of the Soviet Union to the collapse of its external empire. The internal stability of Eastern Europe represented a higher priority for Western political officials and strategists than the region's democratization. This was not the result of great power cynicism: over a period of four decades, the United States and its allies had learned to coexist with the Cold War. Officials in the West feared that the unexpected and uncontrolled disappearance of the Soviet adversary could produce a political vacuum resulting in deep social and ethnic conflicts that might even entail the use of nuclear weapons. In July 1989, the deputy chief of the foreign-policy committee of the Hungarian Socialist Workers' Party, Imre Szokai, remarked with some astonishment: "It is the firm view of our West European partners that to preserve European stability and the historically evolved status quo there should be no regime change in Hungary[;] Hungarian politics should not impinge upon the Soviet Union's security, military and political interests (they consider even mention of exit from the Warsaw Pact a dangerous fiction)."[111] In September 1989, former US national security adviser Zbigniew Brzezinski, one of the country's foremost experts on Eastern Bloc affairs, traveled to Moscow in order to ask Soviet officials to preserve the Warsaw Pact in accordance with US interests.

In East Germany, the small opposition networks that had been working in isolation merged into a political movement in the autumn of 1989. On September 4, the first Monday demonstration was held in Leipzig with the participation of those who had attended the weekly prayer-for-peace at St. Nicholas Church. East German authorities became alarmed at the growing size of these Monday demonstrations and the increasingly sharp debates that occurred during them regarding current political issues. The activity of the opposition associated with the Neues Forum opposition movement reached a turning point with the events that took place on October 9—two days after the official celebration of the fortieth anniversary of the foundation of the German Democratic Republic. Authorities had already prepared to violently suppress the mass demonstrations in Leipzig, though they decided against utilizing the Chinese model to end the protests after reconsidering the political costs of doing so under pressure from the Soviet Union. Both the demonstrators and the international media regarded the decision of the Honecker regime not to use force as evidence that it was teetering toward collapse. Over the following month, demonstrations spread throughout East Germany despite Honecker's resignation and the attempt to renew the SED leadership. Finally, on November 9, party Central Committee member Günter Schabowski committed a fatal communication error during an international press conference, announcing the immediate opening of the border between West Berlin and East Berlin without prior consultation with his superiors. As a result of this ill-considered remark, thousands of Berliners began to move freely across the border that constituted the widely despised symbol of Europe's internal division.[112] That night, the unintentional fall of the Berlin Wall marked the symbolic end of the world order that had been based on the bipolar, competitive political system.

Contrary to the other countries of the Eastern Bloc, the German Democratic Republic lost its intimate legitimacy as a state with the collapse of the communist system, since the GDR had existed in the name of introducing and implementing Soviet-type socialism. Talks regarding the possible reunification of the two German states began in Bonn in the weeks after the collapse of the Berlin Wall. On November 28, 1989, Chancellor Helmut Kohl of West Germany ignored the doubts of the Christian Democratic Union's liberal coalition partner and the open disapproval of the social-democratic and green opposition, introducing his ten-point plan to achieve German unity within a confederative structure.[113] Soviet leaders opposed this plan to reunify Germany primarily because they feared it would lead to the expansion of NATO, while the political establishments of the United Kingdom, France, and Italy regarded it with concern. Even members of the main East German and Polish opposition groups maintained reservations about Kohl's German-reunification plan: many East German dissidents advocated the establishment of a genuinely pluralistic German Democratic Republic or a unified, though neutral Germany, while their Polish counterparts believed that the process of uniting the GDR and the FRG might divert the attention of West German political officials from the changes taking place in Warsaw. According to Mary Elise Sarotte, the rapid and somewhat painful reunification of Germany was the product of a series of "imperfect decisions" resulting from West Germany's haste to take advantage of the singular historical opportunity that had presented itself. The activity of European cooperative organizations and the eastward expansion of NATO served to further deepen the crisis that Gorbachev and his allies within the Soviet leadership had already been confronting for quite some time. Gorbachev faced charges in the Soviet Union that he had permitted the unification of West Germany and East Germany in exchange for a package of economic and financial assistance, which the reeling Soviet economy had immediately consumed.[114]

In November 1989, the East German crisis exercised a destabilizing influence on the steadiest communist regime in Central Europe—that of Czechoslovakia. Communist leaders in Prague were not enthusiastic about perestroika and even attempted to prevent Soviet-style opening.[115] The Jakeš regime was particularly apprehensive about the first Soviet disarmament plans. CPSU officials, in fact, persuaded Gorbachev to reject a March 1987 proposal from his advisors to withdraw Soviet troops from Czechoslovakia and to conduct a positive reappraisal of the Dubček's 1968 reforms on the grounds that such a plan was untimely. Czechoslovakia's economy, though stagnating, showed the greatest degree of stability in the socialist bloc. The Czechoslovak opposition was weak, divided, closely monitored, and apolitical, while the Communist Party had no internal reform faction that was receptive to change.

However, the collapse of the East German regime following the negotiated transitions in Poland and Hungary prompted Czechoslovak citizens to take action to induce political change in their country as well. The hundreds of thousands of civilians who beginning on November 16, 1989, occupied schools, workshops, and factories throughout Czechoslovakia were not protesting against cold and hunger as they would in Bucharest later that year. The outrage caused by the regime's overreaction to a peaceful demonstration rapidly created the national sense of a revolutionary community, whose action was nonviolent, self-organized, and spontaneous. The "gentle" revolutionaries' stated goals were freedom, fairness and, above all, humanity and humaneness.[116]

The moral opposition movement, which the Václav Havel–led Civic Forum managed to provide with political content, caused the collapse of the Czechoslovak communist regime. The Velvet Revolution that took place in Czechoslovakia concluded with the election of Havel to serve as the country's new president and the formation of a new government that for the first time in more than forty years was not under the control of the CPSU. However, as James Krapfl claimed when analyzing opinion polls carried out in late 1989, uncertainty remained as far as the citizens' demand list was concerned. An opinion poll conducted in November 1989 found that 45 percent of interviewed persons would have preferred a socialist development, 47 percent some in-between system, and only 3 percent Western-like capitalism. One month later, these percentages only slightly shifted toward a mixed economic system.[117] Moreover, the vexed issue of Czech and Slovak institutional coexistence reemerged shortly after the establishment of the new, democratic state of Czechoslovakia.

Betrayed Hopes? Romania, 1989–1990

The 1989 Romanian revolution began almost accidentally in the multiethnic city of Timişoara, the capital of the Banat region of western Romania near the borders of Hungary and Yugoslavia, where on December 15, 1989, a few civilians gathered before the home of Reformed assistant pastor László Tőkés, who had entered in conflict with his state-loyal bishop. Romanian authorities used force to disperse demonstrations over the following two days, and the army killed about sixty people in the process, although international news agencies, citing Hungarian and Yugoslav sources, started soon reporting much higher figures. After the bloodshed, Ceauşescu was persuaded by his assistants that the situation was under control in Timişoara. This misperception led him to commit the fatal error to travel to Iran to sign an agreement for the shipment of arms and military equipment. By the time he returned to Romania, Timişoara had been declared a free city and the protests had spread to other big cities and also the capital Bucharest, while the army and the so-called anti-terrorist units of the police began shooting at demonstrators. On December 21, Ceauşescu voiced condemnation of the demonstrations during a speech at a political assembly in Bucharest broadcast live on Romanian television. However, the Romanian dictator's censure of the protests backfired in grotesque fashion. Those gathered at the assembly began to chant anti-regime slogans and attacked the RCP Central Committee headquarters. On December 22, Nicolae and Elena Ceauşescu were forced against their will to board a helicopter that transported them from the besieged Central Committee building and out of Bucharest. The circle appeared to close with the capture of the Ceauşescus and the December 25 verdict of the Revolutionary Court sentencing them to death.[118]

Evaluations of the 1989 Romanian Revolution remain contradictory even two and a half decades after the event. Those who had taken part in the uprising pinpointed its spontaneous, civilian character.[119] Postcommunist governments and cultural elites in search of democratic legitimation overemphasized the positive role of the Romanian Army, underlying the beneficent function played by the only political institution that had emerged from the upheaval, the National Salvation Front (NSF) led by a former Communist functionary, Ion Iliescu.[120] However, how was it possible that the all-powerful Securitate failed to suppress the small demonstration of solidarity in Timişoara? The many logical shortcomings of the official narrative stimulated criticism from both analysts and witnesses already beginning in the early 1990s.[121] Anti-communist revolutionaries from Timişoara and those affiliated with liberal right wing (to further simplify, anti-Iliescu) political parties concede that the 1989 events started as a genuine popular revolt but ended in a hijacked or expropriated revolution.[122] Many scholars regard the overthrow of Ceaușescu and the victory of the unarmed civilian rebels on December 22 as a turning point. They believe that Ion Iliescu and Gorbachevist pro-reform communists coalesced around him seized power on December 22 and expropriated the revolution via the National Salvation Front.

Other critics claimed that the revolutionary events of December 1989 cannot be called a revolution because they would fit into a long-standing Romanian pattern of army-sponsored palace coups. More radical deniers of the popular character of the upheaval that occurred in Romania in December 1989 have produced or sided a third, much bolder hypothesis: the collapse of the communist dictatorship would have the result of a foreign-supported putsch that required the rebellion of the masses to provide cover for their activities.[123] This explanation of the causes of the events that resulted in the overthrow of Ceaușescu are founded on the insufficiently corroborated notion of Soviet and Hungarian diversion. The other suggestive but unconfirmed landmark of this theory concerns the decision to replace Ceaușescu with a more palatable leader, that would have been personally taken by US president George H. W. Bush and Soviet leader Gorbachev at their summit meeting held in Malta on December 2 and 3, 1989.[124] According to archival sources, the Romanian security service informed Ceaușescu that they had full evidence of a deal reached in Malta between the superpowers. Soviet troops would be allowed to enter Romania to support the anti-Ceaușescu movement as an exchange for the Soviet noninterference in Panama.[125] However, the theory fails to explain why President Bush, who was known as a political pragmatist, would have approved such a risky intervention in an almost isolated country that was a member of the Warsaw Pact.

The amount of manipulated or patently false information that have been spread around the 1989 Romanian events might explain why international scholars, rather than formulating a strong independent narrative offer a set of factors as preconditions for a revolution: the breakdown of the state, a permissive international environment, and the mobilization of challengers to the established power.[126] Available evidence refutes the notion of Soviet (and Hungarian) deliberate provocation and rather suggests that the Soviets were too preoccupied with German reunification and separatist movements in the Baltics, the Caucasus, and Central Asia to raise objections with regard to the Romanian question. Although Gorbachev personally detested Ceaușescu's policies and leadership style, the Soviet leader was satisfied to merely urge his Romanian counterpart during their final meeting in Moscow on December 4, 1989, to launch reforms resembling those undertaken throughout the rest of the Eastern Bloc.[127] The Soviet leadership played no direct role in the violent overthrow of a regime that posed no immediate threat to the military and economic interests of the Soviet Union.[128] Quoting a range of contemporary Soviet sources, Constantin Pleshakov asserts that CPSU officials actually declined to intervene in Romania in order to support the National Salvation Front.[129] According to a Polish military file quoted by Adam Burakowski, on December 23, 1989, Soviet officials even rejected an "urgent request for military and political support" from the Iliescu-led provisional Romanian government following Ceaușescu's overthrow.[130] The outbreak of the popular uprising in Romania in December 1989 represented the culmination of a long process. The austerity program caused distress among the people of Romania. By this time, average citizens had begun to question the success of national communism even if they did not deny the legitimacy of the communist system in general.

In the absence of alternative anti-regime movements, many Romanian citizens who had not participated in the events directly connected to the revolution regarded the National Salvation Front as the sole organization capable of undertaking the process of rebuilding the collapsed state.[131] In several Hungarian-inhabited cities of eastern Transylvania the regime change ended up in episodes of crude violence performed by ordinary citizens against the (mostly Romanian) representatives of the most hatred state agency, the Militia, as well in the sacking of public institutions and local facilities.[132] In the rest of the country, the transition to some new form of political setting went remarkably smoothly and the Hungarian community pulled together around the newly established Democratic Alliance of Hungarians in Romania.

However, it was difficult to prevent social and ethnic tensions from exploding into open conflict. The situation escalated following the announcement of the NSF that it had transformed itself into a party to participate in impending national elections. Miners from the Jiu Valley attacked participants in enormous demonstrations that the newly reconstituted historical liberal and peasant parties organized in early 1990. The radical faction of the civilian revolutionary associations convened for the first time in Timișoara on March 11 to issue the demand that former party activists be prohibited from performing official functions—a demand that unambiguously referred to NSF leader Iliescu and former political-police officials.[133]

Moreover, ethnic clashes erupted between Hungarians and Romanians in the city of Târgu Mureș on March 19 and 20, 1990, claiming six casualties and several hundred injuries. Due to the confusion of the period of political transition and the unsatisfied material and emotional needs that had long accumulated within Romanian society, almost all the economic issues that emerged in this mixed-nationality Transylvanian city, from shortages of food and basic necessities and inflation to unemployment and the distribution of foreign relief, assumed an ethnic dimension. Meanwhile, the legitimacy crisis and organizational disintegration of state organs prompted the local Romanian elite to take its fate into its own hands. The conflict between Romanians and Hungarians in Târgu Mureș was the effect of local causes; therefore, it would be a mistake to think that it was merely instigated either from Bucharest or Budapest.[134] It was not in the interest of the Romanian state to transform the most ethnically diverse region of Transylvania into a second Kosovo, particularly considering the rather inauspicious international reputation of Romania with regard to treatment of minority nationalities. The most plausible explanation for the lack of action from central authorities to end the ethnic clashes is that the political parties in Bucharest, which were busy preparing for Romania's May elections, simply lacked the capacity to react to the conflict. Only the belated intervention of the army managed to stabilize the situation in the city.

The National Salvation Front won a landslide victory in national elections held on May 20, 1990, receiving more than two-thirds of all votes cast, while NSF leader Ion Iliescu was elected president with 85 percent of votes. The weak and scattered opposition tried to challenge NSF revolutionary legitimacy by transforming itself into a permanently mobilized anti-communist force through the students' protest in Bucharest and in other major cities. The moral rejection of the Iliescu-led semiauthoritarian system marked the birth of the myth of the unfinished revolution and entrapped the pluralistic public sphere in the binary logic of "us" against "them." Starting from these premises, return of "Stalinist-fascist baroque" after the Târgu Mureş clash anticipated the rise of illiberal civil society as exemplified by the activity of the unofficial pro-NSF militia culminated in the bloody procession of miners through the streets of Bucharest between June 13 and 15, 1990. The first, infamous violent demonstration labeled "Mineriad" claimed dozens of victims and was followed until autumn 1991 by three other episodes of incumbent use of politics by other means. This event marked the end of the long revolution that began in December 1989 and the beginning of a distressing institutional transition in Romania. As Cristian Bogdan Iacob has pointed out, what made the Romanian situation special in an Eastern European comparative perspective was the upward spiral of extrainstitutional pressure from the streets on systemic transformation. Between 1990 and late 1991, the government led by Petre Roman was assigned the impossible task to navigate a heterogeneous coalition of reform socialists and nationalists into the unknown realm of Western-type democracy.[135]

Notes

1. For the international context surrounding *Ostpolitik*, see Melloni, *Il filo sottile*. The secret papers of Vatican's top diplomat Agostino Casaroli are mentioned in Barberini, *La politica del dialogo*.

2. Fink and Schaefer, *Ostpolitik, 1969–1974*.

3. Bange and Niedhart, *Helsinki 1975 and the Transformation of Europe*.

4. Savranskaya, "Human Rights Movement in the USSR," 26–40.

5. See in detail Romano, "Untying Cold War Knots," 163–173.

6. On the substantial change in US foreign policy toward the region, see Miller, Selvage, and Van Hook, *Foreign Relations of the United States*; Kraemer, *Foreign Relations of the United States*.

7. On the relationship between US policy making and the Eastern European diaspora, see Ambrosio, *Ethnic Identity Groups and U.S. Foreign Policy*; Kádár Lynn, *Inauguration of Organized Political Warfare*.

8. Gökay, *L'Europa orientale*, 14.

9. Crampton, *Eastern Europe in the Twentieth Century*, 345.

10. Majtényi, *K-vonal*.

11. See the studies of Stephen Lowell and Paulina Bren on the social function of weekend houses in the Soviet Union and Czechoslovakia in Crowley and Reid, *Socialist Spaces*, 105–140.

12. Freifeld, "Cult of March 15," 276–277.

13. Amanda Swain, "'Freedom for Lithuania'" or 'Freedom for Hippies'?" (paper presented at the "Memories of Stalinism" seminar, University of Bologna, September 29, 2010).

14. Colas et al., *L'Europe post-communiste*, 35.

15. Kotkin, *Uncivil Society*, 11–16.

16. Graziosi, *Guerra e rivoluzione in Europa*, 79.

17. Kligman, *Politics of Duplicity*, 15.

18. Tomka, *Welfare in East and West*, 47–48.

19. Zaslavsky, *Storia del sistema sovietico*, 264.

20. Bacon and Sandle, *Brezhnev Reconsidered*. For a comparative perspective, see Klumbyte and Sharafutdinova, *Soviet Society in the Era of Late Socialism*.

21. Ledeneva, *Russia's Economy of Favours*.

22. Horváth, *Kádár gyermekei*.

23. Romsics, *Hungary in the Twentieth Century*, 386–387.

24. Crampton, *Eastern Europe in the Twentieth Century*, 345–346.

25. On the East German economy, see Stokes, *Constructing Socialism*.

26. Berend, *From the Soviet Bloc to the European Union*, 29–30.

27. Berend, *Storia economica dell'Europa nel XX secolo*, 205.

28. Botos, "Magyarország IMF-csatlakozásának előtörténete," 82–102. For a fresh account based on new sources from the IMF archives, see Mong, *Kádár hitele*.

29. Schröder, "IMF and the Countries of the Council for Mutual Economic Assistance," 87–90; Gabanyi, "Ceaușescu Admits Economic Failures, Eschews Responsibility," 3–8; Kalabinski, "How World Bank Bailouts Aid East European Regimes."

30. Lavigne, *International Political Economy and Socialism*, 344–345.

31. Boughton, *Silent Revolution*, 320–325.

32. IMF Archives, Washington, DC, European Department-EURAI files, Romania, Correspondence and Memos 1988–1989, Memorandum for Files, November 22, 1989, Romania: Recent Development.

33. Ban, "Sovereign Debt, Austerity, and Regime Change," 743–776.

34. See in detail Graziosi, *L'URSS dal trionfo al degrado*, 477–498.

35. Graziosi, "I perché del collasso dell'URSS," 348.

36. Rothschild, *Return to Diversity*, 196–198.

37. Historical Archives of the Hungarian State Security, Budapest (Állambiztonsági Szolgálatok Történeti Levéltára), fond 3.2.5, file 0-8-552, vol. 15, f. 90, Evaluation regarding the possible successors of Pope Paul VI, August 15, 1975.

38. Lipski, *KOR*.

39. Historical Archives of the Hungarian State Security, fond 3.2.5. file 0-8-552, vol. 14, f. 72, On the personality of Pope John Paul II and the consequences of his election, January 2, 1979.

40. Wandycz, *Il prezzo della libertà*, 168.

41. Mark Kramer, "Soviet Deliberations during the Polish Crisis, 1980–1981," 15.

42. Ibid., 25–33.

43. Rothschild, *Return to Diversity*, 210.

44. Kopecek, "Citizen and Patriot in the Post-Totalitarian Era," Tr@nsit online, Institute for Human Sciences in Vienna, http://www.iwm.at/transit/transit-online/citizen-and-patriot-in -the-post-totalitarian-era/ (accessed April 13, 2016).

45. Stehle, *Eastern Politics of the Vatican*, 331–341.

46. See Duray's autobiography, *Kutyaszorítóban*.

47. Mong, *Kádár hitele*, 171–274.

48. On the context of the economic transformation in Eastern Europe, see Szelényi, "New Grand Bourgeoisie under Post-Communism."

49. Kemény, "Unregistered Economy in Hungary," 349–366.

50. Csizmadia, *Diskurzus és diktatúra*, 93–195.

51. On the Hungarian democratic opposition, see Csizmadia, *A magyar demokratikus ellenzék*. See also Bozóki, "A magyar demokratikus ellenzék," 7–45; Csizmadia, "Hungarian Democratic Opposition in the 1980s," 119–138.

52. Fulbrook, *People's State*, 12, 297.

53. Fulbrook, *People's State*, 236.

54. Gieseke, *History of the Stasi*, chapter 4.

55. Fulbrook, *Anatomy of a Dictatorship*, 83–85.

56. Lorenzini, *Il rifiuto di un'eredità difficile*.

57. Zatlin, *Currency of Socialism*, 253.

58. Harrington, and Courtney, *Tweaking the Nose of the Russians*.

59. Novák, *Aranykorszak?*, 64–102.

60. For the cult of personality around Nicolae Ceauşescu and his family, see Gabanyi, *Ceauşescu Cult*; Marin, *Originea şi evoluţia cultului personalităţii lui Nicolae Ceauşescu*.

61. Marin, *Originea şi evoluţia*, 577–578.

62. See Ioanid, *The Ransom of the Jews*; Dobre, Banu, and Stancu, *Acţiunea "Recuperarea."*

63. Deletant, *Ceauşescu and the Securitate*, 139. For the position of Hungary's government toward refugees, see Révész, "'Out of Romania!,'" 8–66.

64. Bottoni, "Find the Enemy: Ethnicized State Violence and Population Control in Ceauşescu's Romania," *Journal of Cold War Studies* (forthcoming).

65. Dobre, *Securitatea*; Moldovan, Anisescu, and Matiu, *"Partiturile" Securităţii*.

66. Tóth, *Ellenpontok 1982*.

67. Petrescu, *From Robin Hood to Don Quixote*, 34.

68. Rus, *Valea Jiului*.

69. Crampton, *Concise History of Bulgaria*, 195.

70. Rothschild, *Return to Diversity*, 215.

71. Hungarian National Archives (Magyar Nemzeti Levéltár), fond XIX-J-1-j, Foreign Ministry 1945–1990, Report from the Hungarian Embassy in Sofia, box 89, file 004519, Visit to Bulgaria of Enrico Berlinguer on October 23, 1973. See also Pons, *Berlinguer e la fine del comunismo*, 33–42.

72. Dimitrov, "In Search of a Homogeneous Nation," 9.

73. Ibid., 11–16.

74. Lampe, *Yugoslavia as History*, 312–315.

75. Pavlowitch, *Serbia*, 234.

76. Franzinetti, *I Balcani dal 1878 a oggi*, 85–86.

77. Lampe, *Yugoslavia as History*, 320–334.

78. Franzinetti, *I Balcani dal 1878 a oggi*, 87.

79. Pavlowitch, *Serbia*, 235.

80. Ramet, *Whose Democracy?*, 141.

81. Malcolm, *Storia della Bosnia*, 289–290.

82. Ibid., 278.

83. Malcolm, *Storia del Kosovo*, 334–340.

84. Franzinetti, *I Balcani dal 1878 a oggi*, 71.

85. On the personal merits of Gorbachev in the new Soviet policy making, see Brown, *Gorbachev Factor*.

86. Kotkin, *Armageddon Averted*, 58–67.

87. On Gorbachev's foreign policy, see the firsthand account of his former adviser Andrei Grachev, *Gorbachev's Gamble*.

88. Graziosi, *L'URSS dal trionfo al degrado*, 503–579.

89. Savranskaya, Blanton, and Zubok, *Masterpieces of History*.

90. Bettanin, "I costi dell'impero," 21–53.

91. Kramer, "Collapse of East European Communism (Part I)," 178–256.

92. "Soviet Policy toward Eastern Europe under Gorbachev," National Intelligence Estimate, May 1988, http://www.cia.gov/library/center-for-the-study-of-intelligence/csi-publications/books-and-monographs/at-cold-wars-end-us-intelligence-on-the-soviet-union-and-eastern-europe-1989-1991/16526pd les/NIE1112-9-88.pdf.

93. Bianchini, *L'Europa orientale*, 6.

94. Staniszkis, *Dynamics of the Breakthrough in Eastern Europe*, 111–116.

95. See Joachim von Puttkamer's ongoing project on state violence and social conflict during the Polish transition (seminar lecture at Imre Kertész Kolleg, Jena, on March 9, 2015, and conference paper at Imre Kertész Kolleg annual conference on June 11, 2015).

96. On the political involvement of the youth, see Junes, *Student Politics in Communist Poland*, 189–252.

97. For more detail, see Hardy, *Poland's New Capitalism*.

98. Szabó, *A magyar államadósság keletkezése*, http://www.penzriport.hu/letoltes/Magyar_allamadossag_keletkezese_1973_1989.pdf.

99. Tőkés, *Hungary's Negotiated Revolution*, 426–427.

100. Csizmadia, *Diskurzus és diktatúra*, 78.

101. Kalmár, *Történelmi galaxisok vonzásában*, 568–605.

102. Romsics, *Hungary in the Twentieth Century*, 431.

103. Bozóki, *Roundtable Talks of 1989*.

104. Oplatka, *Egy döntés története*, 263.

105. Eyal, Szelényi, and Townsley, *Making Capitalism without Capitalists*.

106. Báger and Kovács, *Privatisation in Hungary*, 25.

107. Kornai, *The Road to a Free Economy*.

108. Crampton, *Concise History of Bulgaria*, 210.

109. For the negotiated changes in Bulgaria, see Pleshakov, *Berlino 1989*, 250–255.

110. Franzinetti, *I Balcani dal 1878 a oggi*, 84–85.

111. Borhi, "Reluctant and Fearful West," 64.

112. For the final years of East Germany's existence, see Maier, *Dissolution*.

113. Sarotte, *1989*, 76.

114. Ibid., 119–149.

115. Rothschild, *Return to Diversity*, 235.

116. Krapfl, *Revolution with a Human Face*.

117. James Kraft, "1990 in Czechoslovakia" (paper presented at the annual conference of Imre Kertész Kolleg, Jena, June 11–12, 2015).

118. Siani-Davies, *Romanian Revolution of December 1989*, 97–99.

119. Mioc, *Revoluţia fără mistere*.

120. Scurtu, *Revoluţia română din decembrie 1989 în context international*.

121. On early criticisms of the official interpretation, see Portocala, *Autopsie du coup d'état roumain*; Gabanyi, *Die unvollendete Revolution*; Ratesh, *Romania*.

122. Cesereanu, *Decembrie '89*.

123. See Stoenescu, *Istoria loviturilor de Stat din România*.

124. Susanne Brandstätter, *Checkmate—Strategy of a Revolution*, 2003, documentary film coproduction by ORF/3sat, ZDF/ARTE.

125. Historical Archives of the Hungarian State Security, fond 1.11.4—T-III/89, box 542, f. 221, intelligence cable from Bucharest, December 21, 1989.

126. Siani-Davies, *Romanian Revolution of December 1989*, chapter 4. See also the deconstruction work of Hall, "Uses of Absurdity," 501–542; and id., "Theories of Collective Action and Revolution," 1069–1093.

127. For the minutes of the last Gorbachev-Ceauşescu meeting on December 4, 1989, see Betea, "Ultima vizită a lui Nicolae Ceauşescu la Moscova I-II," 82–88 and 86–92; there is also a reconstruction in Pleshakov, *Berlino 1989*, 269–272.

128. Kramer, "Collapse of East European Communism (Part II)," 26.

129. Pleshakov, *Berlino 1989*, 285–86.

130. Adam Burakowski, "În decembrie 1989, Iliescu şi Brucan au cerut ajutor militar de la sovietici," *Revista 22* (Bucharest), February 2, 2010, http://revista22online.ro/7557/.html (accessed March 25, 2017).

131. For an examination of the cultural legacy of the 1989 Romanian Revolution, see Murgescu, *Revoluţia română din 1989*.

132. New insights are found in Bárdi, Gidó, and Novák, *Primele forme de autoorganizare a maghiarilor din România*.

133. Burcea and Bumbes, "Lustrabilii," 256–257.

134. László and Novák, *A szabadság terhe*.

135. Cristian Bogdan Iacob, "1990 in Romania and Bulgaria" (paper presented at the annual conference of Imre Kertész Kolleg, Jena, June 11–12, 2015).

Chapter 5

Return to Europe?
The Postcommunist Galaxy

1989 and the National Factor

The changes that occurred in the Eastern Bloc in 1989 and 1990 resulted in an astonishingly rapid redrawing of the political map and social landscape of Europe. Several years after this transformation, the philosopher Ralf Dahrendorf asserted that the history of Europe had begun to revolve uncontrollably.[1] Political scientist Timothy Garton Ash, who had been a privileged witness of the dramatic changes that affected Central and Eastern Europe in 1989, coined the oft-quoted definition of *refolutions* to underline the interplay of revolutionary changes and reform-minded peaceful transition.[2] In a later writing, he insisted that "1989 left realities. Yet there was something new; there was a big new idea, and that was the revolution itself—the idea of the non-revolutionary revolution, the evolutionary revolution. That particular motto of peaceful, sustained, marvelously inventive, massive civil disobedience channeled into an oppositional elite—that was the historical novelty of 1989."[3]

More recently, Karol Edward Sołtan suggested that the Eastern European transformations should be placed in the context of a global turn toward a moderate modernity, which eschewed radical transformation in developmental process that included transitional societies placed in different geographical contexts. Vladimir Tismăneanu also argued that the revolutions of 1989, whatever the eventual disappointments they might have caused, embodied, in their pragmatic rejection of millenarian visions of ideal society, a set of universal values based on notions like citizenship and civility.[4] It seems appropriate, then, to start the analysis of the consequences of 1989 by shortly describing the impact the Eastern European changes had on the geopolitical map of the continent.

The most explosive consequence of the fall of the Soviet Bloc was the re-unification of the two German states less than a year after the fall of the Berlin Wall. The memory of the Nazi past imbued German unification, which was not devoid of threat to the stability of Europe, with special importance. One can state without exaggeration that the Helmut Kohl–led Christian-democratic and lib-eral political class created a masterpiece in reunified Germany. The decisive ac-tions of the Franco-German axis and European Commission president Jacques Delors laid the foundations for the conclusion of the Maastricht Treaty (Febru-ary 7, 1992), the introduction of the euro, and a new phase of European economic integration.

While in Western Europe the demise of the Soviet Bloc boosted the suprana-tional integration, in the Eastern part of the continent it prompted an unexpected ethnic and national revival. The de facto secession of these republics exacerbated internal conflicts within the leadership of the Soviet Union. Boris Yeltsin, who became the first president of the Russian Federation in June 1991, advocated the creation of an independent Russia, while CPSU General Secretary Gorbachev, whose social legitimacy was steadily weakening, continued to support the anach-ronistic preservation of a supranational state entity.

Desperate Soviet actions to defend the territorial integrity of the state, most important the attack of Latvia and Lithuania in January 1991, sealed the politi-cal fate of the Soviet Union and jeopardized Gorbachev's leadership at home. At the decisive moment, the formerly progressive Gorbachev embraced similar viewpoints to those of the most conservative wing of the CPSU.[5] On August 19, 1991, shortly before the scheduled signing of the agreement intended to restruc-ture the Soviet Union, conservatives led a putsch against Gorbachev. Although the intervention of Boris Yeltsin and the military thwarted this coup d'état, the disintegration of the Soviet Union had already begun: Estonia and Latvia im-mediately declared independence and by September five other republics of the Soviet Union had done the same. The Communist Party of the Soviet Union was officially banned and its organizations dissolved. The Commonwealth of Inde-pendent States was founded in place of the Soviet Union, but the three Baltic states chose not to join the new federation. On December 25, 1991, Gorbachev resigned from his office as president of the formally dissolved Soviet Union, after which the Soviet flag was lowered at the Kremlin. In its place the Russian tricolor was raised. By this time the Soviet military occupation of large parts of Eastern Europe had peacefully ended, and the Council of Mutual Economic Assistance and the Warsaw Pact had been disbanded (although contention regarding inter-nal debt and the distribution of goods and equipment continued for some years after the 1991 decision).[6]

The imperial legacy in the Eastern European peripheries emerged soon as a major obstacle to their full integration into the new pan-European framework.

The case of Moldova, a small post-Soviet republic with a population of just 3 million, provides a clear example of how the ambiguous legal framework of the Soviet disintegration (the 1977 Soviet Constitution guaranteed the right to self-determination to all republics of the Soviet Union, and this legitimized Moldova's secession) produced nationality conflict even in absence of a local pattern of ethnic or religious hatred.

In the spring of 1992 an armed conflict broke out between the central government of the Republic of Moldova and secessionist militia of the primarily Russian- and Ukrainian-inhabited Transnistria. The small-scale war resulted in several hundred casualties on both sides and eventually required international intervention. In July 1992, President Mircea Snegur of Moldova and President Boris Yeltsin of Russia signed a cease-fire agreement that instituted security zones along the Dniester River and prescribed the deployment of Russian peacekeeping forces. The Snegur-Yeltsin agreement also established the Joint Control Commission, composed of representatives from Moldova, the Transnistria secessionists, Russia, Ukraine, and the Organization for Security and Co-operation in Europe (OSCE). The OSCE peace plan, which the US Senate and various international organizations supported, strengthened Moldova's territorial integrity and called for the withdrawal of Russian troops from the region of conflict.[7] However, Russia did not withdraw its troops by 2002, and relations between Transnistria, which has a population of just over a half million and its capital city in Tiraspol, and Moldova are still unsettled—hence the "frozen conflict" elaborated by scholars of post–Cold War ethnic issues, by which violent ethno-political struggles over secession have led to the establishment of a de facto regime, recognized by neither the international community nor the state from which it seceded.[8]

The former Soviet Union has become a site for great-power competition through geopolitical aspects such as energy, and it remains important to global security. All the ongoing frozen conflicts in that region rest on five overarching themes: sovereignty, also framed as the issue of state and nation building; power and geopolitics; transnational terrorist networks; identity and ethnicity between traditional and postmodern patterns; and finally, structures of patronage and privilege, which cut across and between different governance structures.[9] Following Moscow's goals, Moldova has since become one of the several frozen conflicts of the post-Soviet world, along with other contested regions like Abkhazia and South Ossetia against Georgia, or the Nagorno-Karabakh dispute between Armenia, backed by Russia, and Azerbaijan. Moldova remains important today; it is a model for mastering the much more extensive and military worrisome Ukrainian conflict that erupted in 2014, and it is discussed in the next chapter.

The fall of internationalist communism and the demise of the Soviet empire have also put the notions of ethnicity, nation, and national egoism back on the international agenda, paradoxically just as the Western European consolidated democracies enhanced their cooperation in the European Union. As Map 5.1 shows, between 1991 and 2008 new nation-states emerged or reemerged in Eastern Europe and the former Soviet Union as the result of the disintegration of three multinational states (the Soviet Union, Czechoslovakia, and Yugoslavia): the European, Caucasian, and Central Asian former Soviet republics, seven former Yugoslav republics and regions, and the two former republics of federal Czechoslovakia. Only five states in the region (Poland, Hungary, Romania, Bulgaria, and Albania) preserved their former configuration.

The Western European political elite harbored mixed feelings regarding the supremacy of the sovereignty-based national factor. Many feared that the triumph of the old paradigm of territorial sovereignty in Central and Eastern Europe, as normalized after the Peace of Westphalia in 1648, would lead to catastrophe, as it had during the first half of the twentieth century. The overlap between administrative and ethnic borders, which social anthropologist Ernest Gellner famously called the basic goal of every nationalist movement, was considered legitimate and timely from the perspective of the postcommunist and/or post-Soviet political elites. But the asynchrony of traditional nation-state claims in Eastern Europe with the globalization process and the European supranational integration could not have been more strident. The armed conflict that erupted in Yugoslavia during the summer of 1991 appeared to confirm the most pessimistic expectations regarding the impact of the rebirth of nationalism in Eastern Europe. Many analysts characterized the discord in Eastern Europe, particularly the Balkans, during the 1990s as the typical product of ethnic hatred and nationalist rhetoric. As shown previously in this book, though, nationality-based conflict and rivalry between linguistic and religious groups are an organic component of modern Eastern European history. The communist system failed to address genuine issues related to nationality and was thus able to alleviate them only temporarily—if at all. However, with the notable exception of Yugoslavia, the collapse of multinational states in the east of Europe in the 1990s did not end in catastrophe, instead resulting in the establishment of new democratic or, at the very least, hybrid political systems based on the principle of multiparty pluralism. This result should not be underestimated, considering the recent history of Eastern Europe and accumulated mutual grievances in the region. The peaceful dissolution of Czechoslovakia, for example, put an end to a common state that generations of politicians and intellectuals had struggled to create though had proved unable to serve the often contradictory interests of its various nationalities.[10] Evidence suggests that both the Czech Republic and Slovakia have been able to take greater advantage of the benefits of capitalism and European integration as separate entities rather than as part of a union burdened by permanent conflicts.

Map 5.1. Eastern Europe, 1995. Courtesy Béla Nagy, Hungarian Academy of Sciences.

Naturally, this does not mean that the postcommunist states of Eastern Europe all found reassuring answers to their issues of nationality. The governments of Germany and the Czech Republic maintained disagreements regarding the still-valid Beneš decrees, which provided for the expulsion of Germans from Czechoslovakia following the Second World War and reparations for those expelled and their descendants. In Transylvania, relations between the region's Romanian majority and Hungarian minority remained tense for many years after the collapse of the Ceaușescu regime, although they began to improve in the late 1990s—a circumstance that has exercised a positive impact on bilateral relations between Romania and Hungary.[11] During the 1990s, a number of officials in Eastern Europe exploited nationality conflicts to achieve electoral success. Gheorghe Funar, who served three successive terms as mayor of Cluj-Napoca between 1992 and 2004 and has served as president of the Romanian National Unity Party and, subsequently, general secretary of the Greater Romania Party, is a classic example. In the 1990s, the Romanians who accounted for the majority of the inhabitants of Cluj-Napoca experienced everyday relations between nationalities much differently than did the Hungarians, who constituted about one-sixth of the city's population. However, the identity of the state-supported majority Romanians remained practically "unmarked," as it was regarded to be self-evident. Members of the city's Hungarian community, to the contrary, were much more concerned with issues surrounding their national identity. Only when the Romanians of Cluj-Napoca realized that their Hungarian neighbors posed no threat to their everyday existence and that enveloping the city's public spaces in the colors of the Romanian flag would not draw foreign investment or create local jobs did they withdraw their support from nationalist Funar and elect more pragmatic municipal leaders.[12]

An especially interesting case of belated nation building concerns the Baltic area, which regained its independence after more than half a century under foreign domination. As Andrea Graziosi and Paul Kennedy have demonstrated, the nonviolent nature of this process was not predestined. The largely peaceful independence of Estonia, Latvia, and Lithuania in 1991 was the result of responsible and rational decisions, supported by the overwhelming majority of the local population who acted with civic courage during the struggle with Moscow. On August 23, 1989, 2 million people formed a human chain that linked three capital cities—Vilnius in Lithuania, Riga in Latvia, and Tallinn in Estonia—symbolically marking their condemnation of the infamous Molotov-Ribbentrop Pact on its fiftieth anniversary: the largest political demonstration of any time in Soviet-dominated Eastern Europe. Both the Soviet-Russian and the Baltic-state elites deserve credit for their pragmatism, which made possible the negotiated

resolution of the most important issues connected to secession despite their contradictory interests.[13]

As a result of the Russification that took place in Latvia and Estonia, Russian
is still the native language of a significant proportion of the population in these
countries (almost half the population of both Riga, the capital of Latvia, and Tallinn, the capital of Estonia). After regaining independence in 1991, Latvia and
Estonia restored the pre-1940 citizenship laws on the basis of the legal continuity
of their statehood, and they recognized citizenship according to the principle of
jus sanguinis for those who held citizenship before the Soviet annexation. Most
of those who had settled on the territory of these republics after their incorporation by the Soviet Union and their descendants received the right to obtain
citizenship through naturalization, but they were not granted citizenship automatically. New procedures compelled Russian-speaking Soviet citizens either to
become Russian citizens or to accept the status of stateless. Dual citizenship was
also prohibited, except for those who acquired citizenship by birth. In 2004, both
Estonia and Latvia slightly adjusted their citizenship policies in response to EU
monitoring and requests.[14]

In Search of Stability: The Post-1989 Political System

According to Stephen F. Cohen, the phrase that Western political science devised
to define the process of transformation in Eastern Europe following the collapse
of the Soviet Bloc—"postcommunist transition"—reflects a normative point of
view. The majority of specialists who deal with Eastern Europe regarded the establishment of Western-type capitalist societies to be the natural objective of this
transition in post-Soviet Eastern Europe.[15] A search for scapegoats occurred in
those places where the self-fulfilling prophecy failed to be realized. Was it the
incompetence of the Eastern European political elite or the passivism and nationalism of Eastern European society that caused the unexpected difficulties
connected to the postcommunist transition? European specialist literature has
dealt much less with the mistakes the West made in the export of its own models
than with those that Eastern Europe made in their import. However, the sociologists László Bruszt and David Stark saw clearly that the year 1989 marked not a
transition but a transformation that entailed neither the simple replication of the
old democratic societies of Western Europe nor a return to pre-1945 social structures.[16] In fact, the postcommunist Eastern European elite faced the challenging
task of finding socially sustainable methods of transforming industrialized societies based on the layers of existing socialism.

The most important task in these postcommunist states was to habituate
to democracy Eastern European societies that for generations had functioned

within authoritarian political structures and that during periods of hardship related to democratic transformation tended to seek security in the myth of the
strong man. Even the new leaders of these states were unfamiliar with the
internal mechanisms of the democratic political systems they were operating.
The restoration of monarchy was not plausible even in those Balkan countries
that had deposed kings shortly before the introduction of socialism (Romania,
Yugoslavia, Bulgaria, and Albania). Democratic political formations that had
emerged in Eastern Europe during the interwar periods—such as the independent socialists in Poland, the Beneš-led social nationalists in Czechoslovakia, the
smallholders in Hungary, the peasant parties in Croatia and Romania—and the
social-democratic parties that possessed strong bases of support throughout
the region immediately after the Second World War either failed to resurface after 1990 or played only a marginal role in postcommunist politics. Culturally and
ideologically heterogeneous movements and alliances—which often chose not to
use the word *party* in their official designations to avoid being associated with
the single-party state and because the term had attained a distinctly left-wing
connotation—arose to take the place of these interwar and immediate postwar
political formations. Thus, the overall success of attempts to introduce parliamentary democracy in countries in which it had weak historical traditions must
be praised in historical perspective as the common achievement of the widely
diverse postcommunist governments of Eastern Europe.

A defining aspect of the new Eastern European political movements was
that they rarely possessed a coherent world outlook, and their programs called
for a fuzzy mixture of European Union integration and ethno-cultural nationalism, free-market policies, and economic protectionism.[17] The party structure of
the countries of postcommunist Europe was formally stable and decidedly integrative. However, social support for most political forces was either weak or
temporary. It happened—and still happens—that political movements gained
momentum and then disappeared within some years, that political officials
switched their political affiliations several times as a result of frequent party
splits, or found a new movement with the support of a local media oligarch.[18] This
helps explain why the designations "right wing" and "left wing" in their Western
European sense should be applied cautiously to describe political phenomena
in the postcommunist Eastern Europe. The Czech Republic, where the reconstituted Social Democratic Party and the Communist Party of Bohemia and
Moravia have consistently posted strong election results, is a partial exception to
this rule. The other exception is possibly Slovenia, where the current political left
emerged from the reform wing of the Communist Party and played a primary
role in the establishment of the independent Slovenian state, thus legitimizing
itself in both national and democratic terms.[19]

The comparative analysis of the various types of state structure that have emerged in postcommunist Eastern Europe, which number at least a dozen even without counting those in the former Yugoslavia, does not fall within the scope of the present volume.[20] However, a few general tendencies can be discerned.

The political model toward which the countries of postcommunist Central and Eastern Europe gravitated has long resembled German consensual democracy in their establishment of republics and heads of state that were based on the simple representation of political parties. The new postcommunist democracies of Eastern Europe established balance among the executive, legislative, and judicial branches of government and provided constitutional courts with supervisory and counter-balancing roles not only to conform to European norms but to prevent authoritarian-type restoration attempts as well.[21] Ukraine again departed to the greatest degree from this pattern, introducing a Russian-type constitutional system that provides the head of state with genuine power, whereas Poland and Romania both established semipresidential systems based on the French model. The presidents of the latter republics are elected directly and play a significant role in the formation of foreign and security policy. As in France, the presidents of these countries sometimes serve alongside a prime minister who belongs to a different political party.

Voter participation is often regarded as a gauge of the strength of democracy, although it must be regarded with caution in the context of postcommunist Eastern Europe. The highest rates of voter participation in the first postcommunist elections held in Eastern Europe in 1990 were recorded in the still semiauthoritarian countries of Bulgaria (90 percent) and Romania (86 percent), where political interest groups composed of former communists were able to easily defeat disorganized right-wing rivals that lacked both financial resources and media support. Voter participation was also greater than 80 percent in Czechoslovakia, although in this country the Communist Party took part in elections without using ideological camouflage of any kind. In Hungary and Poland, where the democratic transformation had begun auspiciously and by 1990 citizens had started to seek stability rather than continual political struggle, voter participation in the first postcommunist elections was relatively low, at 65 percent and 43 percent, respectively. However, in subsequent elections held between 1993 and 1996, voter participation declined in those countries where it had been extraordinarily high in 1990 and stabilized or rose moderately in those where it been low, such as Hungary and Poland. Beginning at this time, average voter participation in the countries of Eastern Europe remained steady at around 50 percent to 60 percent, which, though modest, approaches that recorded in most of the countries of Western Europe.

Although communist parties were not usually banned, they recorded poor electoral results throughout Eastern Europe after 1990, with the previously mentioned exception of the Communist Party of Bohemia and Moravia in the Czech Republic. Alternative left-wing movements (e.g., environmentalist, anti-globalist) have never gained significant support in postcommunist elections in Eastern Europe. During the first half of the 1990s, moderate and radical anti-communist coalitions that can generally be classified as right of center on the political spectrum won elections throughout Eastern Europe, with the notable exception of Romania and Bulgaria, where formations connected to the left wing retained power until the years 1996–1997, and Ukraine, where pro-West political forces had to wait until the 2004–2005 Orange Revolution to gain strength.

The return of former communists to power during the second postcommu-nist parliamentary cycles in Eastern Europe was not only foreseeable but also remarkably smooth and fair.[22] In Poland, where the program of economic shock therapy had deeply divided the Solidarity Trade Union, the postcommunist Democratic Left Alliance gained strength beginning in the middle of the 1990s and the party's dynamic leader, Aleksander Kwaśniewski, was elected president of the republic in 1995 and again in 2000. In Hungary, the Hungarian Democratic Forum, which had led the governing coalition during the country's first post-communist parliamentary cycle, won only 12 percent of the vote in 1994 elections, while the Hungarian Socialist Party gained an absolute majority in the National Assembly under the leadership of late 1980s foreign minister Gyula Horn. As the leaders of social-liberal coalitions that advocated the free market and economic reform, President Kwaśniewski of Poland and Prime Minister Horn of Hungary worked with the total support of the West to take their countries closer to Euro-pean institutions.

In the newly independent Slovakia, left-wing parties that opposed compre-hensive privatization won 1994 parliamentary elections. The Movement for a Democratic Slovakia (HZDS), led by Vladimír Mečiar, was the most powerful of these parties. Mečiar, a former Communist Party functionary, dominated Slovak political life for almost a decade, serving as the prime minister of Slovakia during the short-lived Czech and Slovak Federative Republic and of the independent Slo-vak Republic from 1992 to 1998 with just a short interval. Difficulties surrounding the application of political categories devised in the West to conditions in the post-Soviet countries of Eastern Europe become clear when describing the re-gion's former communist and socialist parties, which operate in an environment of multiple nationalities and have inherited a political culture from the party state that combines nationalism with collectivism in the economic sphere. How-ever, in Poland and Hungary, both of which have very small national-minority populations, parties that can be classified as right wing espouse anti-liberal, moderately statist economic policies similar to those of left-wing parties in the West, whereas socialist and liberal parties support neoliberal economic policies.[23]

The final noteworthy political phenomenon in postcommunist Eastern Europe discussed here regards the prolongation of governing cycles and, particularly after the global economic crisis of 2008–2009, the progressive shift of the electoral balance toward right-wing movements. With the exception of the former communist governments in Romania and Bulgaria, no government in Eastern Europe managed to remain in power for two consecutive parliamentary cycles until the late 1990s. However, beginning at that time, certain political parties began to maintain the long-term support of national electorates, such as the right-of-center coalition parties in Slovakia from 1998 to 2006, followed by the long rule of Robert Fico's social-democratic SMER (Direction) Party over the past ten years, or the Donald Tusk–led Civic Platform (Platforma Obywatelska, or PO) in Poland from 2007 to 2015, and the Hungarian Socialist Party in Hungary from 2002 to 2010 under the direction of Péter Medgyessy and later Ferenc Gyurcsány. In this case, social-liberal supremacy was ended by the landslide success of Viktor Orbán's right-wing Fidesz-Hungarian Civic Alliance, whose maverick ideological grounds are discussed in the last chapter.

Economy and Society: The Winners and Losers of Change

The rapid transformation from planned to market economy in Eastern Europe presented even greater challenges than political and institutional reform. The period of transition in the region coincided with incipient crisis within the welfare systems of developed societies. Economic hardship prevented the Western world from launching a program such as the Marshall Plan to provide assistance to the states of Eastern Europe and post-Soviet Russia, although specialists did consider such initiatives. Pessimists believed that the economies of these countries were not developed enough to utilize Western support effectively.[24] International financial organizations that cooperated with them finally proposed an economic-stabilization program for the postcommunist countries of Eastern Europe based on measures that had been implemented to consolidate the economies of Latin America in the 1980s. The fundamental principle of the proposed neoliberal economic policies to be implemented in Eastern Europe was that the state role in regulation of the economy should be decreased to an absolute minimum. Proponents argued that the free flow of goods, services, and capital ensured global economic growth and stability and that individual countries must refrain from using economic instruments to defend their perceived national interests. Advocates of the unrestrained free market supported the comprehensive privatization of state-owned enterprises and the removal of impediments to foreign investment. The US economist John Williamson characterized the proposed neoliberal economic package for Eastern Europe as the "Washington consensus."[25] However, David L. Bartlet has maintained that international financial institutions, though they played an important role in the supervision of policy in postcommunist Eastern Europe, did not exercise as much impact on the course of the economic transition in the region as many would believe. Estonia was the only country in Eastern Europe that implemented the proposed neoliberal economic reforms at the beginning of the 1990s, while in Poland the Balcerowicz Plan was mollified significantly to alleviate social tension and in the Czech Republic the Václav Klaus government adopted an economic-stabilization program that partly incorporated the recommendations of the International Monetary Fund. Governments in Hungary treated the popular institutions of socialist welfare, such as preferential pensions and free social provisions, with much greater caution, and the postcommunist governments in Romania and Bulgaria rejected every proposed structural transformation to their national economies.[26]

The United States and the European Union offered only modest concrete support for measures designed to transform the economies of Eastern Europe during the 1990s. Moreover, Eastern European states proved unable to finance the reconstruction of their economies via direct foreign investment. The magnitude of state ownership varied considerably among the Soviet Bloc states in the late 1980s: in the Soviet Union 99 percent, compared to 98 percent in Yugoslavia and Romania (where property was under nominal social ownership), 97 percent in Czechoslovakia, 81 percent in Poland, and 65 percent in Hungary.[27] German-owned enterprises, which possessed significant know-how and cash flow, were largely preoccupied with business activities related to the reunification of Germany, while the political crisis in Italy after 1992 prevented competitive companies from establishing operations in the region. Multinational companies based in the United States, the United Kingdom, and France showed little interest in Eastern Europe during the early period of economic transition in the region. Not even Hungary, which featured the most open and attractive investment environment in all of Eastern Europe, drew enough foreign investment to cover the cost of its foreign debt until the year 1993.[28]

The frequently changing and ideologically diverse governments of Eastern Europe were left with no viable option other than implementing rapid privatization, which entailed the liberalization of prices and public services, the mass layoff of workers, and the reduction of state subsidies for less profitable sectors of the economy. However, as a result of contradictory elements within Eastern European capital markets, governments in the region were forced to utilize "special privatization techniques."[29] Such techniques to privatize state-owned property included direct sale, public donation, distribution of property vouchers, bankruptcy, and leasing to employees. These methods were used to privatize nearly 150,000 large and medium-sized companies, several hundred thousand small-scale factories, and millions of homes in Eastern Europe in the first decade after the fall of communism.[30]

The distribution of vouchers that provided their holders with a symbolic share in state-owned companies represented a particularly novel means of mass privatization in Eastern Europe. The Klaus government utilized this method of privatization in Czechoslovakia from 1990 to 1992, and the governments of Lithuania, Poland, and Bulgaria did so in 1994 and 1995. The process of mass privatization through these and other means, contrary to the stated objectives, resulted in a high degree of capital concentration and nontransparent economic conditions. The same process took place in Russia, where newly established holding companies accumulated enormous numbers of vouchers during the presidency of Boris Yeltsin, thus permitting their young owners—subsequently branded by the press "oligarchs," "new Russians," and even "kleptocrats"—to enrich themselves at the expense of the fellow Russian population and national economy.[31] Hungary's first democratically elected government put an end to the purchase—through personal connections—of public property to limit the acquisitions via privatization of the economic elite associated with the former state party, many members of which earned their first millions during the immediate postcommunist period. As a result of this measure, foreign interests were temporarily denied access to privatized companies. In 1995, the new socialist-liberal coalition governing in Hungary initiated a more comprehensive privatization campaign following the introduction of an economic-stabilization program formulated according to the demands of international creditors. Following the third privatization wave in Hungary, in the late 1990s, private ownership (domestic or foreign) of property had risen to 75 percent of all property in the country, from 35 percent in 1989.[32]

Despite the macroeconomic successes achieved in Eastern Europe, the countries of the region lost an immense amount of financial resources in the labyrinths of privatization. Using the fitting term that Hungarian scholars have used in various contexts, one can refer to these as "transformational losses," which served not only to transform the economic structure but to increase social inequality as well.[33] According to an official report that Hungary's finance ministry published in 2009, administrative and legal expenses consumed nearly half the net revenue of €11 billion proceeding from the sale of public property between 1990 and 2007.[34] Taking into consideration the widespread grassroots corruption, we can conclude that public property was sold at much less than its true market value not only in Russia but also in countries such as Hungary where governments conducted the privatization process in a more restrained manner.

The transition to the free-market economy and the sudden loss of Soviet markets led to a sharp decrease in exports and national income throughout Eastern Europe. The precise magnitude of this decline is difficult to estimate because of the considerable black-market activity in late socialist economies. Nevertheless, crisis afflicted all sectors of the Eastern European economy between 1989 and 1992, particularly heavy industry, which contracted throughout the region by between 15 percent and 40 percent during those years. Poland was able to record positive economic growth in 1992 as a result of the country's extremely low economic performance base, followed by the Czech Republic, Slovakia, Romania, and Albania in 1993 and Hungary and Bulgaria in 1994.[35] The territories of the former Yugoslavia in which armed conflict was taking place constituted one of the exceptions to the economic-growth pattern in Eastern Europe in 1994, as did Estonia, Lithuania, Macedonia, and, above all, Ukraine. The latter post-Soviet state lost more than 20 percent of its national wealth in 1994 alone and more than 60 percent of its national wealth between 1991 and 1998. Following a few years of economic growth, many Eastern European countries entered a period of decline in 1997 as a result of the economic and financial crises in Asia and Russia. Per capita income in the states of Eastern Europe dropped from 37 percent of that in the West in 1989 to 27 percent a few years later.[36]

The closing of thousands of factories and the complete restructuring of production sectors in Eastern Europe generated immense social hardship in the region. The restructuring of industry resulted in significant unemployment of around 20 percent in the Baltics, Poland, and Slovakia throughout the 1990s. Only in Czech Republic, where the economy rebounded quickly as a result of the country's production of high-quality goods and high degree of labor specialization, did industrial workers continue to compose a significant proportion of the domestic workforce (more than one-third). As a result of the contraction of traditional industrial sectors and the delocalization of logistical and information-technology services, a large proportion of those currently employed throughout Eastern Europe work in the service sector, and a smaller proportion works in the industrial sector. Only a small portion of the active workforce in the region is engaged in the agricultural sector, which has become increasingly focused on intensive private farming.

The economic changes that took place in Eastern Europe resulted in the complete transformation of social practices and the standard of living as well as the intellectual horizons of the region's population. Although it would be impossible to summarize the consequences of the latter phenomenon, one can nevertheless make a few observations. Most of the social dramas that attended the process of transformation in Eastern Europe occurred quietly, apparently unnoticed by the Western media. Mass layoffs, structural changes, and rationalization did not cause long-term or violent protest, with the exception of scattered unrest among miners in Poland, Ukraine, and Romania. Trade unions lost their social support among blue-collar workers and also their material resources, and new interest groups seldom emerged to replace them. Eastern European private-sector employees rarely organized themselves, and multinational companies employed every means at their disposal to demoralize trade-union representatives.

Contrary to the case in Western Europe, strikes and mass demonstrations have been almost unknown in Eastern Europe as a means of promoting the interests of the postcommunist working class.

The rapid pace of economic change has compelled the citizens of postcommunist states to adapt with equal speed. Millions of people in Eastern Europe have been forced to live under circumstances of not knowing when their wages and pensions will be paid. In the early 1990s, most Eastern Europeans wanted to believe that the changes they were enduring, no matter how painful and unjust, would soon lead to a better life for the majority of society. The traditional Eastern European elite that survived communism and many members of the "red bourgeoisie," the large urban white-collar or intellectual middle class that had become the main beneficiary of the late Soviet period, possessed the cultural, social, and political capital necessary to realize their postcommunist dreams.[37] For ordinary members of the old and new Eastern European middle class, the postcommunist transition represented a successful process that brought millions of their fellow citizens closer to the long-coveted Western standard of living.

Apparently, Central and Eastern European countries have been experiencing in the past two decades more sustained economic growth than the old members of the European Union. Nevertheless, as late as 2015 none of these countries had reached the average per capita income, and figures varied significantly between them: 87 percent in Czech Republic; 83 percent in Slovenia; 77 percent in Slovakia; 75 percent in Estonia and Lithuania; 69 percent in Poland; 68 percent in Hungary; 64 percent in Latvia; 58 percent in Croatia; 57 percent in Romania; and 47 percent in Bulgaria. Outside the European Union, per capita income in Serbia and Macedonia was 36 percent of average per capita income of all-European Union member states, and in Bosnia and Herzegovina and Albania it was only around 30 percent.[38] However, these data need to be placed in context to test their validity. First, it is important to consider whether the ongoing scholarly debate as to whether gross domestic product (GDP) is a reliable measure of a nation's economic performance. In the case of postcommunist Eastern Europe, whose economic systems are characterized by a sustained share of foreign investments, multinational companies operating at the periphery are likely to repatriate most of their profits. They contribute to GDP growth but fail to provide added value to the host country. A recent multi-indicator analysis including employment, distribution of incomes, and productivity of labor dismissed the commonly accepted claim of a convergence taking place between Western and Eastern Europe after the first transition period.[39]

Second, the imaginary ranking of Eastern European states in terms of per capita income has not changed significantly over the past century, despite all the political and social changes that have taken place during the same time. The more developed and Western-oriented countries of Estonia, the Czech Republic, and Slovenia have the highest level of average well-being, just as they had in the interwar period and under socialism, followed by the other Central European countries (Poland, Slovakia, Hungary, and Croatia). The Balkan states (Romania, Bulgaria, the southern former Yugoslav republics, and Albania) as well as the post-Soviet republics outside the Baltic area used to have and still have the lowest level of average well-being, with only very slow progress. These data serve to support the critical approach of scholars like Andrew C. Janos to convergence theories. Analyzing the patterns of relative backwardness of the region from the late nineteenth century to the postcommunist period, Janos noted that the social legacy of the past century has played a key role in the outcome of the periodic attempts of Eastern European countries to reach Western levels of development.[40] From a historical perspective, we might conclude that postcommunism has assigned—or rather confirmed—the status of Eastern Europe on the economic periphery. Inter- and intraregional disparities in east-central Europe not only are resistant to political upheavals but also are structural and likely unsolvable.

The changes that have taken place in Eastern Europe since 1990 have generally benefited the younger and more educated generations of people in the region. For those Eastern Europeans who have grown up in a globalized and digital world, market-oriented society has provided previously unimaginable opportunities that have made them the winners of postcommunist transformation: the freedom of movement, the chance to learn Western languages, and almost unlimited exposure to the outside world. In those more socially conservative countries, such as Catholic Poland, the generational changes have also promoted the fast emancipation of women.

However, for Eastern Europeans who were born between the 1930s and 1950s, the postcommunist period has been a collective drama. For entire social groups in the region—former cooperative members, workers from closed-down factories, inhabitants of mining towns—the disappearance of their former home community has resulted in a loss of social status in the strict sense of the term. According to much-debated research published in the medical journal *Lancet*, the 12.8 percent increase in mortality recorded in the states of the former Soviet Bloc between 1989 and 2002 can be explicitly attributed to the ill-conceived implementation of neoliberal economic policies.[41]

Other studies have ascribed the decline in life expectancy measured in the former Soviet Bloc since 1990 to an increase in psychological pressure, stress, alcoholism, inadequate awareness of health issues, and poor diet.[42] This might explain the paradox that the average life expectancy in relatively prosperous Eastern European countries such as Czech Republic and Slovenia is still lower than that in underdeveloped states in the region such as Bosnia and Herzegovina and Albania, where women live into their early eighties and men into their midseventies, on average.

In the Baltic states, Hungary, and Romania, average life expectancy decreased to between 77 and 75 years for women and to between 69 and 67 years for men. Life-expectancy data revealed a catastrophic demographic crisis in the former Soviet republics, falling to 74 years for women and 66 years for men in Moldova, to 76 years for women and 64 years for men in Belarus, to 74 years for women and 62 years for men in Ukraine, and to 73 years for women and 59 years for men in Russia. Although some recover since the 1990s, Ukraine still occupies the 148th place in the world ranking of countries according to average life expectancy, and Russia occupies the inglorious 153th position.[43]

Punishment, Commemoration, or Investigation: Handling the Totalitarian Past

The treatment of those who committed crimes during the Soviet-type socialism represents one of the acute questions of the democratic transition in Eastern Europe. In comparison to other twentieth-century authoritarian systems such as German National Socialism, Italian fascism, and Latin American and Mediterranean right-wing military juntas, the communist system featured an exceptional admixture of ideological agency, technocratic knowledge, and state-security control. On the one hand, the pervasive ruling techniques of Soviet-type socialism exposed a significant part of the civil population to some forms of repression. On the other hand, they transformed millions of ordinary citizens into reluctant or willing collaborators with the communist regimes.[44]

After 1989, Western visitors and former dissidents who had for whatever reason been placed under observation by the secret police wanted to find out the identities of agents and informants who had spied on them and the precise reason secret services had decided to keep them under surveillance.[45] On a general plan, the new democracies of Eastern Europe attempted to confront the past through the so-called processes of lustration, or the exclusion of people who had been affiliated with the communist system from public and political life, and transitional justice, or the provision of moral and material compensation to the victims of communism.[46]

Research on the process of coming to terms with the authoritarian past in Eastern Europe shows that the boundary between rational understanding and indiscriminate lustration has been very thin, indeed.[47] In most instances, the condemnation of the fallen system bore only symbolic significance. Interconnections between the old and new elites made it impossible to remove those who had been affiliated with the communist system from their positions of power and influence. In 2007, a Bulgarian investigative commission determined that President Georgi Parvanov as well as many members of the country's government and diplomatic corps had maintained contacts with the Committee for State Security, although the revelation entailed no serious consequences.[48] In Hungary, Prime Minister Péter Medgyessy was able to retain his office even after admitting in 2002 that he had served in the country's economic counterespionage service in the late 1970s and early 1980s. Shortly thereafter, the European Union did not object to the Hungarian government's nomination of the national police chief László Salgó to serve as deputy director of Europol even though it was common knowledge that he had been involved in political police activities in the 1980s. Several years later, NATO similarly raised no formal objections to the Hungarian government's nomination of Moscow-trained former political police officer Sándor Laborc to serve as chair of the organization's special committee dealing with security issues.[49]

The only exception was the German Democratic Republic, where the political changes resulted in the total collapse of the state structure that had helped get rid of the most compromised members of the former GDR *nomenklatura*. The methods utilized in Germany to handle the GDR's state-security past— lustration, the peaceful assumption of control over archives, and the provision of victims with information as well as moral and material compensation—proved impracticable in those countries where the collapse of the communist political system had not entailed the dissolution of the oppressive state formation.

The Ukrainian case is in many ways unique and deserves a detailed analysis here. After the 2014 Euromaidan revolution that ousted pro-Russian president Viktor Yanukovych, the new governments have engaged in a controversial process of fast-track nation building meant to erase the symbolic presence of the Soviet and communist past. As a Ukrainian scholar noted, stripped-down post-colonial discourse that makes Soviet Russia responsible for the present conditions of the country does not help elaborate a self-reflective national consciousness and exacerbates a symbolic fight in which both sides, the Ukrainian nationalists and the supporters of Russian President Vladimir Putin, "are ready to sacrifice their own and others' lives to eliminate the enemy and ensure the victory of historical justice."[50] Sharper criticism arose after Ukrainian president Petro Poroshenko signed a law in May 2015 that mandated the transfer of the country's main archives from the Soviet organs of repression to a governmental organization, the newly established Ukrainian Institute of National Memory. This new institution would be charged with "implementation of state policy in the field of restoration and preservation of national memory of the Ukrainian people."[51] To achieve this goal, the institute received documents on political dissidents, propaganda campaigns against religion, the activities of Ukrainian nationalist organizations, KGB espionage and counterespionage activities, and criminal cases connected to the Stalinist purges. The ultimate goal of the new politics of memory is to present a radically different view of modern Ukrainian history by constructing a purified past of the role of Ukraine and of the Ukrainians during the Soviet system.

The most controversial issue appears to be a narrative of the Second World War that amplifies Soviet crimes and glorifies Ukrainian nationalist fighters while dismissing the central role they played in ethnic cleansing of Poles and in the local implementation of the Nazi Holocaust.[52]

According to many communist-era dissidents and current specialists, collective remembrance represents the only genuine and feasible form of justice that can avert the repetition of crimes in the posttotalitarian states.[53] However, in postcommunist Eastern Europe, condemnation of the most recent defeated system among all the authoritarian regimes that were in power between the 1930s and 1989 often replaced civil debate, offering a reductive, if not dichotomized, vision of the national past. Today's Eastern Europe is full of historical museums, remembrance places, statues, and commemorative plaques that intend to express a break with the deplorable past and sometimes envisage a teleological history, by which the undesired past might be simply undone.[54]

At the same time, it is worth listening to Tony Judt's sober warning on the misuses of public memory as an instrument of political and moral legitimation:

> Memory is inherently contentious and partisan: one man's acknowledgement is another's omission. And it is a poor guide to the past. The first post-war Europe was built upon deliberate mismemory—upon forgetting as a way of life. Since 1989, Europe has been constructed instead upon a compensatory surplus of memory: institutionalized public remembering as the very foundation of collective identity. The first could not endure—but nor will the second. Some measure of neglect and even forgetting is the necessary condition for civic health.[55]

The stridently anti-communist and anti-Soviet public commemorative culture of democratic Eastern Europe represents the counterpart to nostalgia for the recent past that is also common in the region. The case of Romania is particularly interesting as a result of the well-known ruthlessness of the communist system in this country. Sociological surveys have demonstrated that the economic crisis and frequent political scandals that have taken place over recent years have contributed to increasing social nostalgia for the former system and rejection of capitalism, not only among elderly, less educated residents of rural areas, but among young urbanites who did not experience the Ceaușescu regime directly.[56] Former Securitate officers, who to this day fill important positions in Romanian media, have had an active role in improving the popular conception of the Ceaușescu-era security services. The image of the Securitate promoted in television programs, large-circulation newspapers, and the many autobiographical volumes that have appeared in Romania over the past decades exercise at least as much impact on the formation of the general attitudes toward the secret-police organization as do the educational system and the family. Among all the factors that have influenced the process of confronting the state-security past in Romania, the revolutionary character of the transition period in the country is perhaps the most important. Had the Romanian Communist Party not been dissolved in 1989, one could define the post-Ceaușescu transition as a radical renewal of the party elite. However, the alternative project for implementing change was not the own project of the new leaders as is usually the case with revolutions. The adoption of European norms represented the central objective of this project, which the West supported in written form through documentation regarding European integration. However, Romania's old-new political elite began to reinterpret its mission, objectives, and political identity in the process of putting into practice the principles outlined in the documents. The mimicry and ambiguity that inevitably accompanied the process resulted in either half-hearted or biased confrontation with the communist past in Romania.[57]

How is it possible to deal with the enormous burden of an inglorious collective past? Understanding and rationally elaborating on this story remains the best answer to this question. An unprecedented archival revolution has taken place in Eastern Europe over the past two decades in both depth and breadth. The most highly guarded documents of the communist dictatorships have become accessible throughout the former Eastern Bloc states and their constituent republics.[58] Although these documents must be handled with obvious caution (they are still used for the purposes of political and economic blackmail, denigration, and disinformation), in most cases civilians in Eastern Europe have been happy to receive the right of access to information from the communist era, and researchers have attempted to build the enormous amount of new information into historical narratives.[59]

After 1989, social scientists living on the eastern border of the enlarged West continued to suffer from what sociologists Marina Blagojević and Gad Yair called the catch-22 syndrome, that is, a structural and self-reproducing disadvantage of the postcommunist area vis-à-vis the West in the intertwined facets of academic work, from conceptualization to international research funding.[60] For a long time, these facets have formed "a coherent structure which debilitates, censors, and excludes unique patterns of knowledge from the semi-periphery."[61] It is telling that the only academic institution in Eastern Europe to earn international ranking is the English-language postgraduate Central European University, which has been operating in Budapest since 1991 under the auspices of the Hungarian-born American businessman George Soros.

Notwithstanding these problems, Eastern Europe has tried to exit its former state of marginality in the field of academic research of its own communist past. International conferences no longer focus exclusively on the global aspects of the Cold War from the perspective of the Western powers—instead, they examine relations between state and society during the years of existing socialism; conduct debates regarding the coordination of information networks in Soviet-occupied countries after the Second World War; and analyze Warsaw Pact strategy toward disarmament, religious revival, dissidents, and international terrorism, all from the point of view of the Soviet Union and its satellite states. Debunking the Cold War–inherited frameworks, new historiographical approaches regard the Soviet-type state as a heterogeneous complex of agencies and individual actors, with mixed and at times contradictory interests. This is what makes its social memory so fractured, though also intellectually exciting.

Postcommunism in the Balkans: Catastrophe and Starting Anew

The Disintegration of Yugoslavia

As Josip Glaurdić put it in his excellent analysis of the breakup of Yugoslavia, with the end of the Cold War, Yugoslavia "lost all importance to the West as a bulwark against Soviet advances and as an example of socialism that was not sponsored by the Kremlin."[62]

 The fate of Yugoslavia from the late 1980s to 1992 was primarily decided by Slobodan Milošević's Serbian expansionist project and the failure of the West (Western Europe in particular) to respond effectively to it. Milošević was an educated, multilingual functionary with extensive management experience as director of the Belgrade-based Beobanka financial institution. His appointment as head of the League of Communists of Serbia in 1986 intensified the conflict between the central government in Belgrade and the constituent republics. The new Belgrade strongman believed fervently in the notion of maintaining the unity of Yugoslavia under Serbian leadership. In order to achieve this objective, Milošević initiated in 1988 the purging of the party apparatus, known as the Anti-Bureaucratic Revolution, to reestablish the authority of the federal government in Belgrade over the local governments. In March 1989, a constitutional amendment was adopted that curtailed the authority of the territorial units that composed the Socialist Republic of Serbia. The support of representatives from the Socialist Republic of Slovenia and the Socialist Republic of Croatia for these measures in return for the introduction of the right to strike and economic liberalization provides a clear reflection of the conditions that prevailed in Yugoslavia in the late 1980s. The revocation in 1989 of the autonomy of Kosovo caused an even much greater outcry. The aggressive intervention of Belgrade in Kosovo, the population of which was 90 percent Albanian, sparked ethnic conflict that resulted in the declaration of martial law and the introduction of military control in the province in March 1990. The image that Milošević had created of Serbia as a neglected republic of federal Yugoslavia and of the Serbs as a martyred people won mass support for his leadership, particularly among those with little education. According to Stevan K. Pavlowitch, "While defending Yugoslavia as they saw it—the only state in which all Serbs were gathered—the leadership of Serbia and Serbian nationalists in fact gave the final blow to that state, and thus unwittingly destroyed it."[63]

Nationality-based conflict in Yugoslavia in late 1989 and early 1990 was connected to the emergence of severe economic problems and political pluralism in the country. Slovenia was the first Yugoslav republic to engage in open conflict with Serbia. The rational notion of independence had gradually matured among the communist elite in Slovenia, where political and the linguistic-cultural boundaries had long coincided. Several factors served to nourish secessionism in Slovenia at the end of the 1980s: the growing threat to the Tito-guaranteed autonomy of the republic, the increasing mistrust of the "Serbian" army, press campaigns denouncing the centralism of Belgrade, and concern about the inability of Serbian, Bosnian, Montenegrin, and Macedonian guest workers to integrate into Slovenian society.[64]

In September 1989, the parliament of Slovenia approved constitutional amendments that provided the republic with complete judicial independence and with its proclamation of self-determination articulated the intention to secede from Yugoslavia. In February 1990, the Milan Kučan–led Slovenian delegation withdrew from the fourteenth and final congress of the League of Communists of Yugoslavia, thus prompting remaining delegates to call an end to the assembly. The only serious attempt to fill the void that Marshal Tito had left behind and oversee the country's transition to democracy took place in 1989–1990 under the leadership of Ante Marković, the Croatian prime minister of Yugoslavia who had previously headed several state companies. After coming to office, he implemented a series of reforms, including fixing the exchange rate of the dinar to that of the deutsche mark, thus making the Yugoslav currency partially convertible, and freezing prices to stop inflation. Prime Minister Marković adopted very strict credit policies that were necessary in order to reduce deficits resulting from repayment of the massive debt that the country had accrued in the 1980s and undisciplined spending in certain constituent republics. According to Mark Thompson, Marković stood for an undivided Yugoslavia with a market economy and political pluralism, and he soon gained huge popularity: "This was music to Western ears and to Yugoslavia's own cosmopolitan elite."[65] His pro-federal initiatives sought to debunk resurging nationalism by uncoupling self-managing socialism and political Yugoslavism. In the spring of 1990 it seemed that the economic reforms of the "miracle man" targeting hyperinflation were working. Behind the scenes, however, the Yugoslav federation was going through its strategic dismantling by a large, heterogeneous coalition of national(ist) elites who wanted to recentralize the state and then sought to bring an end to the Yugoslav state itself in order to establish smaller republic-based states.[66]

The first multiparty elections held in Yugoslavia parallel to the dissolution of the Soviet Union between April and December 1990 contributed greatly to the failure of attempts to achieve social and economic consolidation. In Slovenia, a pro-reform and pro-independence coalition under the leadership of the former communist Kučan won parliamentary elections held in the republic in April 1990. In June 1990, the newly elected Slovenian parliament declared Slovenia a sovereign and independent state—a status that won 88 percent approval in a referendum held six months later. The decision of the central government to withhold two billion dollars in federal funding for Slovenia as punishment for this declaration and its subsequent popular confirmation prompted the government of Slovenia to withdraw from Yugoslavia on June 25, 1991.[67] In response, authorities in Belgrade ordered the Yugoslav People's Army to strike the positions of the Slovenian Territorial Defense, although these random and ineffective attacks merely prompted the better-organized and more motivated Slovenian armed forces to launch a counterattack. The so-called Ten-Day War ended with the signing of a cease-fire agreement on July 3. Serbia, in fact, maintained no significant strategic interest in preventing the withdrawal of Slovenia from Yugoslavia, and Milošević himself decided to allow the country to secede following his brief attempt to stifle the Slovenian independence movement.

In Croatia, the Franjo Tuđman–led Croatian Democratic Union nationalist party defeated the pro-Yugoslav League of Communists of Croatia in parliamentary elections in the spring of 1990. However, contrary to the case in the essentially single-nationality state of Slovenia, a large number of Serbs lived in Croatia, constituting around 20 percent of the republic's population. In August 1990, Serbs living in the region of Kninska Krajina bordering Bosnia and Herzegovina called a referendum on autonomy from Croatia. Meanwhile, the Croatian government began transforming the Croatian Territorial Defense and local police into a genuine army, and Serbian civilians in Croatia began to organize armed forces as well. Several events, some of them violent, led to the outbreak of armed conflict in Croatia: the murder of several Serbian civilians in the cities of Zagreb, Osijek, and Vukovar; the secession of the Republic of Croatia from Yugoslavia in January 1991; and the formation of the Republic of Serbian Krajina in April 1991 and that state's self-proclaimed union with Serbia in May 1991. On May 19, the citizens of Croatia voted in favor of independence from Yugoslavia in a referendum that Serbs from the republic boycotted. Finally, on June 25, 1991, Croatia withdrew from Yugoslavia along with Slovenia and declared itself an independent state.

The remaining Yugoslav republics held elections during the final two months of 1990. In Bosnia and Herzegovina, three nationality-based parties—the Alija Izetbegović–led Bosniak-Muslim Party of Democratic Action, the Radovan

Karadžić–led Serb Democratic Party, and the Stjepan Klujić–led Croatian Democratic Union—won 80 percent of the vote. As conflict escalated in Croatia in 1991,
surreal calm prevailed in Bosnia and Herzegovina, where President Izetbegović
formed the so-called Platform on the Future of the Yugoslav Community with
his Macedonian partner Kiro Gligorov, a pro-Tito communist who was concerned about the fate of his small multiethnic republic. The two leaders envis-
aged the preservation of the territorial unity of Yugoslavia as a community of
semi-independent states, provided with a common market according to the rules
of the European Economic Community (EEC) monetary union but entitled to
carry out their own foreign policy.

Although Macedonia began to suffer from an increasing degree of internal
disunity, the communists, led by Gligorov, defeated the nationalist party called
Internal Macedonian Revolutionary Organization–Democratic Party for Macedonian National Unity. After declaring independence in September 1991, Macedonia became the only former Yugoslav republic to continue efforts to integrate
its large Albanian minority. Meanwhile, Macedonia fought to gain official international recognition despite Greece's strenuous insistence that the country's
name was inaccurate from both a historical and cultural standpoint and use of its
European Union veto right vis-à-vis the new state. The difficulties were resolved
when the Republic of Macedonia agreed to accept the somewhat convoluted designation Former Yugoslav Republic of Macedonia (FYROM) as its official name.

In his monograph on the Yugoslav Wars, Jože Pirjevec has examined the
frequently proclaimed opinion that Germany, Austria, and the Vatican bore a
significant responsibility for the disintegration of Yugoslavia. This viewpoint ig-
nores two important factors: first, that Yugoslavia ceased to exist as a political
unit in a de facto sense in 1991; and second, that the international diplomatic
community supported preservation of the status quo during the initial phase of
the Yugoslav Wars and therefore characterized the attempts of Slovenia and Croatia to gain independence as "an anachronistic ethnic-nationalist disease" that
lacked democratic legitimacy.[68] In July 1991, several members of the EEC blocked
a Netherlands-initiated proposal that would have made it possible to suspend
the conflict in Yugoslavia until the convening of an international conference to
resolve territorial issues in the country.[69] The lack of Western diplomatic understanding and failure to provide Yugoslavia with the financial assistance required
to sustain the Marković government's economic measures made inevitable the
Yugoslav disintegration.

The Croatian and Bosnian Wars

Whereas members of the Serb-Yugoslav faction did not regard in 1991 the secession of Slovenia as a threat, they considered Croatia's attempt to withdraw from

the federal state to represent a serious security risk. After the Yugoslav People's Army recognized defeat in the Ten-Day War and withdrew from Slovenia, representatives from Slovenia, Croatia, and the Yugoslav federal government signed the European Economic Community–sponsored Brioni Agreement on July 7, 1991, calling for a three-month delay in the declaration of Slovene and Croatian independence to give the signatories time to find a permanent resolution to territorial disputes between them. However, this belated diplomatic effort failed to prevent the spread of conflict in Croatia. Armed clashes in the regions of Krajina, Slavonia, Istria, and Dalmatia began to assume the character of total war, which spared neither civilians nor World Heritage sites such as the Adriatic port city of Dubrovnik. The Yugoslav People's Army and Serbian irregular forces besieged the Danube River port of Vukovar, the population of which was 44 percent Croatian, 38 percent Serb, and 10 percent "Yugoslav," taking the town in November 1991 at the cost of around 2,000 dead, including more than 1,100 civilians. By the end of 1991, approximately 250,000 Croatians had fled to regions of Croatia that remained under the authority of the country's central government—territories that constituted roughly one-third of the area of the former Socialist Republic of Croatia. The European Economic Community recognized the independence of Slovenia and Croatia only on January 15, 1992. A few days later, the governments of Croatia and Yugoslavia signed a cease-fire agreement that ended the Serbian-Croatian war for years.

The violent disintegration of Yugoslavia contributed significantly to the radicalization of the political conflicts among the three major nationalities in Bosnia and Herzegovina—the Bosniaks, the Croatians, and the Serbs. Between February 29 and March 1, 1992, an EU-instigated referendum was held in Bosnia and Herzegovina in which 99 percent of those participating voted for independence from Yugoslavia—however, almost one-third of the republic's population, primarily Serbs, boycotted the referendum. Antagonism between the nationalities in Bosnia and Herzegovina grew even more intense following the republic's declaration of independence in March 1992. Armed conflict broke out in the capital city of Sarajevo in early April, thereby forcing the international community to take action. The United States and the European Union recognized Bosnia and Herzegovina as an independent state, while Bosnian-Serb leader Radovan Karadžić, who received military support from the Yugoslav government in Belgrade, declared the foundation of the Republika Srpska and placed Sarajevo under siege. A sad novelty of the wars in Croatia and Bosnia and Herzegovina was that, contrary to warfare in modern Europe, the opposing sides fought only partially with regular army units. A significant proportion of the armed forces that waged these wars comprised local civilian volunteers supported by an unquantifiable, though significant, number of foreign mercenaries and adventurers. These forces increasingly focused their attacks on unarmed civilians, transforming widespread

psychological terror into one of the distinguishing characteristics of the Yugoslav Wars. The Bosnian War fought between the spring of 1992 and summer 1995
was the bloodiest armed conflict in Europe since the end of the Second World
War, resulting in 14,000 casualties—half of them civilian—and 50,000 wounded
in Sarajevo alone. According to Steven Burg and Paul Shoup, approximately
140,000 people were killed in the Bosnian War, while the International Criminal
Tribunal for the former Yugoslavia estimated that 102,000 people were killed in
the three-year conflict.[70] The Sarajevo-based Research and Documentation Center has recorded 97,000 killed—62 percent of them Bosniaks, 25 percent of them
Serbs, and 8 percent of them Croats—in its methodically compiled database of
Bosnian War casualties.[71] Hundreds of thousands of people were wounded in the
war, and around 2 million people were forced to seek refuge either elsewhere in
Bosnia and Herzegovina or abroad.

The Bosnian War was an extremely complicated historical phenomenon. The
conflict entailed widespread ethnic cleansing that many observers qualified as
genocide, notably in the town of Srebrenica in the current territory of Republika Srpska, where 25,000 Muslims had taken refuge from Bosnian Serb forces.[72]
On July 11, 1995, Serbian militia units systematically executed around 8,000 Bosniak men near the town.[73] A few years ago, the International Court of Justice at
The Hague determined that Serbia was not guilty of genocide but had failed to
prevent the massacre of Bosniaks near Srebrenica. Available data suggests that
Serbian civilians and armed forces committed the greatest number of atrocities
during the Bosnian War, particularly during the years 1992–1994, and had established and operated two-thirds of the prison camps located in Bosnia and
Herzegovina during the conflict.

The various military alliances that rapidly formed, transformed, and often
disintegrated during the Bosnian War attempted to achieve immediate tactical
advantages and rarely defined long-term strategic objectives. The fragile Bosniak-
Croatian alliance collapsed in early 1993 after the Croatian defense forces that received material support from the Republic of Croatia began conducting military
and ethnic-cleansing campaigns in Bosniak-inhabited territories in Herzegovina
and central Bosnia.

In the meantime, Croatian and Serbian officials conducted intensive negotiations regarding the future of Bosnia and Herzegovina both before and during
the Bosnian War. These talks produced, among others, the Karađorđevo Agreement between Tuđman and Milošević in March 1991 and the Graz Agreement
between President Radovan Karadžić of Republika Srpska and President Mate
Boban of the Croatian Democratic Union of Bosnia and Herzegovina in May
1992.[74] According to a study examining Milošević's monitored telephone conversations, Serbian leaders—unlike their Croatian counterparts—never attributed
great significance to these bilateral Serbian-Croatian talks. While the Western

powers failed to prop up Yugoslavia's continuing existence as intended, the Belgrade leadership felt encouraged to incorporate all of Bosnia and Herzegovina into the territory of the planned new Serbian state at the expense of the Croatians during the critical phases of the war in Croatia in 1991.[75]

The international community had no other choice than to recognize the dissolution of Yugoslavia and attempt to arbitrate a peace settlement between the warring factions. The International Conference on the Former Yugoslavia convened in Geneva under the auspices of the United Nations and the European Union in September 1992. This conference, which functioned under the dual chairmanship of former Secretary of State Cyrus Vance of the United States and former foreign secretary David Owen of the United Kingdom, issued the first comprehensive plan for peace in Bosnia and Herzegovina on January 3, 1993. This so-called Vance-Owen peace plan called for the establishment of nine cantons in country—three Bosniak, three Croatian, and three Serbian— and a demilitarized administrative district centered on the capital city of Sarajevo that would have been under implicit Bosniak control. Implementation of the plan would have left 43 percent of Bosnian Serbs, 30 percent of Bosniaks, and 37 percent of Bosnian Croats living outside the cantons designated for their nationalities. While Bosnian Croats accepted the plan, both the Bosniaks and Bosnian Serbs rejected it immediately—the latter largely because the plan would have reduced the amount of territory in Bosnia and Herzegovina under their control from around 70 percent of the total area of the republic to 38 percent.

Croats and Bosniaks reconstituted their alliance against the Serbs in March 1994 as a result of a Western initiative. The failure of all attempts to find a political settlement to the Bosnian War prompted the Western powers to shift their focus toward the possibility of intervening militarily to end the conflict and to punish the Serbs whom they had declared primarily responsible for it. By September 1994, even the leaders of the Federal Republic of Yugoslavia had abandoned the radical leaders of the Republika Srpska. Milošević refused to provide further military assistance to the self-declared Serbian republic and sealed the border between the Federal Republic of Yugoslavia and Bosnia and Herzegovina. The Croats profited to the greatest degree from the strategic weakness of the Serbs, reoccupying the Serbian Autonomous Oblast of Western Slavonia and incorporating the region into the Republic of Croatia in the spring of 1995.

The increasing military cooperation between the governments of Croatia and Bosnia and Herzegovina fortified the pragmatic alliance between Bosnian Croatians and Bosniaks. The Croatian army strengthened with help from the West, and an increasing number of Muslim foreign volunteers reached Bosnia and Herzegovina illegally, often with the covert support of the United States as part of humanitarian-aid groups from Arab countries, to fight alongside the Bosnian army.[76]

The turning point in the Bosnian War occurred in the summer of 1995, shortly after Dutch soldiers in the UN Protection Force failed to prevent the massacre of Bosniaks near Srebrenica. On August 4, 1995, the Western-supported Croatian Army launched an offensive known as Operation Storm in the vicinity of Knin, the capital of the Republic of Serbian Krajina that resulted in the flight of Serbian armed forces and more than 200,000 civilians from the self-declared state inside the Republic of Croatia. As a result of this offensive, the demarcation lines and the military fronts began to coincide. Combined Croatian and Bosniak armed forces launched their final offensive with NATO air support. The long-awaited Western military intervention helped destroy the military-logistical infrastructure of the Bosnian-Serb armed forces and did not end until 51 percent of the territory of Bosnia and Herzegovina had come under Bosnian Croat and Bosniak control in accordance with the Contact Group plan of May 1994. By the autumn of 1995, the intensity of armed conflict had decreased throughout Bosnia and Herzegovina, and the sides involved in the war entered talks to find a peace settlement. After three weeks of negotiations, representatives from the Republic of Croatia (on behalf of Bosnian Croats and Bosniaks) and the Federal Republic of Yugoslavia finally reached a comprehensive agreement.

From the Dayton Agreement to the Independence of Kosovo

The US-arbitrated Dayton Agreement, concluded at Wright-Patterson Air Force Base near Dayton, Ohio, but formally signed in Paris on December 14, 1995, has been called by Richard Caplan an example of coercive diplomacy.[77] Dayton brought the three-and-a-half-year Bosnia War to an end and modified political-territorial conditions in the relevant territories. The agreement served to solidify the military situation in the regions of Slavonia and Krajina, both of which returned to Croatia after three years of Serbian occupation. Bosnia and Herzegovina was split into two parts: the Croat-Bosniak Federation of Bosnia and Herzegovina, comprising 51 percent of total state territory, and the Serbian Republika Srpska, comprising 49 percent of total state territory. The agreement established ten cantons within the Federation of Bosnia and Herzegovina—five Bosniak, three Croat, and two of mixed nationality.

To this day, an interentity administrative border divides the Federation of Bosnia and Herzegovina and Republika Srpska, which although part of the same state of Bosnia and Herzegovina exercise a significant degree of autonomous authority. Legislatures operate in both constituent entities of Bosnia and Herzegovina—a bicameral parliament in the Federation of Bosnia and Herzegovina capital city of Sarajevo and a unicameral national assembly in the Republika Srpska capital city of Banja Luka. Bosnia and Herzegovina features a collective Bosniak-Croatian-Serbian presidency with a rotating head of state based on a model inherited from the 1980s.

The stabilization of the situation in Bosnia and Herzegovina following the Dayton Agreement paradoxically served to sustain the power of the political elite that had been responsible for the Bosnian War. Milošević deflected blame for Serbian military failures in Croatia and Bosnia and Herzegovina toward the international community, Serbian militias, and "internal enemies," that is, the democratic opposition in order to retain his political legitimacy. In July 1997, Milošević was elected to serve as president of the Federal Republic of Yugoslavia, composed of the Republic of Serbia and the Republic of Montenegro. During his final years in power, Milošević presided over an ideologically syncretic government that included communists, socialists, and right-wing radical nationalists. The opposition Zajedno (Together) coalition had defeated the pro-Milošević government parties in 1996 local elections and faced a wave of student demonstrations protesting government-sponsored fraud in these elections early the following year. However, Milošević survived this unrest through the use of tactics such as raising wages and pensions (which he financed partially through the unscrupulous privatization of the national telecommunication company), the harassment of opposition supporters, and the adoption of laws circumscribing the press freedom.[78]

In Croatia, Franjo Tuđman triumphantly won another term in office as head of state in the 1997 presidential elections. Tuđman, who had overseen the Croatian Army's reincorporation of the secessionist Republic of Serbian Krajina into Croatia, maintained his unquestioned political authority until his death in December 1999. However, Tuđman has since become a very divisive figure: whereas almost everyone recognizes that the independent state of Croatia may not have come into existence without his decisive actions, many associate him primarily with long years of military conflict, war crimes, and authoritarian rule. In Bosnia and Herzegovina, President Alija Izetbegović remained in office until the year 2000, when he retired because of health reasons.

Although ethnic and religious tensions in Kosovo had made it a potential flash point of conflict, Stefan Troebst contends that the Dayton Agreement failed to address political and ethnic problems in this region, which became the nexus of regional conflict beginning in the second half of the 1990s.[79] The new Yugoslav federation of Serbia and Montenegro relinquished the notion of Greater Serbia as the main source of Milošević's political legitimacy following the defeat of pro-Serbian forces in the wars in Croatia and Bosnia and Herzegovina. Milošević had not hesitated to withdraw support for the Serbs living in those countries after having exploited them to promote Serbian nationalism as a means of enhancing his own political power. However, Kosovo—unlike the Republic of Serbian Krajina and Republika Srpska—constituted a province within the Republic of Serbia that President Milošević was prepared to prevent from seceding through the use of all means at his disposal. Following the revocation of Kosovo's autonomous

status in 1989, the Ibrahim Rugova–led Democratic League of Kosovo began boy-
cotting Serb-Yugoslav state institutions and refused to participate in elections.
At the same time, Rugova and his supporters started to build a parallel Albanian
society in Kosovo, establishing an underground educational system, illegal printing presses, and informal cultural centers.[80]

The situation in Kosovo deteriorated in the years 1997–1998, when long-
standing conflict within the Albanian elite between older moderates who had
grown up in Tito's Yugoslavia and younger radicals who had been socialized
in an environment of nationality hatred and cultural deprivation in the 1980s.
Growing political and economic crisis in Albania also contributed to the wors-
ening conditions in Kosovo, discussed later in this chapter. The Albanian internal crisis led to the outbreak of civil war in the spring and summer of 1997.
A large number of weapons subsequently began to circulate from hand to hand
in the country and eventually came into the possession of the Kosovo Liberation Army. This guerilla army conducted a series of attacks on Serbian forces
in Kosovo. The response of Belgrade to these attacks was merciless and dispro-
portionate: by August 1998, Serbian armed forces had killed several hundred
Albanians in Kosovo and forced around 300,000 others to flee from the region to Albania or Macedonia, thus contributing to the destabilization of those
countries.

This time, the Western powers took immediate diplomatic steps to resolve
the conflict in Kosovo. On September 23, 1998, the UN Security Council issued
Resolution 1199 calling for a cease-fire and talks between the factions involved in
the conflict. However, the Serbs did not comply with this agreement. Following
the failure of negotiations to end the Kosovo War held in Rambouillet, France, in
February and March 1999, Western political and diplomatic officials concluded
that Serbia had to be punished. As Adam Roberts put it, the Western initiative
had several notable features, for it involved "the first sustained use of armed
force by the NATO alliance in its 50-year existence; the first time a major use of
destructive armed force with the stated purpose of implementing UN Security
Council resolutions but without Security Council authorization; the first major
bombing campaign intended to bring a halt to crimes against humanity being
committed by a state within its own borders; and the first bombing campaign of
which it could be claimed that it had brought about a major change of policy by
the target government."[81]

On March 24, 1999, NATO aircraft began an intensive bombing campaign
aimed at destroying Serbian military and nonmilitary targets. In response, Serbia accelerated its ethnic-cleansing campaign targeting the 800,000 Albanians
who lived in Kosovo. Around 10,000 Albanians, both civilians and guerilla fighters, were killed during the Kosovo War, including several hundred who died in

NATO air attacks. Authorities from the Republic of Serbia reported that 576 people had been killed in the country, most of them civilians who died in the NATO bombing of targets in Belgrade and other cities.

On June 10, 1999, the UN Security Council issued Resolution 1244 confirming the technical agreement that NATO had concluded with the Federal Republic of Yugoslavia in Kumanovo, Macedonia; on the previous day the Security Council had stipulated the withdrawal of Serbian armed forces from Kosovo and the beginning of a cease-fire in the province. The inclusion of Russia and China in negotiations seeking to end the conflict did not prevent the deployment of the international Kosovo Force to keep peace in Kosovo under the unified command of NATO. Kosovo formally remained part of the Federal Republic of Yugoslavia but was placed under the temporary administrative authority of the United Nations, while Albanian refugees were returned to the province and guerilla fighters were disarmed. Albanian institutions were established in Kosovo as the first step toward comprehensive autonomy in the province.

As Noel Malcom predicted in 1998, all attempts to resolve the Kosovo conflict within the framework of the Yugoslav state proved illusory.[82] Following the war and the largely involuntary departure of Serbs from Kosovo, the population of the province became almost exclusively Albanian. The only Serb-inhabited enclaves that have remained in Kosovo are the town of North Kosovska Mitrovica and areas surrounding Serbian Orthodox Church monasteries. In 2008, the international community regarded Kosovo's US-sponsored secession as the lesser of two evils. In July 2010, the International Court of Justice determined that Kosovo's nonviolent declaration of independence had not violated international law. The Republic of Serbia might even recognize the independence of Kosovo in the not-too-distant future as a condition for its joining the European Union. According to security-policy specialist Francesco Strazzari, independent Kosovo—along with neighboring Montenegro—has become the prime example of a new type of institutionally fragile state that operates under the auspices of economic interest groups and criminal networks that direct the smuggling and the black-market activities that form the foundation of the national economy.[83] According to Strazzari, "In a manner that does not differ from other mafias, those in the Balkans are not born where the state and the market are absent, but, to the contrary, accompany (or direct) the process of establishing market and state structures."[84] The quoted sentence touches on a phenomenon known by scholarly literature as state capture, which occurs when state regulatory agencies make businesses in accordance with the private and often elicit interests of the regulated, to the detriment of the public interest they were supposed to serve. The last chapter of this book analyzes this issue that is so crucial to the postcommunist social history of Eastern Europe.

The Decade After: Between Democratization and Social Tensions

The Kosovo War undermined Milošević's authority in the Federal Republic of Yugoslavia, thus establishing conditions necessary for political change. The national solidarity that had formed among Serbs as a result of the NATO bombing campaign in 1999 did not negate the popular desire for peace and economic stability after eight years of war. Moreover, Russia, which had become weak and marginalized as a result of its financial and economic collapse in 1998, could no longer provide the Milošević regime with adequate support. The Kosovo War had made Serbian government officials in Belgrade aware of the true extent of Serbia's international isolation. US Secretary of State Madeleine Albright and the US ambassador to the United Nations Richard Holbrooke initiated a change in the policy of NATO away from humanitarian intervention against the Milošević regime and toward preservation of the traditional status quo. The downfall of President Milošević was the ultimate result of Yugoslavia's military defeat in 1999, but also of his personal political defeat vis-à-vis Montenegro—Serbia's greatest, and eventually sole, ally. The young, ambitious, and unrestrained president of Montenegro, Milo Đukanović, quickly began steering the country toward independence following his election in February 1998—a course that culminated in a 2006 referendum and Montenegro's subsequent membership in the United Nations.[85]

As an answer to the actions of his last ally, Milošević initiated constitutional amendments intended to reduce the autonomy of Montenegro within the Yugoslav federation, which resulted in widespread protest. In presidential elections in Yugoslavia in September 2000, the Serbian opposition finally managed to unite behind a single candidate—the conservative intellectual Vojislav Koštunica, a moderate advocate of democratic ideals who was acceptable to nationalists and the Serbian Orthodox Church. Milošević attempted unsuccessfully to reverse his defeat in the voting booths through charges of electoral fraud just as he had done a few years previously. On October 5, an enormous crowd symbolically occupied the parliament building in Belgrade, prompting Milošević to recognize Koštunica's victory.[86] The victory of the liberal-democratic coalition under the leadership of former Belgrade mayor Zoran Đinđić in parliamentary elections in December 2000 completed the transfer of political power in Yugoslavia. The Đinđić government formed following the elections differed markedly from its predecessors, seeking rapprochement with the West, authorizing Milošević's extradition to the Netherlands to stand trial on charges of war crimes before the International Criminal Tribunal for the Former Yugoslavia, and attempting to find a peaceful resolution to the conflict in Kosovo. The newly founded Serbian democracy has proven capable of responding effectively to significant challenges such as the secession of Montenegro and of Kosovo despite the destabilization actions of security forces connected to the former regime that resulted in the assassination of several political officials, including Prime Minister Đinđić in 2003, and has maintained its ambition to join the European Union despite the economic crisis and the unresolved issue of Kosovo's contested independence.

Of the former Yugoslav republics, Macedonia has encountered the greatest test to the endurance of its political and social system over the past ten years. Following the Kosovo War, the right-center governing coalition in Macedonia, which included the party representing the sizable Albanian minority, faced the humanitarian catastrophe of 300,000 refugees in a country of 2 million inhabitants. As a result of this massive influx of refugees from Kosovo, the number of Albanians living in Macedonia increased to one-quarter of the total population, and the number of Albanian, Turk, and Roma Muslims increased to one-third of the total population, according to data from the last available census, in 2002. Anecdotal evidence suggests that the demographic trends are rather unfavorable to the Macedonian-majority community, and this might explain the growing concern on this issue by the nationalist circles in Skopje.[87]

Although a large number of the refugees quickly returned to Kosovo, the intensification of contacts between various Albanian communities and the transfer of the Kosovo Liberation Army's operative base to Macedonia have resulted in the radicalization of Macedonian politics. The demands of Albanians living in northern Macedonia assumed a revolutionary character beginning in the autumn of 2000, manifesting in attacks on Macedonian police at various locations along the country's border with Kosovo. This low-intensity conflict—which until then had resulted in a few hundred military and civilian deaths—escalated into open hostility during the first half of 2001 and spread to other regions of Macedonia.

The response of the international community to the escalation of conflict in Macedonia was immediate and proportional, resulting in the launch of Operation Essential Harvest under the auspices of NATO and the initiation of efforts to rebuild the Macedonian social and political structure. On August 13, 2001, the parties involved in the conflict signed an agreement in Ohrid Framework Agreement that obligated the government of Macedonia to recognize Albanian as a second official language of the republic, increase the influence of Albanians within the governing structure, and implement the planned decentralization of state administration. According to Michael S. Lund, the relative success of internal stabilization in Macedonia might be due to a lucky combination of factors. In addition to the already-mentioned pluralist institutional framework, after almost a decade of continuous crisis management in former Yugoslavia, the international actors had finally learned the lesson and introduced conflict-preventive measures in Macedonia soon after its new nationhood.[88]

The agreement at Ohrid also established the conditions necessary for Macedonia to become an official candidate for accession to the European Union in

2005, although negotiations regarding the country's EU membership have not yet begun. Greece vetoed the application of Macedonia for NATO membership in 2008 given the countries' dual claim to the use of the name Macedonia—which also refers to the northern region of Greece (map 5.2).

The Prolonged Albanian Transition

Ramiz Alia, who in 1985 succeeded Enver Hoxha as the first secretary of the Party of Labor of Albania, maintained the national independence policies that his predecessor had initiated in the 1960s. Only in 1990 did the party undertake cautious political liberalization, which resulted in the introduction of minor free-market reforms, the signing of the Helsinki Accords following a fifteen-year delay, the annulment of the law forbidding the practice of religion, the removal of restrictions on the right to travel, and the reinstitution of the previously dissolved justice ministry.[89] As Joseph Rothschild has noted, the political liberalization that occurred in Albania in 1990 was not a response to demands from below but an anticipation of them. In 1991, Alia authorized the organization of opposition parties, the most important of which was the Democratic Party of Albania, which operated under the leadership of Enver Hoxha's former personal physician, Sali Berisha. However, the Party of Labor (which subsequently became the Socialist Party of Albania) defeated the Democratic Party in the parliamentary elections on March 31, 1991. The new opposition party managed to win 38 percent of all votes cast and gained a significant degree of support from the inhabitants of major cities and young people. The political chaos and social and economic hardship that emerged in Albania during the transition period prompted tens of thousands of Albanians to leave the country for Italy.

As in Romania, the collapse of ruthless dictatorship and transition to democracy in Albania during the early 1990s resulted in significant upheaval and the fracturing of politics along generational lines. In Albania, social and geographical fault lines also appeared at this time between those who lived in cities and those who lived in rural areas, as well as between the mostly pro–Democratic Party Gheg ethnic group in northern Albania and the mostly pro–Socialist Party Tosk ethnic group in southern Albania.

The political conflict in Albania resulted in an atmosphere of permanent tension, which the catastrophic economic, social, and environmental conditions in the country served to further intensify. Obsolete mines and, from an aesthetic standpoint, the several hundred thousand bunkers built beginning in the 1950s symbolized the environmental problems that Albania confronted following the country's tumultuous transition to democracy. Nevertheless, the genuine turning point in the process of political transition nevertheless took place earlier in Albania than it did in Romania or Bulgaria: the Democratic Party defeated the

Map 5.2. Yugoslavia, 2008. Courtesy Béla Nagy, Hungarian Academy of Sciences.

Socialist Party in parliamentary elections held in March 1992 and Sali Berisha succeeded Ramiz Alia as president of Albania the following month. During its five years in power from 1992 to 1997, the Democratic Party implemented ultraliberal economic policies (e.g., coupon-based privatization), oversaw a chaotic process of urbanization, and instituted an authoritarian-type presidential system under Berisha's leadership.[90]

During these years, half of all Albanians placed their savings and movable and immovable assets, as well as their returned property and livestock, in banks and financial companies—so-called pyramids—in the hope of quickly enriching themselves. These banks and financial companies offered their clients unrealistically high interest (44 percent per month in 1996, for example), although they covered these exorbitant rates through the acquisition of an ever greater stock of invested assets. The citizens of Albania were so unfamiliar with even basic financial mechanisms that they were unable to recognize that the banks and financial institutions in which they had invested their assets were classic Ponzi schemes. These banks and financial institutions collapsed in February 1997, and those who operated these pyramids took refuge abroad, leaving their accomplices within the Albanian state with enormous wealth and hundreds of thousands of Albanian citizens destitute and lacking access to legal redress.[91]

The collapse of these companies caused popular unrest in Albania, particularly in the Tosk region of the country, which was pro–Socialist Party. This turmoil forced the Democratic Party government to dissolve itself on March 8, 1997, after which the Albanian army and police disintegrated and Albania fell into a state of undeclared civil war. Crowds of civilians plundered military warehouses, and more than 2,000 people were killed in armed clashes between supporters of Berisha, who resigned from his post as president in July 1997, and new Socialist Party prime minister Fatos Nano. Several hundred thousand people fled from Albania as a result of the conflict and disorder, mostly to Italy. The Socialist Party government that came to power in June 1997 enacted economic-stabilization measures to prevent the complete collapse of Albania's state apparatus. This stabilization enabled Albania to accommodate around 500,000 Kosovo Albanian refugees in 1999 despite the country's poverty and underdeveloped infrastructure.

Albania has undergone gradual political normalization over the past decade. After winning 2001 parliamentary elections, the Socialist Party lost to the Berisha-led Democratic Party in 2005 and 2009 elections, which the international community declared to be valid despite evidence of minor electoral fraud. Foreign investment and, to an even greater degree, an enormous sum of remittances from Albanians living abroad, including 500,000 in Italy alone, lifted Albania out of postcommunist transition and subsequent financial collapse in 1997. In 2009, Albania became a member of NATO and applied for membership to the

European Union. Although the accession of Albania to the European Union represents a long-term prospect, the process of European integration could provide enormous benefits to the country's economy, which during the immediate post-communist period had fallen into a miserable state.

Notes

1. Dahrendorf, *1989*, 11.
2. Ash, *Uses of Adversity*, 320.
3. Ash, "Conclusions," 398.
4. Karol Edward Sołtan, "Moderate Modernity and the Spirit of 1989," 69–108.
5. Benvenuti, *La Russia dopo l'URSS*, 33–39.
6. Kramer, "Collapse of East European Communism (Part III)," 3–96.
7. King, *Moldovans*, 188–194.
8. On contemporary ethnic conflict from a theoretical perspective, see McGarry and O'Leary, *Politics of Ethnic Conflict Regulation*. For a comparative analysis of frozen conflicts in the postcommunist region, see Nodia, "Europeanization and (Not) Resolving Secessionist Conflicts."
9. Sussex, "Introduction," 9–11.
10. Kraus and Stanger, *Irreconcilable Differences?*.
11. Bárdi, Fedinec, and Szarka, *Minority Hungarian Communities in the Twentieth Century*, 456–67, and 525–537.
12. Brubaker et al., *Nationalist Politics*.
13. Graziosi, *L'URSS dal trionfo al degrado*, 663–664; see also Kennedy, *Rise and Fall of the Great Powers*, 514.
14. Elsuwege, "Russian-Speaking Minorities in Estonia and Latvia."
15. Cohen, *Failed Crusade*, 21.
16. Bruszt and Stark, *Postsocialist Pathways*, 7–8, 110.
17. See Cortona, *Da uno a molti*.
18. See *Political Parties in Central and Eastern Europe: In Search of Consolidation* (Stockholm: International Institute for Democracy and Electoral Assistance, 2007), http://www.idea .int/publications/pp_c_and_e_europe/upload/Regional_Report_CEE.pdf.
19. Kitschelt et al., *Post-Communist Party Systems*, especially chapters 1 and 2.
20. For an introduction to democracy building, see Dawisha and Parrott, *Consolidation of Democracy in East-Central Europe*.
21. Sadurski, *Constitutional Justice, East and West*.
22. See Argentieri, *Il ritorno degli ex*.
23. Schöpflin, *Nations, Identity, Power*, 66–73.
24. Berend, *From the Soviet Bloc to the European Union*, 108–109.
25. Ibid., 42.
26. Hoen, *Governance in Central and Eastern Europe*, 94–96.
27. Báger and Kovács, *Privatisation in Hungary*, 119.
28. Berend, *From the Soviet Bloc to the European Union*, 111–113.
29. Sárközy, *A privatizáció joga Magyarországon*, 7.
30. Åslund, *How Capitalism Was Built*.

31. Kenney, *Il peso della libertà*, 10–11.

32. Báger and Kovács, *Privatisation in Hungary*, 49–84.

33. Kornai, "Transzformációs visszaesés," 569–599; Csaba, "A rendszerváltozás elmélete és/vagy a közgazdaságtan kudarca?" 1–19; Gyarmati, "A nosztalgia esete a Kádár-korszakkal," 3–21.

34. "Report No. J/8582 of the Government of the Republic of Hungary regarding the Activities of the State Privatization," Budapest, January 2009, http://www.parlament.hu/irom38/08582.pdf.

35. Berend, *From the Soviet Bloc to the European Union*, 168–169.

36. Ibid., 77.

37. For more detail, see Eyal, Szelényi, and Townsley, *Making Capitalism without Capitalists*.

38. See the table at http://ec.europa.eu/eurostat/tgm/table.do?tab=table&plugin=1&language=en&pcode=tec00114. The data refer to GDP per capita in in purchasing power standards expressed in relation to the European Union average.

39. Pogátsa, "No Convergence in the Central Eastern European New Member States," 363–376.

40. Janos, *East Central Europe in the Modern World*.

41. Stuckler, King, and McKee, "Mass Privatisation and the Post-Communist Mortality Crisis," 399–407.

42. Cockerham, "Social Determinants of the Decline in Life Expectancy," 117–130.

43. Estimated life expectancy for 2015 provided by the CIA World Factbook; see http://www.cia.gov/library/publications/the-world-factbooks/fields/2102.html.

44. See the special issue edited by Sándor Horváth, "Everyday Collaboration with the Communist Regimes in Eastern Europe," *Hungarian Historical Review* 4, no. 1 (Spring 2015).

45. Ash, *File*; Verdery, *Secrets and Truths*. An attempt to transpose security files into literature is found in the novel *Javított kiadás* of the Hungarian writer Péter Esterházy, who realized that his father was an informer of the communist secret police.

46. For a comparative examination, see Kritz, *Transitional Justice*; De Brito, González Enriquez, and Aguilar, *Politics of Memory*; Stan, *Transitional Justice in Eastern Europe and the Former Soviet Union*.

47. On the impact of the communist legacy on voting behaviors, see Roper and Fesnic, "Historical Legacies," 119–131. On post-1989 Czechoslovakia, see David, "Transitional Injustice?," 789–812. On Poland, see Aleks Szczerbiak, "Dealing with the Communist Past or the Politics of the Present?," 553–572. On independent Slovakia, Nadya Nedelsky, "Divergent Responses to a Common Past," 65–115.

48. "Bulgarian President Collaborated with Communist Secret Services." *Eurasian Secret Services*, July 23, 2007.

49. "KGB-Trained Hungarian Has NATO Role," *New York Times*, February 4, 2008.

50. Kasianov, "How a War for the Past Becomes a War in the Present," 155.

51. Quotations from "Law of Ukraine: On Access to Archives of Repressive Agencies of Totalitarian Communist Regime 1917–1991." The English translation of the original Ukrainian text is provided at the institution's website: http://www.memory.gov.ua.

52. For an informative introduction to the debate, see Josh Cohen, "The Historian Whitewashing the Ukrainian Past," *Foreign Policy*, May 2, 2016, https://foreignpolicy.com/2016/05/02/the-historian-whitewashing-ukraines-past-volodymyr-viatrovych/.

53. Booth, *Communities of Memory*; Minow, *Breaking the Cycles of Hatred*, 28.

54. On this, see Rév, *Retroactive Justice*.

55. Judt, *Postwar*, 829.

56. See the telling data from the opinion polls realized in Romania after the 2009 economic crisis, avaialable at http://www.balkanalysis.com/romania/2011/12/27/in-romania-opinion-polls-show-nostalgia-for-communism/. For a complex analysis of communist nostalgia in the Romanian context, see the excellent contribution of Cristina and Dragoş Petrescu in Todorova, Dimou, and Troebst, *Remembering Communism*, 43–70.

57. On the misuse of the former Securitate's archives, see Andreescu, *Cărturari, opozanţi şi documente*. On the Romanian "truth commission," see Ciobanu, "Criminalising the Past and Reconstructing Collective Memory," 315–338.

58. In December 2008 representatives from Bulgaria, Czech Republic, Germany, Hungary, Poland, Romania, and Slovakia established the European Network of Official Authorities in Charge of the Secret Police File. More English-language information on the netwok and the founding institutions is available at the website https://eureconciliation.eu/national-institutions-responsible-for-the-investigation-and-archival-of-communist-crimes/.

59. For an introduction to postcommunist historiographical renewal, see Antohi, Trencsényi, and Apor, *Narratives Unbound*.

60. The patent inequality in the distribution of research funds by the European Union has been described by an anonymous but well-informed academic. See "European Research Funding: It's Like Robin Hood in Reverse," *The Guardian*, November 7, 2014, https://www.theguardian.com/higher-education-network/2014/nov/07/european-research-funding-horizon-2020.

61. Blagojević and Yair, "Catch 22 Syndrome," 355.

62. Glaurdić, *Hour of Europe*, 6.

63. Pavlowitch, *Serbia*, 265.

64. Lusa, *La dissoluzione del potere*.

65. Thompson, *Paper House*, 105.

66. This is the main argument of Dizdarevic, *From the Death of Tito to the Death of Yugoslavia*.

67. Franzinetti, *I Balcani dal 1878 a oggi*, 100–101.

68. Pirjevec, *Le guerre jugoslave*, 37.

69. Franzinetti, "Bosnia," 238–239.

70. Burg and Shoup, *War in Bosnia-Herzegovina*, 169.

71. Franzinetti, "Bosnia," 244.

72. For an examination of the suitability of the term *genocide* in the Bosnian War, see Hayden, "'Genocide Denial' Laws as Secular Heresy," 384–407.

73. Suljagić, *Cartoline dalla fossa*, 244.

74. Malcolm, *Storia della Bosnia*, 303–304.

75. Glaurdić, "Inside the Serbian War Machine," 92–93.

76. Schindler, *Jihad nei Balcani*, 229.

77. Caplan, "'Bombing and Negotiating,'" 158–160.

78. Stefan Wagstyl, Irena Guzelova, and Kerin Hope, "Milosevic's Murky Fortune," *Financial Times*, April 4, 2001.

79. Troebst, *Conflict in Kosovo: Failure of Prevention?*

80. A thorough analysis is found in Kostovicova, *Kosovo*.

81. Roberts, "NATO's 'Humanitarian War' over Kosovo," 102.

82. Malcolm, "Kosovo," 23–26.

83. Strazzari, *Notte balcanica*, 69–72.

84. Ibid., 146.

85. Franzinetti, *Balcani dal 1878 a oggi*, 112.

86. Pavlowitch, *Serbia*, 289–290.

87. The following national census was canceled amid political conflicts between the Macedonian center-right government party VMRO and its Albanian coalition member.
88. Lund, "Greed and Grievances Diverted," 231.
89. Rothschild, *Return to Diversity*, 254–255.
90. Franzinetti, *I Balcani dal 1878 a oggi*, 114.
91. Jarvis, "Rise and the Fall of the Pyramid Schemes," 1–29.

Chapter 6

Eastern Europe Today
Western Periphery or Buffer Zone?

The State of Regional and Euro-Atlantic Integration

Beginning in 1989, the countries of Eastern Europe made an enormous effort to put into practice new political, economic, and cultural models adopted from the Western free-market liberal democracies. This goal was mostly pursued through mimetic adaptation to patterns that were often very foreign to the historical legacy and the collective mind-set of the societies that came to be involved in the experiment. The most important challenge was how to build or eventually rebuild a nation-state in the changing context of a globalized world. The new, postcommunist Eastern Europe thus became a dynamic region in which the (re)construction and tardy nationalization of the societal body became intertwined with the ongoing processes of European integration.

During the 1990s, regional-cooperation organizations established with the ultimate goal of boosting European integration, such as the Visegrád Group that Poland, Czechoslovakia, and Hungary founded in 1991 and the Council of the Baltic Sea States instituted in 1992, achieved only modest results. The preference that the European Union gave to individual negotiations emerged soon from the Maastricht Treaty and the Copenhagen and Madrid criteria established in 1993 and 1995, respectively, to determine the preconditions for joining the European Union (stable institutional system, respect for human and minority rights, functioning market-economy, the gradual incorporation of communal achievements into the national legal system).

The road to European Union membership turned out to be long and circuitous. Moreover, the front-runners undertook the process of European integration in competition with one another. In December 1994, the European Council adopted a broad preaccession strategy to bring postcommunist countries closer to the European Union. The European Commission divided the candidates into two groups based on the executive body's appraisal of their democratic institutions: candidate states with sufficiently developed and stable democratic institutions— Estonia, Poland, Czech Republic, Slovenia, and Hungary—that began laborious negotiations in 1998; and candidate states with insufficiently developed democratic institutions—Latvia, Lithuania, Slovakia, Romania, and Bulgaria—that had to implement further reforms before starting them.

Scholars agree that in the second half of the 1990s, the need for collective security in Central and Eastern Europe constituted the primary motive for the parallel and sometimes competitive eastward expansion of the European Union and NATO. US diplomacy during President Bill Clinton's second term in office exploited the weakened Russian influence in Central Europe to unilaterally initiate the settlement of contested issues in the region. Poland, the Czech Republic, and Hungary joined NATO in March 1999 on the eve of the alliance's military intervention in Yugoslavia in which logistical assistance from neighboring Hungary was especially needed—five years before the accession to the European Union granted on May 1, 2004, to ten new members, seven of them former members of the Soviet Bloc. Romania, Bulgaria, Slovakia, Slovenia, and the Baltic countries followed in March 2004, moving the external borders of the Western defensive alliance even closer to Russia.

The American strategic interest for the postcommunist areas of Europe ended with George W. Bush's presidency. The last moment of reciprocal enthusiasm came during the US invasion of Iraq in 2003, when most Eastern European governments and public intellectuals supported the military action and US Secretary of State Donald Rumsfeld compared the "New Europe," loyal toward the United States, to the increasingly hostile and unreliable allies from the Western half of the continent.[1] As the subsequent developments showed, only a few countries in Eastern Europe (grateful Kosovo, as well as security-minded Romania, Poland, and the Baltics) can be defined as unequivocally pro-American. The majority of the population of the other new NATO members pragmatically recognizes the achievements of the United States and expects NATO to provide them with security but opposes taking significant measures to support the Euro-Atlantic alliance and increasing extremely low military expenditures. The perception of the West in the New Europe is strictly linked to the complex relationship between the Eastern European member states of the European Union and Russia. The Baltic countries, Poland, and Romania have always regarded post-Soviet Russia as a potential threat to their national security. These states have become especially concerned about the revival of Russian expansionism following Russia's unilateral annexation of the Crimean Peninsula in 2014. Other EU and NATO member states in Eastern Europe—notably the Czech Republic, Slovakia,

Hungary, and Bulgaria—regard their relations with Russia primarily as an energy issue given their nearly total dependence on the import of Russian gas.[2] This consideration explains the interest that some of these countries expressed in the proposed South Stream pipeline to carry gas from Russia to Eastern Europe, despite opposition to the project from the United States and other Western powers.

A quarter of a century after the end of the Cold War, the inclusion of a region that had long been subject to Soviet competition has been formally successful. As map 6.1 shows, eleven countries that once belonged to the Soviet Bloc, including three that were part of the Soviet Union, joined the European Union between 2004 and 2013, thus shifting the European Union's geopolitical center of gravity eastward, while another four countries are expected to join (Serbia, Macedonia, Montenegro, and Albania). Of these countries, Albania and Montenegro already enjoy NATO member status despite strong Russian disapproval of the latter's move. The peripheral areas (Ukraine, Belarus, and Moldova from the post-Soviet region, as well as Kosovo and Bosnia and Herzegovina) have been excluded so far from the integration process for different reasons that relate not only to their poor economic development but also to institutional fragilities that make their deeper integration unlikely for a long time.

As Timothy Snyder—an advocate of the fast Europeanization of the Eastern peripheries—recently claimed, the European Union can be best understood as a post-imperial economic project led by democratic and multicultural Germany, a country that after dramatically losing its own empire in 1945 was more prepared than any other European power to undertake paradigm shift. This deeply emotional factor destined the European Union to become an empire by invitation, reluctant to grow but continuously forced by external events to do so, and this makes the European Union so attractive to candidate countries despite all negative news coming about the union's internal life. According to this view, the European Union could represent a solution to the problems posed by last century's wars and as a way of solving the "decolonization problem," that is to say, the persistent social inequalities within Europe.[3]

The process of European integration has obliterated much of the Iron Curtain that physically separated Eastern Europe from the rest of the continent during the second half of the twentieth century. In the conclusive chapter of his pioneering attempt to reconstruct a comprehensive social history of contemporary Europe, Béla Tomka puts on the scales discourses on Europe's unity and disunity throughout the last century and argues that "no one can seriously question that a significant body of heritage exists," although "we cannot see the continuous and constant presence of the idea of Europe in the twentieth century." According to Tomka, the European integration process, also referred to as the Europeanization of Europe, has "decisively contributed to the situation in which the question of the existence of a European society could be raised at all." Nevertheless, Tomka

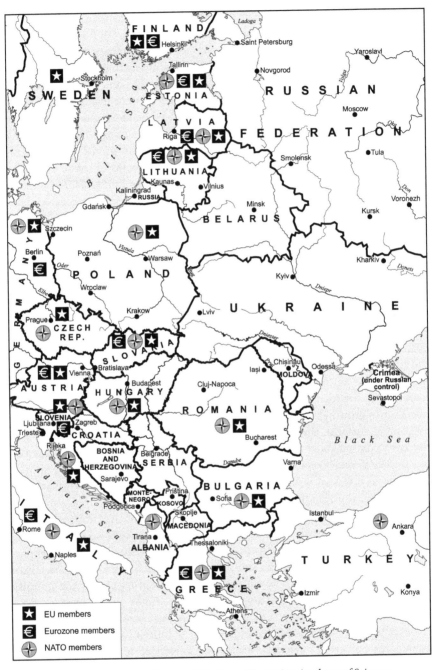

Map 6.1. Eastern Europe, 2016. Courtesy Béla Nagy, Hungarian Academy of Sciences.

warns against transforming the existing set of common European cultural values and social experiences into a self-fulfilling narrative that denies "the openness of the European integration process" and arrives at "teleological interpretations."[4]

The idea that the European integration not only is desirable but also represents the necessary outcome of the inevitable vanishing of the nation-state touches on a controversial point. For many years after 1989, citizens from the European peripheries have been sharing the view that the end of Soviet-type communism paved the way for what Francis Fukuyama famously called "the end of history": a metaphor of the unchallenged worldwide diffusion of Western-style liberal democracy and free market. Despite getting through tough difficulties and painful setbacks, most citizens of the continental periphery have long maintained their trust toward the West as the only viable way out from economic underdevelopment and security threat from Russia.

From a pragmatic standpoint, the most important consequences of European integration have been the free flow of goods and capital and above all the freedom of individual movement within the European space. The legal standardization and highly bureaucratized state mechanism that have emerged as a result of European Union enlargement present neither an intellectual challenge nor the necessity of emotional self-identification, although they may test the adaptive capacities of EU citizens.

Among the Eastern European members of the European Union, only Poland has shown the ambition to play an assertive role in European Union political affairs, and former Polish prime minister Donald Tusk managed to become president of the European Council in December 2014 with the decisive support of Germany. All other Eastern European countries have rarely tried to promote their interests within the European Union during their first decade of membership, and their influence on EU decision-making is negligible. Western European EU member states have frequently behaved in an ambiguous manner with regard to issues ranging from the symbolic condemnation of communism to energy dependence on Russia, which are extremely important for Eastern European member states. With regard to minority issues within the enlarged European Union, Giuliano Amato and Judy Batt warned to no avail already in 1990s that the European Union would have to develop a mechanism through which it could conduct the collective application of human and minority rights as a means of resolving internal ethnic and nationality conflict.[5] However, recent developments within the European Union have decreased the chances of doing this. Longtime members of the European Union, notably France and Greece, as well as many new EU member states have maintained their nation-state mentality (one state equals one nation). Moreover, territorial autonomy established in different states of Europe during the 1970s has resulted in secessionist movements that pose a threat to their unity. The efforts of Scotland and Catalonia to secede from the United

Kingdom and Spain, respectively, have prompted many Europeans to conclude that nationality issues should be resolved through the strict preservation of the nation-state rather than decentralization.

Partly as an answer to this challenge, racist and authoritarian parties have recorded significant successes in legislative elections held in Eastern Europe in the twenty-first century: the Greater Romania Party in 2000 (21 percent of votes), the League of Polish Families in 2001 (7.9 percent), the Attack Party in Bulgaria in 2005 (8.1 percent), the Slovak National Party in 2006 (11.7 percent), and the Jobbik-Movement for a Better Hungary in 2010 and 2014 (16.7 percent and 20.2 percent, respectively). It is to be noted that these parties have not managed to enter the political mainstream or gain significant influence within political institutions, nor have they broken out of the cordon sanitaire in which the domestic media and intelligentsia have enclosed them.[6] Moreover, minority parties such as the Democratic Alliance of Hungarians in Romania, the Movement for Rights and Freedoms, the Turkish party in Bulgaria, and the Democratic Party of Albanians in Macedonia have played a stabilizing role in their countries, taking part in several coalition governments and realizing their demands within the political environment into which they have become integrated.[7] Sherrill Stroschein pinpoints how ethnic protest and contention in postcommunist Eastern Europe transformed into a de facto deliberative process that allowed democratic consolidation to take root in multiethnic areas.[8] However, the ambition of Hungarian minorities in the neighboring countries to gain territorial autonomy has fallen victim to this neo-centralizing logic even though such autonomy would present no significant internal security threat to any neighboring countries. The failure of EU member states in Western Europe to distinguish between indigenous minorities and the Soviet-determined immigrant communities that evolved in the region during the second half of the twentieth century also serves to inhibit the expansion of minority rights within the European Union.

Extending the Boundaries of Democracy? Postcrisis Developments in the European Peripheries

During the 1990s, political scientists characterized many of the Eastern European newly democratic states as still imperfect democracies or even semiauthoritarian hybrid regimes.[9] These political systems, though formally pluralistic, lacked democratic checks and balances, concentrated power and economic resources, and marginalized and often harassed the domestic opposition. After a decade of intensive democratic training, the adoption of EU-advocated norms (the *acquis communautaire*) helped consolidate the legal framework, while the fast propagation of digital technologies and social networks brought an end to the previous state monopoly on public information.

Where the authoritarian structure and mind-set inherited from the communist era proved insensitive to the public call for democracy, the mass mobilization of politically committed citizens succeeded in ousting them in a series of follow-ups of the 1989 revolutions. Illiberal regimes were challenged by color revolutions: nonviolent popular uprisings that forced the power in place to resign or to accommodate themselves to democratic norms. In the second half of the 1990s, two formerly marginalized countries, Romania and Slovakia, both run by ethnocentric protectionist elites, experienced a rapid and peaceful transition to genuine democracy. In both cases, the change came through an electoral process but the outcome was quite different. The unexpected victory of the university professor Emil Constantinescu in the Romanian presidential elections of 1996 did not foster a more effective government for the power coalition, which although committed to the ideals of democracy, lacked competence and unity. The economic collapse of 1998–1999 favored the return of the postcommunist party to power. Paradoxically, it was the patronage-based social democratic government under Prime Minister Adrian Năstase from 2000 to 2004 that managed to get the country closer to the European Union and to become a pivotal military ally of the United States in the region. Năstase was remarkably successful in achieving economic growth via foreign investments while touching nationalist chords in domestic discourse. His government did not improve the quality of Romanian democracy but pragmatically adapted its most controversial features (e.g., the ubiquitous secret services) to the requirements of the new partners.

On the contrary, the parliamentary elections that marked the defeat of Slovak prime minister Vladimír Mečiar led to long-term qualitative changes in the democratic setting of the country between 1998 and 2006 under the leadership of liberal-conservative prime minister Mikuláš Dzurinda, whose farsighted political and economic reforms have helped the country regain its international credibility.[10] Scholars of democratic transition have used the term *electoral revolution* to describe the Slovak case. The anti-Mečiar grassroots campaign of 1998 was based on monitoring government activities and the elections themselves, as well as on an aggressive propaganda campaign. In attempting to oust the political elite in Slovakia, a double campaign was initiated: a positive one to bring people to the polls and a negative one to emphasize the regime's dark side. Slovakia has since become a member of both NATO and the European Union and is one of five EU member states in Eastern Europe that have adopted the euro, along with the Baltic countries and Slovenia. Although the eastern half of Slovakia is significantly poorer and less developed than the western region around the capital city of Bratislava, the Slovak case demonstrates that good governance still matters to the success of a country.

After a majority of the former socialist countries joined the European Union and others seemed to be on the path to follow, Western analysts and decision makers reached the conclusion that the democratic consolidation had become irreversible in Central Europe and entered into an advanced stage in Southeastern Europe and the post-Soviet republics. In the first decade of the twenty-first century, so-called color revolutions took place in Serbia (2000), Georgia (2003), Ukraine (2004), and Moldova (2009) and were soon celebrated as the final triumph of democratic principles over authoritarian rule. The impact of these social movements was rather different from case to case. The model of the color revolution appears to have been effective where the revolutionary nucleus (e.g., Otpor! in Serbia) possessed both financial and logistical backing from Western nongovernmental organizations combined with social support.[11] In Serbia, there was no genuine alternative to Milošević's removal from power following ten years of war and the de facto acceptance of losing Kosovo. But in neither Ukraine nor Moldova was the process of reorientation toward the West irreversible. The young protesters and liberal intellectuals who had initiated the latter process in these countries failed to adequately take into account the fragility of the state and so-called civil society and the lack of effective support from the European Union.

Moreover, the role of Russia in orienting the local political elites was grossly underestimated. After consolidating the internal situation in Russia, around 2005 President Vladimir Putin started to implement an anti-Western foreign policy toward the former Soviet Bloc countries, designed to discourage further NATO expansion and regain some direct influence in the region. The failure of pro-Western governments in Ukraine during the presidency of Viktor Yushchenko after the Orange Revolution of late 2004 foreshadowed the clear victory of the pro-Russian candidate Viktor Yanukovych over his main rival, former prime minister Yulia Tymoshenko, in the runoff of the presidential elections held in early 2010. The victory of Yanukovych in Ukraine at least seemingly embodied the conflict between some semblance of governance and the abstract principles of democracy.

The latent conflict between the "two Ukraines" exploded in November 2013 amid President Yanukovych's refusal under Russian pressure to sign the Ukraine–European Union Association Agreement, which would have brought the country closer the European integration. The civil unrest began with protests of young people in Kyiv's central Maidan Nezalezhnosti (Independence Square) demanding closer European integration. In the following weeks, the scope of the protests expanded, and in February 2014 a series of violent clashes that claimed dozens of victims forced Yanukovych to resign in order to end the bloodshed.[12]

In Ukraine, political cleavages between citizens of Ukrainian and Russian affiliation did not threaten the country's territorial integrity until the outbreak of armed conflict in the spring of 2014, when Russia reacted furiously to the loss of its main partner in the region and Putin used local militias and undercover

Russian army units to start an armed conflict with the new Ukrainian authorities. The Russian-speaking region of Crimea that had been transferred in 1954 to the Ukrainian Soviet Socialist Republic was annexed to Russia, in contravention of international law. Ukraine emerged as the ideal ground for Russia's neo-imperial answer to Western expansion plans in the former Soviet Bloc. In the years 2014–2015, the poorly armed Ukrainian military faced a type of war strategy characterized by Western scholars as "hybrid," which stemmed from nonstate actors and blended conventional warfare, irregular false flag warfare, and cyberwarfare on social media. In the Ukrainian case, the symbol of this hybrid warfare became those masked soldiers—reportedly members of Russian special forces—in unmarked green army uniforms who appeared carrying Russian weapons during the annexation of Crimea on March 18, 2014, and subsequently ravaged the mostly Russian-speaking eastern regions of Donetsk and Luhansk, resulting in thousands of casualties and the displacement of more than 2 million Ukrainians.

Scholars of different orientations have argued over the responsibilities for Ukraine's economic and civil collapse as a state as a consequence of the devastating conflict. Political scientist John J. Mearsheimer put most of the blame for the Ukrainian tragedy on the Western powers:

> Putin's pushback should have come as no surprise. After all, the West had been moving into Russia's backyard and threatening its core strategic interests, a point Putin made repeatedly and emphatically. Elites in the United States and Europe have been blindsided by events only because they subscribe to a flawed view of international politics. They tend to believe that the logic of realism holds little relevance in the twenty-first century and that Europe can be kept whole and free on the basis of such liberal principles as the rule of law, economic interdependence, and democracy. But this grand scheme went awry in Ukraine. U.S. and European leaders blundered in attempting to turn Ukraine into a Western stronghold on Russia's border.[13]

Commenting in this article, Alexander Motyl observed that the West had done too little, not too much, to integrate Ukraine and to avoid its de facto partition (map 6.2):

> Until the Maidan Revolution broke out in late 2013, Western policy toward Ukraine had been characterized by "fatigue" since about 2008, when the reformist energy of the Yushchenko government fully dissipated. Indeed, the EU's development of its Eastern Partnership program and its offer of an Association Agreement to Ukraine were precisely intended to address that policy lacuna without promising Ukraine even the prospect of membership in the EU. Indeed, the striking thing about the EU has been its reluctance for the last two decades to state that Ukraine could, even at some time in the distant future, become an EU member.[14]

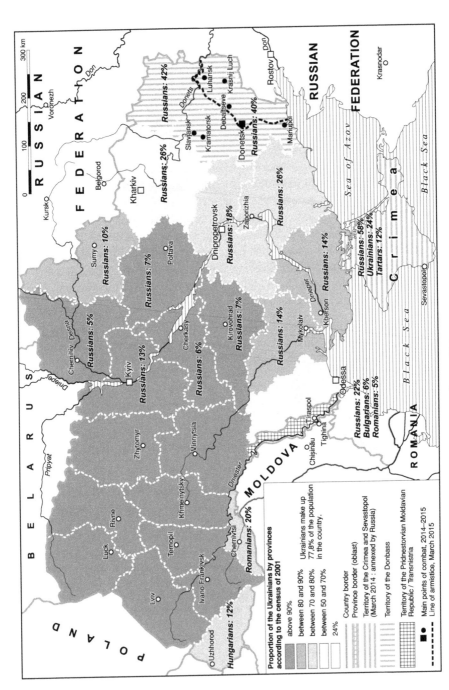

Map 6.2. Ukraine, 2015. Courtesy Béla Nagy, Hungarian Academy of Sciences.

Proportion of the Ukrainians by provinces according to the census of 2001

- above 90%
- between 80 and 90%
- between 70 and 80%
- between 50 and 70%
- 24%

Ukrainians make up 77.8% of the population in the country.

— Country border

···· Province border (oblast)

Territory of the Crimea and Sevastopol (March 2014): annexed by Russia)

Territory of the Donbass

Territory of the Pridnestrovian Moldavian Republic / Transnistria

■ ● Main points of combat, 2014–2015

- - - Line of armistice, March 2015

Russians: 42%
Russians: 26%
Russians: 40%
Russians: 26%
Russians: 18%
Russians: 10%
Russians: 7%
Russians: 5%
Russians: 13%
Russians: 6%
Russians: 7%
Russians: 14%
Russians: 14%
Russians: 58%
Ukrainians: 24%
Tartars: 12%
Russians: 22%
Bulgarians: 6%
Romanians: 5%
Romanians: 20%
Hungarians: 12%

POLAND
BELARUS
RUSSIAN FEDERATION
RUSSIAN FEDERATION
MOLDOVA
ROMANIA
Crimea
Sea of Azov
Black Sea
Black Sea

0 100 200 300 km

Kursk, Voronezh, Belgorod, Rostov, Krasnodar
Don, Donets, Desna, Pripyet, Dnieper, Dniester

Sumy, Kharkiv, Poltava, Chernihiv, Kyiv, Zhytomyr, Vinnytsia, Khmelnytsky, Ternopil, Rivne, Luck, Lviv, Ivano-Frankivsk, Chernivtsi, Uzhhorod, Cherkasy, Kirovohrad, Dnipropetrovsk, Zaporizhia, Mykolaiv, Kherson, Odessa, Tiraspol, Tighina, Chișinău, Sevastopol

Sloviansk, Kramatorsk, Luhansk, Krasnij Luch, Debaltseve, Donetsk, Mariupol

A similar, albeit less violent, script had already played out in another former Soviet republic, Moldova. Here, political upheaval—the Twitter Revolution—in 2009 ousted longtime president Vladimir Voronin's Communist Party, accused of falsifying electoral results, and after a long crisis replaced it with a short-lived coalition known as the Alliance for European Integration. However, according to Henry E. Hale, in a broader perspective Moldova's revolution was nothing more than the product of a succession crisis that happened to hit the regime as the country failed to stop its economic decline which was only partially linked to the global financial crisis.[15] Political and social developments have confirmed this sober judgment. In 2010, Mihai Ghimpu, acting president and former mayor of Chişinău, announced the intention to unite Moldova with Romania, thus angering both the country's minority nationalities and the government of Russia, and leading the country to a long period of political and social unrest, the only internal beneficiary of which seems to have been the wealthiest oligarch of the country, Vladimir Plahotniuc. According to a Polish analyst, during the normalization that followed the upheaval of 2009, the Moldovan power system has evolved from "oligarchic pluralism" to the "personal hegemony" of a single man who reportedly controls the whole political spectrum.[16]

While the Moldovan population was losing all remaining trust in a state that has been captured by the oligarchs and their protégés, in Bucharest and also Washington diplomats started thinking about the future of the country. During his nearly ten years in office between 2004 and 2014, President Traian Băsescu of Romania supported the notion of unification with Moldova, proposing that Moldovans be granted the opportunity to gain expedited Romanian citizenship and declaring during the escalation of conflict in Ukraine that unification represented his country's "next major medium-term objective."[17] Romania needs Western support to realize this goal and would not necessarily gain geopolitical benefit from unification with a much poorer country. Moreover, the status of the self-declared Transnistrian Republic remains unsettled and exposes the otherwise peaceful Moldova to the threat of Russian-orchestrated destabilization.

Another multiethnic state whose medium-term future might not be guaranteed is Bosnia and Herzegovina. This post-Yugoslav federative state has descended into a state of permanent political and social tension, and although there is no imminent threat of renewed armed conflict in the country, the danger of its disintegration is very real. The 1995 Dayton Agreement established an extremely complicated and expensive bureaucratic system in Bosnia and Herzegovina that consumes over half of the state budget without ensuring the effective operations of the state.[18] The failure of Bosnia and Herzegovina to build political and social stability since the end of the Bosnian War can be attributed to several factors: the absence of precise guarantees regarding the return of refugees and the punishment of war criminals, the inefficient and corrupt use of humanitarian assistance, increasing conflict between the country's various nationalities and religious groups, and economic decline. In 2014, Bosnia and Herzegovina recorded 44 percent unemployment rate (and a stunning 57 percent among youth aged 15–24), which not even the massive amount of undeclared labor in the country and remittances from emigrants living in the West could fully mitigate.[19]

The lack of cohesion between the two administrative entities that compose the Republic of Bosnia and Herzegovina—the predominantly Bosniak and Croatian Federation of Bosnia and Herzegovina and the 83 percent Serbian Republika Srpska—represents the most serious problem in the country; the government, army, and security apparatus are also divided along nationality lines. According to the sociologist Darragh Farrell, Bosnia and Herzegovina has fallen victim to its own internal contradictions as well as to Western humanitarian intervention, which attempted to transform the country into a political laboratory of liberalism and centralization where citizens would be instilled with tolerance and the rejection of nationalism. The lack of collective security and alternative political formations in Bosnia and Herzegovina has, predictably, channeled almost all voters toward nationality-based parties and movements. The prospect of joining the European Union has become less attractive among the citizens of Bosnia and Herzegovina and seems to have become very distant. The rejection of Europe overlooked many options that have since become the subject of broad debate, such as the peaceful secession of Republika Srpska and constitutional decentralization. Over the long term, this failure could lead to the counterproductive defense of state unity, as occurred in Yugoslavia in the early 1990s.[20]

The problems of Belarus are of a different nature. Ruled since 1994 by the authoritarian president Alexander Lukashenko, Belarus is a special case among the states of Eastern Europe. Lukashenko won the first and last free election held in Belarus in 1994 on a popular platform of anti-privatization and anti-corruption platform. Since then President Lukashenko has totally dominated politics in Belarus, winning several reelections with more than 80 percent of the vote after an amendment to the country's constitution removed the previous two-term limit for heads of state. The Organization for Security and Co-operation in Europe and various other international organizations rejected the legitimacy of this procedure.[21] Lukashenko won his fourth term in office in December 2010 with 79.7 percent of the vote, although his victory produced massive demonstrations in the capital city of Minsk that police dispersed by force. Five years later, in October 2015 he ran for his fifth term in office and was reelected with almost 85 percent of the popular vote.

Belarus has differed from all other postcommunist states of Eastern Europe in both its political system—the country is often called Europe's last dictatorship—and its state-controlled economic structure. For this reason,

Belarus has been less exposed to the effects of political, social, and economic transformation than other countries of the former Soviet Union. Moreover, Belarus, unlike other states in the region, has maintained strong political and economic relations with Russia and has even accorded the Russian language official status. The Lukashenko regime was able to obtain genuine popular support in spite of its dictatorial inclinations, manifested in the persecution of political opponents and members of the Polish minority, restriction of media freedom and access to the internet, and the boycott of Western institutions.[22] Lukashenko has virtually isolated the country from the most visible setbacks of the postcommunist social order. Even more plastically than Putin's Russia, Belarus represents an example of how a cohesive elite can increase and stabilize the popular support of a patently undemocratic regime left without viable alternatives.[23]

After the 2009 economic crisis, Belarus has experienced deteriorating conditions that have forced the government to raise prices, privatize companies, and conduct unprecedented layoffs. Moreover, Belarus's relations with Russia have soured as a result of a drastic rise in the price of Russian gas and other fundamental bilateral issues.[24] After the Ukrainian war of 2014–2015, Lukashenko multiplied diplomatic gestures toward the West as an attempt to decouple from Russia, given the Western sanctions against Russia.[25] The deterioration in relations between Lukashenko and Putin did not result in the Belarusian president's eventual fall from power, as some analysts had predicted, although the mass demonstration of March 2017 may be a sign that his authoritarian regime is losing its grip on growing segments of the population. The end of his quasi dictatorship might result in the collapse of political stability and the social cohesion that has been maintained by force over the past two decades.

The Uncomfortable Demographic Challenge

Emigration (particularly that of young educated people), rapid population decline, and the failed integration of the Roma represent three of the main challenges on which both the success of Eastern European states in their effort to cope with concrete issues and, to a significant degree the future of the entire continent, depends.

According to a discussion note published by the research staff of the International Monetary Fund, the scale of emigration from Central and Eastern Europe to the West since the early 1990s has been staggering. During the past 25 years, nearly 20 million people (more than 5 percent of the overall population of this area) are estimated to have left the region. The Balkans had experienced the largest outflows, amounting to about 16 percent of the early 1990s population.[26] The accession of Bulgaria and especially Romania to the European Union in 2007 further increased emigration from that country, increasing the number of Romanian citizens residing abroad, notably in Italy and Spain, to around 3.5 million (roughly one of three young adults).

The governments of the wealthy countries of the European Union encouraged the source of inexpensive labor force from Eastern Europe. Immigrants from this region typically integrated linguistically, socially, and economically with relative ease into the countries of Western Europe. In fact, mass emigration has presented the states of Eastern Europe a complex set of problems. On the one hand, emigrants provide an enormous amount of economic support to their family members at home, thus increasing domestic consumption and national income. The remittances of Romanians working abroad, for example, totaled more than €30 billion between 2005 and 2010, constituting around one-tenth of Romania's gross domestic product and significantly exceeding the amount of foreign capital that entered the country during that period. Citizens working abroad are not counted as unemployed, and this also serves to embellish statistics on unemployment data. However, these apparent gains are overshadowed by losses. The states of Eastern Europe receive no direct compensation for the expense of educating and training a skilled labor force. Emigration creates a shortage of professionals, notably physicians, nurses, and information technology specialists, as well as skilled laborers in the region. Emigration has also caused social problems in the already-atomized Eastern European societies, serving to further loosen family ties and increase the dependence of many elderly people and minors on support from the state. Finally, according to the quoted IMF report published in 2016, emigration appears to have lowered potential growth and slowed economic convergence with the European Union, for it negatively affected competitiveness, wage productivity, and income convergence, as well as economic growth in the region:

> Empirical analysis suggests that in 2012, cumulative real GDP growth would have been 7 percentage points higher on average in CESEE in the absence of emigration during 1995–2012, with skilled emigration playing a key contributing factor. In turn, this has slowed per capita income convergence, in particular in South Eastern European countries (Albania, Bulgaria, Croatia, and Romania), which had a high share of young and skilled emigrants in their populations. Significant effects are also observed in the Baltics (Estonia, Lithuania) and in Slovenia.[27]

In fact, uncontrolled migration of workers from the European periphery to the core has created a win-lose situation, as the only real beneficiaries of the persistent in-flow have been Western European host countries.

Population decline is another challenge for Eastern Europe. All the countries of the region with the exception of Kosovo have recorded declining populations since the 1990s as a result of both low birth rates and emigration. According to

Eurostat, the statistical office of the European Union, the population of Bulgaria could decrease by 30 percent between 2010 and 2060; that of Latvia and Lithuania, by around 25 percent; and that of Hungary and Romania, by around 20 percent.[28] The population of Ukraine decreased from around 51 million to about 45 million between 1989 and 2013, and the country's population could drop to 35 million over the coming decades even if the Donbass region does not secede. The population of Moldova without Transnistria has contracted from 4.5 million to less than 3 million in the same period—if the approximately 700,000 Moldovans working abroad are not subtracted.

Nationalist rhetoric throughout Eastern Europe warns that the demographic crisis entails the threat of national extinction. Governments in the region have introduced family subsidies and tax incentives designed to increase birth rates, although these measures have shown only short-term and partial successes. The demographic characteristics and poor economies of countries in Eastern Europe will likely prevent their populations from stabilizing in the near future. One solution to the population decline in Eastern Europe could be for countries in the region to adopt the method that their counterparts in Western Europe have used to resolve their own demographic crises—the import of non-European immigrants. Although a sizable Chinese community lives in Budapest and an increasing number of Vietnamese and Chechens have settled in Warsaw, Eastern Europe is scarcely attractive for non-European economic migrants and asylum seekers.[29]

Finally, the social integration of Roma represents perhaps the most urgent challenge for governments in Eastern Europe. The Roma are the largest minority in the region and can be divided into many linguistic and cultural subgroups. Census data compiled in Eastern Europe consistently underreport the number of Roma for two reasons: Roma citizens frequently decline to identify themselves as such in census questionnaires, and census takers often unilaterally classify them as members of the majority or some other minority nationality. Because census data published in the countries of Eastern Europe tend to report Roma populations of between one-quarter and one-third their estimated actual size, some sociologists and demographers have begun to employ an alternative method of defining Roma identity that, though exceptionally subjective, may be more accurate: Roma are those whom non-Roma identify as such. According to a study by Jean-Pierre Liégeois that the Council of Europe published in 2007, Romania and Bulgaria have the largest populations of Roma in Eastern Europe. An estimated 2 million Roma live in Romania, compared to 621,000 at the time of the 2011 census—around 10 percent of the national population, despite their mass emigration following the country's accession to the European Union in 2007. An estimated 700,000 to 800,000 Roma live in Bulgaria, compared to 370,000 reported in 2001 census data—between 9 percent and 10 percent of the country's population. The number of Roma living in Hungary is also estimated to be between 700,000 and 800,000, compared to 315,000 reported in 2011 census data. An estimated 400,000 Roma live in Serbia, compared to the 147,000 officially reported in 2002. A further 50,000 Roma live in Kosovo—the same number as fled from Serbia following the end of the Kosovo War in 1999. An estimated 400,000 Roma live in Slovakia, compared to 105,000 officially reported in 2011. The number of Roma living in Macedonia is estimated to be between 150,000 and 200,000, compared to official 2002 data reporting 54,000 Roma in the country. An estimated 250,000 Roma live in the Czech Republic, compared to 13,000 reported in the country's most recent census. The number of Roma living in the states of Eastern Europe can be qualified as demographically insignificant in only the following five countries: Ukraine, which has a Roma population of around 200,000 (compared to a total national population of 45 million); Poland, which has a Roma population of less than 50,000; Slovenia, which has a Roma population of between 15,000 and 20,000; and Bosnia and Herzegovina and Croatia, where the Roma population had nearly disappeared first during the Second World War and then during the mass emigration during the Yugoslav Wars in the 1990s.[30] The total population of Roma living in Eastern Europe in the early twenty-first century can be estimated to be between 8 million and 9 million. One must note that the population of Roma living in the region, contrary to that of non-Roma, is growing quickly, mainly as a result of birth rates among Roma that are still between two and three times higher than those among non-Roma.[31]

Roma migrated to Europe, particularly the eastern half of the continent, in the Middle Ages and lived as nomads until the Second World War, when they were subjected to cruel and racist persecution. During the 1950s and 1960s, communist regimes in Eastern Europe enacted totalitarian measures to promote the social integration, assimilation, and acculturation of Roma, compelling them to reside at fixed locations in large cities, to assume regular employment, and—particularly in Czechoslovakia—to force Roma women to undergo involuntary sterilization after having given birth to multiple children.[32] In exchange for their cooperation, communist regimes ensured that Roma would gain access to educational opportunities and social security benefits.

The economic transformation that took place in Eastern Europe after the collapse of communist regimes in 1989 led to mass unemployment and economic hardship within the Roma communities of the region. As a result of the exodus of working and middle-class non-Roma populations from urban areas that had suffered economically as a result of the postcommunist transition, large Roma ghettos emerged in numerous urban and rural areas.

Sociological analyses conducted in Europe over the past decade have tended to focus on the social plight of Roma. According to the conclusions reached by Iván Szelényi and János Ladányi in their cross-country comparative work, Roma constitute an underclass that faces cultural deprivation, and they often live in disadvantaged geographical and economic environments from which it is nearly impossible for them to leave.[33]

Field research done after 1989 shows that infant mortality among Roma is many times higher than that among non-Roma, that the average life expectancy of Roma is less than sixty years and the gap with the average life expectancy is constantly widening, that an enormous number of young Roma are functionally illiterate, and that few Roma continue their education beyond primary school despite the many scholarships that have been established for them.[34]

The majority of adult Roma are unemployed and therefore compelled to subsist on state subsidies and irregular employment. One can estimate that Roma inmates likely constitute a large part of the prison population in certain Eastern European countries (according to a survey financed by the Open Society Research Support Scheme, in Hungary their proportion was of almost 50 percent in 2000).[35] The high incidence of behavior infractions, family violence, drug addiction, and alcoholism among Roma can be attributed only partially to objective poverty. The high degree of criminality among Roma is the product of several interrelated factors: inadequate existential opportunities, deeply entrenched prejudice, and the insufficiency of social-support systems and integration policies. There is a also a memory gap between Roma who grew up in the most inclusive countries of Eastern Europe (e.g., Czechoslovakia, Hungary) during the years of socialist modernization that provided them with secure employment, and Roma who have grown up in the region during the years of postcommunist transition and often rarely encounter a family member or acquaintance who holds a legal steady job.[36] According to Michael Stewart, social scientists do not help in tackling the Eastern European Roma issue when they project their own ideological expectations onto it. He contends that "underclass" theorists focus on social, educational, and welfare policy and practice (taking the image of a Roma community as separate from the rest of society), whereas human rights advocates talk of racial discrimination and suggest that "juridical changes and legal challenges to established practice can offer a road to 'liberation.'"[37]

In fact, what human rights activists and sociologists describe is a constructed image of a nonexistent singular Roma community. Internal divisions within Eastern European Roma communities that are often erroneously regarded as unified serve to increase the difficulty of integration and prevent the establishment of a standardized minority identity. Most Roma in Eastern Europe speak the language of the national majority or that of a national minority rather than Romany in their everyday communications. The failure of the non-Roma majority to understand that many of the problems associated with the Roma minority can be attributed to general social dysfunction rather than to personal inadequacy contributes significantly to the social exclusion of Roma. A misguided sense of fellowship and group cohesion pushes many Roma communities to marginalize integrated, or assimilated Roma from their own ranks. Much of the blame rests with the clan-based Roma elites that in the postcommunist era have focused on obtaining as much international and European Union support as possible to gain personal benefit rather than to improve cultural and social conditions for the broader Roma community.

Since the 1990s, verbal and physical conflicts between Roma and non-Roma have become more frequent in Western Europe following the arrival of a large number of Roma from the Balkans. Authorities in both Germany and France have been regularly deporting Roma living in encampments on the outskirts of large cities under the illusion that doing so will decrease the number of foreign Roma living in their countries. Such measures fail to address the underlying causes of Roma migration and therefore can only temporarily ease problems associated with it. Nongovernmental organizations and human-rights groups dedicated to fighting discrimination have collectively exonerated Roma of guilt for crimes and antisocial behavior, thus suggesting that they are incapable of independent action and bear no responsibility for their deeds. The neglect and disavowal of civic education for Roma has led to social and cultural catastrophe for the Roma communities of Eastern Europe.

According to the Bulgarian-born attorney Iskra Uzunova, European Union–sponsored programs to promote the social integration and identity building of Roma communities in Eastern Europe are doomed to failure because funding allocated to these "imagined communities" are rarely compatible with the realities of the region and, moreover, concentrate excessively on rights and ignore civic education.[38] Eastern European countries that have significant Roma populations have received no concrete advice from European institutions regarding their integration. A typical example is the ill-fated EU Roma Framework for National Roma Integration Strategies in Europe by 2020, adopted by the European Commission in 2011 during the Hungarian presidency. Behind their ritual praise for the efforts put by the European Commission and the national government in addressing this issue, the annual assessment reports show how very little progress has been achieved.[39] Appeals to end discrimination and guarantee equality include no concrete proposals for the policies that might be implemented to achieve such objectives. Nobody has yet been able to identify how a state based on the rule of law should respond to actions that conform to internal models of behavior though are clearly incompatible with national and European laws and social standards.

Taking current demographic trends into consideration, European states must treat the question of Roma integration as a top priority and discard the politically correct approach to this issue that serves only to conceal problems and avoid effective solutions. Moreover, the lack of social integration of Roma in Eastern Europe exacerbates difficulties related to population decline in the region, namely pressure on social security systems because of a declining number of contribution-paying workers and an increasing number of pensioners, unemployed, and others who depend on state support.

The Impact of the Economic Crisis on East-West Convergence

It is a matter of debate whether the Eastern European project of catching up with the European core has led to measurable convergence. Between 2004 and 2015, the gross national product grew by around 10 percent in the twenty-eight countries of the European Union, and the better growth rates were observed among the new member states (Slovakia and Poland with 50 percent; Bulgaria, Lithuania, and Romania with 35 percent; Czech Republic, Estonia, and Latvia with around 30 percent). The only underperformers in the area were Croatia (4 percent growth), Hungary (12 percent), and Slovenia (16 percent).[40] The European Union provided new member states with the opportunity to apply for an apparently enormous amount of structural and cohesion funds: €174 billion during its 2007–2013 seven-year budgetary cycle.[41] Structural funds contributed to the fast economic growth of the region in comparison with the old EU members. In several Slovak or Polish macroregions and in most Eastern European capital regions, GDP per capita relative to the average of the twenty-eight EU countries grew by at least twenty percentage points over the past decade, making them among the most dynamically developing areas of Europe.

As mentioned in the previous chapter, statistical evidence based on GDP figures must be approached cautiously. Multiple-factor analyses show that integration of the eastern half of Europe either has proceeded very slowly or has not even begun in a number of peripheral regions affected by brain drain, growth in territorial inequality, local corruption, and profit outflow. EU funding to new Eastern European member states promoted convergence only in certain domains such as infrastructure and represented—as a sort of belated compensation for the never arrived Marshall Plan—only one-third of that needed for wage convergence. Although no independent research has been produced to date on how rationally the EU funds are being been spent in the new member states of Eastern Europe, the impression from reading local media and the periodical reports of the EU anticorruption agency is that a sizable part of this huge amount of money has been mismanaged or wrongly allocated. Moreover, the productive and political core of the European Union has been emerging as the true long-term beneficiary of the structural funding programs. As Günther Oettinger, the German European commissioner for budget and human resources, candidly admitted to an economic newspaper in early 2017: "The structural funds are for making weak regions more competitive. And a large part of every euro the European Union gives Poland comes back to Germany. The Poles use the money to place orders with the German construction industry, to buy German machines and German trucks. So net contributors such as Germany should be interested in the structural funds. From an economic perspective, Germany isn't a net contributor but a net recipient."[42]

Zoltán Pogátsa pointed out that "Gini coefficients (the decimal quotient of the highest and lowest wages) show the result that social inequalities in the East are smaller than in the West. This result is statistically correct, though conceals the fact that up to one half of society lives under a hypothetical 'European minimum subsistence level.'"[43]

The underdevelopment of regional transportation infrastructure, including both main roads and railways, is another burden remaining from the socialist era. The network of highways in Eastern Europe has remained much less developed than that in Western Europe. Existing and planned pan-European transportation corridors also are a problem: whereas all of these corridors run along an East-West axis, the greatest potential expansion of regional cooperation runs along a North-South axis, from the Baltic Sea to the Mediterranean Sea. The railway connections in Eastern Europe are even less developed than the region's highway network. A look at train schedules shows how little they have changed over the past century, when the Orient Express connected Paris to Istanbul through Hungary and the Balkans. The transportation of freight via railway in Eastern Europe is so slow and circuitous that it can no longer compete with road haulage. The lagging the logistical network and its resulting inability to accommodate globalizing industrial production represents an impediment to investment and economic development in Eastern Europe.

Another reason the Eastern European EU member states have fallen further behind their Western European counterparts in terms of overall competitiveness is that they maintain contrasting interests in several important regards and the viewpoints of the former states seldom prevail as a result of their smaller lobbying power and lower degree of political influence.

The European Union's Common Agricultural Policy (CAP), the implementation of which absorbed a stunning 42 percent of the entire EU budget during the 2007–2013 budgetary cycle, is a primary example of this. Shortly before the Baltics, Poland, the Czech Republic, Slovakia, Slovenia, and Hungary joined the European Union in 2004, the fifteen existing EU member states established common agricultural priorities for the following decade that neglected the needs of their Eastern counterparts. Not surprisingly, those fifteen countries wished to limit the budgetary costs of agricultural support in the new member states, arguing that direct payments were inadequate for transitional economies. Eventually a compromise solution was found that would ensure the inclusion of new members in the system of direct payments, although it was decided that payments would start at 25 percent and reach 100 percent of the level of payments applicable in the fifteen countries only after ten years, in 2013 in the case of the members that joined in 2004 and in 2016 in the case of Bulgaria and Romania.[44] A further issue that would be exploited from the nationalist standpoint concerned land grabbing. Eastern Europe is currently witnessing a massive land concentration process that has a direct and negative impact on small-scale farmers. The land-grabbing wave especially hit new member states like Romania, Bulgaria, and Hungary, but also other Eastern European countries like Poland and Lithuania. As a result of the vague legal environment and circumvention of collaborating local authorities, several million hectares were given up to multinational agribusiness and/or national oligarchs, mostly through pocket contracts—illegal land deals in which the date of purchase remained unspecified and the contract was kept "in the pocket" until the moratorium on land sales was lifted.[45]

The global financial and economic crisis that erupted in the autumn of 2008 ended a prolonged period of economic development in Eastern Europe during which countries in the region had recorded annual GDP growth of between 4 percent and 6 percent, while some countries such as the Baltic states and Slovakia had temporarily posted GDP growth of 10 percent. During the first decade of the twenty-first century, governments in the region attempted to adjust wages and pensions to growing inflation that brought the prices of consumer goods and communal services close to Western standards. Although this effort succeeded only partially (the hourly wages of workers and technicians at vehicle-manufacturing plants in Slovakia amount to a fraction of the hourly salary of their German colleagues, and the percentage drops further with regard to Hungary, Serbia, and Romania), purchasing power did increase significantly in Eastern Europe and a young middle class of professionals came into being. Economic growth heightened demand for nonessential consumer goods and increased real estate investment in the region, factors that paired with lax credit practices among banks, resulted in growing household debt among Eastern Europeans. Moreover, many banks in Eastern Europe disbursed loans denominated in foreign currencies, thus increasing the exposure of both creditors and central banks in the region to global risk factors. Following the onset of the global financial and economic crisis, some countries in Eastern Europe were forced along with Greece to obtain emergency loans from the International Monetary Fund and the World Bank to avoid insolvency. The economies of Eastern Europe, particularly those that depended primarily on the economic activity of multinational companies rather than that of small and medium-sized businesses, have only partially recovered from the crisis. The three Baltic states sustained a particularly catastrophic decline in gross domestic product as a result of the global financial and economic crisis: from the second half of 2008 through the first half of 2010, the GDP of Latvia—formerly regarded as a success story by prominent scholars— contracted by 20 percent, while Lithuania's GDP contracted by 16 percent and

Estonia's GDP by 14 percent. The GDP of Ukraine shrank by 15 percent in 2009—a decline that the country's previous failure to recover from the economic shock resulting from the collapse of the Soviet Union served to exacerbate. GDP contracted by between 6 percent and 8 percent in Slovenia, Hungary, Romania, and Bulgaria, while the economies of the Czech Republic and Slovakia shrank by around 2 percent. Poland is the only country in Eastern Europe that has maintained stable economic growth over the past decade.[46] Economists attribute the economic strength of Poland to policies of Prime Minister Donald Tusk that made the country attractive for foreign investors and used EU funding to create opportunities for local enterprise, as well as to the remittances of Polish citizens working abroad. The access of companies in Poland to relatively cheap domestic labor and the country's adoption of Western business models has made it possible for the Polish service sector and electronics industry to compete with foreign rivals in the low- to medium-range price categories. Poland also profited from the country's underdevelopment benefit to generate rapid economic growth and development.

The global financial and economic crisis weighed the most heavily on those Eastern European countries such as Hungary that depended to the greatest degree on exports and the governments of which had conducted flawed economic policies that undermined their financial credibility.[47] From 1995 to 2005, Hungary recorded the most stable economic growth in Central Europe. Since then Hungary's economy has become one of the weakest in the region. Although analysts disagree regarding the magnitude to which the socialist-liberal and conservative governments of Hungary bear responsibility for the economic decline the country has sustained since joining the European Union in 2004, most regard this downturn to be a common failure. Between 2002 and 2010, in particular, the foreign debt of Hungary rose from 53 percent of GDP to above 80 percent of GDP under the direction of the country's Hungarian Socialist Party-Alliance of Free Democrats coalition governments. The crisis threw hundreds of thousands of Hungarians into a debt spiral resulting from the foreign-currency-denominated loans that they had taken out without receiving enough information regarding the risk of exchange-rate fluctuations from financial supervisory authorities. The prolonged period of political and social unrest that began in Hungary during the autumn of 2006 and resulted in the strengthening of right-wing radicalism and the landslide defeat of the socialist-liberal governing coalition in 2010 parliamentary elections must be seen within this context.[48]

A New Mainstream? State Capture and Illiberal Democracy

Since 2010, Europe has recovered from the recession with moderate economic growth and an improving balance of public finance and foreign debt. Eastern

European countries reacted better than the rest of the European Union thanks to structural funds as well as to fiscal containment and rigorous implementation of the austerity measures agreed to by the national governments with the European institutions. Writing shortly after the most acute phase of the crisis, neoliberal economist and former adviser to several postcommunist governments Anders Åslund argued that populism would fail to gain traction despite the initial shock:

> The East European crisis offers clear insights into the political economy of the crisis. When the going gets tough, politics become a pragmatic matter of solving vital problems, while rational expectations with tradeoffs between various social groups are no longer politically relevant. Instead of widely predicted social unrest, the East European public has accepted their hardship with minimal protest. After many years of high economic growth, people were prepared for some suffering.[49]

The problem with this statement made in 2010 was not its despicable cynicism but its ultimate fallacy. Contrary to the argumentation of Åslund, the global crisis has left a long-lasting impression on the citizens of states in the eastern half of the continent and has deeply reshaped their political attitudes toward the state and capitalism as well as toward liberal democracy as such. Eastern Europeans were forced to realize as a result of the global financial and economic crisis that economic development in capitalist systems is not predictable or equally shared. After nearly fifteen years of (uneven but robust) growth and increasing living standards, many Eastern Europeans regarded the sharp rise in unemployment, the emigration of skilled workers, and the reduction in state social benefits to be the result of personal failure, just as with the economic problems that afflicted the region in the early 1990s. Paradoxically, the crisis that began in 2008 exercised a greater psychological impact on younger generations of Eastern Europeans, who had never experienced the hardship of living in a shortage economy. Moreover, the crisis revived debate that had previously taken place in Eastern Europe at the time of the democratic transition regarding the proper regulatory and initiatory role of the government vis-à-vis the economy. To borrow Kotkin's fitting expression, "uncivil society" requires the control of an authoritative state in order to regulate its internal functions. During the 1980s, opposition intellectuals regarded the Soviet-type state agencies as an objectified enemy. Postcommunist Eastern European countries inherited bureaucracies that suffered from a legitimacy gap (the corrupt practices of the police, secret services, financial organizations, and judiciary were well known) while almost all strategic sectors of the economy had been privatized to foreign companies or local oligarchs. As a result of the crisis, a growing part of the population has come to support the idea that state-imposed regulatory mechanisms are necessary to ensure that market-based economies operate properly.

In a book that attempts to place the postcommunist transition in the historical framework of the impact of the neoliberal canon on both Western and Eastern
European post–Cold War transformation, Philipp Ther makes two important arguments. The first is that the transformative crisis the former socialist countries
had gone through in the years 1989–1993 and after 2008 could serve as a spring-
board for southern European states that find themselves in a similar position.
The second is that the Eastern European left-wing parties and intellectual elites
might play a pivotal role in challenging the discursive hegemony of neoliberalism by endorsing genuine social democratic economic policy and abandoning
conservative flagship projects like the flat-rate tax regime and the privatization
of pension systems.[50] The first point is insightful because it encourages scholars to overcome the artificial geographical cleavage between East and West to
move toward an entangled narrative of the recent history of Europe. It can be
argued that the global economic crisis has redrawn the internal boundaries of
the continent. The dividing line between prosperity and collective failure is no
longer a vertical one from west to east, which would reflect the culturally rooted
intra-European borders famously drawn in the early 1990s by Samuel Hunting-
ton (with "Catholic" Poland, Czechoslovakia, and Hungary opposed to the [Or-
thodox] Balkans and to Russia). It might rather be described as a diagonal cutting
across the continent from north to west, or the productive and political core of
Europe, and the widening peripheral areas located in the southeastern corner including wide regions of Italy, Greece, Spain, and France. On the contrary, Ther's
second point might overestimate the electoral strength and the cultural capacity
of Eastern Europe's fragmented leftist elites. Despite intermittent resurgence at
the polls, the Eastern European left suffers from an excess of heterogeneity. Ideological confusion endures and prevents a progressive approach on a number of
critical issues, including ethnicity, nationalism, and the vague idea of European-
ism. Some parties have been unable to dispel old regime nostalgia, particularly
among the aging electorate. But the most serious problem may be pinning down
the social content of leftist politics, an ambiguous task at best. Analyzing key
economic measures taken by Eastern European governments after the 2009 crisis
demonstrates polarities that are unconnected to the left. These choices are best
represented by moves taken by Poland's Civic Platform and Hungary's Fidesz,
both members of the European center-right. Warsaw has chosen to modernize
using a free-market, market-friendly approach, and Budapest has pressed to re-
nationalize the energy sector and augment national capital in the banking and
telecommunications sectors, an interventionist strategy typical of the classic
European left of the 1960s and 1970s. What Eastern Europe has been witnessing
in the last years is a crisis of the sources of (neo)liberal democratic legitimation,
the main beneficiaries of which are not the pro-European social-democratic parties but a heterogeneous coalition of admittedly right-wing forces. According to

the Eurobarometer surveys, over the past few years public support for the European Union and its institutions has decreased in most East European countries.[51]

Controversies over cultural and ethical issues have been multiplying between the European institutions and the national governments of the new member states (e.g., surrounding the compulsory relocation of asylum seekers from Muslim countries or the recognition of same-sex marriages). Most people in Eastern Europe feel they live in a "nationalized," monocultural cultural space even when their country is in fact a multiethnic one and look with suspicion upon the rapid transformation going on in the same Western metropolises that many of them have moved to as economic migrants. In contrast, decision makers in the Western capitals share the perception that Eastern European societies remain not only more traditional but also, and more regretfully, backward and uncompassionate as the result of a series of historical and related burdens.[52] These mutual negative perceptions are in some regards exaggerated, but they undermine mutual trust, as the different perception of the social role of religion and public morals shows.

The strengthening of the public role of religion in postcommunist Eastern Europe was a foreseeable phenomenon following a long period of official atheism and religious persecution. However, the revival of many ecclesiastical institutions and organizations after 1990 (e.g., monasteries, hospitals, schools, universities, charitable groups, media) has not served to reverse the trend toward secularization that began in Eastern Europe during the communist period, nor has it resulted in the commonly expressed concern that religious fundamentalism could gain ground in the region. Poland was a deeply religious country even before 1989 and has remained so since then, particularly in rural areas, even if Brian Porter-Szűcs has recently contended that "the linkage between Catholicism and an articulated ethnic identity is supported by a deeply ingrained but highly selective telling of national history."[53] In Hungary, less than one-third of the population is affiliated to a religious denomination, whereas in the Czech Republic indifference toward religion has become widespread and in Slovakia the long-suppressed Roman Catholic Church regained strength in the early postcommunist period though has failed to attract the country's young and urban populations.[54]

Although traditionally Eastern Orthodox countries have undergone an intensive secularization process on the model of Soviet Russia, surveys indicate that the church, along with the military, still represents among the most honored public institutions among ordinary citizens. However, whereas the Romanian Orthodox Church continues to play a vital role in maintaining national cohesion and receives significant support from the state, the Serbian Orthodox Church and, especially, the Bulgarian Orthodox Church have lost much of their former political influence.[55] Meanwhile, Islamic fundamentalism has surfaced among the younger generations of Muslims in Bosnia and Herzegovina, Kosovo,

Macedonia, and more recently Bulgaria as a result of trauma from the post-Yugoslav wars and indifference from the West.

One might argue that the peaceful consolidation that took place in the region during the 1990s served to reinforce the ultimately false notion that Fukuyama's triumph of liberalism had arrived in the post-Soviet world, thus bringing an end to a long period of instability. However, the wheels of history began to turn again after 2009. Until very recent times, most analysts were convinced that Central and Eastern Europe would have not been affected by the democratic setback that occurred in Russia in the late 1990s. Here the population asked for the end of savage capitalism and ultimately got from President Putin a more predictable and prosperous, albeit repressive and illiberal, state. In the past years, the picture has significantly changed, and we are witnessing to the rise of new, hybrid democratic and undemocratic situations all over the region. One can identify two regional variants. The Balkan states from Croatia to Albania have witnessed the rise of budding autocracies governed by nonideological parties or coalitions of parties. Their only stable predicament appears to be keeping power and draining public resources to secure the support of local oligarchs. According to Besnik Pula, a political scientist highly critical of neoliberalism, these new autocrats "operate under a different, savvier playbook than those of the 1990s: Internationally, they enthusiastically embrace the EU in their foreign policy. With the exception of Serbia, they express the same fervor for NATO. They are well-coached in telling Western diplomats what they want to hear, while blatantly undermining democratic principles and the rule of law at home."[56] As so many times over the past century, this region plays a marginal role in the international chessboard, and Western policy makers prefer to turn a blind eye to corruption and informal power techniques in exchange for unconditional geopolitical loyalty, as in the case of controversial longtime Montenegrin power holder Milo Đukanović:

> The goal of the diplomatic push by the West has been to counter Russian influence in the region and ensure the consolidation of democratic regimes and the rule of law there. But a closer look at this presumed success reveals that the fruit may be rotten. The apparent Westernization of the region, it's now clear, has come at great cost.[57]

A similar analysis could be made with regard to Bulgaria, where the prime minister in office since 2009 is the leader of a party (Graždani za evropejsko razvitie na Bălgarija, or GERB) that is a member of the European People's Party, the largest and most influential political family within the European Parliament. A former staff member of the Bulgarian communist security service, Boyko Borissov, has long dominated domestic political life with a law-and-order program amid frequent accusations of corruption, connections with organized crime, and money laundering. Commenting on the wave of grassroots student protest that rocked the country in 2013, John O'Brennan claimed that the movement lacked ideological ballast and could be better described as an anti-politics rebellion that contained a populist discourse that divided society into the corrupt and parasitical elites versus the people.[58] The subsequent wave of spontaneous mass protests in Macedonia, Kosovo, Bosnia and Herzegovina (2015–2016), and Romania (2017) have revealed widespread popular discontent with corrupt states that fail to provide their citizens with job opportunities and the most basic services like health care and education. This renewed commitment to public affairs might be interpreted as a sign that parts of the society have become ready for qualitative changes. Nevertheless, the protests largely remain a testimony to civil courage notwithstanding the lack of alternative elites enforced with the administrative skills and the necessary financial resources to implement their utopian projects.

In the case of Romania, its pivotal role in US regional foreign policy ensures closer Western attention and prevents organized crime from fully capturing the political structures. The price for relative macrostability is a lack of democratic governance based on competitive visions of the future, because none of the elected officials seems to have any. The weak legitimacy of the political class as a whole has made possible the silent counterrevolution carried out by the many and mutually antagonistic security services that represent the real bulk of the Romanian power structure. In 2013, the public budget allocated to these security agencies was reportedly twice as large as that granted to the Ministry of Health, and their operations staff totaled 15,000 people—by far the highest density in democratic Europe.[59]

To better understand how the Balkans are ruled in the postcommunist era, one might recall the seminal research of Ryan Gingeras on organized crime as a crucial prism through which to consider the state-building process in Turkey from the late Ottoman era to the present day. Despite the many and obvious differences between the case of post-Ottoman Turkey and postcommunist Eastern Europe, a common feature can be detected: the formally elected power elites enter into close collusion with the "deep state," represented by those oligarchs and power groups that have effective control over domestic policy with the assistance of the country's secret services.[60]

The second variant of the new illiberal trend might be described as local contestation of the post–Cold War global order. After the global economic crisis, several Central European political forces have started challenging the Western discursive monopoly over modernization and social security on more ideological grounds. In the immediate aftermath of the EU integration of the Central European states, the first country to experience a divisive controversial governmental rule in a full-fledged democracy was Poland. The Justice and Freedom Party (Prawo i Sprawiedliwość, or PiS) won the 2005 elections and entered in coalition with another right-wing party, Self-Defense of the Republic of Poland

(Samoobrona Rzeczpospolitej Polskie) on a program that rested on traditional Christian values enforced with anti-Russian and anti-German bias. PiS originated in the 1980s Polish opposition movement, and the party's leaders gave voice to a defensive reaction of the rural world against the challenges that European integration imposed on the collective mind-set of Polish society. What Polish President and PiS leader Lech Kaczyński (2005–2010) asserted was the existence of a Polish *Sonderweg* between Soviet-type socialism and globalized turbo-capitalism. After only two years, the fragile PiS-Samoobrona coalition split and a long period of pro-European governments followed in Poland under the leadership of a centrist, pro-European politician, Donald Tusk, the leader of the Civic Platform (Platforma Obywatelska, or PO, from 2007 to 2015). The country was the only major European economy to avoid the recession, and the economy continued to grow in the following years. In spite of this, in 2015 Polish voters turned their backs on the coalition. Despite stubborn efforts by Poland to attach itself to the German locomotive and the efficient absorption of EU development funds, the Polish miracle left too many out from prosperity, and PiS entered its second term in office with the idea of replicating the anti-liberal reforms the Hungarian ruling party Fidesz had introduced since it gained power in 2010. Over the past few years, mainstream democratic mass parties like Hungary's Fidesz and Poland's Law and Justice have implemented a series of highly controversial constitutional, economic, and cultural measures. According to many observers, their ruling style confirmed the somber prediction of Fareed Zakaria: "Western liberal democracy might prove to be not the final destination on the democratic road, but just one of many possible exits."[61]

Why did they choose to go this route, and what are the possible consequences of their autocratic turn on the rest of the region? The last section of this chapter analyzes how a small, strategically unimportant country as Hungary could become the "black beast" of Western European liberal-democratic public opinion. And paradoxically, how it could do so well after the country's EU accession under the guidance of a Western-trained former dissident of the communist regime who during his first term in office (1998–2002) governed with the vision of building a Hungary filled with economically independent citizens? As already explained, Hungary emerged from the first years of EU membership as the least successful Central European country, plagued by recession, corruption, high unemployment, and rising crime rates, especially in the countryside and its eastern region, where the Roma minority is concentrated. As had already happened in Poland, voters punished the ruling left wing, and the rightist opposition leader Viktor Orbán won a landslide, two-thirds victory in 2010 elections that he replicated four years later. After the 2010 vote, Hungarian political analyst Péter Tölgyessy wrote that many had supported Orbán not out of ideological conviction but because they believed that Fidesz was the only rational alternative following several years of domestic chaos. The success of Fidesz rested in the pragmatic capacity of his uncontested leader to govern the country out of the economic crisis and, even more important, to increase the accountability of a ruling system that looked like a permanent revolution that devours its own cadres, selecting the new ones according to the only criterion of absolute loyalty.[62] Several years after, Tölgyessy came up with a more radical explanation. The ultimate result of Orbán's six-year government would have been a new regime change that over-wrote the consensual end of Soviet-type communism. According to Tölgyessy, Orbán managed to set up a state-driven capitalist system based on "distributive neo-patrimonialism." Parliamentary democracy has not been abolished, and the opposition parties have retained some chance to win the following elections in 2018 or perhaps 2022, but the state apparatus has been more deeply reshaped than during the previous regime change of 1990, and it works in full compliance with the needs of the ruling party.[63] Political scientist András Körösényi made a case for not calling the Orbán government a "system"—a normative defini-tion that usually implies a stable, predictable set of values and practices. Instead, he labeled Orbán's rule a regime: not to stress its dictatorial tendencies but to emphasize that this surprisingly unideological regime is so strictly linked to Orbán's personal charisma that no officials in the party believe that it could sur-vive without its creator. According to Körösényi, the Orbán regime is both un-willing and unable to consolidate itself. The very content of Orbán's governance is improvisational crisis management, which absorbs all the energies of the state apparatus and prevents it from achieving the internal stability that ensured long-term survival to the consolidated system of János Kádár.[64]

In the past few years, several scholars have tried to grasp the reasons for Orbán's success and to put his government in comparison with other illiberal de-mocracies, notably Putin's Russia. Among them, Iván Szelényi and Tamás Csillag underlined that both experiences share the interplay of neoconservative ideologi-cal settings and everyday practices of managed capitalism. These two countries seem to shift from consensual democracy to mixed regimes in which guaran-teed private property tends to be a converted benefice through a mechanism called neo-prebendalism. The democratic principle of majoritarian rule is not denied but is strongly managed and sometimes arranged. Finally, in both coun-tries the ruling elites operate with a legitimating neoconservative ideology that emphasizes the value of patriotism, religion, and the traditional family model.[65] Scholars investigating the political economy of Hungary since Orbán's rise to power cautioned against overestimating the social impact of the political turn toward a more temperate capitalism. The so-called system of Orbánomics can be described as an eccentric mix of selective protectionism to create a national capitalism in the public utilities and agrarian sectors, neoconservative economic policy through the support granted to multinational companies that invest in

Hungary, and sustained fiscal consolidation. These unorthodox policies might have improved the capacity of the country to resist external financial shocks, but they severely hit the poorest segments of the society through their cuts to social assistance and public services.[66]

The sociologist and former left-wing liberal politician Bálint Magyar has gone so far as to define this new institutional framework as a power pyramid, a "mafia state." While the classical mafia channeled wealth and economic players into its spheres of interest by means of direct coercion, Hungary is ruled by Orbán as a patriarchal family, and this unprecedented concentration of wealth and vertical power deeply influences parliamentary legislation, legal prosecution, tax authority, and to a incomparably lesser extent than in Putin's Russia, police forces. In the mafia state, the postcommunist relationship between the ruling party and the criminal underworld is reversed: it is no longer the case that private wealth is acquired to help the party's need for financial support gained from illegitimate sources; rather, the political party's decision-making potential is to be used to seize private property.[67]

A more fitting explanation of the Hungarian version of illiberal democracy was produced by historian Balázs Trencsényi. Departing from the definitions of hybrid democracy, electoral democracy, and managed democracy, Trencsényi argues that after 2010 and to an even greater degree under Viktor Orbán's second consecutive mandate in office, Hungary has developed a syncretic power system that retains the basic elements of formal democracy and the multiparty system with free elections and the presence of an assertive, albeit numerically marginal, civil society. Parliamentary and nonparliamentary opposition have free access to the public space and the social networks, even if control on public and also private media has become tight. According to Trencsényi, Hungary is currently neither a Western-type democracy nor a Russian-style autocratic regime; it lives in a gray zone along with several other countries of the postcommunist area. The unsettled fate of a formerly stable democracy might presage the end of the liberal consensus in Central and Eastern Europe. It certainly marks the epistemological collapse of the academic belief in the inevitable triumph of liberal democracy in the region.[68]

In a controversial 2014 speech, Orbán pointed to authoritarian Russia, Turkey, and Singapore as successful examples of nation and state building. He did not claim that nondemocratic policies ought to be implemented in Hungary, but he warned that the country needed to consider whether following the Western path is the only possible answer to the aspirations of Central and Eastern European societies. In that speech, Orbán claimed that a nation "is not a simple sum of individuals, but a community that needs to be organized, strengthened and developed," and he called the state he was building "an illiberal state, a nonliberal state." It must be noted that Orbán consistently uses the word *liberal* as a synonym for *socialist* or *leftist* in terms of social and ethical issues. In Orbán's view, the postliberal state "does not deny foundational values of liberalism, as freedom, etc. But it does not make this ideology a central element of state organization, but applies a specific, national, particular approach in its stead."[69] Thus, he made the intellectually exciting, albeit perilous, case for a new kind of representative democracy, and showed how entangled global politics has become in a postideological world. The anthropologist Chris Hann observed that the radical, law-and-order stand of Hungary and other Eastern European countries during the 2015 European refugee crisis was as much about the idea of "Europe" as it was about internal politics: "Orbán claims to be defending the values of Christian Europe when he builds fences and internment camps. In response, his secular liberal critics in Budapest claim they are the ones who represent humanist European values. In short, Europe is claimed by both sides."[70]

Although this and other public statements of similar tone have been widely interpreted as an attempt to put Hungary on a Russia-like track of vehemently anti-Western authoritarianism and cultural isolation, one might observe that from an analytical point it makes little sense to compare Russia to Orbán's Hungary. The first consistently labeled itself a "sovereign democracy" (a term first used by Russian political strategist Vladislav Surkov in 2006) with reference to the increased capacity of Russia to pursue its geopolitical goals without the interference of the West. On the contrary, Hungary is a small Central European state that lacks both natural resources and a powerful army and security services, and its economy is defined as one of the most open in Europe because of its strong dependency on exports and European Union structural funds. This might explain why Orbán's Hungary has remained so far and despite the constant criticism to Europe an integral part of the Euro-Atlantic system of alliances (Fidesz a member of the largest European political family, the center-right European People's Party). The Hungarian prime minister's muscular national rhetoric may be disturbing to many, and it certainly constitutes a warning sign for the European cultural mainstream that a professional, postmodern, and deeply illiberal political culture has planted its roots all over the region, such that more and more local politicians look at Orbán as a model and copy his ways.

Orbán's anti-Brussels rhetoric fits well with the media offensive launched by Russia in Central and Eastern Europe on the topic of national sovereignty. In terms of diplomacy, the rational geopolitics of the Cold War has made a spectacular comeback, with Central European countries attempting to forge bilateral ties with the United States and even more so with Vladimir Putin's ambitious Russia. Moscow, though, might not offer a viable alternative path of modernization and sustainable growth. As a consequence of the Ukrainian war and the sanctions imposed by the West, the Russian economy has significantly contracted. However, the anti-Western, traditionalist, if not openly racist, narrative of the present offered by the Kremlin and propagated worldwide through social media seems to find more fertile ground than ever in disillusioned Europe, including the Central and Eastern European peripheries.

Notes

1. Kenney, *Il peso della libertà*, 155–156.
2. For a comprehensive analysis on the early Putin era, see Baev, *Russian Energy Policy and Military Power*. On the latest developments, including the consequences of the military conflict with Ukraine on Russia's energy policy, see Gusev and Westphal, "Russian Energy Policies Revisited."
3. Timothy Snyder, keynote lecture at the "Revolution and War: Ukraine in the Great Transformations of Modern Europe" conference of the German-Ukrainian Historical Commission, Berlin, May 28–29, 2015.
4. Tomka, *Social History of Twentieth-Century Europe*, 431–439.
5. Amato and Batt, *Minority Rights and EU Enlargement to the East*.
6. Rupnik, "From Democracy Fatigue to Populist Backlash," 17–25.
7. Bárdi, "History of Relations," 58–84.
8. Stroschein, *Ethnic Struggle, Coexistence, and Democratization in Eastern Europe*.
9. See the comparative analysis in Berglund, *Handbook of Political Change in Eastern Europe*.
10. Haughton, "Other New Europeans," 56–71.
11. Beacháin and Polese, *Colour Revolutions in the Former Soviet Union*, 5–6.
12. A balanced assessment is found in Marples and Mills, *Ukraine's Euromaidan*.
13. Mearsheimer, "Why the Ukraine Crisis Is the West's Fault," 77–89.
14. Motyl, "Ukraine Crisis according to John J. Mearsheimer."
15. Hale, "Did the Internet Break the Political Machine?," 481–505.
16. Calus, "Moldova."
17. See "Moldovenii de peste Prut răsplătiți cu cetățenie română la minut," *Cotidianul*, August 2, 2010, http://www.cotidianul.ro/moldovenii-de-peste-prut-rasplatiti-cu-cetatenie-romana-la-minut-121120/. See also Băsescu's statement on Romanian television station TVR 1 on November 26, 2013, available at http://unimedia.info/stiri/video-basescu-anunta-urmatorul-proiect-al-romaniei-unirea-cu-republica-moldova-68881.html/.
18. Bieber, *Post-War Bosnia*.
19. See the World Bank data at http://data.worldbank.org/indicator/SL.UEM.1524.ZS?locations=BA. Youth unemployment 1991–2004, modeled on the database of the International Labour Organization.
20. Farrell, "Failed Ideas for Failed States?"
21. Wilson, "East Europeans," 102.
22. Ioffe, *Understanding Belarus*.
23. On the Russian case, see Rose, Mishler, and Munro, *Popular Support for an Undemocratic Regime*.
24. Marples, "Belarus: Europe's Last Dictator Gets a Little Lonelier."
25. http://www.ndtv.com/world-news/belarus-lukashenko-looks-to-eased-sanctions-but-osce-queries-poll-1231258.
26. Ruben Atoyan et al., *Emigration and Its Economic Impact on Eastern Europe*, IMF Staff Discussion Note, July 2016, 8, http://www.imf.org/external/pubs/ft/sdn/2016/sdn1607.pdf.

27. Ibid., 22.

28. See Eurostat, "Population Projections 2010–2060," News Release 80/2011, June 8, 2011; and id., "Demography Report 2010," Staff Working Document, European Commission Directorate-General for Employment, Social Affairs and Inclusion, http://epp.eurostat.ec.europa .eu/portal/page/portal/population/.../report.pdf.

29. Nyíri, *Chinese in Eastern Europe and Russia.*

30. Liégeois, *Roma in Europe.*

31. According to data presented to the press in 2011 by Vasile Ghețău, director of the Romanian Institute of Statistics, the birth rate among Roma women is 2.5 times higher than among non-Roma women (3.0 percent versus 1.3 percent). See the website http://www.gandul .info/magazin/o-romanca-naste-in-medie-1-3-copii-o-romanca-de-etnie-roma-3-copii-cum -va-arata-romania-in-2050-7862914. The director of the Institute for Minority Studies of the Hungarian Academy of Sciences, Attila Z. Papp, in a 2011 study estimated at 15 percent the proportion of Roma-descent children in the Hungarian primary schools (twice their population share in Hungary). See Papp, "A roma tanulók," 229–231.

32. Barany, *East European Gypsies,* 112–156.

33. Ladányi and Szelényi, *Patterns of Exclusion.*

34. Barany, *East European Gypsies,* 171–176.

35. Póczik, "Magyar és cigány bűnelkövetők a börtönben," 426–435.

36. Barany, *East European Gypsies,* 151–153.

37. Stewart, "Deprivation, the Roma and the 'Underclass,'" 145.

38. Uzunova, "Roma Integration in Europe," 283–323.

39. See the assessment reports of the EU Roma Framework for National Roma Integration Strategies in Europe by 2020, adopted by the European Commission in 2011, at http:// ec.europa.eu/justice/discrimination/roma/index_en.htm. For the national level in every EU country, see http://ec.europa.eu/justice/discrimination/roma-integration/index_en.htm.

40. See the statistics on real GDP growth rate at the website of the European Commission: http://ec.europa.eu/eurostat/tgm/refreshTableAction.do?tab=table&plugin=1&pcode=tec00011 5&language=en.

41. "Gyorsan kötünk, lassan költünk," *Népszabadság,* July 23, 2014.

42. Full text of the interview with Günther Oettinger is available on the website of the German economic newspaper *Handelsblatt,* at https://global.handelsblatt.com/politics/oettinger -germany-may-have-to-pay-more-to-e-u-714934.

43. Pogátsa, *Magyarország politikai gazdaságtana,* 111–117.

44. Kosior, "Impact of Central and Eastern Europe on the Common Agricultural Policy," 116–147.

45. A comparative analysis is found in Franco and Borras, *Land Concentration,* 114–190.

46. "Economics & FI/FX Research: CEE Quarterly," Unicredit Bank, October 7, 2010.

47. Dan Bilefsky, "A Crisis Is Separating Eastern Europe's Strong from Its Weak," *New York Times,* February 23, 2009.

48. Ágh, "Triple Crisis in Hungary," 25-51. For a different perspective, see Bottoni, "L'Ungheria di Viktor Orbán," 1006–1014.

49. Åslund, *Last Shall Be the First,* 112.

50. Ther, *Europe Since 1989.*

51. See *Standard Eurobarometer 83* carried out in May 2015 in the European Union Member States and in five candidate countries, at http://ec.europa.eu/public_opinion/archives/eb/eb83 /eb83_en.htm.

52. Ivan Krastev, "Eastern Europe's Compassion Deficit," *New York Times,* September 8, 2015.

53. Porter-Szűcs, *Faith and Fatherland*, 5.

54. Tomka, *Church, State and Society in Eastern Europe.*

55. Murzaku, *Quo vadis Eastern Europe?*

56. Pula, "Budding Autocrats of the Balkans."

57. Ibid.

58. John O'Brennan, "Bulgarians under the Yoke of Oligarchy," unpublished paper, 2014, https://www.maynoothuniversity.ie/sites/default/files/assets/document/New_Left_Review_Bulgarians_under_the_Yoke_of_Oligarchy.pdf.

59. Data are available at http://www.antena3.ro/en/romania/how-many-spies-romania-has-got-the-budgets-allocated-to-the-intelligence-services-could-provide-the-235384.html.

60. The scholarly literature on the post-Ottoman deep state is very large. See Ryan Gingeras's *Heroin* on the role of the deep state in modern Turkey; he explores the relationship between the interconnected underground criminal network of transnational heroin traders and Turkish politicians and security officers. For a detailed analysis of the oligarchs' control, see Gallagher, *Romania and the European Union.*

61. Zakaria, "Rise of Illiberal Democracy," 24.

62. Tölgyessy, "A Fidesz és a magyar politika lehetséges új iránya," 310–345.

63. For the audio record of Tölgyessy's interview, see http://inforadio.hu/arena/2016/05/02/arena-tolgyessy_peter/.

64. Körösényi, *A magyar politikai rendszer.*

65. Szelényi and Csillag, "Drifting from Liberal Democracy," 18–48.

66. Pogátsa, *Magyarország politikai gazdaságtana*, 173–202; Tóth, "Coming to the End of the Via Dolorosa?," 233–252.

67. Magyar, *Post-Communist Mafia State.*

68. Trencsényi, "Minek nevezzelek?," 49–68.

69. The integral text in English translation is available at the website of Budapest Beacon, a US-based English-language news portal specializing in Hungary's current events that is very critical of the right-wing government: http://budapestbeacon.com/public-policy/full-text-of-viktor-orbans-speech-at-baile-tusnad-tusnadfurdo-of-26-july-2014/10592.

70. Chris Hann, "Beleaguered Pseudo-Continent: Happy Birthday, Europe!" March 29, 2017, http://www.focaalblog.com/2017/03/29/chris-hann-beleaguered-pseudocontinent-happy-birthday-europe/.

Epilogue

Unreflective Mimicry and National Egoism

The EASTERN EUROPEAN political and cultural elites have long believed in (Western) European integration as the only desirable future for their country. After the global crisis, and as a consequence of their subordinate position in the new globalized society, a mostly silent but palpable reflection has started to catch up with the West without having to renounce the fundamental attribute of the nation-state and sovereignty over sensitive public issues. Shall we conclude that the days of rampant neoliberalism are numbered and top-down enlightened reforms are likely to be undone by social populism? In the past years, this debate went beyond think tanks to receive unprecedented political articulation in countries like Poland and Hungary, but also throughout the Balkans—most likely because of Russian inspiration. Still, its premises are in the permanent contrast that Hungarian political thinker István Bibó described in the 1940s between the two behavioral patterns of the Eastern European elites: unreflective, mimetic reception of foreign models versus ethno-protectionist national egoism.[1]

In the past century, the Eastern European pendulum has swung between these extremes. After three decades spent posing as model pupils who are learning about democracy and the market economy, many educated Eastern Europeans and some of their governments changed their mind about the future of their countries, becoming disenchanted and possessing national biases, notwithstanding that this correction does not affect their ultimate goal of catching up with the Western quality of life. There is a basic contradiction in the way Eastern European citizens, encouraged by their national public discourse, spend considerable time criticizing everything Brussels, Berlin, and/or Washington does while they sustain an ultimate ambition to live as ordinary people do in a small, quiet Alpine town. But their frustration stems from the awareness that the golden era of the

European welfare state and social inclusion is ending without their having ever enjoyed it.

From this perspective, there is a rationale in the fact that mounting anti-politics and anti-elite behaviors in Eastern Europe go hand in hand with Euroskepticism and anti-Western tirades. Writing in 2012, Dorothee Bohle and Béla Greskovits could still express optimism about the capacity of resilience of the neoliberal model, as when they argued that the backsliding of democracy in east-central Europe was connected to the different models of economic government after the 2009 economic crisis ("neo-corporatism" in Slovenia; "embedded liberalism" in the four countries of the Visegrád group; "neoliberalism" in the Baltic states).[2] At the time this epilogue is being edited, in spring 2017, it seems that the issue of hollowing democracy has lost its original character of academic debate on economic and social policies in Eastern Europe. The issue of Eastern Europe has gained momentum, turning into a comprehensive vision, a deeply rooted rejection of the Western developmental model. Regional experts such as Ivan Krastev speak of deglobalization as the outcome of the emergence of populist and nationalist movements in both Western and Eastern Europe, but they warn against the peculiar role the latter area might play—as it already did in the interwar period and during the Cold War—as a laboratory of authoritarian politics. According to Krastev, there is a growing chance that at least several countries of Eastern Europe become full-fledged authoritarian, albeit not totally dictatorial, systems. In these countries, the boundaries between democratic rule and autocracy have been fading, and open borders guaranteed by the Schengen Treaty paradoxically help authoritarian leaderships to survive because, unlike during the communist times, dissidents and unsatisfied citizens can just leave and settle down into another European Union member state.[3] To further complicate this, one of the unintended consequences of the economic support provided by the European Union to the new member states is that a sizable portion of the allocated money ends up in the pockets of local politicians and oligarchs. The cohesion funds have neither decreased regional differences nor significantly contributed to improving political culture throughout the region. And so far, the European Union has proved unable to sanction those member states whose policies conflict with its principles.

More than twenty-five years after the beginning of the economic and political transition of this region, hybrid political cultures and peculiar, neither Western nor fully Eastern power practices seem to have taken root in the European semiperipheries, not only in the postcommunist area but also in the more consolidated democracies of southern Europe. Belorussian sociologist Evgeny Morozov has emphasized the role of digital media and social networks in stimulating among youngsters a sense of disillusion with liberal democracy and "Western values," first in post-Soviet Russia, then in Central and Eastern Europe. As he brilliantly showed as early as 2011, the widespread use of digital platforms has become a formidable instrument for authoritarian leaderships in the age of the general crisis of the democratic model in Europe. Illiberal governments and their media proxies skillfully use the new technologies to influence public opinion and control their citizens' behavior.[4]

The dilemma is whether to come to terms with this, acknowledging the right of certain countries either to enact a discount version of liberal democracy or to stick to the original plan and feign full-hearted integration into the West. The stakes are no less than including or excluding Central and Eastern Europe from the strengthened cooperation of the European core countries within a reformed European Union, a perspective that would likely represent the first step toward a European superstate. The collective pessimism that has spread about the future of the region is in fact a self-fulfilling prophecy: the incorrect expectation that the societal behavior and the material conditions of these countries will soon resemble those of the Western model.

At the end of its long socialist journey Eastern Europe has found itself once again on the fringes of the Western productive and cultural core, just as it was in the interwar period.[5] The young Polish writer Jacob Mikanowski might have a point when he perceives among many people of his generation the vanishing of the very idea of Eastern Europe as the "shared experience of occupation and exclusion, the permanent-seeming weight of economic backwardness, treasured memories of defeat."[6] It is also true that the urban landscape has gone through tremendous changes over the past decades, and that capital cities of Eastern Europe are becoming more and more attractive for professionals, students, and young hipsters. But is it enough to move a few miles away from the vibrant city centers to the desolate anthropic landscape of the urban peripheries and depopulated rural areas to experience Eastern Europe as a physical entity?

As depressing as is sounds, the challenge Eastern Europe must face over the coming years resembles the old intellectual debate among Romanian intellectuals of the nineteenth century between the "Westerners" (or synchronists) and the "traditionalists"—the latter blaming the uncritical reception of Western attitudes from an evolutionist standpoint. One must note that old and new discourses on national specificity in Eastern Europe share the notion that a nation has to transcend its own past and aspire to universality.[7] Since 1989, the proliferation in Eastern Europe of Western "forms without substance"—to borrow the famous words of Romanian intellectual Titu Maiorescu, written in 1868 to denounce the mimicry of Western civilization in a totally different context—has increased the gap between the elite and fellow citizens. It was the paradoxical blend of nationalism and universalism that contributed to the emergence of the different brands of Eastern European (and Soviet) authoritarianism in the region throughout the past century. And the same paradoxical blend of anti-globalist nationalism makes possible now a reloaded, postmodern, digital version of the same old dilemma of Westernization.

The overall project to integrate the Central and Eastern European region into the globalized West and avoid transforming it into a buffer zone contended over by superpowers and regional powers has suffered serious setbacks, although it is still standing. Its failure would mean condemning the whole region to another unsuccessful run-up after those of the past century and would lead it into a new era of catastrophe.

Notes

1. Dénes, *Art of Peacemaking*, 1–24.
2. Bohle and Greskovits, *Capitalist Diversity*.
3. Lecture of Ivan Krastev at the opening event of Zois (Zentrum für Osteuropa und Internationale Studien), a new think tank for expertise on Eastern Europe, Berlin, March 26, 2017.
4. Morozov, *Net Delusion*.
5. Berend, *Central and Eastern Europe*, 361–362.
6. Mikanowski, "Good Bye Eastern Europe!" *Los Angeles Review of Books*, February 23, 2017.
7. See Trencsényi, *Politics of "National Character."*

BIBLIOGRAPHY

Abrams, Bradley. "The Politics of Retribution: The Trial of Jozef Tiso in the Czechoslo-vak Environment," in Deák, István, Gross, T. Jan, and Judt, Tony, eds., *The Politics of Retribution in Europe: World War II and Its Aftermath*. Princeton, NJ: Princeton University Press, 2000.

———. *The Struggle for the Soul of the Nation: Czech Culture and the Rise of Commu-nism*. Lanham, MD: Rowman & Littlefield, 2004.

Ágh, Attila. "The Triple Crisis in Hungary: The 'Backsliding' of Hungarian Democracy after Twenty Years." *Romanian Journal of Political Science* 13, no. 1 (2013): 25–51.

Albrecht, Ulrich. *The Soviet Armaments Industry*. Philadelphia: Harwood Academic Press, 1993.

Amar, Cyril Tarik. *The Paradox of Ukrainian Lviv: A Borderland City between Stalinists, Nazis, and Nationalists*. Ithaca, NY: Cornell University Press, 2015.

Ambrosio, Thomas, ed., *Ethnic Identity Groups and U.S. Foreign Policy*. Westport, CT: Praeger, 2002.

Andreea, Andreescu, Lucian, Nastasă, and Andrea, Varga, eds. *Maghiarii din Româ-nia (1945-1955)*. Cluj-Napoca (Romania): Centru de Resurse pentru Diversitate Etnoculturală, 2002.

Andreescu, Gabriel. *Cărturari, opozanți și documente: Manipularea Arhivei Securității*. Iași (Romania): Polirom, 2013.

Antohi, Sorin, and Tismăneanu, Vladimir. *Between Past and Future: The Revolutions of 1989 and Their Aftermath*. Budapest: Central European University Press, 2000.

Antohi, Sorin, Trencsényi, Balázs, and Apor, Péter, eds. *Narratives Unbound: Historical Studies in Post-Communist Eastern Europe*. Budapest: Central European Univer-sity Press, 2007.

Anušanskas, Arvydas, ed. *The Anti-Soviet Resistance in the Baltic States*. Vilnius: Du Ka, 2000.

Apor, Balázs, Apor, Péter, and Rees, Arfon E., eds. *The Sovietization of Eastern Europe: New Perspectives on the Postwar Period*. Washington, DC: New Academia, 2008.

Apor, Balázs, Behrends, Jan, Jones, Polly, and Rees E., Arfon, eds. *The Leader Cult in Communist Dictatorships: Stalin and the Eastern Bloc*. Basingstoke, UK: Palgrave Macmillan, 2004.

Applebaum, Anne. *Iron Curtain: The Crushing of Eastern Europe, 1944–1956*. New York: Anchor Books, 2012.

Argentieri, Federigo, ed. *Il ritorno degli ex: Rapporto CeSPI sull'Europa centrale e orien-tale*. Rome: Editori Riuniti, 1996.

Ash, Timothy Garton. *The File: A Personal History*. London: Random House, 1997.

———. *The Uses of Adversity: Essays on the Fate of Central Europe*. London: Random House, 1989.

Åslund, Anders. *How Capitalism Was Built: The Transformation of Central and Eastern Europe, Russia, and Central Asia.* Cambridge: Cambridge University Press, 2007.
——. *The Last Shall Be the First: The East European Financial Crisis, 2008–10.* Washington, DC: Peterson Institute for International Economics, 2010.
Baberowski, Jörg. "Criticism as Crisis; or, Why the Soviet Union still Collapsed." *Journal of Modern European History* 9, no. 2 (2011): 148–166.
Bacon, Edwin, and Sandle, Mark, eds. *Brezhnev Reconsidered.* Basingstoke, UK: Palgrave, 2002.
Baczoni, Gábor, and Bikki, István. "Egyesített állambiztonsági adattár—A SZOUD." In Gyarmati, György, ed., *Az átmenet évkönyve 2003/Trezor 3.* Budapest: Állambiztonsági Szolgálatok Történeti Levéltára, 2004.
Baev, K. Pavel. *Russian Energy Policy and Military Power: Putin's Quest for Greatness.* London: Routledge, 2008.
Báger, Gusztáv, and Kovács, Árpád. *Privatisation in Hungary: Summary Study, Research and Development.* Budapest: Institute of the State Audit Office of Hungary, 2004.
Baier, Hannelore. *Deportarea etnicilor germani din România in Uniunea Sovietică.* Bucharest: Forumul Democrat al Germanilor din România, 2004.
Balogh, Margit. *Mindszenty József I-II.* Budapest: MTA Bölcsészettudományi Kutatóközpont, 2015.
Ban, Cornel. "Sovereign Debt, Austerity, and Regime Change: The Case of Nicolae Ceausescu's Romania." *East European Politics and Societies* 26, no. 4 (November 2012): 743–776.
Bán, D. András. *Pax Britannica: Wartime Foreign Office Documents Regarding Plans for a Postbellum East Central Europe.* Boulder, CO: Social Science Monographs, 1997.
Banač, Ivo. *The National Question in Yugoslavia: Origins, History, Politics.* Ithaca, NY: Cornell University Press, 1984.
——. "Political Change and National Diversity." *Daedalus* 116, no. 1 (Winter 1990): 141–159.
——. *With Stalin against Tito: Kominformist Splits in Yugoslav Communism.* Ithaca, NY: Cornell University Press, 1988.
Bange, Oliver, and Niedhart, Gottfried, eds. *Helsinki 1975 and the Transformation of Europe.* New York: Berghahn, 2008.
Bank, Barbara, Palasik, Mária, and Gyarmati, György, eds. *"Állami titok": Internáló- és kényszermunkatáborok Magyarországon, 1945–1953.* Budapest: ÁBTL-L'Harmattan, 2012.
Banu, Florian. *Asalt asupra economiei României: De la Solagra la Sovrom (1936–1956).* Bucharest: Editura Nemira, 2004.
Barany, Zoltan. *The East European Gypsies: Regime Change, Marginality, and Ethnopolitics.* Cambridge: Cambridge University Press, 2002.
Baráth, Magdolna, ed. *Szovjet iratok Magyarországról, 1953–1956.* Budapest: Napvilág Kiadó, 2002.
Barberini, Giovanni, ed. *La politica del dialogo: Le carte Casaroli sull'Ostpolitik vaticana.* Bologna: Il Mulino, 2008.
Bárdi, Nándor. "The History of Relations between Hungarian Governments and Ethnic Hungarians Living beyond the Borders of Hungary," in Kántor, Zoltán, Majtényi, Balázs, Ieda, Osamu, Vizi, Balázs, and Halász, Iván, eds., *The Hungarian Status*

Law: Nation Building and/or Minority Protection, 58–84. Sapporo: Hokkaido University Slavic Research Center, 2004.

Bárdi, Nándor, Fedinec, Csilla, and Szarka, László, eds. *Minority Hungarian Communities in the Twentieth Century*. Boulder, CO: East-European Monographs, 2011.

Bárdi, Nándor, Gidó, Attila, and Novák, Csaba Zoltán, eds. *Primele forme de autoorganizare a maghiarilor din România, 1989–1990*. Cluj-Napoca (Romania): Editura Instititului pentru Studierea Problemelor Minorităților Naționale, 2014.

Batt, Judy, and Amato, Giuliano. *Minority Rights and EU Enlargement to the East: European University Institute*. RSC Policy Paper No. 5. Florence: European University Institute, 1998.

Bauquet, Nicolas, and Bocholier, François, eds. *Le communisme et les élites en Europe centrale*. Paris: Presses Universitaires de France, 2006.

Behrends, Jan C. "Nations and Empire: Dilemmas of Legitimacy during Stalinism in Poland (1941–1956)." *Nationalities Papers* 37, no. 4 (July 2009): 443–466.

Békés, Csaba. *Európából Európába. Magyarország konfliktusok kereszttüzében, 1945–1990*: Budapest: Gondolat, 2004.

Békés, Csaba, Byrne, Malcolm, and Rainer, M. János, eds. *The 1956 Hungarian Revolution: A History in Documents*. Budapest: Central European University Press, 2002.

Bencsik, Péter, and Nagy, György. *A magyar úti okmányok története 1945–1989*. Budapest: Tipico Design, 2005.

Benvenuti, Francesco. *La Russia dopo l'URSS: Dal 1985 ad oggi*. Rome: Carocci, 2007.

Berend, T. Iván. *Central and Eastern Europe, 1944–1993: Detour from the Periphery to the Periphery*. Cambridge: Cambridge University Press, 1996.

———. *From the Soviet Bloc to the European Union: The Economic and Social Transformation of Central and Eastern Europe since 1973*. Cambridge: Cambridge University Press, 2009.

———. *The Hungarian Economic Reforms, 1953–1988*. Cambridge: Cambridge University Press, 1990.

———. *Storia economica dell'Europa nel XX secolo*. Milan: Bruno Mondadori, 2008.

Berend, T. Iván, and Ránki, György. *Economic Development in East-Central Europe in the 19th and 20th Centuries*. New York: Columbia University Press, 1974.

Berglund, Sten, et al., eds. *The Handbook of Political Change in Eastern Europe*. 3rd ed. Cheltenham, UK: Elgar, 2013.

Betea, Lavinia, ed. *21 august 1968: Apoteoza lui Ceaușescu*. Iași (Romania): Polirom, 2009.

———. "Ultima vizită a lui Nicolae Ceaușescu la Moscova I-II." *Sfera Politicii* 142 (2009): 82–88, and 143 (2010): 86–92.

Bettanin, Fabio. *Stalin e l'Europa: La formazione dell'impero esterno sovietico (1941–1953)*. Rome: Carocci, 2006.

———. "I costi dell'impero," in Panaccione, Andrea, ed. *Vent'anni dopo (1989–2009)*. Milan: Unicopli, 2010.

Bianchini, Stefano. *Le sfide della modernità: Idee, politiche e percorsi dell'Europa orientale nel XIX e XX secolo*. Soveria Mannelli: Rubbettino, 2009.

———, ed. *L'autogestione jugoslava*. Milan: Franco Angeli, 1982.

Bibó, István. *Válogatott tanulmányok, II: 1945–1949*. Budapest: Magvető Könyvkiadó, 1986.

————. *Válogatott tanulmányok, IV: 1935–1979.* Budapest: Magvető Könyvkiadó, 1990.
Bideleux, Robert, and Jeffries, Ian. *A History of Eastern Europe: Crisis and Change.* 2nd ed. London: Routledge, 2007.
Bieber, Florian. *Post-War Bosnia: Ethnicity, Inequality and Public Sector Governance.* London: Palgrave, 2005.
Bîtfoi, Dorin Liviu. *Petru Groza, ultimul burghez: O biografie.* Bucharest: Compania, 2004.
Blagojević, Marina, and Yair, Gad. "The Catch 22 Syndrome of Social Scientists in the Semiperiphery: Exploratory Sociological Observations, *Sociologija* 52, no. 4 (2010): 337–358.
Blaive, Muriel. *Une déstalinisation manquée: Tchécoslovaquie 1956.* Paris: Éditions Complexe, 2005.
Boda, Zsolt, and Körösényi, András, eds. *Trendek a magyar politikában.* Budapest: MTA TK Politikatudományi Intézete, 2013.
Boeckh, Katrin, and Völkl, Ekkehard. *Ucraina: Dalla rivoluzione rossa alla rivoluzione arancione 2007.* Trieste: Beit, 2009.
Bohle, Dorothee, and Greskovits, Béla. *Capitalist Diversity on Europe's Periphery.* Ithaca, NY: Cornell University Press, 2012.
Booth, W. James. *Communities of Memory: On Witness, Identity, and Justice.* Ithaca, NY: Cornell University Press, 2006.
Borhi, László. *Hungary in the Cold War, 1945–1956: Between the United States and the Soviet Union.* Budapest: Central European University Press, 2004.
————. *Magyar-amerikai kapcsolatok 1945–1989: Források.* Budapest: MTA Történettudományi Intézet, 2009.
————. *Dealing with Dictators—The United States, Hungary, and East Central Europe, 1942–1989.* Bloomington: Indiana University Press, 2016.
————. "A Reluctant and Fearful West. 1989 and Its International Context." *Hungarian Quarterly* 193, no. 1 (Spring 2009): 62–76.
Borodziej, Włodzimierz, Kochanowski, Jerzy, and Puttkamer von Joachim, eds. *"Schleichwege": Inoffizielle Begegnungen sozialistischer Staatsbürger zwischen 1956 und 1989.* Cologne: Böhlau, 2010.
Botos, Katalin. "Magyarország IMF-csatlakozásának előtörténete." *Valóság* 49, no. 10 (October 2005): 82–102.
Bottoni, Stefano. *Transilvania rossa: Il comunismo romeno e la questione nazionale, 1944–1965.* Rome: Carocci, 2007.
————. *Stalin's Stalin's Legacy in Romania:The Hungarian Autonomous Region, 1952–1960.* Lanham, MD: Lexington Books.
————. "Reassessing the Communist Takeover in Romania. Violence, Institutional Continuity, and Ethnic Conflict Management." *East European Politics and Societies* 24, no. 1 (Spring 2010): 59–89.
————. "L'Ungheria di Viktor Orbán." *Il Mulino* 61, no. 6 (November–December 2011): 1006–1014.
Bottoni, Stefano, László, Márton, László, Réka, Lázok, Klára, and Novák, Zoltán, eds. *Az 1956-os forradalom és a romániai magyarság (1956–1959).* Csíkszereda (Miercurea Ciuc, Romania): Pro-Print, 2006.
Boughton, James M. *Silent Revolution: The International Monetary Fund, 1979–1989.* Washington, DC: International Monetary Fund, 2001.

Bozgan, Ovidiu. *Cronica unui eşec previzibil: România şi Sfântul Scaun în epoca pontificatul lui Paul al VI-lea (1963–1978)*. Bucharest: Curtea Veche, 2004.

Bozóki, András. "A magyar demokratikus ellenzék: önreflexió, identitás és politikai diskurzus." *Politikatudományi Szemle* 19, no. 2 (2010): 7–45.

——. *The Roundtable Talks of 1989: The Genesis of Hungarian Democracy*. Budapest: Central European University Press, 2002.

Brent, Jonathan, and Naumov, Vladimir. *Stalin's Last Crime: The Plot against the Jewish Doctors, 1948–1953*. New York: HarperCollins, 2003.

Brix, Emil, Koch, Klaus, and Vyslonzil Elisabeth, eds. *The Decline of Empires*. Munich: Oldenbourg, 2001.

Brown, Archie. *The Gorbachev Factor*. Oxford: Oxford University Press, 1996.

Browning, Cristopher. "A New Vision of the Holocaust." *New York Review of Books* 62, no. 15 (October 8, 2015): 41–43.

Brubaker, Rogers. *Nationalism Reframed: Nationhood and the National Question in the New Europe*. Cambridge: Cambridge University Press, 1996.

Brubaker, Rogers, Feischmidt, Margit, Fox, Jon, and Grancea, Liana, eds. *Nationalist Politics and Everyday Ethnicity in a Transylvanian Town*. Princeton, NJ: Princeton University Press, 2006.

Bruszt, László, and Stark, David, eds. *Postsocialist Pathways: Transforming Politics and Property in East Central Europe*. Cambridge: Cambridge University Press, 1998.

Brzezinski, Zbigniew. *The Soviet Bloc: Unity and Conflict*. Cambridge, MA: Harvard University Press, 1967.

Bucur, Maria, and Wingfield, Nancy M., eds. *Staging the Past: The Politics of Commemoration in Habsburg Central Europe, 1848 to the Present Europe*. Lafayette, IN: Purdue University Press, 2001.

Bugge, Peter. "The Use of the Middle. Mitteleuropa vs. Střední Evropa." *European Review of History* 6, no. 1 (Spring 1999): 15–35.

Burcea, Mihai, and Bumbeş, Mihail. "Lustrabilii." *Anuarul Institutului de Investigare a Crimelor Comunismului în România*. Iaşi (Romania): Polirom, 2006.

Burg, Steven L., and Shoup, Paul S., eds. *The War in Bosnia-Herzegovina: Ethnic Conflict and International Intervention*. New York: Sharpe, 1999.

Caccamo, Francesco. *Jiri Pelikan: Un lungo viaggio nell'arcipelago socialista*. Venice: Marsilio, 2007.

Całus, Kamil. "Moldova: From Oligarchic Pluralism to Plahotniuc's Hegemony." *OSW Commentary*, no. 208, April 7, 2016, http://www.osw.waw.pl/en/publikacje/osw-commentary/2016-04-11/moldova-oligarchic-pluralism-to-plahotniucs-hegemony.

Caplan, Richard. "'Bombing and Negotiating,'" in Cohen, Ben, and Stamkoski, George, eds., *With No Peace to Keep: UN Peacekeeping and the War in the Former Yugoslavia*. London: Grain Press, 1995.

Case, Holly. *Between States: The Transylvanian Question and the European Idea during World War II*. Stanford, CA: Stanford University Press, 2009.

Cassese, Antonio. *I diritti umani nel mondo contemporaneo*. Bari: Laterza, 1994.

Caşu, Igor. *Duşmanul de clasă: Represiuni politice, violenţă şi rezistenţă în R(A)SS Moldovenească, 1924–1956*. Chişinău: Cartier, 2014.

——. "Political Repressions in Moldavian SSR after 1956: Towards a Typology Based on KGB files." *Dystopia: Journal of Totalitarism Ideologies and Regims* 1, nos. 1–2 (2012): 89–127.

Cattaruzza, Marina. *L'Italia e il confine orientale, 1866–2006*. Bologna: Il Mulino, 2007.

Cesereanu, Ruxandra. *Decembrie '89: Deconstrucţia unei revoluţii*. Iaşi (Romania): Polirom, 2009.

Chiper, Ioan. "Considerations on the Numerical Evolution and Ethnic Composition of the Romanian Communist Party, 1921–1952." *Totalitarianism Archives* 34–35, nos. 1–2 (2002): 9–29.

Ciobanu, Monica. "Criminalising the Past and Reconstructing Collective Memory: The Romanian Truth Commission." *Europe-Asia Studies* 61, no. 2 (2009): 315–338.

Clementi, Marco. *Cecoslovacchia*. Milan: Unicopli, 2007.

Clesse, Armand, Cooper, Richard, and Sakamoto, Yoshikazu, eds. *The International System after the Collapse of the East-West Order*. Dordrecht: Nijhoff, 1994.

Cockherman, William C. "The Social Determinants of the Decline in Life Expectancy in Russia and Eastern Europe: A Lifestyle Explanation." *Journal of Health and Social Behavior* 38, no. 2 (1997): 117–130.

Cohen, Ben, and Stamkoski, George, eds. *With No Peace to Keep: UN Peacekeeping and the War in the Former Yugoslavia*. London: Grain Press, 1995.

Cohen, Lenard, and Dragović-Soso, Jasna eds. *State-Collapse in South-Eastern Europe: New Perspectives on Yugoslavia's Disintegration*. West Lafayette, IN: Purdue University Press, 2008.

Cohen, Shari J. *Politics without a Past. The Absence of History in Post-Communist Nationalism*. Durham, NC: Duke University Press, 1999.

Cohen, Stephen F. *Failed Crusade: America and the Tragedy of Post-Communist Russia*. New York: Norton, 2000.

Colas, Dominique, et al. *L'Europe post-communiste*. Paris: Presses Universitaires de France, 2002.

Connelly, John. *Captive University: The Sovietization of East German, Czech, and Polish Higher Education, 1945–1956*. Chapel Hill, NC: University of North Carolina Press, 2000.

———. "The Paradox of East German Communism," in Tismăneanu, Vladimir, ed., *Stalinism Revisited: The Establishment of Communist Regimes in East-Central Europe*. Budapest: Central European University Press, 2009.

Courtois, Stéphane, ed. *Il libro nero del comunismo: Crimini, terrore, repressione*. Milan: Mondadori, 1998.

———. *Il libro nero del comunismo europeo: Crimini, terrore, repressione*. Milan: Mondadori, 2006.

Crampton, Richard J. *Bulgaria*. Oxford: Oxford University Press, 2007.

———. *A Concise History of Bulgaria*. Cambridge: Cambridge University Press, 1997.

———. *Eastern Europe in the XXth Century—And After*. 2nd ed. London: Routledge, 1997.

Craveri, Marta. *Resistenza nel Gulag: Un capitolo inedito della destalinizzazione in Unione Sovietica*. Soveria Mannelli: Rubbettino, 2003.

Crowley, David, and Reid, Susan E., eds. *Socialist Spaces: Sites of Everyday Life in the Eastern Bloc*. Oxford, UK: Berg, 2002.

Csaba, László. "A rendszerváltozás elmélete és/vagy a közgazdaságtan kudarca?" *Közgazdasági Szemle* 46, no. 1 (1999): 1–19.

Cseh, Bendegúz Gergő, ed. *Documents of the Meetings of the Allied Control Commission for Hungary, 1945–1947*. Budapest: MTA Jelenkorkutató Bizottság, 2000.

Csizmadia, Ervin. *Diskurzus és diktatúra: A magyar értelmiség vitái Nyugat-Európáról a késő Kádár-rendszerben*. Budapest: Századvég, 2001.

———. "The Hungarian Democratic Opposition in the 1980's: External and Internal Effects and Resources." *Intersections: East European Journal of Society and Politics* 1, no. 4 (2015): 119–138.

———. *A magyar demokratikus ellenzék (1968–1988)*. Budapest: T-Twins, 1995.

Cummings, Richard H. *Cold War Radio: The Dangerous History of American Broadcasting in Europe, 1950–1989*. Jefferson, NC: McFarland, 2009.

Dahrendorf, Ralf. *1989: Riflessioni sulla rivoluzione in Europa*. 1990; Bari: Laterza, 1999.

David, Roman. "Transitional Injustice? Criteria for Conformity of Lustration to the Right of Political Expression." *Europe-Asia Studies* 56, no. 6 (2004): 789–812.

Davies, Norman. *Storia d'Europa*. 1996; Milan: Bruno Mondadori, 2001.

Dawisha, Karen, and Parrott, Bruce ed., *The Consolidation of Democracy in East-Central Europe*. Cambridge: Cambridge University Press, 1997.

Deák, István, Judt, Tony, and Gross, Jan T. *The Politics of Retribution in Europe: World War II and Its Aftermath*. Princeton, NJ: Princeton University Press, 2000.

De Brito, Alexandra Barahona, González Enríquez, Carmen, and Aguilar, Paloma, eds. *The Politics of Memory: Transitional Justice in Democratizing Societies*. Oxford: Oxford University Press, 2001.

Deletant, Dennis. *Ceaușescu and the Securitate: Coercion and Dissent in Romania, 1965–1989*. London: Hurst, 1995.

———. *Communist Terror in Romania: Gheorghiu-Dej and the Police-State, 1948–1965*. London: Hurst, 1999.

Deletant, Dennis, and Ionescu, Mihai. *Romania and the Warsaw Pact, 1955–89*. Working Paper No. 43. Washington, DC: Cold War International History Project, 2004.

Dénes, Iván Zoltán, ed. *The Art of Peacemaking: Political Essays by István Bibó*. New Haven, CT: Yale University Press, 2015.

Dimitrov, Vesselin. "In Search of a Homogeneous Nation: The Assimilation of Bulgaria's Turkish Minority, 1984–1985." *Journal on Ethnopolitics and Minority Issues in Europe* 4, no. 1 (2000): 1–22.

Dizdarević, Raif. *From the Death of Tito to the Death of Yugoslavia*. Sarajevo: Šahinpašic, 2009.

Djilas, Milovan. *Conversations with Stalin*. New York: Harcourt Brace Jovanovich, 1962.

———. *The New Class: An Analysis of the Communist System*. San Diego: Harcourt Brace Jovanovich, 1957.

Dobre, Florica Banu, Duică, Florian Camelia, Moldovan B. Silviu, Neagoe, Elisa, and Țăranu, Liviu, eds. *Bande, bandiți și eroi: Grupurile de rezistență din munți și Securitatea (1948–1968)*. Bucharest: Editura Enciclopedică, 2003.

———. *Securitatea: Structuri, cadre, obiective și metode, 1948–1989 I–II*. Bucharest: Editura Enciclopedică, 2006.

Dobre, Florica, Banu, Florian, Banu, Luminița, and Stancu, Laura, eds. *Acțiunea "Recuperarea": Securitatea și emigrarea germanilor din România (1962–1989)*. Bucharest: Editura Enciclopedică, 2011.

Dobrincu, Dorin. "Historicizing a Highly Disputed Theme: Anti-Communist Armed Resistance in Romania," in Tismăneanu, Vladimir, ed., *Stalinism Revisited: The Establishment of Communist Regimes in East-Central Europe*. Budapest: Central European University Press, 2009.

Duray, Miklós. *Kutyaszorítóban.* New York: Püski, 1983.

Esterházy, Péter. *Javított kiadás.* Budapest: Magvető, 2002.

Eyal, Gil. *The Origins of Postcommunist Elites: From Prague Spring to the Breakup of Czechoslovakia.* Minneapolis: University of Minnesota Press, 2003.

Eyal, Gil, Szelényi, Iván, and Townsley, Eleonor. *Making Capitalism without Capitalists: The New Ruling Elites in Eastern Europe.* London: Verso, 1998.

Falanga, Gianluca. *Non si può dividere il cielo: Storie dal Muro di Berlino.* Rome: Carocci, 2009.

Farrell, Darragh. *Failed Ideas for Failed States? Liberal International State-Building in Bosnia and Herzegovina.* Working Paper. Graz: University of Graz, Center for Southeast Europe, 2009. http://www.uni-graz.at/ofre2www_csee_1.pdf.

Fava, Valentina. *Storia di una fabbrica socialista: Saperi, lavoro, tecnologia e potere alla Skoda auto (1918–1968).* Milan: Guerini e Associati, 2010.

Fejérdy, András. *Pressed by Double Loyalty: Hungarian Attendance at the Second Vatican Council, 1959–1965.* Budapest: Central European University Press, 2016.

Ferge, Zsuzsa, Sik, Endre, Róbert, Péter, and Albert, Fruzsina, eds. *Social Costs of Transition: International Report on the Social Consequences of the Transition—A Survey Coordinated by the Institute for Human Studies.* Vienna: Institut für die Wissenschaften vom Menschen, August 1997.

Ferrara, Antonio. "Esodi, deportazioni e stermini. La 'Guerra-Rivoluzione europea' (1939–1953)." *Contemporanea* 9, no. 4 (October 2006): 653–680.

Filitov, Alexei. "Problems of Post-War Construction in Soviet Foreign Policy Conceptions during World War II," in Gori, Francesca, and Pons, Silvio, eds., *The Soviet Union and Europe in the Cold War, 1943–1953*, 3–22. London: Palgrave, 1996.

Fink, Carol, and Schaefer, Bernd, eds. *Ostpolitik, 1969–1974: European and Global Responses.* Washington, DC: German Historical Institute, 2009.

Fowkes, Ben. *L'Europa orientale dal 1945 al 1970.* Bologna: Il Mulino, 2004.

Franco, Jennifer, and Borras, M. Saturnino, Jr., eds., *Land Concentration, Land Grabbing and People's Struggles in Europe*, 114–190. Amsterdam: Transnational Institute (TNI) and Hands off the Land Network, April 2013. https://www.tni.org/files/download/land_in_europe-jun2013.pdf.

Franzinetti, Guido. "Bosnia: Guerre civile, sterminio, genocidio." *900: Per una storia del tempo presente*, no. 2 (July 2009): 235–249.

———. *I Balcani dal 1878 a oggi.* Roma: Carocci, 2010.

———. "Mitteleuropa in East-Central Europe: From Helsinki to EU Accession (1975–2004)." *European Journal of Social Theory* 11, no. 2. (2008): 219–235.

Freifeld, Alice. "The Cult of March 15: Sustaining the Hungarian Myth of Revolution, 1849–1999," in Bucur, Maria, and Meriwether Wingfield, Nancy, eds., *Staging the Past: The Politics of Commemoration in Habsburg Central Europe, 1848 to the Present.* Lafayette, IN: Purdue University Press, 2001.

Frommer, Benjamin. *National Cleansing: Retribution against Nazi Collaborators in Postwar Czechoslovakia.* Cambridge: Cambridge University Press, 2005.

Fulbrook, Mary. *Anatomy of a Dictatorship: Inside the GDR, 1949–1989.* Oxford: Oxford University Press, 1997.

———. *The People's State: East German Society from Hitler to Honecker.* New Haven, CT: Yale University Press, 2005.

———. *Power and Society in the GDR, 1961–1979: The "Normalisation of Rule"?* New York: Berghahn Books, 2009.

Fülöp, Anna. *La Transylvanie dans les relations roumano-hongroises vues du Quai d'Orsay: Septembre 1944–décembre 1947.* Cluj-Napoca: Centrul de Resurse pentru Diversitate Etnoculturală, 2006.

Fülöp, Mihály. *La paix inachevée.* Budapest: Association des Sciences historiques de Hongrie, 1998.

Gabanyi, Anneli Ute. "Ceauşescu Admits Economic Failures, Eschews Responsibility." *Radio Free Europe Research* (Munich), no. 44., November 6, 1987.

———. *The Ceauşescu Cult: Propaganda and Power Policy in Communist Romania.* Bucharest: Fundaţia Culturală Română, 2000.

———. *Die unvollendete Revolution: Rumänien zwischen Diktatur und Demokratie.* Munich: Piper, 1990.

Gagyi, József. *A krízis éve a Székelyföldön: 1949.* Csíkszereda (Miercurea Ciuc, Romania): Pro-Print, 2004.

Gallagher, Tom. *Romania and the European Union: How the Weak Vanquished the Strong.* Manchester: Manchester University Press, 2009.

Garthoff, Raymond L. *When and Why Romania Distanced Itself from Warsaw Pact.* Bulletin No. 5. Washington DC: Cold War International History Project, 1995.

Gati, Charles. *The Bloc That Failed: Soviet-East European Relations in Transition.* Bloomington: Indiana University Press, 1990.

———. *Failed Illusions: Moscow, Washington, Budapest, and the 1956 Hungarian Revolt.* Stanford, CA: Stanford University Press, 2006.

Germuska, Pál. *Unified Military Industries of the Soviet Bloc: Hungary and the Division of Labor in Military Production.* Harvard Cold War Studies. Lanham, MD: Lexington Books, 2015.

Gerrits, André. *The Myth of Jewish Communism: A Historical Interpretation.* New York: Peter Lang, 2009.

Gieseke, Jens. *The History of the Stasi: East Germany's Secret Police, 1945–1990.* New York: Berghahn, 2014.

Gingeras, Ryan. *Heroin, Organized Crime, and the Making of Modern Turkey.* Oxford: Oxford University Press, 2014.

Glatz, Ferenc, ed. *Magyarok és szerbek—Együttélés, múltfeltárás, megbékélés / Hungarians and Serbs: Coexistence, Revealing the Past, Reconciliation.* Budapest: MTA Bölcsészettudományi Kutatóközpont, 2013.

Glaurdić, Josip. *The Hour of Europe: Western Powers and the Breakup of Yugoslavia.* New Haven, CT: Yale University Press, 2011.

———. "Inside the Serbian War Machine. The Telephone Intercepts, 1991–1992." *East European Politics and Societies* 23, no. 1 (2009): 86–104.

Gluchowski, Lech. "The Defection of Josef Swiatlo and the Search for Jewish Scapegoats in the Polish United Workers' Party, 1953–1954." *Intermarium: Columbia University Electronic Journal of Modern East Central European Postwar History.* http://www.columbia.edu/cu/ece/research/intermarium/vol3no2/gluchowski.pdf.

Gluchowski, Lech, and Polonsky, Antony, eds. *1968: Forty Years After.* Studies in Polish Jewry. Oxford: Littman Library of Jewish Civilization, 2008.

Gökay, Bülent. *L'Europa orientale dal 1970 ad oggi.* 2001; Bologna: Il Mulino, 2005.

Gough, Roger. *A Good Comrade: János Kádár, Communism and Hungary.* London: I. B. Tauris, 2006.

Grachev, Andrei. *Gorbachev's Gamble: Soviet Foreign Policy and the End of the Cold War.* Cambridge, UK: Polity Press, 2008.

Grahek Ravančić, Martina. "Controversies about the Croatian Victims at Bleiburg and in Death Marches." *Review of Croatian History* 1, no. 2 (2006): 27–46.

Granville, Johanna. *The First Domino: International Decision Making during the Hungarian Crisis of 1956.* College Station: Texas A&M University Press, 2004.

Graziosi, Andrea. *Guerra e rivoluzione in Europa, 1905–1956.* Bologna: Il Mulino, 2001.

———. *L'URSS di Lenin e Stalin.* Bologna: Il Mulino, 2007.

———. *L'URSS dal trionfo al degrado: Storia dell'Unione Sovietica, 1945–1991.* Bologna: Il Mulino, 2008.

———. "Il mondo in Europa: Namier e il Medio Oriente europeo, 1815–1948." *Contemporanea* 10, no. 2 (2007): 193–228.

———. "I perché del collasso dell'URSS." *Storica* 43–45 (2009): 345–370.

Grilli Di Cortona, Pietro. *Da uno a molti: Democratizzazione e rinascita dei partiti in Europa orientale.* Bologna: Il Mulino, 1997.

Grob, Thomas. "The Concept of Eastern Europe in Past and Present." *Uninova: University of Basel Research Magazine*, October 2015), 16–17.

Gross, Jan T. *Revolution from Abroad: The Soviet Conquest of Poland's Western Ukraine and Western Belorussia.* Princeton, NJ: Princeton University Press, 2002.

Grúňová, Alexandra, ed. *NKVD/KGB Activities and Its Cooperation with Other Secret Services in Central and Eastern Europe, 1945–1989: Anthology of the International and Interdisciplinary Conference.* Bratislava: Nation's Memory Institute, 2008.

Gusev, Alexander, and Westphal, Kirsten. "Russian Energy Policies Revisited: Assessing the Impact of the Crisis in Ukraine on Russian Energy Policies and Specifying the Implications for German and EU Energy Policies." Research Paper No. 2015/RP 08, Stiftung Wissenschaft und Politik (Berlin), December 2015. https://www.swp -berlin.org/fileadmin/contents/products/research_papers/2015RP08_gsv_wep.pdf.

Gyarmati, György. "A nosztalgia esete a Kádár-korszakkal." *Metszetek: A Debreceni Egyetem Politikatudományi és Szociológiai Intézetének online társadalomtudományi folyóirata"* 1, nos. 2–3 (2013): 3–21.

Györkei, Jenő, and Horváth, Miklós eds. *Soviet Military Intervention in Hungary, 1956.* Budapest: Central European University Press, 1999.

Hale, E. Henry. "Did the Internet Break the Political Machine? Moldova's 2009 'Twitter Revolution That Wasn't.'" *Demokratizatsiya: The Journal of Post-Soviet Democratization* 21, no. 3 (Fall 2013): 481–505.

Halecki, Oskar. *Borderlands of Western Civilization: A History of East Central Europe.* New York: Ronald Company, 1952.

Hall, John A., ed. *The State of the Nation: Ernest Gellner and the Theory of Nationalism.* Cambridge: Cambridge University Press, 1998.

Hall, Richard A. "Theories of Collective Action and Revolution. Evidence from the Romanian Transition of December 1989." *Europe-Asia Studies* 52, no. 6 (September 2000): 1069–1093.

———. "The Uses of Absurdity: The Staged War Theory and the Romanian Revolution of December 1989." *East European Politics and Societies* 13, no. 3 (Fall 1999): 501–542.

Hanák, Péter. *The Garden and the Workshop: Essays on the Cultural History of Vienna and Budapest.* Princeton, NJ: Princeton University Press, 1998.

Hanebrink, Paul. *In Defense of Christian Hungary: Religion, Nationalism, and Antisemitism, 1890–1944.* Ithaca, NY: Cornell University Press, 2006.

Harbutt, J. Fraser. *Yalta 1945: Europe and America at the Crossroads.* Cambridge: Cambridge University Press, 2010.

Hardt, John P., and Kaufman, Richard F. *East-Central European Economies in Transition.* London: M. E. Sharpe, 1995.

Hardy, Jane. *Poland's New Capitalism.* London: Pluto Press, 2009.

Harrington, F. Joseph, and Courtney, Bruce J. *Tweaking the Nose of the Russians: Fifty Years of American-Romanian Relations, 1940–1990.* Boulder, CO: East European Monographs, 1991.

Haughton, Tim. "The Other New Europeans," in White, Stephen, Lewis, Paul G., and Batt, Judy, eds., *Developments in Central and Eastern European Politics.* Basingstoke, UK: Palgrave Macmillan, 2007.

Hayden, Robert M. "'Genocide Denial' Laws as Secular Heresy: A Critical Analysis with Reference to Bosnia." *Slavic Review* 67, no. 2 (Summer 2008): 384–407.

Heimann, Mary. *Czechoslovakia: The State That Failed.* London: Yale University Press, 2009.

Herbstritt, Georg, and Olaru, Stejărel. *Stasi şi Securitatea.* Bucharest: Humanitas, 2005.

Hodos, George. *Show Trials: Stalinist Purges in Eastern Europe, 1948–1954.* New York: Praeger, 1987.

Hoen, Herman W., ed. *Good Governance in Central and Eastern Europe: The Puzzle of Capitalism by Design.* Cheltenham, UK: Edward Elgar, 2001.

Hoffmann, David L. *Stalinist Values: The Cultural Norms of Soviet Modernity, 1917–1941.* Ithaca, NY: Cornell University Press, 2003.

Höhmann, Hans Hermann, Michael Kaser, and Karl C. Thalheim, eds. *The New Economic Systems of Eastern Europe.* London: Hurst, 1975.

Holloway, David. *Stalin and the Bomb: The Soviet Union and Atomic Energy, 1939–1956.* New Haven, CT: Yale University Press, 1994.

Horváth, Sándor. *Stalinism Reloaded: Everyday Life in Stalin-City, Hungary.* Bloomington: Indiana University Press, 2017.

———. *Kádár gyermekei: Ifjúsági lázadás a hatvanas években.* Budapest: Nyitott Könyvműhely, 2009.

———, ed. *Az ügynök arcai: Mindennapi kollaboráció és ügynökkérdés.* Budapest: Libri, 2014.

Hroch, Miroslav. *Social Preconditions of National Revival in Europe.* Cambridge: Cambridge University Press, 1985.

Hunyadi, Attila, ed. *State and Minority in Transylvania, 1918–1989: Studies on the History of the Hungarian Community.* New York: Columbia University Press, 2013.

Ioanid, Radu. *The Holocaust in Romania: The Destruction of Jews and Gypsies under the Antonescu Regime, 1940–1944.* Chicago: Ivan R. Dee, 2000.

———. *The Ransom of the Jews: The Story of the Extraordinary Secret Bargain between Romania and Israel.* Chicago: Ivan R. Dee, 2005.

———, ed. *Lotul Antonescu în ancheta SMERŞ, Moscova, 1944–1946: Documente din arhiva FSB.* Iaşi (Romania): Polirom, 2006.

Ioffe, Grigory. *Understanding Belarus and How Western Foreign Policy Misses the Mark.* Boston: Rowman & Littlefield, 2008.

Iordachi, Constantin, and Dobrincu, Dorin, eds. *Transforming Peasants, Property and Power: The Collectivization of Agriculture in Romania, 1949–1962.* Budapest: Central European University Press, 2009.

Irving, David. *Uprising! One Nation's Nightmare: Hungary 1956.* London: Hodder & Stoughton, 1981.

Ivaničková, Edita, and Simon, Attila, eds. *Mad'arská revolúcia 1956 a Slovensko: Az 1956-os magyar forradalom és Szlovákia.* Somorja (Šamorín, Slovakia): Forum, 2006.

Janowski, Maciej, Iordachi, Constantin, and Trencsényi, Balázs. "Why Bother about Historical Regions? Debates over Central Europe in Hungary, Poland and Romania." *East-Central Europe* 1, nos. 1–2 (2005): 5–58.

Jarvis, Christopher. "The Rise and the Fall of the Pyramid Schemes in Albania." *IMF Staff Papers* 47, no. 1 (2000): 1–29.

Jelavich, Barbara. *History of the Balkans.* Vol. 2, *Twentieth Century.* Cambridge: Cambridge University Press, 1983.

Judt, Tony. *Postwar: A History of Europe since 1945.* New York: Penguin, 2005.

Junes, Tom. *Student Politics in Communist Poland: Generations of Consent and Dissent.* London: Lexington Books, 2015.

Kádár Lynn, Katalin, ed. *The Inauguration of Organized Political Warfare: Political Organizations Sponsored by the National Committee for a Free Europe/Free Europe Committee.* Saint Helena, CA: Helena History Press, 2013.

Kalabinski, Jacek. *How World Bank Bailouts Aid East European Regimes.* Washington, DC: Heritage Foundation, 1988. http://www.policyarchive.org/handle/10207/bitstreams/12626.pdf.

Kalmár, Melinda. *Ennivaló és hozomány: A kora kádárizmus ideológiája.* Budapest: Magvető, 1998.

———. *Történelmi galaxisok vonzásában: Magyarország és a szovjetrendszer: 1945–1990.* Budapest: Osiris, 2014.

Kamiński, Łukasz, and Persak, Krzysztof, eds. *A Handbook of the Communist Security Apparatus in Eastern Central Europe 1944–1989.* Warsaw: Institute for National Remembrance, 2005.

Kaplan, Karel. *Dans les archives du comité central: 30 ans de secrets du Bloc soviétique.* Paris: Albin Michel, 1978.

Karsai, László. "The People's Courts and Revolutionary Justice in Hungary, 1945–46," in Deák, István, Gross, T. Jan, and and Judt, Tony, *The Politics of Retribution in Europe: World War II and Its Aftermath,* 233–252. Princeton, NJ: Princeton University Press, 2000.

Kasianov, Georgiy. "How a War for the Past Becomes a War in the Present." *Kritika: Explorations in Russian and Eurasian History* 16, no. 1 (Winter 2015): 149–155.

Kemény, István. "The Unregistered Economy in Hungary." *Soviet Studies* 34, no. 3 (July 1982): 349–366.

Kemp-Welch, Anthony. *Poland under Communism: A Cold War History.* Cambridge: Cambridge University Press, 2008.

Kenez, Peter. *Hungary from the Nazis to the Soviets: The Establishment of the Communist Regime in Hungary, 1944–1948.* Cambridge: Cambridge University Press, 2006.

Kennedy, Paul. *The Rise and Fall of the Great Powers: Economic Change and Military Conflict from 1500 to 2000.* New York: Random House, 1987.

Kenney, Padraic. *Il peso della libertà: L'Europa dell'Est dal 1989.* 2006; Turin: EDT, 2008.

King, Charles. *The Moldovans: Romania, Russia and the Politics of Culture.* Stanford, CA: Hoover Institution Press, 2000.

King, R. Robert. *Minorities under Communism: Nationalities as a Source of Tension among Balkan Communist States.* Cambridge, MA: Harvard University Press, 1973.

Kirschbaum, Stanislav. *A History of Slovakia: The Struggle for Survival.* New York: St. Martin's Press, 1995.

Kitschelt, Herbert, et al., eds. *Post-communist Party Systems: Competition, Representation, and Inter-Party Cooperation.* Cambridge: Cambridge University Press, 1999.

Kligman, Gail. *The Politics of Duplicity: Controlling Reproduction in Ceausescu's Romania.* Berkeley, CA: University of California Press, 1998.

Klumbyte, Neringa, and Sharafutdinova, Gulnaz. *Soviet Society in the Era of Late Socialism, 1964–1985.* Lanham, MD: Lexington Books, 2012.

Kochanowski, Jerzy. "Pioneers of the Free Market Economy? Unofficial Commercial Exchange between People from the Socialist Bloc Countries (1970–1985)." *Journal of Modern European History* 8, no. 2 (2010): 196–220.

Kohn, Hans. *The Idea of Nationalism.* New York: Macmillan, 1944.

Kolakowski, Leszek. *Il marxismo e oltre: responsabilità e storia.* Cosenza: Lerici, 1979.

Kopecek, Mihal. "Citizen and Patriot in the Post-Totalitarian Era: Czech Dissidence in Search of the Nation and Its Democratic Future." *Transit Online.* The "Brave New World" after Communism. 1989: Expectations in Comparison (December 2009).

Kornai, János. *Overcentralization in Economic Administration: A Critical Analysis Based on Experience in Hungarian Light Industry.* Oxford: Oxford University Press, 1959.

———. *The Road to a Free Economy: Shifting from a Socialist System—The Example of Hungary.* New York: Norton, 1990.

———. "Transzformációs visszaesés: Egy általános jelenség vizsgálata a magyar fejlődés példáján." *Közgazdasági Szemle* 40, nos. 7–8 (1993): 569–599.

Körösényi, András. *The Hungarian Political System.* Budapest: Central European University Press, 1999.

———, ed. *A magyar politikai rendszer—Negyedszázad után.* Budapest: Osiris, 2015.

Kőrösi, Zsuzsanna, and Molnár, Adrienne. *Carrying a Secret in My Heart: Children of Political Victims of the Revolution in Post–1956 Hungary—An Oral History.* Budapest: Central European University Press, 2003.

Kosior, Katarzyna. "The Impact of Central and Eastern Europe on the Common Agricultural Policy." *Romanian Journal of Political Science* 14, no. 1 (September 2014): 116–147.

Kostovicova, Denisa. *Kosovo: The Politics of Identity and Space.* London: Routledge, 2005.

Kotkin, Stephen. *Armageddon Averted: The Soviet Collapse, 1970–2000.* Oxford: Oxford University Press, 2001.

———. *Uncivil Society: 1989 and the Implosion of the Communist Establishment.* New York: Modern Library, 2009.

Kovács, Gábor. *Az európai egyensúlytól a kölcsönös szolgáltatások társadalmáig: Bibó István, a politikai gondolkodó*. Budapest: Argumentum Kiadó-Bibó István Szellemi Műhely, 2004.

Kovács, József Ö. *A paraszti társadalom felszámolása a kommunista diktatúrában: A vidéki Magyarország politikai társadalomtörténete*. Budapest: Libri, 2012.

Krahulcsán, Zsolt. "A magyar politikai rendőrség és a szocialista országok állambiztonsági szervei közötti kapcsolatok szabályozása (1956–1989)." *Levéltári Szemle* 59, no. 3 (2009): 3–19.

Kramer, Mark. "The Collapse of East European Communism and the Repercussions within the Soviet Union (Part 1)." *Journal of Cold War Studies* 5, no. 4 (Fall 2003): 178–256.

———. "The Collapse of East European Communism and the Repercussions within the Soviet Union (Part 2)." *Journal of Cold War Studies* 6, no. 4 (Fall 2004): 3–64.

———. "The Collapse of East European Communism and the Repercussions within the Soviet Union (Part 3)." *Journal of Cold War Studies* 7, no. 1 (Winter 2005): 3–96.

———. "The Early Post-Stalin Succession Struggle and Upheavals in East-Central Europe. Internal-External Linkages in Soviet Policy Making." *Journal of Cold War Studies* 1, no. 1 (Winter 1999): 3–55.

———. *Soviet Deliberations during the Polish Crisis, 1980–1981*. Working Paper No. 1. Washington, DC: Cold War International History Project, 1999.

———. "The Soviet Union and the 1956 Crises in Hungary and Poland: Reassessments and New Findings." *Journal of Contemporary History* 33, no. 2 (April 1998): 163–214.

Kraemer, Peter, ed. *Foreign Relations of the United States, 1969–1976, Volume E-15, Part 1, Documents on Eastern Europe, 1973–1976*. Washington, DC: US Government Printing Office, 2008.

Kraus, Michael, and Stanger, Allison, eds. *Irreconcilable Differences? Explaining Czechoslovakia's Dissolution*. Lanham, MD: Rowman & Littlefield, 2000.

Kritz, Neil J. *Transitional Justice*. Washington, DC: US Institute of Peace, 1995.

Kundera, Milan. "The Tragedy of Central Europe." *New York Review of Books*, April 26, 1984, 33–38.

Ladányi, János, and Szelényi, Iván. *Patterns of Exclusion: Constructing Gypsy Ethnicity and the Making of an Underclass in Transnational Societies of Europe*. New York: Columbia University Press, 2006.

Lampe, John R. *Yugoslavia as History: Twice There Was a Country*. Cambridge: Cambridge University Press, 2000.

László, Márton, and Novák Csaba, Zoltán. *A szabadság terhe: Marosvásárhely, 1990, március 16-21*. Csíkszereda (Miercurea Ciuc, Romania): Dr. Bernády György Közművelődési Alapítvány-Pro-Print Könyvkiadó, 2012.

Lavigne, Marie. *International Political Economy and Socialism*. Cambridge: Cambridge University Press, 1991.

———. *The Socialist Economies of the Soviet Union and Europe*. London: Martin Robertson, 1974.

Ledeneva, Alena V. *Russia's Economy of Favours: Blat, Networking, and Informal Exchanges*. Cambridge: Cambridge University Press, 1998.

Leuştean, Lucian. *Orthodoxy and the Cold War: Religion and Political Power in Romania, 1947–65*. Basingstoke, UK: Palgrave Macmillan, 2009.

Levy, Robert. *Ana Pauker: The Rise and Fall of a Jewish Communist.* Berkeley: University of California Press, 2001.

Liégeois, Jean-Pierre. *Roma in Europe.* Strasbourg: Council of Europe Publishing, 2007.

Linz, J. Juan., and Stepan, Alfred. *Problems of Democratic Transition and Consolidation: Southern Europe, South America, and Post-Communist Europe.* Baltimore, MD: Johns Hopkins University Press, 1996.

Lipski, Jan-Józef. *KOR: A History of the Workers' Defence Committee in Poland, 1976–1981.* Berkeley: University of California Press, 1985.

Lorenzini, Sara. *Il rifiuto di un'eredità difficile: La Repubblica Democratica Tedesca, gli ebrei e lo Stato di Israele.* Florence: Giuntina, 1998.

Lund, S. Michael. "Greed and Grievances Diverted: How Macedonia Avoided Civil War 1990–2001," in Collier, Paul, and Sambanis, Nicholas, eds., *Understanding Civil War: Evidence and Analysis: Europe, Central Asia and Other Regions,* vol. 2, 231–257. Washington, DC: World Bank, 2005.

Lusa, Stefano. *La dissoluzione del potere: Il partito comunista sloveno ed il processo di democratizzazione della Repubblica.* Udine: Kappa Vu, 2007.

Magocsi, Paul Robert. *Historical Atlas of Central Europe.* 2nd ed. Toronto: University of Toronto Press, 2002.

Magyar, Bálint. *Post-Communist Mafia State: The Case of Hungary.* Budapest: Central European University Press, 2015.

Maier, Charles S. *Dissolution: The Crisis of Communism and the End of East Germany.* Princeton, NJ: Princeton University Press, 1997.

Majtényi György. *K-vonal: Uralmi elit és luxus a szocializmusban.* Budapest: Nyitott Könyvműhely, 2009.

Malcolm, Noel. *Storia della Bosnia: Dalle origini ai giorni nostri.* 1994; Milan: Bompiani, 2000.

———. *Storia del Kosovo: Dalle origini ai giorni nostri.* 1998; Milan: Bompiani, 1999.

———. "Kosovo: Only Independence Will Work." *National Interest* 54 (Winter 1998–1999): 23–26.

Márai, Sándor. *Memoir of Hungary, 1944–1948.* Budapest: Corvina, in association with Central European University Press, 1996.

Marceva, Ilyiana. "Change of the Guard: The Struggle for Power in Bulgaria, 1953–1962, Part 1." *Études Balkaniques* 36, no. 1 (2000): 59–78.

———. "Change of the Guard: The Struggle for Power in Bulgaria, 1953–1962, Part 2." *Études Balkaniques* 36, no. 2 (2000): 36–57.

Marchi, Marzia, and Tonini, Carla, eds. *Da Berlino a Samarcanda: Città in transizione.* Rome: Carocci, 2009.

Marin, Manuela. *Originea și evoluția cultului personalității lui Nicolae Ceaușescu 1965–1989.* Alba Iulia (Romania): Editura Altip, 2008.

Mark, Eduard. *Revolution by Degrees: Stalin's National-Front Strategy for Europe, 1941–1947.* Working Paper No. 31. Washington DC: Cold War International History Project, 2001.

Mark, James. "Remembering Rape: Divided Social Memory and the Red Army in Hungary, 1944–1945." *Past and Present* 188, no. 1 (August 2005): 133–161.

Marples, R. David. "Belarus: Europe's Last Dictator Gets a Little Lonelier." *Central Europe Digest,* September 15, 2010. http://www.cepa.org/ced/view.aspx?record_id=263.

Marples, R. David, and Mills, V. Frederik, eds. *Ukraine's Euromaidan: Analyses of the Civil Revolution*. New York: Columbia University Press, 2015.

Martin, Terry. *The Affirmative Action Empire: Nations and Nationalism in the Soviet Union, 1923–1939*. Ithaca, NY: Cornell University Press, 2001.

Mastny, Vojtech. *Il dittatore insicuro: Stalin e la guerra fredda*. 1996; Milan: Corbaccio, 1998.

Mastny, Vojtech, and Byrne, Malcolm, eds. *A Cardboard Castle? An Inside History of the Warsaw Pact, 1955–1991*. Budapest: Central European University Press, 2005.

Mazower, Mark. *Hitler's Empire: Nazi Rule in Occupied Europe*. London: Penguin, 2008.

———. *Le ombre dell'Europa*. 1999; Milan: Garzanti, 2001.

McGarry, John, and O'Leary, Brendan, eds. *The Politics of Ethnic Conflict Regulation*. London: Routledge, 1993.

Mearsheimer, J. John. "Why the Ukraine Crisis Is the West's Fault: The Liberal Delusions That Provoked Putin," *Foreign Affairs* 93, no. 5 (September–October 2014): 77–89.

Mëhilli, Elidor. "Defying De-Stalinization: Albania's 1956." *Journal of Cold War Studies* 13, no. 4 (Fall 2011): 4–56.

Melegh, Attila. *On the East-West Slope: Globalization, Nationalism, Racism and Discourses on Central and Eastern Europe*. Budapest: Central European University Press, 2006.

Melloni, Alberto. *L'altra Roma: Politica e S. Sede durante il concilio Vaticano II (1959–1965)*. Bologna: Il Mulino, 2000.

———, ed. *Il filo sottile: L'Ostpolitik vaticana di Agostino Casaroli*. Bologna: Il Mulino, 2006.

Mevius, Martin. *Agents of Moscow: The Hungarian Communist Party and the Origins of Socialist Patriotism, 1941–1953*. Oxford: Oxford University Press, 2005.

———. "Reappraising Communism and Nationalism." *Nationalites Papers* 37, no. 4 (2009): 377–400.

Milin, Miodrag, and Stepanov, Liubomir. *Golgota Bărăganului pentru sârbii din România, 1951–1956*. Timișoara: Uniunea Democratică a Sârbilor și Carașovenilor din România, 1996.

Miller, E. James, Selvage, E. Douglas, and Van Hook, Laurie, eds. *Foreign Relations of the United States, 1969–1976*. Vol. 29, *Eastern Europe; Eastern Mediterranean, 1969–1972*. Washington, DC: US Government Printing Office, 2007.

Mink, András. "David Irving and the 1956 Hungarian Revolution." *Hungarian Quarterly* 14, no. 4. (Fall 2000): 117–128.

Minow, Martha. *Breaking the Cycles of Hatred: Memory, Law, and Repair*. Princeton, NJ: Princeton University Press, 2002.

Mioc, Marius. *Revoluția fără mistere: Începutul revoluției române: cazul László Tőkés*. Timișoara: Editura Almanahul Banatului, 2002.

Moldovan, Silviu B., Anisescu, Cristina, and Matiu, Mirela. *"Partiturile" Securității: Directive, ordine, instrucțiunii (1947–1987)*. Bucharest: Editura Nemira, 2007.

Mong, Attila. *Kádár hitele: A magyar államadósság története*. Budapest: Libri, 2012.

Morozov, Evgeny. *The Net Delusion: How Not to Liberate the World*. London: Allen Lane, 2011.

Motyl, Alexander. "The Ukraine Crisis according to John J. Mearsheimer: Impeccable Logic, Wrong Facts," *European Leadership Network*, October 31, 2014. http://

www.europeanleadershipnetwork.org/the-ukraine-crisis-according-to-john-j-mearsheimer-impeccable-logic-wrong-facts_2079.html.

Munteanu, Mircea. "When the Levee Breaks: The Impact of Sino-Soviet Split and the Invasion of Czechoslovakia on Romanian-Soviet Relations, 1967–1970." *Journal of Cold War Studies* 12, no. 1 (Winter 2010): 43–61.

Murgescu, Bogdan, ed. *Revoluția română din 1989: Istorie și memorie*. Iași (Romania): Polirom, 2007.

Murzaku, Ines Angeli, ed. *Quo Vadis Eastern Europe? Religion, State and Society after Communism*. Ravenna: Longo, 2009.

Muyhtar, Fatme. *The Human Rights of Muslims in Bulgaria in Law and Politics since 1878*. Sofia: Bulgarian Helsinki Committee, 2003.

Naimark, M. Norman. *The Russians in Germany: A History of the Soviet Zone of Occupation, 1945–1949*. Cambridge, MA: Harvard University Press, 1995.

———. *La politica dell'odio: La pulizia etnica nell'Europa contemporanea*. 2001; Rome: Laterza, 2002.

Naimark, M. Norman, and Gibianski, Leonid, eds. *The Establishment of Communist Regimes in Eastern Europe, 1944–1949*. Boulder, CO: Westview, 1997.

Namier, B. Lewis. *Conflicts: Studies in Contemporary History*. London: Macmillan, 1942.

Nastasă, Lucian., ed. *Minorități etnoculturale: Mărturii documentare—Evreii din România (1945–1965)*. Cluj-Napoca (Romania): Centru de Resurse pentru Diversitate Etnoculturală, 2003.

Nedelsky, Nadya. "Divergent Responses to a Common Past: Transitional Justice in the Czech Republic and Slovakia." *Theory and Society* 33, no. 1 (February 2004): 65–115.

Niederhauser, Emil. *A History of Eastern Europe since the Middle Ages*. Boulder, CO: Social Science Monographs, 2003.

———. *Nemzetek születése Kelet-Európában*. Budapest: Kossuth, 1976.

———. *A nemzeti megújulási mozgalmak Kelet-Európában*. Budapest: Akadémiai Kiadó, 1977.

Nodia, Ghia. "Europeanization and (Not) Resolving Secessionist Conflict." *Journal of Politics and Minority Issues in Europe* 5, no. 1 (2004): 1–15.

Novák, Csaba Zoltán. *Aranykorszak? A Ceaușescu-rendszer magyarságpolitikája, 1965–1974*. Csíkszereda (Miercurea Ciuc, Romania): Pro-Print, 2011.

Nuti, Leonardo, ed. *The Crisis of Détente in Europe: From Helsinki to Gorbachev, 1975–1985*. London: Routledge, 2009.

Nyíri, Pál. *Chinese in Eastern Europe and Russia: A Middleman Minority in a Transnational Era*. London: Routledge, 2007.

O'Brennan, John. "Bulgarians under the Yoke of Oligarchy." Unpublished paper, 2014. https://www.maynoothuniversity.ie/sites/default/files/assets/document/New_Left_Review_Bulgarians_under_the_Yoke_of_Oligarchy.pdf.

Okváth, Imre. *Bástya a béke frontján: Magyar haderő és katonapolitika, 1945–1956*. Budapest: Aquila, 1998.

Olti, Ágoston, and Nagy, Mihály Zoltán, eds. *Érdekképviselet vagy pártpolitika? Iratok a Magyar Népi Szövetség történetéhez 1944–1953*. Csíkszereda (Miercurea Ciuc, Romania): Pro-Print, 2009.

Oplatka, András. *Egy döntés története: Magyar határnyitás—1989, szeptember 11, nulla óra*. Budapest: Helikon, 2008.

Oprea, Marius. *Banalitatea răului: O istorie a Securității în documente 1949–1989*. Iași (Romania): Polirom, 2002.

———. *Bastionul cruzimii: O istorie a Securității (1948–1964)*. Iași (Romania): Polirom, 2008.

Ostermann, Christian, ed. *Uprising in East Germany, 1953*. Budapest: Central European University Press, 2001.

Ouimet, J. Matthew. *The Rise and Fall of the Brezhnev Doctrine in Soviet Foreign Policy*. Chapel Hill: University of North Carolina Press, 2003.

Pach, Zsigmond Pál. *Nyugat-európai és magyarországi agrárfejlődés a XV–XVII: Század-ban*. Budapest: Kossuth, 1963.

Papo, Adriano. *L'Ungheria contemporanea: Dalla monarchia dualista ai giorni nostri*. Rome: Carocci, 2008.

Papp, Z. Attila. "A roma tanulók aránya Magyarországon és a tanulói teljesítmények az általános iskolai oktatásban," in Bárdi, Nándor, and Tóth Ágnes, eds., *Asszimi-láció, integráció, szegregáció: Párhuzamos értelmezések és modellek a kisebbségku-tatásban*, 227–264. Budapest: Argumentum, 2011.

Pavlowitch, K. Stevan. *Serbia: La storia al di là del nome*. 2002; Trieste: Beit Editore, 2010.

Pearson, Owen. *Albania as Dictatorship and Democracy: From Isolation to the Kosovo War, 1946–1998*. London: Centre for Albanian Studies and I. B. Tauris, 2006.

Pence, Katherine, and Betts, Paul. *Socialist Modern: East German Everyday Culture and Politics*. Ann Arbor: University of Michigan Press, 2008.

Percival, Mark. "Churchill and Romania: The Myth of the October 1944 'Betrayal.'" *Contemporary British History* 12, no. 3 (1998): 41–61.

Petkova, Lilia. "The Ethnic Turks in Bulgaria: Social Integration and Impact on Bulgarian-Turkish Relations, 1947–2000." *Global Review of Ethnopolitics* 1, no. 4 (2002): 42–59.

Pike, David. *Lukács and Brecht*. Chapel Hill: University of North Carolina Press, 1985.

Piotrowski, Tadeusz. *Poland's Holocaust: Ethnic Strife, Collaboration with Occupying Forces and Genocide in the Second Republic, 1918–1947*. Jefferson, NC: McFarland, 1998.

Pirjevec, Jože. *Le guerre jugoslave, 1991–1999*. Turin: Einaudi, 2001.

———. ed. *Foibe: Una storia d'Italia*. Turin: Einaudi, 2009.

Pittaway, Mark. *Eastern Europe, 1939–2000*. London: Arnold, 2004.

Pleshakov, Konstantin. *Berlino 1989: La caduta del muro*. Milan: Corbaccio, 2009.

Póczik, Szilveszter. "Magyar és cigány bűnelkövetők a börtönben," *Magyar Tudomány* 45, no. 4 (2000): 426–435.

Pogátsa, Zoltán. *Magyarország politikai gazdaságtana és az északi modell esélye*. Buda-pest: Osiris, 2016.

———. "No Convergence in the Central Eastern European New Member States: A Multi Indicator Analysis," in Rustam Jamilov, and Yusaf H., Akbar, eds., *Neo-Transna-tional Economics*, 363–376. Bingley: Emerald, 2015.

Pók, Attila. *The Politics of Hatred: Scapegoating in Twentieth-Century Hungary: History and Historiography*. Szombathely: Savaria University Press, 2009.

Polese, Abel, and Beacháin, Donnacha Ó., eds. *The Colour Revolutions in the Former Soviet Union: Successes and Failures*. London: Routledge, 2010.

Polian, Pavel. *Against Their Will: The History and Geography of Forced Migrations in the USSR.* Budapest: Central European University Press, 2004.

Pons, Silvio. *Berlinguer e la fine del comunismo.* Turin: Einaudi, 2006.

Popély, Árpád. *A (cseh) szlovákiai magyarság történeti kronológiája 1944–1992.* Somorja: Fórum Kisebbségkutató Intézet, 2006.

Porter-Szűcs, Brian. *Faith and Fatherland: Catholicism, Modernity, and Poland.* Oxford: Oxford University Press, 2011.

Privitera, Francesco. *Jugoslavia.* Milan: Unicopli, 2007.

Procacci, Giuliano, ed. *Cominform: Minutes of the Three Conferences 1947/1948/1949.* Milan: Annali della Fondazione Giangiacomo Feltrinelli, 1994.

Puddington, Arch. *Broadcasting Freedom: The Cold War Triumph of Radio Free Europe and Radio Liberty.* Lexington: University Press of Kentucky, 2003.

Pula, Besnik. "The Budding Autocrats of the Balkans." *Foreign Policy,* April 15, 2016. http://foreignpolicy.com/2016/04/15/the-budding-autocrats-of-the-balkans-serbia-macedonia-montenegro/.

Pupo, Raoul. *Il lungo esodo: Istria: le persecuzioni, le foibe, l'esilio.* Milan: Rizzoli, 2005.

Rainer, M. János. *Bevezetés a kádárizmusba.* Budapest: L'Harmattan Kiadó, 2011.

———. *Imre Nagy: A Biography.* London: I. B. Tauris, 2009.

Rákosi, Mátyás. *Visszaemlékezések 1945–1956.* Budapest: Napvilág, 1997.

Ramet, P. Sabrina. *Whose Democracy? Nationalism, Religion, and the Doctrine of Collective Rights in Post-1989 Eastern Europe.* Lanham: Rowman & Littlefield, 1997.

Ratesh, Nestor. *Romania: The Entangled Revolution.* New York: Praeger, 1991.

Rév, István. *Retroactive Justice: Prehistory of Post-Communism.* Stanford, CA: Stanford University Press, 2005.

Révész, Bela. "'Out of Romania!' Reasons and Methods as Reflected in State Security." *Regio English Issue,* no. 7 (2008): 8–66.

Révész, Sándor. *Aczél és korunk.* Budapest: Sík, 1997.

Riccardi, Andrea. *Il Vaticano e Mosca.* Bari: Laterza, 1992.

Rieber, J. Alfred. "Civil War in the Soviet Union." *Kritika: Explorations in Russian and Eurasian History* 4, no. 1 (2003): 129–162.

Roberts, Adam. "NATO's 'Humanitarian War' over Kosovo." *Survival* 41, no. 3 (Autumn 1999): 102–123.

Roberts, Geoffrey. *Stalin's Wars: From World War to Cold War, 1939–1953.* New Haven, CT: Yale University Press, 2006.

Roccucci, Adriano. *Stalin e il patriarca: Chiesa ortodossa e potere sovietico, 1917–1958.* Turin: Einaudi, 2011.

Romano, Angela. ""Untying Cold War knots: The EEC and Eastern Europe in the long 1970s." *Cold War History* 14, no. 2 (2013): 153–173.

Romsics, Ignác. "Economic Reforms in the Kádár Era." *Hungarian Quarterly* 187, no. 3 (Autumn 2007): 69–79.

———. *Hungary in the Twentieth Century.* Budapest: Corvina, 1999.

———. *Wartime American Plans for a New Hungary: Documents from the Department of State, 1942–44.* Boulder, CO: Atlantic Research and Publications, 1992.

Roper, D. Steven, and Fesnic, Florin. "Historical Legacies and Their Impact on Post-Communist Voting Behaviour." *Europe-Asia Studies* 55, no. 1 (January 2003): 119–131.

Rose, Richard, Mishler, William, and Munro, Neil, eds. *Popular Support for an Undemocratic Regime: The Changing Views of the Russians.* Cambridge: Cambridge University Press, 2011.

Rothschild, Joseph. *East Central Europe between the World War.* Vol. 9. *A History of East Central Europe.* Seattle: University of Washington Press, 1974.

———. *Return to Diversity: A Political History of East Central Europe since World War II.* 3rd ed. Oxford: Oxford University Press, 2000.

Rupnik, Jacques. "From Democracy Fatigue to Populist Backlash." *Journal of Democracy* 18, no. 4 (2007): 17–25.

Rus, Alin. *Valea Jiului—o capcana istorică: Studiu de antropologie culturală.* Bucharest: Realitatea Românească, 2003.

Rutar, Sabine, ed. *Beyond the Balkans: Towards an Inclusive History of Southeastern Europe.* Berlin: LIT, 2014.

Sadurski, Wojciech, ed. *Constitutional Justice, East and West: Democratic Legitimacy and Constitutional Courts in Post-Communist Europe in a Comparative Perspective.* The Hague: Kluver Law International, 2002.

Sárközy, Tamás. *A privatizáció joga Magyarországon (1989–1993).* Budapest: Akadémiai Kiadó, 1993.

Sarotte, E. Marie. *1989: The Struggle to Create Post-Cold War Europe.* Princeton, NJ: Princeton University Press, 2009.

Savranskaya, Svetlana. "Human Rights Movement in the USSR after the Signing of the Helsinki Final Act, and the Reaction of Soviet Authorities," in Nuti, Leopoldo, ed., *The Crisis of Détente in Europe: From Helsinki to Gorbachev, 1975–1985,* 26–40. London: Routledge, 2009.

Savranskaya, Svetlana, Blanton, Thomas, and Zubok, Vladislav, eds. *Masterpieces of History: The Peaceful End of the Cold War in Europe, 1989.* Budapest: Central European University Press, 2010.

Schindler, R. John. *Jihad nei Balcani: Guerra etnica e Al-Qa'ida in Bosnia, 1992–1995.* 2007; Gorizia: Goriziana, 2009.

Schlögel, Karl. *Leggere il tempo nello spazio: Saggi di storia e geopolitica.* 2003; Milan: Bruno Mondadori, 2009.

Schöpflin, George. *Nations, Identity, Power: The New Politics of Europe.* London: Hurst, 2000.

———. *Politics in Eastern Europe, 1945–1992.* Oxford, UK: Blackwell, 1993.

Schöpflin, George, and Wood, Nancy, eds. *In Search of Central Europe.* Cambridge, UK: Polity Press, 1989.

Schröder, Karl. "The IMF and the Countries of the Council for Mutual Economic Assistance." *Intereconomics* 17, no. 2 (March 1982): 87–90.

Schumann, Dirk, and Bessel, Richard, eds. *Life after Death: Approaches to a Cultural and Social History of Europe during the 1940s and 1950s.* Cambridge: Cambridge University Press, 2003.

Scurtu, Ioan. *Revoluția română din decembrie 1989 în context internațional.* Bucharest: Editura Enciclopedică and Editura Institutului Revoluției Române din Decembrie 1989, 2006.

Scurtu, Ioan, ed. *România. Retragerea trupelor sovietice—1958.* Bucharest: Editura Didactică și Pedagogică, 1996.

Seton-Watson, Hugh. *The East European Revolution*. London: Methuen, 1950.

Shevel, Oxana. "Nationality in Ukraine: Some Rules of Engagement." *East-European Politics and Societies* 16, no. 2 (2002): 387–413.

Siani-Davies, Peter. *The Romanian Revolution of December 1989*. Ithaca, NY: Cornell University Press, 2005.

Sitariu, Mihaela. *Oaza de libertate: Timișoara, 30 octombrie 1956*. Iași (Romania): Polirom, 2004.

Skilling, H. Gordon. *Czechoslovakia's Interrupted Revolution*. Princeton, NJ: Princeton University Press, 1976.

Slezkine, Yuri. "The USSR as a Communal Apartment, or How a Socialist State Promoted Ethnic Particularism," in Fitzpatrick, Sheila, ed., *Stalinism: New Directions*, 313–347. London: Routledge, 1999.

Snyder, Timothy D. *Black Earth: The Holocaust as History and Warning*. New York: Tim Duggan Books, 2015.

———. *Bloodlands: Europe between Hitler and Stalin*. New York: Basic Books, 2010.

Solonari, Vladimir. *Purifying the Nation: Population Exchange and Ethnic Cleansing in Nazi-Allied Romania*. Washington, DC: Woodrow Wilson Center Press, 2009.

Sołtan, Karol Edward. "Moderate Modernity and the Spirit of 1989," in Tismăneanu, Vladimir, and Iacob C., Bogdan eds., *The End and the Beginning: The Revolutions of 1989 and the Resurgence of History*, 69–108. Budapest: Central European University Press, 2012.

Staar, F. Richard. "Elections in Communist Poland." *Midwest Journal of Political Science* 2, no. 2 (May 1958): 200–218.

Stalin, Joseph. "Marxism and the National Question," in Franklin, Bruce, ed., *The Essential Stalin: Major Theoretical Writings, 1905–52*, 54–84. London: Croom Helm, 1973.

Stan, Lavinia. *Transitional Justice in Eastern Europe and the Former Soviet Union*. London: Routledge, 2008.

Standeisky, Éva. *Gúzsba kötve. A kulturális elit és a hatalom*. Budapest: 1956-os Intézet Állambiztonsági Szolgálatok Történeti Levéltára, 2005.

Stănescu, Mircea. *The Reeducation Trials in Communist Romania*. Boulder, CO: East European Monographs, 2011.

Staniszkis, Jadwiga. *The Dynamics of the Breakthrough in Eastern Europe: The Polish Experience*. Berkeley: University of California Press, 1991.

———. *Poland's Self-Limiting Revolution*. Princeton, NJ: Princeton University Press, 1984.

Stark, Tamás. "Deportation of Civilians from Hungary to the Soviet Union." *Annali dell'Istituto storico italo-germanico in Trento* 18 (2002): 605–618.

———. *Hungary's Human Losses in World War II*. Uppsala: Centre for Multiethnic Research, 1995.

———. *Hungarian Jews during the Holocaust and after the Second World War, 1939–1949*. New York: Columbia University Press, 2000.

Stehle, Hansjakob. *Eastern Politics of the Vatican, 1917–1979*. Athens: Ohio University Press, 1981.

Stewart, Michael. "Deprivation, the Roma and the "underclass," in Hann, Chris M., ed., *Postsocialism: Ideals, Ideologies, and Practices in Eurasia*, 133–156. New York: Routledge, 2002.

Stoenescu, Alex Mihai. *Istoria loviturilor de Stat din România: Revoluția din decembrie 1989—o tragedie românească, IV.* Bucharest: Rao Editura, 2005.

Stokes, R. Gale. *Constructing Socialism: Technology and Change in East Germany, 1945–1990.* Baltimore: Johns Hopkins University Press, 2000.

Stolarik, M. Mark, ed. *The Prague Spring and the Warsaw Pact Invasion of Czechoslovakia, 1968: Forty Years Later.* Mundelein, IL: Bolchazy-Carducci, 2010.

Strazzari, Francesco. *Notte balcanica: Guerre, crimine, stati falliti alle soglie d'Europa.* Bologna: Il Mulino, 2008.

Stroschein, Sherrill. *Ethnic Struggle, Coexistence, and Democratization in Eastern Europe.* New York: Cambridge University Press, 2012.

Stuckler, David, King, Lawrence, and McKee, Martin. "Mass Privatisation and the Post-Communist Mortality Crisis: A Cross-National Analysis." *Lancet* 373, no. 9661 (2009): 399–407.

Sugar, F. Peter, and Lederer, J. Ivo, eds. *Nationalism in Eastern Europe.* Seattle: University of Washington Press, 1969.

Suljagić, Emir. *Cartoline dalla fossa: Diario di Srebrenica.* Trieste: Beit, 2009.

Sussex, Matthew, ed. *Conflict in the Former USSR.* Cambridge: Cambridge University Press, 2012.

Swain, Nigel. *Hungary: The Rise and Fall of Feasible Socialism.* London: Verso, 1992.

Szabó, Csaba. *A Szentszék és a Magyar Népköztársaság kapcsolatai a hatvanas években.* Budapest: Szent István Társulat-Magyar Országos Levéltár, 2005.

Szakolczai, Árpád, and Varga, László Á., eds. *A vidék forradalma, 1956,* 2 vols. Budapest: Budapest Főváros Levéltára, Budapest, 2003–2006.

Szczerbiak, Aleks. "Dealing with the Communist Past or the Politics of the Present? Lustration in Post-Communist Poland." *Europe-Asia Studies* 54, no. 4 (June 2002): 553–572.

Szelényi, Iván. *The New Grand Bourgeoisie under Post-Communism: Central Europe, Russia and China Compared.* Working Paper No. 63. Helsinki: UNU World Institute for Development Economics Research, 2010.

Szelényi, Iván, and Csillag, Tamás. "Drifting from Liberal Democracy: Neo-conservative Ideology of Managed Illiberal Democratic Capitalism in Post-Communist Europe." *Intersections: East European Journal of Politics and Societies* 1, no. 1 (2015): 18–48.

Szűcs, Jenő. *Vázlat Európa három történeti régiójáról.* Budapest: Magvető, 1983.

Tănase, Stelian. *Elite și societate: Guvernarea Gheorghiu-Dej, 1948–1965.* Bucharest: Humanitas, 1998.

Taubman, William. *Khrushchev: The Man and His Era.* New York: Norton, 2003.

Ther, Philipp. *Europe since 1989: A History.* Princeton, NJ: Princeton University Press, 2016.

Ther, Philipp, and Siljak, Ana, eds. *Redrawing Nations: Ethnic Cleansing in East-Central Europe, 1944–1948.* Lanham, MD: Rowman & Littlefield, 2001.

Thompson, Mark. *A Paper House: The Ending of Yugoslavia.* London: Vintage Books, 1992.

Tismăneanu, Vladimir. *Fantasies of Salvation: Democracy, Nationalism, and Myth in Post-Communist Europe.* Princeton, NJ: Princeton University Press, 1998.

———. *Stalinism for All Seasons: A Political History of the Romanian Communism.* Berkeley: University of California Press, 2003.

Tismăneanu, Vladimir, Vasile, Cristian, and Dobrincu, Dorin, eds. *Comisia prezidențială pentru analiza dictaturii comuniste din România: Raport final.* Bucharest: Humanitas, 2007.

Tismăneanu, Vladimir, ed. *Stalinism Revisited: The Establishment of Communist Regimes in East-Central Europe.* Budapest: Central European University Press, 2009.

Tismăneanu, Vladimir, and Bogdan, C. Iacob, eds. *The End and the Beginning: The Revolutions of 1989 and the Resurgence of History.* Budapest: Central European University Press, 2012.

Todorova, Maria. *Immaginando i Balcani.* 1997; Lecce: Argo, 2002.

Todorova, Maria, Dimou, Augusta, and Troebst, Stefan, eds. *Remembering Communism. Private and Public Recollections of Lived Experience in Southeast Europe.* Budapest: Central European University Press, 2014.

Tőkés, L. Rudolf. *Hungary's Negotiated Revolution: Economic Reform, Social Change, and Political Succession, 1957–1990.* New York: Cambridge University Press, 1996.

Tomka, Béla. *A Social History of Twentieth-Century Europe.* London: Routledge, 2013.

———. *Welfare in East and West: Hungarian Social Security in an International Comparison, 1918–1990.* Berlin: Akademie Verlag, 2004.

Tomka, Miklós. *Church, State and Society in Eastern Europe.* Washington, DC: Council for Research in Values and Philosophy, 2005.

Tonini, Carla. *Operazione Madagascar: La questione ebraica in Polonia.* Bologna: Clueb, 1999.

Tönnes, Bernhard. "Religious Persecution in Albania." *Religion, State and Society* 10, no. 3 (Winter 1982): 242–255.

Tóth, Ágnes. *Telepítések Magyarországon 1945–1948 között: A németek kitelepítése, a belső népmozgások és a szlovák-magyar lakosságcsere összefüggései.* Kecskemét (Hungary): BKMÖL, 1993.

Tóth, András. "Coming to the End of the Via Dolorosa? The Rise of Selective Economic Nationalism in Hungary," in Lehndorff, Steffen, ed., *Divisive Integration: The triumph of Failed Ideas in Europe—Revisited,* 233–252. Brussels: European Trade Union Institute, 2015.

Tóth, Károly Antal, ed. *Ellenpontok 1982.* Csíkszereda (Miercurea Ciuc, Romania): Pro-Print, 2000.

Trencsényi, Balázs. *The Politics of "National Character": A Study in Interwar East European Thought.* London: Routledge, 2012.

Trencsényi, Balázs. "Minek nevezzelek? A magyar demokrácia válsága—regionális értelmezési keretben." In Bálint, Magyar, ed. *Magyar Polip 2,* 49–68. Budapest: Noran Libro, 2015.

Troebst, Stefan. *Conflict in Kosovo: Failure of Prevention? An Analytical Documentation, 1992–1998.* Working Paper No. 1. Flensburg: European Centre for Minority Issues, 1998.

Uhl, Matthias, and Ivkin, I. Vladimir. *"Operation Atom": The Soviet Union's Stationing of Nuclear Missiles in the German Democratic Republic.* Working Paper No. 12–13. Washington, DC: Cold War International History Project, 2001.

Ungváry, Krisztián. *Battle for Budapest: 100 Days in World War II*. London: I. B. Tauris, 2006.

Uzunova, M. Iskra. "Roma Integration in Europe: Why Minority Rights Are Failing." *Arizona Journal of International and Comparative Law* 27, no. 1 (2010): 283–323.

Vadkerty, Katalin. *A kitelepítéstől a reszlovakizációig: Trilógia a csehszlovákiai magyarság 1945–1948 közötti történetéről*. Pozsony (Bratislava, Slovakia): Kalligram, 2001.

Van Brabant, M. Jozef. *Economic Integration in Eastern Europe*. New York: Harvester Wheatsheaf, 1989.

Van Elsuwege, Peter. *Russian-Speaking Minorites in Estonia and Latvia: Problems of Integration at the Treshold of the European Union*. Working Paper No. 20. Flensburg: European Center for Minority Issues, April 2004.

Varga, Zsuzsanna. *Politikai, paraszti érdekérvényesítés és szövetkezetek Magyarországon, 1956–1967*. Budapest: Napvilág, 2001.

Vasile, Cristian. *Intre Vatican și Kremlin: Biserică Greco-Catolică în timpul regimului comunist*. Bucharest: Curtea Veche, 2003.

Verdery, Katherine. *National Ideology under Socialism Identity and Cultural Politics in Ceausescu's Romania*. Berkeley: University of California Press, 1991.

———. *Secrets and Truths: Ethnography in the Archive of Romania's Secret Police*. Budapest: Central European University Press, 2014.

Vickers, Miranda. *Between Serb and Albanian: A History of Kosovo*. New York: Columbia University Press, 1998.

Völgyes, Ivan. *Politics in Eastern Europe*. Chicago: Dorsey Press, 1986.

Vučetić, Radina. "Violence against the Antiwar Demonstrations of 1965–1968 in Yugoslavia: Political Balancing between East and West," *European History Quarterly* 45, no. 2 (2015): 255–274.

Wallerstein, Immanuel. *The Capitalist World-Economy*. Cambridge: Cambridge University Press, 1979.

Wandycz, S. Piotr. *Il prezzo della libertà: Storia dell'Europa centro-orientale dal Medioevo a oggi, 1992*. Bologna: Il Mulino, 2001.

Ward, James Mace. *Priest, Politician, Collaborator: Jozef Tiso and the Making of Fascist Slovakia*. Ithaca, NY: Cornell University Press, 2013.

Wasserstein, Bernard. *Vanishing Diaspora: The Jews in Europe since 1945*. Cambridge, MA: Harvard University Press, 1996.

Webb, Alfred. *The Routledge Companion to Central and Eastern Europe since 1919*. London: Routledge, 2008.

Williams, Kieran. *The Prague Spring and Its Aftermath: Czechoslovak Politics, 1968–1970*. Cambridge: Cambridge University Press, 1997.

Wilson, Andrew. "The East Europeans: Ukraine, Belarus and Moldova," in White, Stephen, Lewis, G. Paul, and Batt, Judy, eds., *Developments in Central and Eastern European Politics*, 79–101. Basingstoke, UK: Palgrave Macmillan, 2007.

Wingfield, M. Nancy. *Flag Wars and Stone Saints: How the Bohemian Lands Became Czech*. Cambridge, MA: Harvard University Press, 2007.

Wolff, Larry. *Inventing Eastern Europe: The Map of Civilization on the Mind of the Enlightenment*. Stanford, CA: Stanford University Press, 1994.

Wróbel, Piotr. *Historical Dictionary of Poland 1945–1996. 1998*; London: Routledge, 2013.

Yaffe, Helen. *Che Guevara: The Economics of Revolution.* London: Palgrave, 2009.

Yurchuk, Yuliya. *Reordering of Meaningful Worlds. Memory of the Organization of Ukrainian Nationalists and the Ukrainian Insurgent Army in Post-Soviet Ukraine.* Stockholm: Södertörn University, 2014.

Zakaria, Fareed. "The Rise of Illiberal Democracy." *Foreign Affairs* 76, no. 6 (November–December 1997): 22–43.

Zaslavsky, Viktor. *Storia del sistema sovietico: l'ascesa, la stabilità, il crollo.* 1985; Rome: Carocci, 2001.

Zaslavsky, Viktor, and Aga Rossi, Elena. *Togliatti e Stalin: Il PCI e la politica estera italiana negli archivi a Mosca.* Bologna: Il Mulino, 2007.

Zatlin, R. Jonathan. *The Currency of Socialism: Money and Political Culture in East Germany.* Cambridge: Cambridge University Press, 2007.

Zeljko, Bjeljac, and Lukic, Vesna. "Migrations on the Territory of Vojvodina between 1919 and 1948." *East European Quarterly* 42, no.1 (March 2008): 69–93.

Zhdanov, Andrei. "Soviet literature: The Richest in Ideas, the Most Advanced Literature," in Scott, H. F., ed., *Problems of Soviet Literature: Reports and Speeches at the First Soviet Writers' Congress.* New York: International Publishers, 1935.

Zinner, Tibor. *A kádári megtorlás rendszere.* Budapest: Hamvas Béla Kultúrakutató Intézet, 2001.

Zubkova, Elena. *Russia after the War: Hopes, Illusion, and Disappointments, 1945–1957.* Armonk, NY: M. E. Sharpe, 1998.

Zwass, Adam. *The Council for Mutual Economic Assistance: The Thorny Path from Political to Economic Integration.* London: Sharpe, 1989.

INDEX

Gabčíkovo-Nagymaros Dam, 144
Gellner, Ernest, 4, 134, 180
General Agreements on Tariffs and Trade, 117
Geneva Summit, 84
genocide, 10–11, 13–14, 16, 20, 23, 76, 202; Holocaust, 13, 96, 195; Srebrenica, 202, 204
Georgia, 179, 224
Georgiev, Kimon, 34
German communities, in Czechoslovakia, 17–18, 20, 23, 25, 35, 41, 44, 79, 182; in Hungary, 17, 20; in Poland, 17; in Romania, 17–18, 35, 40, 77, 150; in Yugoslavia, 17–18, 22, 35, 41
German Democratic Republic (GDR), 28, 64, 67, 81, 98, 103, 106–107, 111, 115–116, 124, 131–132, 137, 140, 142–143, 148–149, 159, 164, 167, 194; Lutheran Church, 64, 148; Oder-Neisse border with Poland, 105, 131
Germany, 2, 3, 6–7, 10–11, 13–14, 16–17, 20, 24–25, 27–29, 33, 35, 37, 39, 49–50, 60, 66, 126, 167, 178, 182, 188, 194, 200, 215, 219, 221, 234–236; Christian Democratic Union, 131, 167
Gerő, Ernő, 91–93
Gheorghiu-Dej, Gheorghe, 41, 77, 83, 102–103, 112
Ghimpu, Mihai, 227
Gibiansky, Leonid, 30
Gierek, Edward, 141–142
Gieseke, Jens, 147–148, 129n57
Gingeras, Ryan, 243
Gini coefficients, 236
Glasnost, 158, 165
Glaurdić, Josip, 197
Gligorov, Kiro, 200
Goma, Paul, 152
Gomułka, Władysław, 20, 74, 89–91, 94–95, 105, 119–120, 140
Gorbachev, Mikhail, 132, 134, 139, 158–160, 162, 166–168, 170, 175n85, 178
Gottwald, Klement, 43–46, 81
Graziosi, Andrea: 97, 140, 173n34, 182
Greater Romania Party, 182
Greece, 3, 12–13, 24, 26, 50–51, 80, 84, 110, 113, 200, 210, 221, 237, 240; Thessaloniki, 27
Greek-Catholic Church, in Romania, 65; in Slovakia, 66; in Ukraine, 32
Greskovits, Béla, 252
Grósz, Károly, 163
Groza, Petru, 34, 39–42, 63
gulag, 76, 80
Gyurcsány, Ferenc, 187

Hájek, Jiří, 144
Hale, Henry E., 227
Halecki, Oskar, 5
Hanák, Péter, 5
Hann, Chris, 247
harassment, 101, 123, 152, 205
Harbutt, Fraser, 26
Havel, Václav, 6, 144, 168
Helsinki Final Act, 132–134, 141
Historiography, 13, 197; Czechoslovak, 105; Hungarian, 5; Romanian, 41; Soviet, 64
Hitler, Adolf, 12–14, 34, 39
Hoffmann, David L., 58
Holbrooke, Richard, 208
Homo sovieticus, 62
Honecker, Erik, 107, 131, 147–148, 167
Horn, Gyula, 186
Horváth, Sándor, 60
Hull, Corden, 24
human rights, 132–133, 144, 146, 151–152, 233–234
Hungarian Democratic Forum, 163, 186
Hungarian minorities, 19, 101, 147, 222; in Czechoslovakia, 17–18, 44–45, 47, 63, 79, 144; in Romania, 19, 40, 47, 63–64, 182; in Yugoslavia/Vojvodina, 18
Hungarian Revolution, 1956, 91–96, 102, 104, 107, 123, 128n39, 135, 146–147; Colonel Pál Maléter, 93, 100; Hegedüs, András, 85, 93; massacres of Budapest, Miskolc and Mosonmagyaróvár, 93; Petőfi Circle, 91
Hungarian Socialist Party, 186–187, 238
Hungarian Autonomous Region in Romania (HAR), 64, 103
Hungary, 4–7, 11–14, 17–20, 22–27, 30–35, 42–43, 46–49, 51, 53n12, 54n31, 56n100, 60, 63–68, 70, 72–76, 78–79, 81–83, 85, 89, 91–97, 99–103, 106, 112–120, 122, 124, 126, 128n30, 131, 135, 197–138, 140, 142–147, 150–151, 153–154, 159–160, 162–166, 168–169, 178, 182, 184–194, 217–219, 222, 231, 233, 235–238, 240–241, 244–247, 251; Budapest, 20, 34, 46, 79, 82, 92–95, 101, 146–147, 172, 196, 231, 240, 247; Hungarian Communist Party, 19, 47–49; Hungarian Socialist Workers' Party (HSWP), 94, 100–101, 116–118, 145–146, 162–164, 166; Civic Democratic Party, 47; Independent Smallholders Party, 47–48; Hungarian Fraternal Community, 48; Lake Balaton, 126; Monor, 163; National Peasant Party, 47; Hungarian Workers' Party (HWP), 49, 59, 76, 79, 82, 85,

STEFANO BOTTONI is Senior Fellow at the Center for the Humanities of the Hungarian Academy of Sciences. His research concerns the political usage of nationality, and his work has been published in several languages.

SEAN LAMBERT is a freelance Hungarian-to-English translator, with ten years of experience as an English-language journalist in Hungary. He has also translated Stefano Bottoni's forthcoming *Stalin and the Székelys: History of the Hungarian Autonomous Region.*

CPSIA information can be obtained
at www.ICGtesting.com
Printed in the USA
BVHW081450311218
536773BV00012B/1322/P